VOICES OF REVOLUTION

VOICES OF REVOLUTION

THE DISSIDENT PRESS IN AMERICA

RODGER STREITMATTER

COLUMBIA UNIVERSITY PRESS · NEW YORK

COLUMBIA UNIVERSITY PRESS

Publishers Since 1893

New York   Chichester, West Sussex

Copyright © 2001 Rodger Streitmatter

Library of Congress Cataloging-in-Publication Data

Streitmatter, Rodger.
   "Spirit of revolt" : the dissident press in America / Rodger
Streitmatter.
      p. cm.
   Includes bibliographical references and index.
   ISBN 0–231–12248–9 (alk. paper)—ISBN 0–231–12249–7 (pbk. :
alk. paper)
      1. Underground press—United States—History—20th century.
      2. Underground press—United States—History—19th century.
      1. Title.

PN4888.U5 S77 2001
071'.3—dc21

2001017099

Casebound editions of Columbia University Press books are printed on
permanent and durable acid-free paper.
Printed in the United States of America
Designed by Lisa Hamm
C 10 9 8 7 6 5 4 3 2 1
P 10 9 8 7 6 5 4 3 2 1

Grateful acknowledgment is made for permission to reprint the illustrations that appear in this book, and full acknowledgments appear with the captions to those illustrations. However, several of the illustrations are from publications that are no longer in existence. Therefore, the author and publisher would be interested to hear from anyone not here acknowledged.

To my son Matt and my daughter Kate, who have, on more than one occasion, been known to raise their very own "voices of revolution."

CONTENTS

Introduction   ix

PART 1 SPEAKING UP FOR THE DISENFRANCHISED

1   Fighting for the Rights of American Labor   3
2   Awakening a Nation to the Sins of Slavery   20
3   Setting a Revolutionary Agenda for Women's Rights   36

Dissident Voices/Common Threads I   54

PART 2 STRUGGLING TO FORM A MORE PERFECT UNION

4   Promoting "Free Love" in the Victorian Age   61
5   Crusading Against the Barbarism of Lynching   80
6   Educating America on the Merits of Socialism   97
7   Following Anarchy Toward a New Social Order   115

Dissident Voices/Common Threads II   135

PART 3 RISING FROM A LONE VOICE TO A MASS MOVEMENT

8   Propelling Black Americans Into the Promised Land   141
9   Demanding Wider Access to Birth Control Information   159

Dissident Voices/Common Threads III   176

PART 4 CHANGING THE WORLD IN A SINGLE GENERATION

10   Opposing America's "Dirty War" in Vietnam   183
11   Defining a Counterculture of Sex, Drugs, Rock 'n' Roll . . . and Social Justice   200
12   Standing Tall and Tough Against Racial Oppression   220
13   Creating an Agenda for Gay and Lesbian Rights   238
14   Liberating the American Woman   256

    Dissident Voices/Common Threads IV   275

15   Dissidence in a New Millennium   279

    Acknowledgments   285
    Notes   287
    Index   327

INTRODUCTION

In the spring of 1984, I was a hard-charging young assistant professor in pursuit of tenure. The project on which I pinned my hopes was a first-of-its-kind study of how the American news media were covering AIDS, then still in its infancy. My study looked at coverage by the titans of American journalism—the *New York Times*, the *Washington Post*, *Newsweek*, *Time*, ABC, CBS, NBC. I succeeded in having my research published in a highly respected journal of media criticism, and I subsequently received the praise from both journalists and scholars that led to my securing academia's Holy Grail.[1]

After the study was published, however, I received a letter from a gay physician who was not as laudatory of my research as other readers had been. He pointed out that my study was, in fact, woefully incomplete because I had overlooked a huge body of AIDS reporting that had appeared not in the mainstream press but in the *gay* press.

The guy was right. Like most journalism scholars, I had confined my study to the elite news media. Because of those narrow parameters, I had failed to document that the earliest and best AIDS coverage was not in the Brahmins of American journalism but in the 20,000-circulation *New York Native*. Not only was the gay bi-weekly a month and a half ahead of the mainstream press in reporting the existence of the new disease, but it also was the first news outlet in the country to tell readers what doctors suspected about how the disease was being spread. A tiny gay newspaper, in short, had out-reported the biggest and wealthiest journalistic voices in the country. In the process—and even more importantly—the *Native* had saved the lives of an untold number of gay men who read the paper.[2]

Because I had followed the conventional approach of confining my study to mainstream American journalism, I had ignored the *Native*'s noble contribution.

That error was the impetus for this book.

My omission more than fifteen years ago alerted me, for the first time, to the contributions that publications outside the mainstream of American journalism can make. Indeed, since receiving that first wake-up call, I have discovered numerous other instances during which dissident publications have not only served their readers well but, in many cases, have also been instrumental in shaping the history of this nation.

Fourteen of those episodes are illuminated in the chapters that follow. And impressive case studies they are:

- In the 1860s, *The Revolution* pioneered a radical agenda for women's rights, having the temerity to discuss such explosive topics—then as well as now—as sexual harassment, domestic violence, and abortion.
- Between 1916 and 1919, the *Chicago Defender* helped propel one of the most dramatic demographic shifts in this nation's history, persuading hundreds of thousands of black Americans to abandon the South and relocate in the North.
- In the early years of the twentieth century, Margaret Sanger's publications *Woman Rebel* and *Birth Control Review* ignited a social movement that transformed America's consciousness regarding the controversial issue of a woman's right to control her own body.
- During the turbulent 1960s, multiple genres of the dissident press helped spread a social revolution unprecedented both in force and in scope— fueling opposition to the Vietnam War as well as supporting the counterculture, black power, gay and lesbian rights, and women's liberation.

Because of these and other achievements by the dissident press during the last 200 years, it is absurd to dismiss non-mainstream publications as irrelevant rags and oddball journals, even though that is how most smug mainstream journalists and many myopic media scholars see them.

This book tells a different story. It documents that the dissident American press has, for almost two centuries, served as a robust and effectual force that has had substantial impact on the social and political fabric of this nation. In fact, a strong argument can be made that the dissident press has played a more vital role in shaping American history than has the mainstream press—which, at least in recent decades, has become part of the establishment rather than a watchdog over it.

Before I launch the reader into the history of the dissident press, I want to articulate the dimensions of this project.

My dictionary says that dissidence means "thinking or feeling differently; disagreeing; differing." Consistent with that definition, all of the publications discussed in this book offered views that differed from those served up by the conventional press. Indeed, in order for a publication to merit the mantle of "dissident," at least in this book, it not only had to offer a differing view of society but also had to seek to *change society* in some discernible way. That publication had to set out—intentionally and without apology—to champion a particular cause. The publication's primary purpose must have been, in short, *to effect social change.*

This motivation to transform society is a crucial one, as it separates dissident publications from the much larger category of alternative ones. The way I see it, all dissident publications are alternative publications, but many of those alternative publications are not dissident. For example, I see the weekly tabloids that have proliferated in the bohemian sections of American cities in recent decades—such as the *Village Voice* in New York City, the *City Paper* in Washington, D.C., and *Isthmus* in Madison, Wisconsin—as alternative publications that differ from mainstream newspapers. I have not written about those publications in this book, however, because they were not created, at least in my opinion, in order to *change* society in any fundamental way—they do not represent the voice of any specific social movement. Likewise, I do not include *The Masses*, the alternative journal of the early twentieth century known for its artwork and literary content, because it did not concentrate on advancing any one particular issue or movement.

Several genres of the dissident press that I highlight involve chapters in the American experience that I believe are important to document, even though those movements ultimately failed to change society to any significant degree. Sexual reform journals, for example, added considerable spice to the late nineteenth century by advocating what they termed "free love," but they made little real headway toward their primary goal of destroying the sanctified institution of marriage. Likewise, the leading socialist weekly at the turn of the century, the *Appeal to Reason*, achieved a circulation of a staggering 760,000, but it did not succeed in halting the growth of its major nemesis: capitalism.

If either the existence of these advocacy publications or their accomplishments are unfamiliar to you, do not despair. Thousands of such non-mainstream publications have been either ignored or relegated to a sentence or two in the standard histories of American journalism. Indeed, even the handful of histories of alternative journalism that have been published have overlooked most of the publications illuminated in the pages of this book. In short, then, all but a few scholars of journalism history have treated these presses with the same dismissive attitude that the mainstream press of their day regarded—or rather *dis*regarded—them.[3]

For each of these presses crusaded for change so radical that the establishment press was not willing to provide a forum for the discussion. As dissident journalist Upton Sinclair observed early in the twentieth century, America's largest and best-known newspapers generally do not champion fundamental social change but, in reality, construct a "concrete wall" between the American public and alternative thinking.[4]

So, many of the men and women who have sought to transform society in significant ways have been forced to create their own channels of communication in the form of their own particular brand of dissident journalism.

Those activists-cum-journalists often paid a high price for their social insurgency. In almost every case, the malcontents who edited and wrote for these publications suffered economic deprivation, as they were denied both the advertising revenue and the circulation revenue that support mainstream media. Many of these agents of change also had to endure the emotional pain of name-calling, harassment, intimidation, and public ridicule. Some of them also paid the heavy price of freedom itself, as creating their journalistic venues was so threatening to American society that it landed them in jail.

Throughout the chapters in this book, I have been particularly interested in the human story. I have, in other words, been concerned with the personal as well as the public lives of these women and men who demonstrated the courage to defy conventional standards of behavior and to endure hardship, humiliation, and abuse for the sake of principle. Because of the importance that many of these nonconformist journalists placed on individual freedom and self-reliance, the persons who come to life in these pages often display strong personalities—they lived life large.

In a few cases, in fact, a single individual was such a commanding force in creating and then leading a specific genre of the dissident press that I have written the chapter primarily as his or her biography. In several other chapters, a particular newspaper so dominated a movement that I have focused almost exclusively on that one publication. In the remaining chapters, the specific genre of the dissident press at hand is observed through the matrix of several publications; in no instance, however, have I created a mind-numbing list of the dozens or hundreds of publications that sometimes have supported a particular effort to change society.

As the pages that follow will show, the willingness to rebel against convention in the hopes of improving the quality of life for all people has not merely existed in the nature of individual Americans—men as well as women—but from time to time has erupted from its slumber and emerged in the form of a dynamic dissident press. In telling the stories of these courageous and visionary enemies of orthodoxy, I have quoted extensively from their writing. I have been committed to creating a narrative that draws on their own words not only because dissident journalists write with passion, and sometimes with eloquence, but also because I believe their words can speak to the present generation, across the gulf of time, with undiminished relevance. Their struggle for economic security, social justice, personal liberty, and freedom of expression remains part of the noble human effort that continues today.

Structurally, the bulk of this book consists of fourteen largely independent case studies that I have grouped into four broad chronological periods: the early to middle nineteenth century, the late nineteenth century, the early twentieth century, and the middle to late twentieth century. At the end of each of these four sections, I have inserted an essay that identifies and briefly discusses some of the distinctive characteristics shared by the genres of the dissident press that rose to prominence in that particular period—and, ultimately, the dissident press writ large.

A concluding essay looks at the current and future landscape of journalistic dissent in America, with particular attention to the rise of zines during the 1980s and the communication revolution that is taking place today because of the Internet.

As my final statement before beginning the reader's odyssey into the dissident press, I want to remove the cloak of scholarly detachment that I try to wear through the remainder of this book and speak for a moment—with something of an authorial flight of fancy—about how I have come to see, during the years since I wrote that apocryphal article about early AIDS coverage, the women and men who have pioneered in the journalism of nonconformity.

The persons illuminated in this book labored on the social frontier, clearing new ground and sowing new ideas. They were powered by burning convictions and a faith so strong that they were willing to sacrifice their time, their energy, their material well-being, and their own health. But sometimes—not always, but sometimes—they helped to bring about the social change that drove their very being.

On occasion, the change rushed forward at torrential speed; far more often, the process was so slow that it was almost imperceptible as these tribunes of a better tomorrow gradually wore away the granite structure of the past—tiny grain by tiny grain.

Some of these dissident journalists were blown off course by what was almost always formidable opposition. They were smashed on the rocks of tradition, and they faded from the public eye and mind. They were a speck, an oddity, an item of ephemera on history's rarefied scrolls.

But other of these spirited revolutionaries proved strong enough, single-minded enough, and fortunate enough to witness the new thought or new approach that they championed rise from a ripple to a wave to a universal force that swept away all their enemies and succeeded in becoming part of the American consciousness.

When that happened, they changed the world.

PART 1
SPEAKING UP FOR
THE DISENFRANCHISED

The Declaration of Independence is one of the most powerful statements of human freedom and equality ever composed. The historic document, with simplicity and directness, captures the essence of the ideas and the ideals on which the world's greatest democracy was founded. John Adams wrote his wife Abigail that the date the Founding Fathers adopted the magnificent manifesto—July 4, 1776—"ought to be solemnized with pomp and parade, with shows, games, sports, guns, bells, bonfires and illuminations, from one end of the continent to the other, from this time forward forevermore."

A growing number of Americans soon came to realize, however, that both the document and the new nation itself had a limited definition of exactly which citizens were, in fact, unencumbered in their rights to life, liberty, and the pursuit of happiness.

The declaration's own words—"all men are created equal"—excluded women from its particular brand of egalitarianism. Unstated but clearly understood was the further omission of both men and women of African descent. And by the early decades of the nineteenth century, critics of industrialization were charging that the masses of common laborers had joined, for all intents and purposes, the ranks of the politically and economically disenfranchised.

It was this realization—that America was not living up to the bedrock principle of equality that it purported to value—that gave birth to the first generation of the dissident press during the early to middle nineteenth century.

1 FIGHTING FOR THE RIGHTS OF AMERICAN LABOR

As the United States entered the nineteenth century, the highly skilled artisans who worked in their own homes to create customized items for individual patrons were replaced by large-scale operations in which unskilled workers produced identical units in quantity and at lower cost. Rarely did these laborers ever meet the men and women who ultimately purchased their goods. A single cobbler no longer made the entire shoe; in his place was a series of faceless workers, each completing one discrete function. By the mid-1820s, not only shoes but also such items as furniture, carriages, rope, barrels, brushes, cigars, hats, and candy were all being produced in factories. At the same time, a growing supply of women, children, and recent immigrants depressed the wages being paid to workers, forcing them to toil longer and longer hours. Only by pooling the earnings of husband, wife, and children could a family eke out even a bare subsistence—people who fell into debt would, like serfs from medieval times, be thrown into prison.

The new system of production created class distinctions that were inconsistent with the democratic principles laid down by the Founding Fathers only a few decades earlier. For in stark contrast to the burgeoning multitudes of common laborers, there emerged a new class of "merchant capitalists" to reap the rewards of the first generation of Americans who earned their livelihoods not by making goods but by hiring and managing workers, by selling the products at whatever price the market would bear, and by investing those profits to accumulate enormous wealth. American laborers, suddenly confronted by developments that seemed beyond their control and feeling powerless in the hands of their increasingly prosperous employers, formed the nation's first trade unions.

The country's leading newspapers had scant regard for the struggling new movement launched by the laborers, siding instead with the merchant capitalists and the growth that they symbolized as harbingers of what eventually would become an American version of the Industrial Revolution that had taken fire in England. The leaders of the fledgling Labor Movement in the United States recognized the need to communicate with their members, so they founded an early instance of the dissident press. During the late 1820s and early 1830s, some fifty labor weeklies appeared, most of them in the industrializing Northeast.[1]

The earliest and most important of the labor papers was the *Mechanic's Free Press* in Philadelphia, published from 1828 to 1831; although the paper survived only three years, it boasted a circulation of 2,000—an impressive figure during a time when even the largest New York daily claimed a circulation of only twice that number. A second significant labor paper was the *Free Enquirer*, published in New York City from 1828 to 1835. The most long-lasting of the dissident voices was the *Working Man's Advocate*, published in New York City from 1829 to 1849.[2]

The rise of a dissident press created by American laborers coincided with the period of democratic revolution credited to Andrew Jackson, the first self-made man to ascend to the presidency. In concert with the themes popularized by the rough-hewn Tennessean who was elected to the White House in 1828, the labor publications reflected the concerns of an awakened working class during a time of social, economic, and political turbulence. The common purpose of the publications was to ensure that American workers did not become an industrial underclass merely adding to the power and abundance of their overlords, the merchant capitalists. The papers called for an end to economic conditions that were making life intolerable for American workers, while also identifying and crusading for reforms that were key to the well-being of the American everyman.

The dissident papers quickly attracted a devoted following. Because many workers were illiterate, men and women with some education often purchased the papers for their co-workers and read them out loud on street corners and in churches, town halls, and other gathering places to crowds that often numbered 100 or more. Indeed, the fact that laborers came together to hear what the various editors had to say served to stimulate a sense of fraternity among the increasingly disenfranchised workers.

AMERICAN LABORERS UNITE

The Labor Movement made its first appearance in Philadelphia in 1827 when representatives of fifteen trades—from carpenters and machinists to hatters and shoemakers—formed the Mechanics' Union of Trade Associations. The union, which soon attracted some 2,000 members, was primarily concerned with what the founders saw as a lack of democracy in political affairs; elected officials were catering to the rich, the union men said, while ignoring the poor.

Movement leaders recognized the value of disseminating their concerns to a larger audience through a dissident press, calling for the creation of labor publications in each and every community of consequence in the United States. That desire took an important step forward in April 1828 with the founding of the *Mechanic's Free Press*.[3]

After Philadelphia workers organized, the Labor Movement next expanded to New York, where it encompassed not only urban workers but also farmers in rural areas. These laborers, like their Pennsylvania counterparts, placed a priority on establishing their own dissident publications, including the *Free Enquirer* and *Working Man's Advocate*. Neither of the papers confined its circulation to New York state but also attracted subscribers in Connecticut, Massachusetts, and New Hampshire.[4]

The movement spread rapidly to other areas, with workers organizing in some sixty cities and towns by the early 1830s. Many of the groups recognized the important role that communication plays in the stability and growth of a social movement, so they committed the energy and resources necessary to establish their own papers. Voices of worker discontent founded between 1828 and 1832 included the *Spirit of the Age* in Rochester, *Workingmen's Advocate* in Boston, and *Delaware Free Press* in Wilmington.[5]

In a phenomenon that would be repeated throughout the history of the dissident press, mainstream newspapers greeted the labor papers with hostility. The *Commercial Advertiser*, a New York City daily, labeled the labor editors "poor and deluded" men who were "the slime of this community," and the *Wayne County Patriot* in rural New York state called the working-class press "rabble" and demeaned the working-men-turned-journalists by calling them members of the "Dirty Shirt Party."[6]

The harsh words came as no surprise to the labor editors, who considered the mainstream press an enemy of the American worker. The *Mechanic's Free Press* said point blank that general-circulation newspapers spoke only for the "aristocracy of wealth" and "either entirely neglected" poor people or spoke about common men and women "only with contempt. The great mass of newspapers and periodicals are thus mischievously involved in doing worse than nothing" for the poor because their driving mission was to "pay court to the rich." The *Working Man's Advocate* criticized mainstream papers as well, accusing them of speaking exclusively for the capitalist "gentry" who had "grown fat" by oppressing the working class.[7]

SPEAKING UP FOR THE AMERICAN WORKER

The labor editors assured their readers that they would be unremitting in support of the common worker. *Mechanic's Free Press* editor William Heighton told readers that he had founded his paper to help "raise the productive classes to that condition of true independence and equality which their practical skill and ingenuity, their immense utility to the nation, and their growing intelligence demand." Heighton, a shoemaker by trade, was not afraid to flex his editorial muscle, boldly stating that "the working classes are the blood, bone, and sinew of the nation," while the merchant capitalists were modern-day "money changers" who must be driven "from the temple of freedom."[8]

When the *Free Enquirer* added its voice to the nascent dissident press, it also pledged to speak up on behalf of American labor, urging the men and women of the working classes to "Arise then in your strength." The New York weekly

Although no image of William Heighton survives, the masthead that he created for the *Mechanic's Free Press* provides a visual symbol of the dissident labor press of the early 1800s.

consistently criticized the nation's power elite, saying: "The poor have no laws; the laws are made by the rich and of course *for* the rich."[9]

The *Working Man's Advocate* echoed the sentiments of its two journalistic predecessors. Workers had been "entirely excluded from the advantages derivable from our free institutions," the New York weekly said, promising that it would be unflagging in its support of the poor: "It will be our object to draw the line as distinctly as possible between society living luxurious and ideal lives, and those groaning under oppression and miseries." The *Advocate* stated unequivocally that it was prepared to engage in open rebellion on behalf of American labor. "The Working classes have taken the field, and never will they give up the contest till the power that oppresses them is annihilated," the *Advocate* thundered. "We discern symptoms of a revolution which will be second to none save of '76."[10]

The *Advocate* stated with confidence: "A new and important era is about to take place, an era fraught with good to the producing classes. To aid in hastening the approach of this political millennium shall be our aim."[11]

CRUSADING FOR THE TEN-HOUR WORKDAY

One specific issue the labor press championed was reducing the number of hours that employees worked. As the United States had begun to industrialize, factory owners had succeeded in gaining widespread acceptance of the "sun to sun" system of labor; workers were expected to be on the job before sunrise and not to leave until after sunset. What's more, the stern New England spirit invested the "industrious habit" of working twelve or more hours a day, six days a week with the sacred character of a moral—if not a religious—precept.[12]

So when the labor papers advocated a shorter workday, they ran counter not only to the interests of the factory owners but also to the teachings of the church. The fact that supporting the ten-hour workday became a goal of the labor press demonstrated that this early instance of dissident journalism, like others that would follow, had no intention of shying away from uphill struggles.

Taking the lead in this contentious battle, as he would in many others, was William Heighton of the *Mechanic's Free Press*. Born in England in 1800, Willy Heighton came to America with his family when he was still a toddler. Like many newcomers arriving during that early wave of immigration, the Heightons came without much means but with an abundance of determination. Everyone in the family went to work in the shoemaking trade that Willy's father had mastered in the old country, with the youngest member of the family playing with wooden blocks and a favorite cloth ball only a few feet from where his mother cut and stitched leather in the small cottage that doubled as the Heighton home and workplace. Although Willy soon joined his parents and siblings in creating finely crafted footwear, the family could not compete with the factories that produced more boots at a lower price. While still an adolescent, Willy was sent into a boot factory so that at least one member of the family would be earning a steady wage.[13]

Every day for the next fifteen years, Willy Heighton crawled out of bed in the morning darkness so he would be at his machine by 5 a.m. He then cut the heels for men's boots—two and seven-eighths inches wide, three and three-eighths inches long, one and one-fourth inch thick—for seven hours, stopping for half an hour at midday to eat the lunch his mother had packed for him. Willy then resumed the monotonous cutting, careful to keep his fingers away from the sharp blade—there was no such thing as insurance or workman's compensation in case of injury—for either six or seven more hours, depending on how many boot orders had piled up. Regardless of whether he left the factory at 6:30 or 7:30 p.m., it was already dark as he walked home. So Sunday was the only day of the week that the young man had any chance whatsoever of seeing the sunlight in the crowded south Philadelphia neighborhood where he and the other laborers lived.

Willy Heighton sacrificed his boyhood and early manhood to the boot factory, receiving no formal classroom education and learning to read only because he studied by the light of a candle after his workday had ended.

At the age of twenty-eight, the spirit of revolt took hold.

By then married to the former Ann Beckley, a fellow factory worker, and the father of a young daughter, Heighton could not bear the thought that his wife—and, he knew, eventually their daughter as well—would lose both her health and her looks before she turned thirty unless he found a way for them to escape from industrial slavery. So he quit his job, used his scant savings to buy a used printing press, and launched what he could justly claim to be the first dissident newspaper in America. With Ann working at his side setting the lead type, Heighton published his first issue. "To the working public generally we appeal for support in consideration of the fact that this is the only journal now in existence," Heighton wrote in his debut issue, "devoted to their interest."[14]

Heighton asked laborers to pay two dollars a year for a subscription and to purchase the items they saw advertised in his paper. The *Free Press*'s large circulation within Philadelphia's working class, Heighton assured his readers, "renders it a valuable medium through which buyers and sellers can make known their wishes"—his four pages were dotted with small ads for clothing, pencil cases, and the services of a blacksmith. The paper's finances were always tenuous, however, and Heighton's requests for support from his readers became increasingly intense as time passed and revenue grew scarce. "Your patronage is most desperately desired," he wrote in 1830. In exchange for the support of his readers, Heighton promised to fight tirelessly for increased rights for American labor—beginning with a ten-hour day.[15]

Heighton asserted that "thousands yet unborn will reap the advantages, should the labourer succeed" in shortening the workday. With regard to the precise rationale for reducing the standard hours of labor, Heighton argued that workers needed more time to learn to read and then to educate themselves about current issues—essential steps, he charged, if workers were to fulfill their obligations as informed citizens. As long as the "sun to sun" work schedule prevented laborers from becoming informed, the former shoemaker wrote,

The *Working Man's Advocate* used a drawing of a brawny fist clutching a hammer to communicate the strength of the early labor press.

employers would succeed in "perpetuating amongst us invidious and artificial class distinctions, unnatural and unjust inequalities."[16]

The issue of the ten-hour workday also gave Heighton the opportunity to demonstrate his commitment to creating an open forum—that is, providing space not only for the editor's opinion but also for those of his readers—that would become a hallmark of the dissident press. Heighton made room, for example, for a lengthy letter from a man who was so outraged by the long workday that he insisted that European laborers were better off than American ones. "In this free country (as they call it)," the man wrote, he worked "from 5 o'clock in the morning until 7:30 in the evening," while his workday in Europe had been 6 a.m. until 6 p.m. Even though he worked two and a half hours longer in the United States, the man continued, his income was exactly the same as in his homeland.[17]

Like other dissident editors who would follow in his path, Heighton was not satisfied merely to argue on paper, as he also appealed directly to the Philadelphia City Council. In his many face-to-face encounters with the councilmen, Heighton demanded that the elected officials make "ten hours the standard day's work."[18]

The other labor papers joined the *Free Press* campaign. The *Free Enquirer* expanded on the concept that Heighton had initiated with the city council by preparing resolutions for several northeastern state legislatures on the subject of shortening the workday—and then lobbying hard for their passage. The *Working Man's Advocate* also published a flood of editorials on the subject, insisting that forcing workers to labor twelve and fourteen hours was a "gross imposition" on their freedom.[19]

OPPOSING CHILD LABOR

Another issue that appeared prominently in the early labor press revolved around the legions of youngsters who, with the rise of industrialization, had joined the work force. Of primary concern was the fact that the factories robbed boys and girls of their childhoods—and often their health—when they were only ten years old, or even younger.

Considering William Heighton's personal experience of being sent into factory work at an early age, it was not surprising that his *Mechanic's Free Press* spearheaded the attack on this issue. In 1830, he published the first study that documented the relationship between child labor and illiteracy. According to the findings, only one in six children employed in Philadelphia factories was able to read or write his or her own name. The study revealed other grim realities related to child labor as well. It reported that some impoverished parents who knew they could not educate all of their offspring decided to select one child to send to school while the other members of the family continued to work. The plan failed, however, when the greedy merchant capitalists got wind of it; employers adopted a policy that if parents took even one child from the factory, the entire family would be fired.[20]

Fueled partly by his own frustration at having lost his childhood to factory work, Heighton went far beyond simply reporting the facts, as he also wrote blistering editorials against factory owners who took advantage of working-class youths. "Unless something is done by our government to compel those misanthropes to treat the children in their employ like human beings," the editor raged, "the result of their present infamous practices will be grievously destructive to the liberties of the people."[21]

The *Free Press* was not the only journalistic voice raised against child labor. The *Free Enquirer* reported that a staggering forty percent of American factory workers were between the ages of seven and sixteen. The only time working-class children could study, the paper continued, was on Sunday and after nine o'clock at night the other six days of the week, when the children were too exhausted to concentrate. "The opportunities allowed for children and youth employed in manufactures to obtain an education suitable to the character of American freemen," the *Free Enquirer* protested, "are altogether inadequate." The editors of the paper also drafted recommendations and sent them to several state legislatures, insisting that the elected officials pass laws to reduce the number of children employed in factories.[22]

Coverage of child labor in the *Working Man's Advocate* took a strongly human approach that reflected the experiences of its editor, George Henry Evans. Born into a middle-class English family in 1806, Evans emigrated to America at age fourteen and began working at a New York printing plant. Having endured ten years of manual labor before founding the *Advocate*, Evans was fully aware of the conditions that working-class boys and girls faced. "Scarcely time allows them to take their scanty meals, they retire to their beds at night worn down and exhausted with excessive labour; hence they are deprived of any privilege except working, eating and sleeping." The *Advocate* used this bleak image to blame child labor for the problems that were increasingly plaguing the nation. "Is it to be wondered at," the paper asked, "that our country has become the great theatre of mobs—yea, we may say murderers too—when we remember that the poor and their children in manufacturing towns and districts are kept in ignorance and regarded but little superior to the beasts that perish?"[23]

DEMANDING TAX-SUPPORTED SCHOOLS

Closely related to the campaign to reduce child labor was one to guarantee that every American child received an education. In the 1820s, only the vaguest consideration was given to the needs of children who could not afford tuition to private institutions, with at least one million youngsters between the ages of five and fifteen "scarcely knowing what a school was." Working-class parents realized, however, that unless their children received an education, those boys and girls would be doomed to the same back-breaking labor and deprivation that the parents were forced to endure. So the demand that the government provide every child, regardless of the family's socioeconomic position, with the opportunity to attend school was paramount to the emerging Labor Movement—and labor press.[24]

William Heighton wrote in his *Mechanic's Free Press* that securing a proper education for every working-class child was "the first and most important" objective of his paper. "This is the rock on which the temple of moral freedom and independence is founded; any other foundation than this will prove inadequate to the protection of our liberties." Heighton called the lack of schooling for poor children flagrant proof that "the labourer has been defrauded" of his rights as an American citizen. The editor wrote and submitted two bills to the Pennsylvania legislature calling for universal education, and then propelled them forward with rhetorical muscle: "The productive classes of the nation will be united; and their union will obtain that which has so long been cruelly denied them—a general and republican system of education!"[25]

The importance the *Working Man's Advocate* placed on universal education was clear from the motto it carried each week at the top of page one: "All children are entitled to equal education," and from the item it positioned as number one on its list of measures that working men sought: "Equal Universal Education." The paper repeated its demand for state-supported schools hundreds of times. "The very existence of a free, popular government," read a typical editorial, "depends upon the distribution of knowledge."[26]

The *Free Enquirer* agreed with its two journalistic cohorts that educating working-class children was the top priority; the paper differed with the other labor voices, however, as to exactly what kind of educating was needed.

Robert Dale Owen, co-editor of the *Enquirer*, had been educated in a progressive boarding school in Switzerland, and was convinced that all American children, whatever their class, should have the same experience. So the *Enquirer* demanded that the federal government create boarding schools where all children would receive not only the same instruction but also the same food, clothing, and housing—all at public expense under a system of state guardianship.[27]

Standard day schools would not guarantee the children of laborers an equal education, Owen argued, because their living conditions would remain deficient. "If the children from these state schools are to go every evening, the one to his wealthy parent's soft carpeted drawing room, and the other to his poor father's or widowed mother's comfortless cabin, will they return the next day as friends and equals? He knows little of human nature who thinks they will."[28]

Although neither the *Mechanic's Free Press* nor the *Working Man's Advocate* directly endorsed the *Enquirer*'s boarding-school proposal, each gave its subtle support. When Owen wrote a series of essays explaining the benefits of the concept, the *Free Press* and *Advocate* both reprinted the series on their front pages.[29]

Mainstream papers, by contrast, attacked the boarding-school proposal with a vengeance. New York City's *Evening Journal* called the idea "one of the wildest fancies that ever entered into the brain of any fanatic!" Focusing on the controversial fact that creating boarding schools would mean that children would have to live apart from their parents, the *Evening Journal* accused Owen of attempting "to sever those strong ties of affection that keep families together."[30]

But it was not just the boarding-school proposal that the mainstream press criticized, as many papers attacked any form of tax-supported education. They complained not only that building and maintaining public schools would be too heavy of a financial drain on taxpayers but also that the time necessary to educate all Americans would destroy the country. "The peasant must labor during those hours of the day which his wealthy neighbor can give to the abstract culture of his mind," wrote Philadelphia's *National Gazette*, "otherwise, the earth would not yield enough for the subsistence of all: the mechanic cannot abandon the operations of his trade for general studies." If poor children were allowed to attend school, the upper classes would soon lose "most of the conveniences of life," the establishment paper continued, and, before long, "languor, decay, poverty, and discontent would be visible among all classes."[31]

The labor publications were not deterred, continuing to demand an education for every American child. "Let every man remember that it is not for himself alone that he acts, but for posterity," Owen wrote in the *Free Enquirer*. "If it be too late to secure the blessings of education for himself, it is time he was up and doing to secure them for his children." To the mainstream press argument that tax-supported schools would be too expensive, Owen reacted with outrage: "The funds that should have been appropriated to a rational system of general education at the expense of the state have been shamefully squandered and misapplied."[32]

ABOLISHING IMPRISONMENT AS THE PENALTY FOR DEBT

The antiquated practice of throwing people into jail because they could not meet their financial obligations was still very much in effect in 1820s America. Imprisonment for debt clearly burdened only members of the working class— indeed, threatened to turn more than a few citizens of the world's greatest democracy into vassals—and, therefore, became another target of the early labor press. The scope of the phenomenon was, indeed, appalling. At the close of the decade, some 75,000 people nationwide were being jailed each year because of debts, with most of the cases involving sums of less than twenty-five dollars.[33]

The *Mechanic's Free Press* again took the lead on this issue. William Heighton, as a former shoemaker and now as a newspaper editor, knew all too well that financial stability was fragile for the American worker, forever subject to the whims of a fluctuating economy over which the individual man or woman had scant control. So Heighton attacked the imprisoning of debtors as unfair. "A law that makes poverty a crime and a poor man a felon, after those very laws have made poverty inevitable," he wrote, "is not only cruel and oppressive, but absurd." As would be the case with other dissident journalists and their efforts to change society, Heighton took direct action by drafting and sending to the Pennsylvania legislature a resolution to abolish the medieval punishment.[34]

The *Working Man's Advocate* joined the battle. "Imprisonment for debt we believe to be a remnant of the feudal system," one editorial read, "calculated only for barbarians, disgraceful to the age and country in which we live." The labor weekly supported its commentary by providing compelling examples of exactly how preposterous some of the cases were. One item reported that poverty was so widespread in New York State's Monroe County that each year one person in every ten families was imprisoned because of unpaid bills, with one case involving an outstanding payment of a mere twenty-five cents. Another *Advocate* article disclosed that a man who owed only two cents was forced to remain behind bars for thirty days. In perhaps the most outrageous instance of all, a woman was thrown into jail and her children placed in an orphanage because she owed less than four dollars.[35]

All of the instances of injustice described in the *Free Press* and the *Advocate*—those related to imprisonment for debt as well as other issues—involved white workers, as neither paper spoke up on behalf of the group of American laborers who were, during the period, suffering under the most heinous form of human oppression: chattel slavery. The two papers were entirely silent about white men buying, selling, and abusing Americans of African descent, opting not to give their editorial support to the Abolition Movement that was in its beginning stages in the 1820s. The *Free Enquirer* was the only early labor paper to condemn slavery. The *Enquirer* insisted that "every friend of liberty must earnestly long to see some peaceful but effectual mode suggested and adopted to wash off this stain [of slavery] from the escutcheon of American freedom."[36]

TRANSFORMING LABOR INTO A POLITICAL FORCE

The most broad-based initiative undertaken by the embryonic labor press was to help make the working class a major player in American politics. This effort had the potential not only to allow laborers to regain their status as first-class citizens that the early stages of industrialization had taken from them, but also to advance the various other issues that the workers and their papers valued. Shortening the workday, reducing child labor, creating state-supported schools, abolishing imprisonment for debt—they could all be achieved if labor could be transformed from a mass of powerless individuals into a united political force that the major parties could ignore only at their own peril.

The dissident labor papers were so dissatisfied with the state of American politics in the late 1820s that they urged workers to reject both major parties of the day and nominate their own candidates. "So long as the people will be satisfied with the sound of a name, such as Federalist or Democrat," William Heighton wrote in his *Mechanic's Free Press*, "so long will they have the shadow instead of the substance."[37]

Heighton began the effort to politicize American labor soon after founding his paper in the spring of 1828, counseling readers that "the ordinary mode of effecting nominations of candidates, and of conducting elections" for Philadelphia City Council and the Pennsylvania legislature tended "to concentrate in the hands of a few, what should be the property of all." As with other issues, Heighton did not confine his endeavor to newsprint, however, but plunged directly into the rough-and-tumble of political activism. In this instance, that meant crafting a resolution urging the members of Philadelphia's various trade societies to come together to nominate candidates "to represent the interests of the working class" and thereby to found a third political party. The workers heeded Heighton's call, gathered for the meeting, and formed the Working Men's Party—with the *Free Press* as its official organ.[38]

By the fall of 1828, Heighton's effort had reaped its first dividends, with the new party electing twenty-one candidates to local offices in Philadelphia and the surrounding communities. The shoemaker-cum-editor-cum-political operative was jubilant: "The result has been equal to our most sanguine expectations."[39]

A year later, Philadelphia laborers once again had cause for celebration, having successfully elected another twenty of their own to local offices. "It is the finish of the glorious work of the [American] revolution," Heighton boasted. The 1829 labor victory was so decisive, in fact, that even a mainstream paper, the *Free Trade Advocate*, acknowledged that the *Mechanic's Free Press* had achieved two impressive feats—a weekly circulation of 2,000 and "so formidable an attack upon the ranks of both the political parties" that the workers controlled "the balance of local power."[40]

Buoyed by the Philadelphia victories, the Labor Movement expanded its political influence into other parts of Pennsylvania. Testifying to the central role that the labor press played in the emergence of the working class as a political force, the first step the leaders took was to circulate the *Free Press* in localities around the state, including Lancaster, Harrisburg, Erie, Carlisle, and Pittsburgh, as well as in Ohio.[41]

Meanwhile, the Labor Movement also gained a foothold in New York State—with labor papers again in the vanguard. The *Working Man's Advocate* argued that the only elected officials who would truly represent workers were "those who live by their own labour, AND NONE OTHER." So the *Advocate* called its working-class readers to action: "Awake, then, from your slumbers; and insult not the memories of the heroes of '76 by exhibiting to the world that what they risked their lives, their fortunes, and their sacred honour to obtain you do not think worth preserving."[42]

New York laborers began to taste success late that fall when they elected one of their own to the state legislature. The *Advocate* rejoiced, gloating that the victory had come despite the opposition of establishment papers and four men running against the labor candidate. "We have done more than could reasonably have been expected at this election," the *Advocate* wrote. "We have, to a certainty, paved the way to future victory."[43]

Leaders of the New York branch of the Working Men's Party expanded into a number of cities around the state, and the results of local elections in the spring of 1830 continued to be impressive. The entire labor ticket won in Syracuse, and all but one worker candidate won in both Troy and Albany.[44]

The workers soon triumphed in cities outside of Pennsylvania and New York, too. Three candidates were elected to local offices in Newark, New Jersey, eighteen to local offices in Wilmington, Delaware, three to the state legislature from Levy County, Delaware, one to the New Hampshire state legislature, and several to local offices and one to the state legislature from New London, Connecticut. The *Advocate* was so elated with the numerous victories that it boasted that the Working Men's Party would soon be in a position to nominate candidates for President and Vice-President of the United States.[45]

Then the bottom fell out.

After laborers had proven themselves to be a formidable force at the ballot box three years in a row, the major political parties decided that the time had come to put the brakes on the upstart new party. After independent strategy sessions, both the Federalists and the Democrats decided the Working Men's Party was most vulnerable on the fact that it had become affiliated in the public mind with America's devil incarnate: Frances "Fanny" Wright.

Robert Dale Owen's co-editor at the *Free Enquirer*, Wright was a well-educated Scottish woman of independent means. She had arrived in the United States in 1818 and soon had committed her considerable energies and financial resources to several controversial reform efforts. In 1825, she established a commune in Tennessee to prove that African Americans would thrive if they were freed and properly educated. Wright also endorsed marriages between blacks and whites, then outlawed in every state, as the best way to solve America's race problem. Next, Wright stunned the nation by publicly announcing that women were fully equal to men and should, therefore, participate in all areas of public life.[46]

But Wright was only warming up. In 1827, during a time when propriety banned women from even mentioning the word "sex," Wright described carnal desire as "the strongest and noblest of human passions" and the source of "the best joys of our existence," causing her to become known nationwide as the "High Priestess of Infidelity." Wright next denounced organized religion, proclaiming herself an avowed atheist and arguing that it was wasteful for people to spend their money building churches while the needy went hungry. Wright also campaigned for a redistribution of wealth in which all Americans would give their property and other possessions to the state to be divided equally among members of the various socioeconomic classes.[47]

Owen shared Wright's commitment to atheism and several other of her iconoclastic views. But it was primarily their mutual support of the American working class that brought the two radical thinkers together first to found the *New Harmony Gazette* in Indiana and then, in 1828, the *Free Enquirer* in New York City.

When the Federalists and Democrats launched their assaults on the Working Men's Party in 1830, they focused on Fanny Wright because she was an outspoken woman in an era when American society considered it an offense against God and nature for women to engage in activities outside the home. Mainstream politicians recruited the country's major newspapers to join their anti-labor campaign, prompting a savage editorial onslaught.

In Philadelphia, the *Daily Advertiser* called labor leaders "advocates of infidelity," and the *American Sentinel* accused the Working Men's Party of nominating candidates known to be Wright's "disciples." In New York City, the *Courier and Enquirer* charged the laborers with promoting the cause of "infidels," the *Evening Journal* said the labor press supported universal education only so the editors could "get the children into public schools, and then teach them infidelity," and the *Commercial Advertiser* labeled laborers "ravenous wild beasts," "followers of a crazy atheistical woman," and miserable beings who were "lost to society, to earth and to heaven, godless and hopeless" because of their association with Wright, a woman guilty of "incest, robbery, and murder."[48]

The attacks succeeded in derailing the Labor Movement's early political progress. By the 1831 election, not a single labor candidate nominated for office was elected, and by 1832 the Working Men's Party had ceased to exist.[49]

Another defeat played out not at the polls but in an editorial office in south Philadelphia. There, the vicious attacks in the nation's newspapers followed by the voters' rejection of labor candidates thrust *Mechanic's Free Press* editor William Heighton, the founding father of both the labor press and the labor party, into a state of deep depression. As a result, Heighton returned to shoe-making, refusing ever again to commit his time or his talent either to journalism or to the Labor Movement.[50]

AMERICAN WORKERS ARE HEARD

Although the triple losses of the Working Men's Party, William Heighton, and the *Mechanic's Free Press* represented severe setbacks for the pioneering labor press, this early instance of dissident journalism had not, by any means, been conquered. With regard to the specific issues at the center of the Labor Movement, the Federalists and the Democrats, as well as the mainstream newspapers that supported the two parties, had come to recognize the power that a unified working class could wield. So, as the *Working Man's Advocate* observed at the time, "Many of the reforms called for by the Working Men are now acknowledged to be just and reasonable, and are even advocated by several of the presses which have hitherto supported the party in power." Indeed, leaders of the major parties and the generations of politicians who were to follow them succeeded in attracting working men and women into their ranks by adopting labor's most popular demands as their own. Ideas initially discussed only in the labor press became planks in the platforms of the dominant parties—and were transformed from proposals to realities.[51]

By 1831, the ten-hour workday had already been established in Philadelphia and, within a few years, became the standard in factories in many cities throughout the country. In 1832, Pennsylvania adopted its first child labor laws, four years later Massachusetts did the same, and ultimately the effort to curtail the number of youngsters working in American industry spread to many other states—a movement that labor historians repeatedly traced to the pages of the *Mechanic's Free Press*. In 1834, Pennsylvania passed a law creating tax-supported public schools for all children, an initiative that evolved into the U.S. educational system that liberals and conservatives alike would ultimately look upon with pride. Abolishing imprisonment as a punishment for debt was accomplished in Philadelphia and New York City in 1831, and soon one state after another fell into line and relegated this feudal relic to the Middle Ages where it belonged—another achievement labor historians credited to the early labor press. As for the effort by the labor papers to transform working men and women into a united force at the ballot box, no one familiar with the political history of the United States during the last two centuries can question that labor did, in fact, become a powerful player in American politics.[52]

One of the most important legacies of the *Mechanic's Free Press, Free Enquirer,* and *Working Man's Advocate,* then, was their role in successfully transforming measures that were unpopular in the 1820s into key elements in the nation's progress toward increased democracy during the 1830s and beyond. In addition, the trio of newspapers paved the way for the hundreds of labor papers, including at least fifteen dailies, that would be published during the late 1800s and early 1900s when the American Labor Movement was at its peak. Finally, the three pioneering publications proved—and unequivocally so—that dissident journalism could produce major rewards for the disenfranchised readers that it served, while also having profound impact on the affairs of the nation as a whole.[53]

2 AWAKENING A NATION TO THE SINS OF SLAVERY

In the early decades of the nineteenth century, economic factors related to the issue of slavery developed to create a geographic fault line that divided the United States into two distinct sections. The North began to industrialize, with the rapid growth of urban-based factories producing a broad range of consumer products; the South retained its largely agrarian economy that relied on the production of cotton and tobacco, both of which rested squarely on the back of slave labor.

To the religious zealots at the vanguard of the Abolition Movement, even more important than the economic dimension of slavery was the moral one. To these highly committed and often self-righteous men and women, slavery was abhorrent not merely because it exploited Africans who had been captured and brought to America but also because slaves could not benefit from the fruits of their own labor, were not guaranteed the right to participate in the domestic relations of marriage and parenthood, and were not allowed to control their conduct in sufficient degree to prepare the immortal soul for eternity. So in the eyes of the abolitionists, slaves were denied the opportunity to live their lives as the children of God. Slavery was a sin.

Southern apologists saw the institution of slavery from a strikingly different perspective. They argued that slave owners introduced Americans of African descent to Christianity and civilized behavior, while also guaranteeing this helpless and dependent people—the vast majority of whites believed that black people were so intellectually inferior that they were closer to animals than human beings—the food, clothing, shelter, and security during sickness and old age that northern factory workers were ruthlessly denied.

Abolitionists intent upon propagating their point of view chose the newspaper as their primary method of communication for two reasons. First, newspapers could bridge the geographic gaps that separated anti-slavery advocates from each other, helping to build and galvanize a unified social movement. By publicizing upcoming activities, reprinting speeches and minutes from meetings and conventions, and publishing news items about movement leaders, anti-slavery newspapers could help build a national abolitionist community and then keep the faithful united.

Second, abolitionists were committed to the power of moral suasion. They sincerely believed that all Americans were reasonable people who, when the sinful nature of slavery was explained to them, would immediately support the nation cleansing itself of the dastardly institution, regardless of the economic consequences. Newspapers offered a venue in which to articulate that information to the sons and daughters of democratic thinking.

Because slavery and its inevitable collision of economics and morality created the most contentious issue of the era, mainstream newspapers opted not to devote a great deal of space to the topic, certainly not as much space as abolition leaders wanted. So those resolute men and women created their own communication network. Dozens of abolitionist papers, most of them based and distributed in the North, were published between 1800 and 1865.

By far the best known and most influential of the anti-slavery newspapers was *The Liberator*. Founded in 1831 and published without interruption for thirty-five years—ceasing publication only after slavery was abolished in 1865—this cacophonous advocacy journal dominated the genre like no other. Thanks to William Lloyd Garrison, the paper's bombastic editor and chief prophet of the abolition crusade in the United States, *The Liberator* became synonymous with the abolitionist press. In addition to filling the Boston weekly's four pages with strident commentary, Garrison devised innovative techniques to ensure that his paper became the focal point of the entire Abolition Movement. Today *The Liberator* is remembered, and rightly so, as the epitome of dissident journalism in American history.

WILLIAM LLOYD GARRISON: DIEHARD ABOLITIONIST EDITOR

Garrison was born into a working-class family in Newburyport, Massachusetts, in 1805. Poverty forced young William to leave school at the age of ten and become an apprentice printer whose classroom was the pressroom—his education was confined to reading the lead type in the printing press. While helping abolitionist Benjamin Lundy edit the *Genius of Universal Emancipation* during the 1820s, Garrison grew increasingly vehement in his attacks on American slave

From his position as editor of *The Liberator*, William Lloyd Garrison emerged as the chief prophet of the Abolition Movement. (Courtesy of Boston Public Library)

traders, raging against the barbarities they routinely performed—kidnap, rape, murder.

In 1829, Garrison undertook a journalistic campaign against Francis Todd, who transported slaves to Louisiana sugar plantations aboard his ship, the *Francis*. Under the heading "Black List," Garrison denounced Todd for mistreating his slaves. "Any man can gather up riches, if he does not care by what means they are obtained," Garrison wrote. "The *Francis* carried off seventy-five slaves, chained in a narrow place between decks." Todd sued Garrison for libel, charging that the slaves had not been chained but had been free to move below deck—in fact, had been allowed to conduct their own daily prayer meetings—and that Garrison had relied on hearsay for his article. The jury agreed with Todd. Garrison probably could have avoided a jail sentence if he had shown any sign of remorse, but he did not.[1]

After serving forty-nine days behind bars, Garrison moved to Boston, and on January 1, 1831, he founded what soon became the country's most visible and volatile journalistic adversary of chattel slavery. *The Liberator*'s editor was a single-minded man of courage and conviction who was destined to preach the anti-slavery credo to an entire generation of Americans.

Garrison was irascible and sometimes irresponsible, a man imbued with righteous indignation. Most abolitionists acknowledged the South's economic dependence on slavery and therefore were willing to compromise by supporting gradual emancipation over a period of several years—first in the border states, eventually in the Deep South. But Garrison would have none of it; he demanded nothing less than immediate and total freedom for all slaves. "I will be as harsh as truth and as uncompromising as justice," he wrote in the militant manifesto that appeared in his inaugural issue. "On this subject, I do not wish to think, or speak, or write, with moderation. No! No! Urge me not to use moderation in a cause like the present. I am in earnest—I will not equivocate—I will not excuse—I will not retreat a single inch—AND I WILL BE HEARD."[2]

One of the most controversial themes to erupt in the pages of *The Liberator* involved Garrison's stand on violence. Although he preached Christianity and swore that he was committed to peaceful activism only, his critics charged that the editor encouraged slaves to revolt against their owners. Some of Garrison's rhetoric did, indeed, seem to promote violence. Typical was the message communicated in a verse titled "The Insurrection":

Woe if it come with storm, and blood, and fire,
When midnight darkness veils the earth and sky!
Woe to the innocent babe—the guilty sire—
Mother and daughter—friends of kindred tie!
Stranger and citizen alike shall die![3]

Such statements understandably made Garrison unpopular among people who continued to support slavery, and in the 1830s and 1840s the vast majority of Americans remained securely in that camp. One of *The Liberator*'s early letters to the editor read, "Your paper cannot much longer be tolerated. Shame on the freemen of Boston for permitting such a vehicle of outrage and rebellion to spring into existence among them!" Other letters contained obscenities so foul that the mores of the time dictated that the caustic words be replaced with dashes. One screamed, "O! you pitiful scoundrel! you toad eater! you d—d son of a ——! hell is gaping for you! the devil is feasting in anticipation! you are not worth ——."[4]

But when Garrison received such letters, he did not shudder in fear; he rejoiced. Opting for a route that would be followed by many of the dissident editors who would follow him, Garrison reprinted the charges. The angry letters became so voluminous, in fact, that *The Liberator* began carrying a weekly section set aside specifically for them.

Garrison published the letters because one of *The Liberator*'s hallmarks, as in the labor press, was providing an open forum in which readers—those who agreed with the editor as well as those who did not—could voice their opinions. Garrison, never a modest man, boasted that his paper "admitted its opponents to be freely and impartially heard through its columns—as freely as its friends. I have set an example of fairness and magnanimity, in this respect, such as has never been set before."[5]

Proof of Garrison's pledge to provide an open forum came in the form of the letters from the opposition that he published in *The Liberator*—most of them on the front page. In one, a slavery advocate argued that the Bible "beyond all question" endorsed slavery; in another, the author called abolitionists "instigators of treason." Garrison was a favorite target of many of the writers. He was, at various times, labeled a "fanatical traitor" and "as mad as the winds"; on another occasion, a letter writer demanded that the radical editor be hanged.[6]

In addition to the emotional pain resulting from such ad hominem attacks, Garrison made other personal sacrifices. He often worked sixteen hours a day, six days a week in a small, dingy office—only tiny streams of light entering through ink-spattered windows. Besides writing his fiery editorials, he also set the type, operated the press, wrote the addresses of subscribers on the printed papers, and delivered the bundles to the post office. In his early days as an editor, the gaunt and bespectacled Garrison, who was twenty-five years old when he founded *The Liberator*, lived chiefly on water and stale bread from a nearby bakery.

Garrison's paper was rag-tag in appearance. The layout was erratic, with readers complaining that articles were thrown in "higgledy-piggledy." Issues were rarely complete; matters were often left at loose ends with the promise of "more next week"—but that promise went unfulfilled. The time lag between news stories on page one and editorials on page three often stretched to several weeks, and many important elections passed without Garrison ever finding the time to comment on them.[7]

Finances were another problem. *The Liberator* carried only a few small advertisements—for books, medicines, boarding houses—and therefore received scant revenue from the monetary mainstay of most publications. Nor did *The Liberator* attract substantial revenue from circulation; the initial print run was only 400, and the number of persons paying the two dollars for an annual subscription never exceeded 2,500. Garrison paid his printing and mailing costs primarily from the fees that he charged for giving lectures. He was much in demand as a speaker, averaging one public address a week through the three and a half decades he published *The Liberator*, partly because slavery supporters enjoyed publicly humiliating him. For the passionate words that he spoke, most of them having previously appeared in his newspaper, were almost always accompanied by jeering and heckling from pro-slavery demonstrators. "They came equipped with rotten eggs and brickbats, firecrackers and other missiles," he wrote matter-of-factly after being pelted with eggs during a speech in Pennsylvania. "One of the eggs bespattered my head and back somewhat freely."[8]

Garrison endured the attacks because he was convinced that he had been placed on this Earth to free the slaves and that *The Liberator* was the tool best suited to awakening apathetic Americans to their sins. "The people, at large, are astonishingly ignorant of the horrors of slavery," he wrote. "Let information be circulated among them, and they cannot long act and reason as they now do."[9]

To save his newspaper from financial ruin, in 1832 Garrison founded the New England Anti-Slavery Society and, a year later, the American Anti-Slavery Society. He hoped that contributions from the two groups would give *The Liberator* fiscal stability. Garrison's revenue-raising strategy only partially succeeded, though, because many diehard abolitionists questioned whether publishing a radical newspaper of such small circulation was judicious use of the movement's limited resources.[10]

And yet, despite the small number of subscribers and lukewarm support of many movement leaders, there is no question that *The Liberator* influenced the nation's attitude toward slavery. "I have seen my principles embraced, cordially and unalterably, by thousands of the best men in the nation," the immodest Garrison wrote in 1834. "What else but the Liberator *primarily* (and of course instrumentally) has effected this change? Greater success no man could obtain."[11]

The most salient indication of the influence that the paper was having on the American conscience came not from Garrison's boasting but from the numerous governmental bodies that took extreme measures in hopes of preventing *The Liberator*'s publication and distribution. The Georgia legislature offered a bounty of $5,000 to anyone who kidnapped and brought Garrison before the legislators to answer for his misdeeds, and a group of slave owners in Mississippi

THE LIBERATOR.

VOL. I.]	WILLIAM LLOYD GARRISON AND ISAAC KNAPP, PUBLISHERS.	[NO. 1.

BOSTON, MASSACHUSETTS.]   OUR COUNTRY IS THE WORLD—OUR COUNTRYMEN ARE MANKIND.   [SATURDAY, JANUARY 1, 1831.

THE LIBERATOR
IS PUBLISHED WEEKLY
AT NO. 6, MERCHANTS' HALL.
WM. L. GARRISON, EDITOR.
Stephen Foster, Printer.

TERMS.

Two Dollars per annum, payable in advance.

Agents allowed every sixth copy gratis.

No subscription will be received for a shorter period than six months.

All letters and communications must be POST PAID.

THE LIBERATOR.

THE SALUTATION.

To date my being from the opening year,
I come, a stranger in this busy sphere,
Where some I meet perchance may pause and ask,
What is my name, my purpose, or my task?

My name is 'LIBERATOR'! I propose
To hurl my shafts at freedom's deadliest foes!
My task is hard—for I am charged to save
Man from his brother—to redeem the slave!

...

WILLIAM LLOYD GARRISON.

BOSTON, January 1, 1831.

DISTRICT OF COLUMBIA.

...

THE SLAVE TRADE IN THE CAPITAL.

...

Today *The Liberator*, published each week for thirty-five years, is remembered as the archetype of dissident journalism in America.

later upped that ante to $20,000. Elected officials in South Carolina offered a reward to any person who apprehended *Liberator* distributors, and the city of Georgetown in the District of Columbia was among several jurisdictions that made it illegal for free blacks to read the paper. On the federal level, Postmaster General Amos Kendall openly condoned southern vigilante groups that rifled mail sacks to destroy copies of *The Liberator*.[12]

Boston took its own action. On several occasions, pro-slavery townspeople showed their hatred of Garrison by erecting a gallows in front of his office. Then, in the fall of 1835, a mob of some 100 men assembled outside a hall where the editor was speaking and threatened to tar and feather him. Fearing for his safety, Garrison slipped out a back window and sought refuge in a carpenter shop where he hid behind a pile of lumber. The crowd tracked him down, looped a rope around his neck, and dragged him through the streets of Boston as onlookers screamed, "Lynch him!" Several men then stripped Garrison naked, carried him to the second floor of a building and, with the rope still coiled around his neck, threatened to hang him by hurling him out an open window. Just as the mob was poised to end Garrison's irritating behavior once and for all, a delegation of moderate abolitionists came to his rescue.[13]

Such acts of intimidation did not cause Garrison's radicalism to abate—but to escalate. At the same time that the nation's more even-tempered statesmen struggled to forge a road of compromise that would keep the North and the South united as a single nation, Garrison used *The Liberator* to demand an opposite route. Fully fifteen years before the Civil War finally ripped the country apart, the dissident paper insisted that readers could no longer pledge their allegiance to a slaveholding government and that all non-slaveholders must secede from the union. "The existing national compact should be instantly dissolved," Garrison wrote in 1844. "Secession from the government is a religious and political duty. The motto inscribed on the banner of Freedom should be, NO UNION WITH SLAVEHOLDERS."[14]

As the years passed and the nation's leading politicians continued to strive to preserve the fragile peace, Garrison became increasingly outspoken in his support of violence. In 1859 after radical abolitionist John Brown led his band of rebels in an attack on the U.S. military arsenal at Harper's Ferry, virtually every newspaper in the country—including most abolitionist papers—condemned Brown's action, which had led to the deaths of ten men. Garrison, to the contrary, praised Brown as a man of courage for killing other white men in the cause of ending slavery. After Brown was captured and hanged, Garrison wrote: "I cannot but wish success to all slave insurrections."[15]

Although *The Liberator* certainly was not the sole catalyst for the armed conflict between the North and the South, the strident statements that the newspaper disseminated clearly hastened the division among the American people on the slavery issue. By identifying abolition as a struggle between an open society with a free intellectual market and a closed society that feared change and new ideas, *The Liberator* exposed the American people to the disconnect between the bedrock democratic ideals that the United States had been founded on and the unjust treatment it continued to mete out to Americans of African descent.

By the mid-1840s, Garrison had not only a journalistic venue in which to preach his gospel of abolition, but also a domestic one. He married Helen Eliza Benson, who then joined her husband in inviting prospective abolitionists into the Garrison home—she filled their stomachs with beef and biscuits; he filled their heads with items he read aloud from *The Liberator*. The combination of generous hospitality and unrelenting rhetoric proved so successful in adding converts to the cause, in fact, that wealthy abolition leaders began stocking Helen Garrison's pantry. "I see you have a houseful of people," one supporter scribbled on a note attached to a barrel of flour. "Your husband's position brings him many guests and expenses." She accepted the contributions gladly, as the constant stream of visitors to feed and the growing Garrison family to care for—she had seven children—on her husband's paltry income was taxing. The Garrisons drifted from one house to another until 1855 when a supporter gave them a house to provide a permanent address for what some observers dubbed the "Garrison Anti-Slavery Hotel."[16]

MISSION ACCOMPLISHED

Garrison welcomed the Civil War as a necessary step toward freeing the slaves; soon after the fighting began, he headlined one front-page story "Hurrah for the War!" Although the dissident journalist never went to the battlefront, he wrote articles about the war as if he had. Describing the Confederate soldiers as "debased and dastardly minions of the Slave Power," he crafted exaggerated passages about how Union soldiers were being savagely abused. "We hear of the wounded on the battlefield thrust through and through with bowie-knives and bayonets, and otherwise mangled—in some instances their bodies quartered, and in others their heads cut off, and made foot-balls of by their fiendish enemies."[17]

More than 600,000 Americans died in the Civil War, the most wrenching and costly event—in the human terms of the number of lives lost and the number of families destroyed—in the history of the nation. And then finally, after four years of battle, General Robert E. Lee surrendered at Appomattox in the spring of 1865 to bring an end to the fighting, and ratification of the Thirteenth Amendment to the Constitution later that year abolished slavery in America.

With Garrison's life-long goal achieved, the sixty-year-old editor ceased publishing *The Liberator*, with the final issue dated December 29, 1865.

The praise for the paper's role in transforming public sentiment on the most controversial issue of the era began immediately. *The Nation* magazine wrote that *The Liberator* "has dropped its water upon the nation's marble heart. Its effect on the moral sentiment of the country was exceedingly great. It went straight to the conscience, and it did more than any one thing beside to create that power of moral conviction which was so indomitable." Of Garrison's commitment to the Abolition Movement, *The Nation* said, "It is, perhaps, the most remarkable instance on record of single-hearted devotion to a cause." The *New York Tribune*, one of the progressive newspapers that had joined the abolition cause twenty years after *The Liberator* had led the way, also praised Garrison's journalistic triumph. "We lead such aimless and unlovely lives, so void of earnestness and daily beauty," the paper said. "But now and then comes a man like Mr. Garrison to show us our mistake; to prove what virtue there is in fidelity to a single labor; to accomplish some great work vital to the progress of man."[18]

Officials at the highest level of government joined in lionizing Garrison. Secretary of War Edwin Stanton invited him to Washington for a private interview. U.S. Senators Charles Sumner and Henry Wilson ushered Garrison to a place of honor on the floor of the Senate. President Abraham Lincoln wrote a letter of appreciation to Garrison, signaling his respect for the editor by signing the message, "Your friend and servant." And in the ultimate statement of honor, President Lincoln twice invited Garrison to the White House for sessions in which the two men talked privately.[19]

In recognition of Garrison's contribution to abolishing slavery, he was invited to Charleston for a great jubilee. The climax of the day came when a throng of liberated slaves hoisted Garrison triumphantly onto their shoulders and carried him to a platform, surrounded by thousands of African American women and men who understood what he had done for them. Black orator and activist Frederick Douglass spoke for the multitude, calling Garrison "the man to whom more than any other in this Republic we are indebted for the triumph we are celebrating today."[20]

STRATEGY OF AGITATION

One of the most intriguing questions related to *The Liberator* is how a publication of decidedly limited circulation—and with most of the 2,500 subscribers being free northern blacks of scant political or economic power—became such an influential force on one of the most important social movements in American history.

The answer involves Garrison's masterful skill as a provocateur. He designed a calculated and remarkably modern strategy of agitation to ensure that the sentiments he expressed in his newspaper did not lie sedately on the page to be ignored and forgotten. Instead, he saw to it that his printed words commanded massive public attention and successfully provoked discussion as well as action. Since Garrison's death in 1879, some historians have glorified him as the moral conscience of the nation while others have vilified him as a nettlesome egotist, but admirers as well as detractors have paid tribute to the editor as a dissident journalist without peer. Gilbert H. Barnes, one of the harshest of Garrison's scholarly critics, wrote, "As a journalist he was brilliant and provocative."[21]

The most sustained technique Garrison employed to boost *The Liberator*'s rapid ascent into the national spotlight began in January 1831. He exchanged copies of that premier issue with newspapers being published by some 100 other editors—most of them, like most Americans at the time, adamant defenders of slavery. The editors who received Garrison's *Liberator* were so offended by his words that they quoted him at length, accompanied by their own statements of outrage, to inform their readers of the extreme nature of the abolitionist credo.[22]

When Garrison received his copy of a paper in which an editor had berated him, he celebrated. For Garrison then reprinted the editorial attack, along with his own vehement rebuttal. So by the end of this carefully orchestrated editorial chain reaction, Garrison had not only provided his own subscribers with a double dose of lively reading, but he also had introduced readers of a pro-slavery paper to *The Liberator* and the anti-slavery ideology it promulgated.

For instance, after the editor of the *Middletown Gazette* received and read Garrison's inaugural editorial salvos against slavery, the Connecticut editor first repeated, word for word, Garrison's passionate insistence that he would be as harsh as truth and as uncompromising as justice in his battle to ensure that all slaves were freed. The *Gazette* editor then added contemptuously: "Mr. Garrison can do no good, either to the cause of humanity or to the slaves, by his violent and intemperate attacks on the slaveholders. That mawkish sentimentality which weeps over imaginary suffering, is proper to be indulged by boarding school misses and antiquated spinsters; but men, grown up men, ought to be ashamed of it." In the next issue of *The Liberator*, Garrison reprinted his original words plus the *Gazette*'s harsh ones, and then he used typography to ridicule the pro-slavery newspaper's suggestion that slavery did not cause pain, repeating the phrase in disbelief: "*IMAGINARY suffering!!*" Garrison then denounced the *Gazette* for having betrayed the progressive nature of the region of the country that it and *The Liberator* shared, "Such sentiments, if emanating from the south, would excite no surprise; but being those of New-England men, they fill us with disgust."[23]

Consequently, within a matter of weeks after Garrison had founded his dissident newspaper, he was engaged in high-pitched verbal combat with dozens of editors in far-flung sections of the country. These battles continued throughout the long life of *The Liberator* as Garrison argued with pro-slavery editors in states as far south as Georgia and Mississippi and as far west as Ohio and Michigan—all the while building his paper's reputation across that same vast geographic spread.[24]

A second technique Garrison used to bring attention to his newspaper, as well as himself and his cause, involved broadening his crusade to end slavery into a crusade to protect the civil liberties of the American citizenry writ large.

Garrison began this expansion in 1837 after hearing that the editor of an abolitionist newspaper in Alton, Illinois, had been killed by a pro-slavery mob. The Rev. Elijah P. Lovejoy was from a prominent New England family and had earned his divinity degree from the prestigious Princeton Theological Seminary; the tragedy of his death at age thirty-five and leaving a wife and young child was compounded by the failure of law enforcement officials to arrest anyone for the murder. The astute Garrison immediately recognized that Rev. Lovejoy's death and the circumstances surrounding it, if packaged properly, could propel the Abolition Movement in an exciting new direction.[25]

So in an emotional editorial outlined in a heavy black border, Garrison shrewdly exploited the murder of "a representative of Justice, Liberty and Christianity" to condemn the United States as a nation "diseased beyond recovery." Garrison maintained the passionate tone of his editorial by swearing that Rev. Lovejoy's death would serve his crusade against slavery as well as his defense of a free press. "In destroying his press, the enemies of freedom have compelled a thousand to speak out in its stead," Garrison raged. "In attempting to gag his lips, they have unloosed the tongues of tens of thousands of indignant souls. They have stirred up a national commotion which causes the foundations of the republic to tremble. O most insane and wicked of mankind!"[26]

Through the highly charged campaign that Garrison launched with that editorial and maintained with numerous others—his sensational headlines included "Horrid Outrage!" and "Lovejoy Murdered!!!"—during the months that followed, he succeeded in transforming the relatively narrow issue of attempting to win freedom for a disenfranchised racial minority into the much broader crusade of defending the civil liberties of all Americans—white as well as black, free as well as oppressed.[27]

Garrison's editorials sent shockwaves through the nation, igniting a tide of indignation, resentment, and anger that spread like wildfire. Within a matter of weeks, hosts of people across the country had adopted *The Liberator*'s interpretation of Rev. Lovejoy's death. Hundreds of ministers who eulogized the martyred clergyman from their pulpits mentioned Garrison's paper, and thousands of the men and women who organized public protests supporting free expression and civil liberties also suddenly were talking about the brave journalistic defender of the principles on which America had been founded. As the throngs of patriots previously indifferent to the issue of slavery realized for the first time that their own rights might be imperiled, local anti-slavery societies burst into existence and new members flocked into the national network that was suddenly infused with new life and energy. And the unparalleled surge all could be traced back to Garrison's finely crafted editorials in support of a free press.[28]

A third creative technique Garrison originated to keep his dissident publication securely positioned in the nation's consciousness involved his staging of what today would be labeled "media events"—activities designed to capture the imagination of the American public.

The most shocking of the public exhibitions that Garrison orchestrated came on the Fourth of July in 1854 during what he had billed in advance as a "religious rite." Henry David Thoreau first addressed those gathered in the picnic grove in Framingham, Massachusetts, but on this day Garrison would upstage even one of America's most celebrated literary and intellectual giants. The dissident editor first read several passages from the Bible. Then he spoke to the crowd in the slow and steady tones that a minister might use to prepare his congregation for the taking of the sacrament. Telling his listeners that he would now perform an act that would be the testimony of his soul, he lit a candle on the table before him, and, picking up a copy of the Fugitive Slave Law, touched a corner of it to the flame and held it aloft, intoning the words, "And let the people say, Amen." The crowd dutifully echoed his "Amen." Finally, Garrison proceeded to undertake the single most sensational gesture of his life. Grasping a copy of the Constitution and lifting it high above his head so everyone in the crowd could see it, he cursed the document as "the source and parent of all the other atrocities, a covenant with death and an agreement with hell." Garrison then—during this patriotic observance—set fire to the document that, more than any other, symbolized the democratic form of government. As the Constitution burst into flames, the radical editor defiantly declared, "So perish all compromises with tyranny! And let all the people say, Amen!" A few hisses and protests from members of the crowd were eclipsed by a tremendous shout: "Amen!"[29]

Garrison's multi-pronged strategy to ensure that *The Liberator* attracted massive public attention—his exchanges with pro-slavery editors, his expansion of the cause of abolition to a campaign to preserve all civil liberties, and his staging of attention-grabbing media events—was a spectacular success. The various techniques garnered exactly what the provocateur had hoped: spirited discussions of both his paper and the Abolition Movement in kitchens and public meeting places in large cities and small town across the country.

The discussions extended into newsrooms—and onto newspaper front pages from coast to coast. Garrison firmly believed that the American people, North and South, would embrace the anti-slavery cause if they were fully informed about the evils of the "peculiar institution," and, thanks to the dissident editor's strategy, the mainstream press accommodated with extensive news coverage of *The Liberator* and the abolition ideology.

Although the coverage was largely negative, it succeeded in shining the public spotlight onto the Abolition Movement as never before. Typical was a story spread over three columns on page one of the pro-slavery *New York Herald*, one of the country's largest and most influential papers. The article, which reported on an anti-slavery meeting where Garrison had spoken, contained denigrating references to the editor's "bald head, miserable forehead, and comical spectacles" and was even more disparaging to the African Americans who attended the meeting, describing them as "thick-lipped, pig-faced, woolly-headed, baboon-looking negroes." The article lambasted the meeting as well, saying, "It was one of the most amusing, lamentable, laughable, ridiculous, disgusting and jumbled up affairs that we have had for some time."[30]

In addition to these outrageous insults, however, the article also contained highlights from Garrison's speech—including arguments that were central to the Abolition Movement. Right there on the front page of one of the premier newspapers in the country were words that the abolitionists gladly would have paid a princely sum—if they could have afforded it—to have published so prominently. "If the cause of abolition fails, the world will fall to ruin," Garrison was quoted as saying. "Our fathers spared nothing to free the country from British yoke, and the freedom of the black slaves is as holy a cause as that of the Revolution!" Another quotation could have come straight from an anti-slavery recruiting brochure: "The abolition army is increasing all over the world; our banner streams on every hill; we are marshalling on every plain by thousands and tens of thousands." The story—it measured thirty column inches—also reproduced the dramatic jeremiad with which Garrison had ended his rousing speech: "Everyone who is not an abolitionist—no matter how many prayers he says daily; no matter how many church ceremonies he goes through, he is a liar and a hypocrite. He is an enemy to all mankind, and a disgrace to the nation!"[31]

The *Herald* was among a legion of mainstream papers—including the most important shapers of public opinion in the country—that provided extensive coverage of Garrison, his dissident newspaper, and the Abolition Movement. Within a matter of months after Garrison had begun publishing, the *National Intelligencer* in Washington, D.C., reported that *The Liberator* was being distributed "in great numbers"—a flattering statement, though incorrect—and that the atrocities that slaves had to endure "have already caused the plains of the South to be manured with human flesh and blood." Other major dailies followed suit. After a crowd of slavery supporters disrupted an anti-slavery meeting, the *Philadelphia Ledger* adopted Garrison's concept of civil liberties and editorialized: "It was not an offense against the abolitionists that the mob committed when they broke up Garrison's meeting, but an offense against the Constitution, against the Union, against the people, against popular rights, and the great cause of human freedom." The *Boston Courier* continued to disagree with Garrison on the slavery issue, and yet it praised him as a man of principle and tenacity: "We never read a speech or an article of Mr. Garrison's without a consciousness of the power which his deep and fervid convictions give him." By 1854, the *New York Times* was even printing verbatim transcripts of Garrison's speeches; so the publication that was well on its way to becoming the nation's newspaper of record was allowing Garrison to state, boldly and without denunciation: "I am an abolitionist. Hence, I cannot but regard oppression in every form—and most of all, that which turns a man into a thing—with indignation and abhorrence." Garrison's speech was spread over five full columns of the *Times*, building to the crescendo: "Living or dying, defeated or victorious, be it ours to exclaim, 'No compromise with Slavery! Liberty for all, and forever!' "[32]

AROUSING THE NATIONAL CONSCIOUSNESS

The Liberator did not single-handedly bring slavery to an end, but there is no question that the constant and often compelling drumbeat coming from the pages of a widely known and widely talked about abolitionist newspaper week after week, month after month, year after year for three and a half decades helped turn the American consciousness against the sins of slavery. As *The*

Nation asserted in its celebration of *The Liberator*'s achievements: "Its effect on the moral sentiment of the country was exceedingly great. It went straight to the conscience . . . to create that power of moral conviction which was so indomitable." *The Nation*'s comments about William Lloyd Garrison's accomplishments are worth repeating as well: "It is, perhaps, the most remarkable instance on record of single-hearted devotion to a cause."[33]

Between 1831 and 1865, this radical Boston newspaper led the abolitionist press, as well as the Abolition Movement, in successfully articulating the moral indictment of slavery that precipitated the Civil War and that ultimately forced the institution of slavery into a dark corner of American history. In so doing, *The Liberator* also set a singular standard that would be difficult for the publications that followed it to match. Along with that challenge, however, *The Liberator* also gave future generations of dissident journals an example of an editorial commitment combined with a strategy for gaining public notice that together had defined a stunning success.

3 SETTING A REVOLUTIONARY AGENDA FOR WOMEN'S RIGHTS

The American woman of the nineteenth century was widely perceived to be incapable of rational thinking—resolutely helpless and inferior to her male counterpart. She was thought to require man's protection and was, in legal terms, under the guardianship of her father, then her husband. No woman was allowed to vote, and a married woman was not permitted to own property because she was not considered an independent citizen but an appendage who assumed her place in society based on her husband's identity and her biological ability to reproduce the species. She married at sixteen and gave birth to a child every two years through her thirties, losing a third of those children to early death and losing her own health—as well as her looks—by her mid-twenties.

Woman's limited role in society was promulgated through the newspapers that formed the media establishment of the era. Fundamental to that system of communication was the message that man's sphere encompassed all of business and politics, while woman's sphere was limited to the domestic one strictly defined by the four walls of the home. A Philadelphia newspaper succinctly captured the role of the American woman of the nineteenth century when it stated: "A woman is nobody. A wife is everything."[1]

Into this atmosphere was born *The Revolution*.

Founded in 1868 by two women who would challenge the social, political, and economic restrictions placed on the American woman as few people before or since, the dissident newspaper carried the bold motto "Men, Their Rights and Nothing More; Women, Their Rights and Nothing Less." The paper's editorial content created an agenda that contained many of the high-voltage issues that today—more than a century later—still form the epicenter of the contemporary Women's Rights Movement: Job discrimination. Equal pay for equal work. Sexual harassment. Inadequate political representation. Domestic violence. Abortion.

The Revolution lived up to its name not only through the volatile agenda it advanced but also because of its ambitions as a publishing venture. During a time when few women were allowed to write for newspapers or see their issues discussed in newsprint, Elizabeth Cady Stanton and Susan Brownell Anthony took the audacious step of establishing themselves as, respectively, editor and publisher of *The Revolution*. Stanton wrote the fiery editorials and edited the numerous submissions from readers; Anthony ran the office, paid the bills, and hired the printers. The only male presence in the operation was Parker Pillsbury, who helped Stanton with her editing chores.

The New York-based weekly was daunting in its vision and scope as well. Stanton and Anthony brazenly proclaimed that they would produce sixteen pages per issue—four times the size of *The Liberator*—and would distribute their paper nationally to build a circulation of 100,000. "Nothing short of this ensures our complete success," Stanton wrote. They also projected not a quiet voice but a boisterous one, telling women who wanted to write for the paper: "Don't preach. Don't even exhort. Don't philosophize. Above all, don't sentimentalize. Give us facts and experience in words, if you please, as hard as cannon balls."[2]

Although circulation peaked at 3,000 and the publishing venture survived only two and a half years in its dissident form, there is no question that *The Revolution* fired an astonishing number of editorial cannon balls. "I am delighted to learn that we are to have a paper," a Massachusetts woman wrote in the second issue. "It is what we most need." A Michigan woman added, "God speed you in the cause of justice, Equal Rights, and human liberty. Revolution! How I *like* that name." And an Iowa woman wrote succinctly: "Go on and revolve the whole wheel!"[3]

THE REVOLUTIONARIES

By the time Elizabeth Cady Stanton began editing *The Revolution*, she already had been revolving the wheel toward women's rights for twenty years. She was born into a middle-class New York family in 1815 and during her youth was a voracious reader. Her marriage to lawyer and abolitionist Henry B. Stanton was a happy one that produced seven children, but her husband's work often took him away from home; in the isolated community of Seneca Falls in upstate New York, she grew bored with the limited dimensions of homemaking. Stanton first won her place in history in the summer of 1848 when she organized and hosted the event that marked the beginning of the Women's Rights Movement in the United States. The Seneca Falls Convention brought together some

With Elizabeth Cady Stanton (left) as editor and Susan Brownell Anthony as publisher, *The Revolution* created a dissident agenda for American women's rights. (Courtesy of the Smithsonian Institution)

300 progressive-minded women and men who resolved that liberty was not the province of men alone but was—or should be—the birthright of women as well. The tangible product of their historic event was a paraphrase of the Declaration of Independence that read, "We hold these truths to be self-evident: that all men *and women* are created equal." The feminists who attended the meeting challenged the concept of sex-segregated spheres, crafting resolutions that encouraged women to enter the professions and that called for women to be granted suffrage, as well as property and child custody rights.[4]

During the 1850s, Susan Brownell Anthony crossed paths with Stanton at various suffrage activities while emerging as a movement leader in her own right. Born into a middle-class Massachusetts family in 1820, Anthony initially committed her energies to temperance and abolition but eventually focused on women's rights. Unmarried and willing to devote her abundant talents to the movement, Anthony brought particular strengths as an intellect and organizer.

Together, Stanton and Anthony formed a dynamic partnership at the vanguard of the nascent Women's Rights Movement. They helped orchestrate hundreds of women's rights meetings, public lectures, and petition drives across the country and organized a national convention each year until the outbreak of the Civil War in 1861, when they placed the movement on hold because of the crisis on the battlefield. After the war ended, the women intensified their campaign for women's rights.

One of the major impediments to the march toward gender equality was the news media. For by the mid-nineteenth century, the Fourth Estate was firmly established as a body overwhelmingly peopled by, and largely committed to serving, *men*. American newspapers either ignored the Women's Rights Movement or treated it with a toxic mixture of outrage, contempt, and derision—all designed to prevent women from gaining a share of the male power base. James Gordon Bennett of the *New York Herald*, one of the most influential papers in the country, dubbed the Seneca Falls Convention the "Woman's Wrong Convention" that proved that America's "political and social fabric is crumbling." The *New York Times* took the position that women already possessed so much political power through their husbands that to grant them any more would deny men an equal share in governance. "The time has come," the *Times* contended, "for the organization of a 'Rights of Man Association' to withstand the greedy appropriativeness of womankind."[5]

RAISING A VOICE OF THEIR OWN

Stanton and Anthony realized that if the Women's Rights Movement was to succeed, it would have to follow the example of the Abolition Movement and create its own communication network. So in January 1868, the two women—both in their fifties—entered the tumultuous world of dissident journalism. Stanton and Anthony printed 10,000 copies of that first issue, distributing them nationwide at suffrage meetings and lectures. The paper's primary purpose was, the premier issue stated without apology, to ignite the fire of indignation in the hearts of its readers. "We think 'The Revolution' a fitting name for a paper that will advocate radical reform," Stanton and Anthony announced. "The name speaks its purpose. It is to revolutionize. It is Radicalism practical, not theoretical."[6]

The first major dispute *The Revolution* became embroiled in did not involve its editorial content, however, but its finances. Initial capital for the newspaper was provided by George Francis Train, a controversial millionaire. Train was particularly unpopular among abolitionists because he refused to denounce slavery. An early issue of *The Revolution* carried a letter from William Lloyd Garrison criticizing the paper for accepting Train's money. With his characteristic vehemence, Garrison called Train a "crack brained harlequin and semilunatic!" Stanton and Anthony defended their financial angel, saying that he was willing to support women's rights when most men would not. "It would be right and wise to accept aid from the devil himself," Stanton said, "provided that he did not tempt us to lower our standard."[7]

The passionate debate gave *The Revolution* national notoriety while also beginning its long struggle with money. Unlike other editors of the day, Stanton refused to accept advertisements for patent medicines—she called them "quack remedies"—because she believed that the unregulated elixirs contained so much alcohol that they were dangerous. Nor was the paper's fiscal status helped by the fact that most businesses refused to be associated with such a controversial journal, preferring to place their ads in moderate publications that were less likely to offend potential buyers of their products. (One exception was an advertisement for the Woodhull Claflin & Co. Brokerage House; it was the first firm on Wall Street founded by women, sisters Victoria Woodhull and Tennessee Claflin.)[8]

The paper's finances also suffered because very few women in the 1860s enjoyed the economic resources that allowed them to subscribe to a newspaper, and few husbands supported the idea of their wives reading such a revolutionary publication. Although neither Stanton nor Anthony drew a salary, the annual subscription rate of two dollars still did not produce sufficient revenue to pay the printing and mailing expenses. The women followed Garrison's example and subsidized their newspaper by giving public lectures, but the debts continued to mount.

The Revolution's editorial agenda was too radical even for most supporters of women's suffrage. The newspaper insisted that women securing the vote—an unpopular position until well into the twentieth century—was merely the first step in the Women's Rights Movement. "The ballot is not even half the loaf," the paper argued. "It is only a crust—a crumb."[9]

This stand led to a split in the movement, propelling the more moderate Lucy Stone and her husband Henry Blackwell to found *Woman's Journal,* a far less abrasive journalistic endeavor than *The Revolution,* in 1870. The Boston-based *Woman's Journal* remained tightly focused on suffrage and such middle-

The Revolution.

PRINCIPLE, NOT POLICY: JUSTICE, NOT FAVORS.—MEN, THEIR RIGHTS AND NOTHING MORE: WOMEN, THEIR RIGHTS AND NOTHING LESS.

VOL. I.—NO. 3.   NEW YORK, WEDNESDAY, JANUARY 22, 1868. $2.00 A YEAR.

The Revolution;

THE ORGAN OF THE

NATIONAL PARTY OF NEW AMERICA.

PRINCIPLE, NOT POLICY—INDIVIDUAL RIGHTS AND RESPONSIBILITIES.

THE REVOLUTION WILL DISCUSS:

1. IN POLITICS—Educated Suffrage, Irrespective of Sex or Color; Equal Pay to Women for Equal Work; Eight Hours Labor; Abolition of Standing Armies and Party Despotisms. Down with Politicians—Up with the People!

2. IN RELIGION—Deeper Thought; Broader Ideas; Science not Superstition; Personal Purity; Love to Man as well as God.

3. IN SOCIAL LIFE.—Practical Education, not Theoretical; Fact, not Fiction; Virtue, not Vice; Cold Water, not Alcoholic Drinks or Medicines. Devoted to Morality and Reform, THE REVOLUTION will not insert Gross Personalities and Quack Advertisements, which even Religious Newspapers introduce to every family.

4. THE REVOLUTION proposes a new Commercial and Financial Policy. America no longer led by Europe. Gold, like our Cotton and Corn, for sale. Greenbacks for money. An American System of Finance. American Products and Labor Free. Foreign Manufactures Prohibited. Open doors to Artisans and Immigrants. Atlantic and Pacific Oceans for American Steamships and Shipping; or American goods in American bottoms. New York the Financial Centre of the World. Wall Street emancipated from Bank of England, or American Cash for American Bills. The Credit Foncier and Credit Mobilier System, or Capital Mobilised to Resuscitate the South and our Mining Interests, and to People the Country from Ocean to Ocean, from Omaha to San Francisco. More organised Labor, more Cotton, more Gold and Silver Bullion to sell foreigners at the highest prices. Ten millions of Naturalized Citizens DEMAND A PENNY OCEAN POSTAGE, to Strengthen the Brotherhood of Labor. If Congress Vote One Hundred and Twenty-five Millions for a Standing Army and Freedman's Bureau for the Blacks, cannot they spare One Million for the Whites, to keep bright the chain of friendship between them and their Fatherland?

Send in your Subscription. THE REVOLUTION, published weekly, will be the Great Organ of the Age.

TERMS.—Two dollars a year, in advance. Ten names ($20) entitle the sender to one copy free.

ELIZABETH CADY STANTON,
PARKER PILLSBURY, } Eds.

SUSAN B. ANTHONY, PROPRIETOR.
37 Park Row (Room 17), New York City.
To whom address all business letters.

WESTWARD.

BY GEORGE FRANCIS TRAIN.

EPIGRAM HISTORY OF THE WORLD, IN NINE ACTS.

[WRITTEN on the summit of the Rocky Mountains. Inspired on witnessing the moon set as the sun rose Nov. 13, 1837.]

Westward! Ever Westward, for a thousand generations,
Civilization marching onward, peopled the Ancient Nations,
When woman sold her jewels, 'twas in Fourteen Ninety-two,
That Columbus left the Old World, and landed in the New.
Again in Sixteen Twenty, Miles Standish on the dock,
Founded our Mighty Empire, where he anchored on a rock!
Westward! Ever Westward, seven score and sixteen years,
We worked and toiled, and grew beyond the British House of Peers.
Oppressive taxes—wrath aroused—then Charon crossed the Styx,
Up with the flag—down with the Tea—cried Men of Seventy-six.
Westward! Ever Westward, in Eighteen Sixty-one,
Our people roused from lethargy at sound of Sumter gun.
And then our old arch-enemy went tottering to the grave,
England loosed her grip of death when we set free the slave.
Westward! Ever Westward, in December Sixty-three,
I broke the ground at Omaha, half way from sea to sea.
Westward! Ever Westward, in the following month of May,
The Railroad King Durant pushed on, two miles or more a day.
'Tis morn! on Rocky Mountains' top, whose columns reach the skies,
We see the moon retire to rest! The sun in splendor rise!
Eastward! Presto! Eastward, let my Fenians share the praise,
When Asia visits Europe in less than thirty days!

WHAT THE PRESS SAYS OF THE REVOLUTION.

SUNDAY TIMES.

THE LADIES MILITANT : It is out at last. If the women, as a body, have not succeeded in getting up a revolution, Susan B. Anthony, as their representative, has. Her "Revolution" was issued last Thursday as a sort of New Year's gift to what she considered a yearning public, and it is said to be "charged to the muzzle with literary nitro-glycerine."

If Mrs. Stanton would attend a little more to her domestic duties and a little less to those of the great public, perhaps she would exalt her sex quite as much as she does by Quixotically fighting windmills in their gratuitous behalf, and she might possibly set a notable example of domestic idiotry. No married woman can convert herself into a feminine Knight of the Rueful Visage and ride about the country attempting to redress imaginary wrongs, without leaving her own household in a neglected condition that must be an eloquent witness against her. As for the spinsters, we have often said that every woman has a natural and inalienable right to a good husband and a pretty baby. When, by proper "agitation," she has secured this right, the best honors herself and her sex by leaving public affairs be-hind her, and by endeavoring to show how happy she can make the little world of which she has just become the brilliant centre.

Ah! sir, in recommending to our attention domestic economy, you have assailed us in our stronghold. Here we are unsurpassed. We know—what not one woman in ten thousand does know—how to take care of a child, make good bread, and keep a home clean. We never harbor rats, mice, or cockroaches, ants, fleas, or bed bugs. Our children have never run the gauntlet of sprue, jaundice, croup, chicken-pox, whooping-cough, measles, scarlet-fever or fits, but they are healthy, rosy, happy, and well-fed. Pork, salt meat, mackerel, rancid butter, heavy bread, lard, cream of tartar and soda, or any other culinary abominations are never found on our table. Now let every man who wants his wife to know how to do likewise take THE REVOLUTION, in which not only the ballot, but bread and babies will be discussed.

As to spinsters, our proprietor says, that just as soon as she is enfranchised, and the laws of marriage and divorce are equal for man and woman, she will take the subject of matrimony into serious consideration, perhaps call on the editor of the Sunday Times.

N. Y. CITIZEN.

THE REVOLUTION, advocating "love to man as well as God," is edited by Miss Parker Pillsbury, and two gay young fellows named Mrs. Elizabeth Cady Stanton and Miss Susan B. Anthony. It advocates "Equal pay to women for equal work." But why does it not go for equal justice to all, irrespective of sex or color, and also demand " Equal pay to men for equal work with women?" This, we take it, would save a good many good dollars to a good many good fellows. As society is now organized, we men have to do all the work and the women get all the money. In the dictionary of Fifth avenue, the word husband is thus defined : " Husband—a useful domestic drudge ; a machine that makes dollars."

Exact justice to all, irrespective of sex and color, is precisely what we advocate. We do not forget our sons in demanding the rights of our daughters. When all girls are educated for self dependence, men will cease to be mere machines for making money, while the wealth of the nation will be doubled.

CAMBRIDGE PRESS.

A LIVE NEWSPAPER.—THE REVOLUTION is a great fact. All the leaders in the nation will take it. It is the organ of Temperance—of one hundred thousand School Teachers—of morality, and a new system of Finance. The subscription-list already contains the President and Cabinet of the United States—the Vice-President and Senate—the Speaker and the members of the House of Representatives—all the Governors, Bankers and Brokers. Ten thousand first number.

THE REVOLUTION will be the Organ of the National Party of New America, based on individual rights in political, religious and social life. It will be devoted to Principle, not Policy. It will be backed by the Credit Foncier of America, the Credit Mobilier of America, the Pacific Railroad Company, and half of Wall street ; with Mrs. Elizabeth Cady Stanton and Parker Pillsbury as editors, and Miss Susan B. Anthony as general manager and proprietor.

Let the one hundred thousand school teachers send in their subscriptions. We intend that two million dollars spent yearly in the

The radical concepts that the early women's rights newspaper advocated were reflected in the paper's bold name: *The Revolution*.

class efforts as establishing women's clubs and encouraging women to obtain higher educations. The newspaper's views appealed to a broader base of women, giving *Woman's Journal* the support it needed to build a circulation of 6,000, achieve financial solvency, and publish without interruption until 1933.

The Revolution and *Woman's Journal* were joined by several dozen other women's rights publications, most of which served local communities and were short-lived. None of the other publications approached the topic of women's rights with an agenda nearly as radical as the one that erupted from the pages of *The Revolution*.[10]

Like *The Liberator* before it, *The Revolution* received substantial attention in the mainstream press—most of it negative. New York's *Commercial Advertiser* demeaned *The Revolution* by calling it "Amazonian," and the *New York Times* called Stanton and Anthony's paper "meaningless," "foolish," and "a victim of illogical thinking."[11]

Establishment newspapers were even more hostile toward the founders of the radical women's rights paper, being particularly harsh toward Anthony. In 1870, the *Utica* [New York] *Herald* wrote sardonically: "Who does not feel sympathy for Susan Anthony? She has striven long and earnestly to become a man. She is sweet in the eyes of her own mirror, but her advanced age and maiden name deny that she has been so in the eyes of others." Anthony was positioned in the cross hairs of the mainstream press primarily because she did not marry and, therefore, defied the conventions of the nineteenth-century social order. Papers routinely referred to the publisher by such degrading terms as "poor creature," "unfortunate woman," and "unsexed woman," and the *New York Sun* portrayed Anthony and other unmarried contributors to *The Revolution* as sexual freaks, stating, "The quiet duties of daughter, wife or mother are not congenial to these hermaphrodite spirits who thirst to win the title of champion of one sex and victor over the other."[12]

Despite the scornful tone that mainstream papers adopted, Stanton believed all publicity was good publicity because it ultimately would familiarize more readers with the women's rights agenda that *The Revolution* advocated. She wrote in her personal correspondence: "There is no danger of the Woman Question dying for want of notice. Every paper you take up has something to say about it." Opting for the point of view that it was better to be deplored than ignored, Stanton continued: "Imagine the publicity given to our idea by thus appearing in a widely circulated sheet like the [*New York*] *Herald*. It will start women thinking, and men too; and when men and women think about a new question, the first step in progress is taken." Lucretia Mott, who wrote for *The Revolution*, expressed a similar sentiment. She acknowledged that mainstream newspapers "ridiculed and slandered us" but was convinced that the press goes "through three stages in regard to reforms; they first ridicule them, then report them without comment, and at last openly advocate them. We seem to be still in the first stage."[13]

Mockery aside, *The Revolution*'s provocative content attracted some notable readers. President Andrew Johnson was an early subscriber; he read the radical paper even though he opposed its initiatives, because he believed that it could have profound impact on the voting public. Divinity students at Harvard College read the paper as well. When the Harvard subscription request arrived at *The Revolution* office, Stanton did not pass up the opportunity to let loose an editorial attack on the educational restraints placed upon American women, telling the sons of Harvard: "To be sure we will send it to you FREE. Though the daughters of the land in darkness and ignorance sit weeping at the college doors, still barred against them, yet women will be true to you."[14]

The acerbic comments that Stanton sent to the ivy-covered halls of Harvard were mild, however, compared to the red meat she served up on the pages of *The Revolution*.

JOB DISCRIMINATION

Although the popular ideal for American womanhood during the era called for full-time devotion to domesticity, many women either needed or wanted to work outside the home. But when women sought paid employment, they were allowed to work in an exceedingly narrow range of jobs. African American and immigrant women could work as domestics, at needlework, or in factories; native-born white women with more status could work as teachers or store clerks. So one of *The Revolution*'s most sustained editorial crusades was against the practice of barring women from the vast majority of occupational fields.

The paper initiated this campaign by publishing a working women's call to arms that focused specifically on the fact that thousands of women were destroying their eyesight by working long hours six and seven days a week in clothing factories. "Working women, throw your needles to the winds," the article began. "If women are to have a place in this world, they must get right out of the old grooves and do new and grand things. We have looked through the eye of a needle long enough. It is time for THE REVOLUTION."[15]

The second phase of the crusade against job discrimination consisted of articles illuminating occupations that, according to *The Revolution*, women should consider entering. "If you have a telegraph office in your town, study that business and then look for a position [as a telegraph operator] in some large city," one article argued. "Study medicine or buy some land and raise fruit and vegetables for the New York market. Chickens and eggs pay well." Other items encouraged women to consider jobs as undertakers, railroad and streetcar conductors, architects, real estate brokers, and lawyers. Another said, "We heard of a family of daughters out West who, being left suddenly to depend on themselves, decided to ignore all woman's work at low wages, so they donned male attire. One went to work in a lumber yard, one on a steamboat, one drove a hack in a Western city, and in a few years with economy they laid up enough to buy a handsome farm where they now live in comfort."[16]

In another article highlighting new fields that women should consider entering, Anthony wrote: "There are a thousand things for women to do besides making shirts and night-caps. The entire advertising agency business ought to be in their hands, and, when they have got some money to put in it, they will want a bank—a woman's savings bank—the president, directors and employees all women. They will also want a Woman's Life Insurance Company, but not until they have a vote and their lives are worth insuring."[17]

To nudge American women toward the realms of business and public affairs, *The Revolution* created editorial departments composed of financial and political news, including reports of President Andrew Johnson's impeachment trial and the proposal to replace gold and silver coins with paper currency.[18]

EQUAL PAY FOR EQUAL WORK

Closely connected to the issue of job discrimination was the extreme pay differential between what women and men were paid. The issue of equal pay for equal work was so important to Anthony that she became one of the country's first female labor organizers, helping to found the Working Women's Association "for the purpose of doing everything possible to elevate women, and raise the value of their labor." Anthony conducted the group's initial meetings in *The Revolution*'s business office.[19]

The paper publicized Anthony's labor activities as part of its equal-pay-for-equal-work campaign. In one article, Stanton boasted that her feminist partner's organization had attracted more than 200 working-class women who were meeting monthly to devise ways to raise their pay. "They propose," Stanton reported, "to demand an increase of wages in all those trades where they now work beside men for half pay. This can only be done by combination, for one person alone demanding higher wages can effect nothing, but 5,000 women in any one employment, striking for higher wages, would speedily bring their employers to terms."[20]

Another element in the campaign for pay equity was to bring public attention to particularly egregious instances of wage discrimination. In one poignant article, *The Revolution* reproduced a comprehensive set of salary figures. The material was attributed to the U.S. Superintendent of Public Instruction and documented not merely an occasional example of sexual inequality in one or two communities but a systemic pattern of discrimination nationwide. In Connecticut, male teachers were paid $28 per month; female teachers were paid $16. The figures for other states were just as shocking. In Illinois, $30 for men, $19 for women. In Wisconsin and Ohio, $36 for men, $22 for women. The figures for Maine were the worst of all: $28 for men, $10 for women. After providing the statistics, *The Revolution* added a single sentence of eloquently simple commentary: "Robbery is not all committed in the night, nor on the highway."[21]

SEXUAL HARASSMENT

Women's rights advocates of the nineteenth century were forced to endure not only the unjust and degrading treatment in the workplace that the phrase "sexual harassment" brings to mind today, but other types of mistreatment as well. If a woman dared to speak or write boldly, to think independently, or to dress in defiance of convention, she risked being derided, condemned, intimidated, physically abused, or even arrested and punished by the legal system—all effective methods of maintaining the male-dominated social order. *The Revolution* provided the first published record of the breadth of the sexual harassment meted out against progressive women, and also expressed consistent outrage at the phenomenon in all its forms.

Typical was an anecdotal article written by Eleanor Kirk, a reader who took advantage of *The Revolution*'s open-forum approach to publishing. "A young lady, educated and talented, is compelled to earn her own bread and butter and be of some assistance in a relative's family of which she is a member," Kirk wrote. After "meeting with success" as a writer and "looking forward to a brilliant career," the article continued, the young woman secured a contract with a male editor for "the very handsome sum of $25 for a weekly article." The situation soured, however, when the "smooth-tongued editor" propositioned "the dumbfounded girl, in language which admitted of no misunderstanding, to become his mistress." When the young woman refused, the editor canceled her publishing contract. Kirk concluded the piece with a lament that could just as easily have been written a century later about any sexual harassment case: "Now, we ask, what can a woman do under such circumstances?"[22]

The most frequent cases of sexual harassment documented in *The Revolution* came in response to women attempting to break free from the constraints of proper fashion. The newspaper decried the health hazards of women wearing long, heavy dresses—a typical outfit weighed twelve to twenty pounds—with tightly laced corsets that constricted the diaphragm and made breathing more difficult. The paper also advised readers who were trying to move into new occupations to take drastic measures if their clothes interfered: "If your petticoats stand in the way of bread, virtue and freedom, cut them off." But, at the same time, the paper documented that women who wore looser clothing were often targeted for public censure. News items told of women in Minnesota, Ohio, and New York all being arrested when they wore loose-fitting pantaloons or bloomers, prompting *The Revolution* to protest: "We should like to know under what statute women are prosecuted for wearing a convenient dress?"[23]

INADEQUATE POLITICAL REPRESENTATION

Although *The Revolution* had a much broader agenda than simply campaigning for women to win suffrage, a substantial portion of its editorial space was, nevertheless, devoted to this issue. Abuse of power was rampant in all levels of government, the paper charged, and women voters were needed to bring about the civil service reform that was necessary to prevent the country from being stolen away from its citizens. "Wherever woman goes, reform is sure to follow," one article stated. The widespread corruption proved, Stanton wrote, that men were incapable of running a democratic society without the assistance of women. "The man idea of government is the sword, the gallows, the whip, and toe of the boot. Against all this, woman is working to usher in a new day of love, peace, equality, and mercy."[24]

Many of Stanton's editorial tirades, however, sounded neither loving nor peaceful—but belligerent and hostile. She argued that women not being allowed to vote was tantamount to "the tyranny of taxation without representation" that had driven American colonists to rebel and separate from England. The firebrand editor argued that the ballot would not merely give women a political tool but would represent a new definition of womanhood as fully part of the human race that, throughout history, had been the exclusive domain of white manhood. "Ignorant negroes and women may not use the ballot wisely, but they could not do worse than white men in the past have done for them," she wrote, calling white men "lawless" and "evil-minded" beings who had used the ballot "to grind women and negroes to powder."[25]

Although Stanton clearly opposed racial discrimination, her primary concern was with gender. This ranking of priorities led to her most controversial political position: that black suffrage should not be approved until women's suffrage was also approved. Therefore, she adamantly opposed the Fifteenth Amendment to the Constitution that was proposed at the end of the Civil War to grant African American men the right to vote. Stanton argued that extending the vote to all men, black as well as white, would more deeply embed the sexual caste system and create what she termed an "aristocracy of sex," making every American woman the political inferior of every American man, regardless of the individual's class, occupation, or education. "We have no reason to suppose that the black man understands the principles of equity, or will practice the Christian virtues, better than his Saxon masters."[26]

Stanton moved beyond words. In November 1868, she reproduced a sample petition on *The Revolution*'s front page, urging her readers to circulate the document in their local communities and then send it, along with as many signatures as they could collect, to Washington, D.C. The call for equal suffrage read: "To the Senate and House of Representatives, in Congress Assembled: The Undersigned citizens earnestly but respectfully request, that in any change or amendment of the Constitution you may propose, to extend or regulate Suffrage, there shall be no distinction made between men and women." Within two months, the pages of *The Revolution* were filled with letters from subscribers around the country who had heeded Stanton's call. Typical was one that said, "I send you by this mail a petition for Equal Suffrage, signed by one hundred and eighty-five names."[27]

Stanton's ardent comments and the flood of signatures notwithstanding, Congress passed the Fifteenth Amendment in February 1869.

That setback did not, however, dissuade the women of *The Revolution* from promoting concrete political action. Stanton would, during the life of her hard-hitting newspaper, reproduce more than one petition on the front page. Even if those petitions did not produce immediate victory, Stanton was a savvy political operative who knew that circulating each petition was exposing a larger and larger number of women to the issues of the day, to the political process, and to the fact that a grassroots social movement was gradually gaining momentum. The woman who sent the petition containing 185 signatures ended her letter by saying, "I have obtained them myself, by going from house to house. It is a slow process, so few have heard anything of the movement, and the whole thing has to be explained to each person."[28]

DOMESTIC VIOLENCE

One of the most troubling phenomena *The Revolution* exposed was the physical violence that often was part of nineteenth-century marriage. Indeed, this revelation was one of the paper's most important contributions to the Women's Rights Movement. The paper showed that, contrary to popular belief, husbands did not always protect their wives from danger but often perpetrated acts of domestic violence. The various states, at the time, either had no laws against wife beating or, if laws existed, opted not to enforce them.

Although divorce was a possible resolution to domestic violence, the stigma attached to ending a marriage was more onerous than any law. Even if a woman sought a divorce on the grounds of physical cruelty, "good society" whispered that she must somehow have been to blame for the abuse, dramatically diminishing her chances to remarry. It was not just her reputation and her future prospects that a woman lost in divorce, however, but also her children—the law stated they belonged to their father. So a physically abused woman had two choices. She could remain unhappily married and abused while retaining her home, financial security, and children. Or she could obtain a divorce and lose her place in society, whatever property she possessed, and her children. Not surprisingly, most women decided to stay married—and victims of domestic violence.

The Revolution published a startling record of women being victimized by the men who claimed to love and protect them. A typical article reported the circumstances of a Wisconsin woman. "The first week after their marriage, he brought a whip into the house and gave his wife to understand that whenever she failed to please him it should be used upon her, and true to his original promise, it has, time and again, been used upon the slightest provocation. And yet, notwithstanding all this abuse, this woman feels that she is obliged to continue living with this brutal husband."[29]

Eleanor Kirk wrote a gripping piece titled "A Word to Abused Wives" that related the regrettable details of her own life. "Ten miserable years of married life, in which every article of the wifely contract was performed to the letter—ten years of abuse, drunkenness, infidelity." Kirk went on to describe her husband repeatedly cursing and kicking her.[30]

Kirk's advice to other women who suffered similar abuse was to leave their husbands, taking their children with them. She had done exactly that and had found that her husband did not try to retrieve the children, apparently glad to be rid of them. Kirk then had succeeded, although not without difficulty, in supporting herself and her children by publishing books and writing for magazines.

On the subject of domestic violence, she wrote with fervency: "Who ordained that man can violate every marriage obligation—drink, abuse, and then be *obeyed*? Who declared that woman must live with a wretch through all sorts of personal ill-treatment? Don't believe a word of such stuff; it is the most ridiculous balderdash that ever was repeated. Free yourself, refuse to live with him. Wake up!" Kirk further advised abused women to form consciousness-raising groups to gain the emotional support they needed to live independently. "Form a club. See how many women you have in town who can be depended upon," she wrote. "Frequent discussings, comparing notes with each other, reading aloud articles from 'The Revolution' will give you a breadth and earnestness."[31]

Stanton took an even more controversial position, not only advocating that an abused woman leave her husband but that she also, despite the condemnation that the action would provoke from the press and the pulpit, go through the legal process of suing her husband for divorce on the grounds of physical abuse. Such proceedings would bring attention to the epidemic of domestic violence that *The Revolution* had uncovered, the fearless editor argued, and ultimately force divorce laws to be liberalized.

Happily married herself, Stanton argued that divorce was essential to end unhappy unions and thereby preserve marriage and family as respected and honorable institutions. "You all know marriage is, in many cases, a mere outward tie, impelled by custom, policy, interest, necessity; founded not even in friendship, to say nothing of love." As letters from readers made Stanton increasingly aware of the number of women who endured miserable marriages defined by physical and psychological abuse, she became more strident in her support of divorce, stating that the laws forcing women to remain in unhappy marriages "are exactly parallel with the slave code on southern plantations."[32]

Stanton's most extreme article on the subject of divorce was headlined "Marriages and Mistresses." In it, she described the role of mistress as superior to that of wife, insisting that, "The 'legal position' of a wife is more dependent and degrading than any other condition of womanhood can possibly be."[33]

ABORTION

Mainstream newspapers of the mid-nineteenth century seldom mentioned the crime of abortion, although it was widely acknowledged to be a serious social problem. Aborting a fetus or allowing a newborn infant to die was not only illegal and punishable by death but also was considered the most heinous crime a woman could commit. *The Revolution*'s major contribution on the topic, beyond the fundamental one of discussing it at all, was to object to the common practice of blaming abortions on the depravity of the women who had them. It was not moral degeneracy that led a woman to end an unwanted pregnancy, the paper argued, but sexual exploitation by the man who had impregnated her.

The Revolution used the case of a recent immigrant, Hester Vaughan, to raise the abortion issue. As Stanton, with no small amount of melodrama, told the story: "Not long ago, a pretty English girl, poor and friendless, was wandering in the streets of Philadelphia, seeking employment. Seeing a respectable-looking man, she asked him if he could tell her where she could find a good place to work. Yes, he promptly replied, he would take her to his country home. So she went with him and remained in his family several months." As with any good drama, conflict soon entered Stanton's story. "But alas! her protector proved her betrayer." Specifically, after the married employer (despite the national notoriety that the case eventually received, he was never named) had taken the young girl into the country, he seduced her. And when she became pregnant, he fired her. "She was turned into the street at the very time she needed shelter, love and care. With the wages she had saved, for she was an industrious, frugal girl, she took a small room in a tenement house." Stanton then painted a vivid picture of how, "in the depth of winter, without a fire, a bed, or one article of furniture," one morning young Hester "was found in a fainting condition, and the child dead by her side."[34]

The young woman was then tried, convicted, and sentenced to be hanged for allowing her baby to die. It was at this point that Stanton began a campaign on the young woman's behalf, arguing not that women had the right to have an abortion but that women—particularly young immigrant women—were victims of the system. "If that poor child of sorrow is hung, it will be deliberate, downright murder," Stanton wrote. "She is the child of our society and civilization, begotten and born to it, seduced by it." The editor pleaded with the women of Pennsylvania to take pity on the servant girl, "In the name of womanhood, we implore the mothers of that state to rescue that defenseless girl from her impending fate. Oh! make her case your own."[35]

Stanton did not stop with words but took the unprecedented step—during a time when it was considered a disgrace for a woman to participate in public issues—of meeting personally with the governor of Pennsylvania to plead that he pardon Hester Vaughan. As the governor deliberated, Stanton increased the emotional pitch of the already highly charged atmosphere surrounding the case—and turning up the heat on the governor—by leading a delegation of women who visited Hester in prison. After the visit, Stanton was "more than ever convinced of her innocence. She has a quiet, self-possessed manner and is gentle in her movements and speech." Stanton and Anthony mobilized still more public support for Hester Vaughan by organizing what today would be called a "media event" in the form of a mass rally in New York City to protest the double standard applied to the woman and the man involved in an abortion case. And then, finally, with Stanton and Anthony having whipped public fury to a fever pitch, the governor announced his decision: Hester Vaughan was pardoned.[36]

In Stanton's last entry in her four-month editorial campaign, she spoke not with hubris for winning this battle but with a call for sisterhood that crossed class lines. "This case carries with it a lesson for the serious thought of every woman, as it shows the importance that women of wealth, education and leisure study the laws under which they live, that they may defend the unfortunate of their sex in our courts of justice."[37]

THE RADICAL VOICE GOES SILENT

George Francis Train's financial support of *The Revolution* did more for the paper's notoriety than for its fiscal stability. Soon after the paper began publishing, Train traveled to England and was sent to prison for publicly backing the Irish rebels there. His infusion of funds to *The Revolution* gradually declined, with his association ending completely by May 1869.

Without its angel, the paper quickly amassed a substantial debt. Stanton and Anthony insisted on producing a quality product, and that meant expensive paper and high-salaried typesetters—Anthony hired as many women as possible and insisted on paying them the wages they deserved. Stanton's strict policy against patent medicines kept advertising revenue to a minimum. What's more, the paper's ideology was far too radical to attract large numbers of subscribers; articles about abortion, in particular, caused many potential readers to condemn the paper as pornographic and to banish it from their homes for fear that children might read it.

After two years of meeting weekly deadlines but not meeting expenses, Stanton was open to the possibility of giving up the paper. Anthony, on the other hand, was determined to keep the paper alive. According to one observer, Anthony "worked like a whole plantation of slaves" giving lectures, soliciting contributions, and pouring every available cent into the publication. She even borrowed several thousand dollars from her family. None of it was enough.[38]

In June 1870, Anthony finally gave up. She reluctantly transferred possession of the paper to Laura Curtis Bullard, a suffragist who had written several articles for *The Revolution*, for one dollar. Anthony then assumed the paper's $10,000 debt and spent the next six years repaying it through her lecture fees.

Under Bullard, *The Revolution* became a mainstream literary and social journal, adding columns such as "Household," "Gossip," and "Children's Corner." Bullard's publication also attracted a larger variety of advertisers—including the patent medicine companies that Stanton abhorred. The newspaper was sold again in early 1872 and published its final issue that February.

LASTING LEGACY

Although *The Revolution* survived as a dissident voice for only two and a half years and its circulation never exceeded 3,000, Elizabeth Cady Stanton and Susan Brownell Anthony's journalistic offspring clearly boosted the Women's Rights Movement. More than half a century before the citizenship of women was finally acknowledged through the Nineteenth Amendment in 1920, *The Revolution* fired a volley of editorial "cannon balls" that championed a stunning list of unpopular causes related to women's rights. It brought attention to the plight of working women. It promoted the professional, political, and educational advancement of women, and it provided a public venue in which such factious issues as sexual harassment, domestic violence, and abortion could be discussed in print.

Public humiliation and personal peril be damned, Stanton and Anthony stood tall as agents of change and opponents of gender-based injustice. They took strong editorial positions in their paper and, when necessary, stepped boldly into the bare-knuckled world of politics and public upheaval, encouraging readers to circulate petitions in their local communities and, in the Hester Vaughan case, lobbying the governor of Pennsylvania and holding a public rally to advance their cause.

The Revolution's greatest contributions were not to the women who read it between 1868 and 1870, however, but to those women and men in the future who would continue to read, discuss, and draw inspiration from its radical agenda—and from the fact that the paper had the courage to articulate such ideas as early as the 1860s. The newspaper set down for the first time in a major national forum arguments for women's equality that are still being used more than 100 years later. That agenda has been kept alive in the plethora of biographies that have been written about Stanton and Anthony, as well as in the numerous scholarly studies of *The Revolution* itself—including a 300-page book entirely devoted to reprinting articles that originally appeared in the paper.[39]

The Revolution made contributions to the institution of American journalism as well, helping to initiate the tradition of publishing political news and commentary written from a woman's perspective. The dissident newspaper inspired the founding of several other nineteenth-century women's rights publications, including the venerable *Woman's Journal,* and established a model for the hundreds that would follow in the twentieth century. Mary Ashton Livermore, founder of the Chicago suffrage newspaper *The Agitator,* said she intended her paper to be "the twin sister of *The Revolution,* whose mission is to turn everything inside out." After *The Revolution* ceased publication, Stanton found solace in her paper's historic role. "I have the joy of knowing that I showed it to be possible to publish an out-and-out woman's paper," she wrote, "and taught other women to enter in and to reap where I have sown." As *The Revolution*'s progeny have multiplied and flourished during the years that have passed since Stanton wrote those words, they simultaneously have kept alive the agenda for women's rights born on the pages of their rebellious foremother.[40]

The three earliest genres of the American dissident press crusaded on behalf of very different causes—labor rights, the abolition of slavery, and women's rights—and were spread over a time span of almost half a century—from William Heighton founding the *Mechanic's Free Press* in 1828 to Elizabeth Cady Stanton and Susan Brownell Anthony selling *The Revolution* in 1870. Despite these distinctions, the first generation of dissident publications not only shared several common traits but also established themes that would continue to define the journalistic "voices of revolution" for the next two centuries.

THE DISSIDENT PRESS SPEAKS ON BEHALF OF THE OPPRESSED

Factory workers, slaves, and women were all members of poor and powerless groups that the prevailing forces in American society had, by the early to middle nineteenth century, shunted to the margins of society. African Americans and women could neither vote nor otherwise participate, in any meaningful way, in public life; laborers were rapidly being disenfranchised, too, because of the growing economic and political dominance of what Heighton so poignantly labeled the "aristocracy of wealth." The men and women who founded the nation's first voices of journalistic dissent refused to accept these limitations and set out to level the playing field.

THE DISSIDENT PRESS GENERALLY FACES SEVERE FINANCIAL HARDSHIP

Publications seeking social change are driven by a commitment to and passion for a particular cause, not by the profit motive that propels most commercial media. Many dissident papers are started on a shoestring and remain financially unstable throughout their often-truncated lives. Because the three earliest genres of the dissident American press crusaded on behalf of concepts that were unpopular with the dominant segments of society, the editors of the publications faced severe monetary problems. Denied the revenue that mainstream papers received from major advertisers and large circulations, the editors were forced to beg their readers for support, to endure lives of poverty and deprivation, and to incur onerous debts.

William Heighton pleaded with his readers to subscribe to his paper and patronize his small stable of advertisers—"Your patronage is most desperately desired," he wrote in 1830. William Lloyd Garrison lived on the edge of destitution; before he was married, he survived on water and stale bread, and when he had a wife and seven children, he depended on wealthy patrons to give him barrels of flour and other foodstuffs to feed his family. *The Revolution*'s founders had to sell their paper after only two and a half years of publication, leaving Susan Brownell Anthony with such a hefty debt that it took her six years of making speeches to pay it off.

THE DISSIDENT PRESS RECEIVES NEITHER SUPPORT NOR SYMPATHY FROM THE MAINSTREAM PRESS

The experiences of the editors of the nonconformist papers published in the early to middle 1800s established that the Brahmins of American journalism would be consistent detractors of their radical counterparts. Commercial papers in New York denigrated the early labor editors as "rabble" and "the slime of this community." The *New York Herald* was no less critical of William Lloyd Garrison, ridiculing the abolitionist editor by referring to his "bald head, miserable forehead, and comical spectacles," while demeaning the slaves he was so determined to free by describing them as "thick-lipped, pig-faced, woolly-headed, baboon-looking negroes." Mainstream papers were hostile toward female dissident journalists as well, referring to Susan Brownell Anthony as a "poor creature," "unfortunate woman," "unsexed woman," and "hermaphrodite spirit."

THE DISSIDENT PRESS DIFFERS FROM ITS ESTABLISHMENT COUNTERPARTS BY ADOPTING THE CONCEPT OF AN OPEN FORUM

Having themselves been denied access to mainstream newspapers, the earliest dissident editors were committed to publishing not only their own ideas but also those of their readers—including ideas in direct conflict with their own. William Heighton demonstrated this concept when he made room for a lengthy letter from a man who was so outraged by the long workday in Philadelphia factories that he insisted that—despite Heighton's clear opinion to the contrary—European laborers were better off than American ones. The editors who advocated the abolition of slavery and equal rights for women followed Heighton's lead. William Lloyd Garrison was so determined to provide an open forum, in fact, that he published items from readers that degraded the editor himself—one such article described Garrison as a "fanatical traitor" and another demanded that he be hanged.

DISSIDENT EDITORS ARE PROACTIVE AGENTS OF CHANGE

As men and women who were passionate—sometimes to the point of being obsessed, perhaps even fanatical—about their chosen cause, the first generation of advocacy editors demonstrated that theirs would be a brand of journalism so dedicated to effecting social change that they would not limit their activities merely to printing newspapers. For them, journalism was not a professional calling for its own sake but a means to reach people with ideas, a way to organize and propagandize for a cause.

William Heighton and fellow labor editors Robert Dale Owen and Frances "Fanny" Wright of the *Free Enquirer* and George Henry Evans of the *Working Man's Advocate* not only reported and editorialized against injustices—such as long work days—but also took their demands directly to the Philadelphia City Council and prepared resolutions for several state legislatures, then lobbying for the proposals to be enacted. Indeed, Heighton plunged into the rough-and-tumble of political activism by calling for the creation of a third party for working men—with his *Mechanic's Free Press* serving as its official organ.

William Lloyd Garrison, Elizabeth Cady Stanton, and Susan Brownell Anthony expanded on Heighton's model by creating media events, provoking contentious debates, organizing public rallies, making personal appeals to elected officials, and presenting thousands of speeches on behalf of the causes to which they dedicated not just their newspapers but their very lives.

THE DISSIDENT PRESS HAS IMPACT

Although each of the causes championed by the first generation of journalistic rebels was initially, when the publications were founded, far too radical for the majority of the public to accept, the bold ideas that were put forth in the publications eventually filtered into the mainstream of American thought—some decidedly more slowly than others—to become embraced by society as a whole.

That laborers should have rights, that slavery is an abomination, that women are fully equal to men—they all became precepts that were not only accepted by reasonable-thinking Americans but were also integrated into the definition of democracy.

MANY OF THE ISSUES CHAMPIONED BY THE DISSIDENT PRESS ARE TIMELESS

Although great strides were taken to right the wrongs illuminated by the early labor press, abolitionist press, and women's rights press, the concepts underlying this triumvirate of crusades continue to be very much alive more than a century after the publications helped propel them onto the national agenda. *The Liberator* was fundamentally concerned with race, *The Revolution* with gender, and the labor publications with class. If asked to identify the three most impenetrable issues facing the American people today, many observers of contemporary society would still automatically list race, gender, and class.

PART 2
STRUGGLING TO FORM
A MORE PERFECT UNION

The end of the nineteenth century witnessed the emergence of four genres of the dissident press propelled by a gallery of larger-than-life individuals who were concerned that the United States was not fulfilling its birthright as the exemplar of democratic principles.

These often-idiosyncratic men and women, whose thinking was not in step with the vast majority of society, feared that dangerous forces were at work in the nation—and had to be stopped.

The culprits that the various dissident journalists struggled to defeat seem, at first glance, to bear no relation to each other. The institution of marriage, for example, does not appear to be connected in any discernible way to the hanging of innocent black men. Further, neither holy matrimony nor unholy lynching is, on its face, linked to the Industrial Revolution and the burgeoning growth of capitalism that took place during the late 1800s.

And yet the dissident journalists who surfaced either slightly before or slightly after the nation's 100th birthday shared the common vision that the U.S. Constitution had so poignantly articulated: "To form a more perfect union." What's more, these reform-minded men and women were determined to make that powerful manifesto much more than a hollow phrase.

4 PROMOTING "FREE LOVE" IN THE VICTORIAN AGE

Elizabeth Cady Stanton and other feminists who raised their dissident voices in *The Revolution* had, in the late 1860s, begun to question the sanctity of the vows that permanently bound a wife to her husband. They challenged the concept of a woman finding her identity solely through the man she married, often when she was little more than an adolescent, and pointed out that too often a husband ended up not being his wife's protector—but her abuser. Stanton went so far as to advocate that in cases of domestic violence, often the only viable solution was divorce.

In the 1870s, the reform-minded individuals who focused their attention on improving the union between husband and wife went the next radical step of proposing that wives and husbands should not be bound to an unhappy marriage until death did them part, but should be free to marry or divorce at will, according to the ebb and flow of their love for each other. This concept of a person being free to move in and out of marriage based solely on love—or the lack of it—led to the reformers being identified by the provocative label of "free lovers," a term the iconoclastic crusaders eagerly embraced. "Yes, I am a free lover," Victoria Woodhull shamelessly announced in 1871. "I have an inalienable, constitutional and natural right to love whom I may, to love as long or short a period as I can, to change that love every day if I please. And with that right neither you nor any law you can frame have any right to interfere."[1]

For three decades, the sexual reform press sought to convince the American public that marriage was not always a sacred institution but sometimes a profane one. The dozen sexual reform publications that existed during this period challenged the social mores that dominated American life by asserting that sexual intercourse should occur only when both partners were willing: A woman had the right to deny her body to anyone, including her husband. Choice rather than coercion or a sense of duty should be the only basis upon which a woman would have sex. Victoria Woodhull wrote in the journal she founded, "I believe it is my duty and my mission to carry the torch to light up and destroy the heap of rottenness which, in the name of religion, marital sanctity and social purity, now passes as the social system."[2]

Although the dissident voices advocating free love began their conversation by articulating the weaknesses of wedlock, they soon broadened that discussion. In 1872, the sexual reform press used the details of a prominent minister's affair to expose the hypocritical lifestyles of Victorian men, igniting one of the most sensational scandals in the history of American religion. After that incident, the publications continued to tackle ever more explosive subjects—explicit sexual language, sex education, abortion, promiscuity, and couples living together without being married.

One of the earliest of the sexual reform papers was *Woodhull & Claflin's Weekly*, published by Victoria Woodhull and her sister Tennessee Claflin in New York City from 1870 to 1876. Another leading publication was *The Word*, which played a key role in broadening the discussion to new topics; it was published by Ezra and Angela Heywood from 1872 to 1893 in rural Massachusetts. A third important voice was *Lucifer, the Light-Bearer*, published by Moses Harman from 1883 to 1907, first in rural Kansas and later in Chicago.

The story of the sexual reform publications must begin with the stories of the women and men who were the driving forces behind them. These social rebels dared to illuminate topics that polite society would not admit to discussing even in private, let alone in print. For choosing a road less traveled, the editors ultimately paid a high price—including being sent to prison and dying early deaths.

MRS. SATAN

Victoria Claflin's colorful life began in 1838 in Homer, Ohio, where she was one of ten children born to shiftless parents who turned exploitation and petty crime into a way of life. While the comely Victoria and her equally lovely sister Tennessee were still adolescents, their father sent them into the work world as psychics, telling fortunes and communing with the dead at a dollar a hit. Sometimes he even starved the girls for days at a time because he thought the ill treatment heightened their spiritual powers.[3]

At the age of fourteen, Victoria tried to escape her miserable life by marrying a handsome doctor twice her age. After the nuptial knot had been firmly tied, however, she learned that "Dr." Canning Woodhull was, in fact, a medical quack and an alcoholic who was incapable of supporting himself, much less his wife and

Victoria Woodhull dressed in the rich fabrics that helped define the proper conventions of Victorian America; her ideas regarding sexual activity, however, were far from conventional. (Courtesy of Special Collections Department, Vassar College Libraries)

the two children the couple soon brought into the world. So it fell to the winsome and resourceful Victoria to put food on the Woodhull table by plying her diverse talents as a clairvoyant, a stage actress, a public orator, and a prostitute.

A twenty-six, Victoria Woodhull met Colonel James Blood, a Civil War veteran and fellow spiritualist. In short order, the two lovers divorced their respective spouses and married each other. For the next decade, Blood served as impresario for the various ventures undertaken by his wife—who retained the name Woodhull. Those endeavors veered in a new direction when the spirits who appeared at one of Victoria Woodhull's séances told her to leave the Midwest and move to New York. So to the big city she went.

In 1868, Woodhull forged a lucrative friendship with Commodore Cornelius Vanderbilt, a seventy-year-old widower with more money than sense. She ministered to the millionaire industrialist's soul by putting him in touch with his dead mother and satisfied his lust by placing her sister Tennessee Claflin, and sometimes herself, in his bed. Woodhull gained so much control over Vanderbilt that he financed the creation of Woodhull Claflin & Co. Brokerage House. Leading newspapers, in turn, were so bedazzled by the novelty of the stunningly beautiful Victoria Woodhull and Tennessee Claflin becoming the first women on Wall Street—the *New York World* gushed about their "shrewd management and business acumen," even though neither woman had any experience in finance—that the sisters attracted legions of clients and, therefore, were soon able to buy a mansion in the exclusive Murray Hill section of the city.[4]

It was in May 1870 that the sisters founded *Woodhull & Claflin's Weekly* as a champion for free love, proclaiming on its flag "Progress! Free Thought! Untrammeled Lives!" The thrilling nature of the paper's editorials and essays combined with the voluptuous sisters' ability to charm reporters resulted in massive public attention. The *New York Times* praised *Woodhull & Claflin's Weekly* as a "sprightly, well-edited sheet," and the *New York Globe* predicted that the women's venture would "make many friends." Aided by the positive coverage, the *Weekly* was able to boast, after only six months, that its circulation had reached 20,000—six times that of either *The Liberator* or *The Revolution* before it.[5]

Finances were not a problem for the *Weekly* because Commodore Vanderbilt acted as its angel, paying the printing and mailing costs while also sending free copies to major newspapers and influential people who traveled in his elite social circle. In return, Tennessee Claflin hand delivered copies of the paper to Vanderbilt and then stayed to read the articles aloud to him—while propped up on the pillows in his bed. Claflin also was the paper's revenue "rainmaker," using her seductive powers to secure advertising contracts from any number of major companies. Before long, the paper overflowed with ads for Tiffany watches, Steinway pianos, and Brooks Brothers suits.

Late in the spring of 1870, Woodhull made political history by becoming the first woman to seek the office of President of the United States. The *Weekly* promised to "support Victoria C. Woodhull for President, with its whole strength," going on to detail her plan to run on a platform that promised female suffrage, divorce reform, and full support of free love. Woodhull's announcement again catapulted her paper and her evocative ideas onto the front pages of the nation's leading newspapers. The *New York Herald* alone ran ten Woodhull stories in the four months following the announcement of her candidacy.[6]

Woodhull had still more breakthroughs to make.

In early 1871, she told the U.S. Congress that it should legalize female suffrage under the terms of the Fifteenth Amendment, which had given African American men the right to vote. Woodhull's appearance before the House Judiciary Committee was a triumph—she was the first woman in history to address a congressional committee—that produced another round of flattering newspaper articles. Although the bill ultimately was tabled and then forgotten, Elizabeth Cady Stanton and other suffragists praised Woodhull for advancing the cause of American women.

The next round of news coverage that Woodhull received, however, was disastrous. The episode began when Woodhull's mother filed a lawsuit against Colonel Blood, claiming that her son-in-law had threatened to kill her. During the trial, Victoria Woodhull was accused—in sensational testimony that played on the front pages of newspapers nationwide—of having ongoing sexual relations with both her current and her former husbands. When she admitted that she, Colonel Blood, and Canning Woodhull did, in fact, sleep in the same room, the *ménage à trois* horrified the nation. *Harper's Weekly* captured—and contributed to—the nation's collective gasp of moral outrage by depicting Victoria Woodhull as a disgraceful harpy. The caption for the cartoon pinned a label on Woodhull that she would spend the rest of her life trying to shake: "Mrs. Satan."[7]

THE PROPER VICTORIAN COUPLE

Compared to Victoria Woodhull, Ezra and Angela Heywood lived a decidedly conventional life. In concert with the proper standards among New England families securely positioned in the middle class, Ezra earned a degree from Brown University in preparation for a career as a Congregational minister, while Angela developed the skills necessary to fulfill the domestic duties of wife and mother. The vital statistics of the Heywood marriage reinforced the couple's success at filling the roles of Victorian husband and Victorian wife; they married in 1865, lived together in a monogamous relationship for twenty-seven years, and raised two daughters and two sons.

As other details about the Heywoods are added to this basic description, however, the image of nineteenth-century propriety quickly crumbles. Ezra opted not to use his talents as a writer and orator to keep a small congregation walking on the stairway to Heaven. Instead, he built the forty-room Mountain Home in the rolling hills of central Massachusetts to provide a resort where visitors from Boston and New York could rest their weary bodies while also giving him a captive audience for his lectures on the merits of free love. Ezra tried to convince his guests that the institution of marriage had to be abolished, insisting that lovers should not be bound by a legal contract or church vows but should have the right "to make and dissolve their own contracts" as they think best. He also called for "the unconditional repeal of the laws against adultery and fornication."[8]

Angela Heywood, for her part, wrote long treatises arguing that women should be more than household drudges and sex objects. Angela was more radical than most feminists, however, as she also introduced several startling concepts. She defied Victorian America's belief that sexual intercourse should be engaged in solely for procreation; she insisted that "sexuality is divine," both for reproduction and for "personal exhilaration," thereby endorsing what today would be labeled recreational sex. Angela also broke new ground by acknowledging that sexual activity was not pleasurable for men only, but for women as well; she wrote, "Woman may pretend she does not want anything of man, but her lady-nature knows it is the very great *everything* she wants to do *with* man." The most memorable aspect of Angela's writing evolved from her insistence upon using explicit language; she said, for example, that every man "should have solemn meetings with, and look seriously at, his own penis until he is able to be lord and master of it, rather than it rule as lord and master of him."[9]

Ezra and Angela Heywood built their resort in Princeton in 1871 and began publishing *The Word* a year later. Their monthly sexual reform journal, like the dozens of books and pamphlets the couple produced, treated sexuality with a daunting degree of candor. The Heywoods were soon boasting that *The Word*'s circulation had surpassed 3,000. Profits from the Mountain Home covered the journal's printing and mailing costs; advertisements were few, limited mainly to promotions for reform-oriented books.

The Heywoods met their fellow free love advocate Victoria Woodhull in 1872 and immediately pledged their support to her crusade against conventional marriage and the various abuses that too often accompanied that institution. Ezra and Angela Heywood then helped found the New England Free Love League in 1873 for the purpose of sponsoring lectures by Woodhull, as the crowds eager to listen to Mrs. Satan had grown so large—often surpassing 2,000—that there were few indoor spaces large enough to accommodate them. The Heywoods also reprinted many items from *Woodhull & Claflin's Weekly* in *The Word*.[10]

But unlike Woodhull and her publication, the Heywoods and theirs were vilified in the mainstream press. The *Boston Globe* called *The Word* "a flow of filth," and another Massachusetts paper, the *Worcester Press*, told readers that the Heywoods were publishing "smut" and called for Princeton's townspeople to close down *The Word*.[11]

THE SEX RADICAL

Moses Harman's early life was every bit as conventional as those of Ezra and Angela Heywood, except that as a young boy growing up in Missouri he suffered a farming accident. The incident seriously damaged Moses's right leg, and for the rest of his life he walked with a pronounced limp. Confined to the indoors, he became an inveterate reader.

At twenty-one, Harman began teaching at a rural high school, and his first questioning of the institution of marriage came in the late 1860s when he was preparing to wed Susan Scheuck. Before the ceremony, the groom insisted that he and his bride repudiate all powers legally conferred on married couples by the state and, instead, base their relationship solely on love and individual commitment. The Harmans then settled on a Missouri farm and had two children. Moses continued to teach and to read, with his tastes moving steadily to the left on the ideological continuum.

In 1877, Susan Scheuck Harman died while attempting to give birth to her third child. Distraught and desperate to escape the memories of the past, Moses Harman secured a new teaching position and moved with his son and daughter to the frontier town of Valley Falls in eastern Kansas.

It did not take long for the new school teacher to develop a reputation as an abrasive zealot. When the local newspaper found Harman's letters to the editor criticizing Victorian mores too radical to print, he decided to create his own publishing venue.

So in 1883, at the age of fifty, Moses Harman launched his career as a dissident journalist. He named his bi-weekly newspaper *Lucifer, the Light-Bearer* after the archangel who was cast out of Heaven for leading a revolt of the angels. By this stage in his life, Harman looked the part of the social revolutionary he had become, standing tall and thin with stern facial features and a shock of flowing white hair.

One article that appeared in *Lucifer* captures Harman's particular stripe as a publishing provocateur. The Department of Agriculture was mailing, to anyone who requested it, a book about how to treat ailing horses. If descriptions contained in the book were applied to human organs, *Lucifer* argued, postal authorities would have censored them. Why should the federal government be allowed to distribute medical facts about *horse* procreation, Harman's editorial asked, but a private citizen was prevented from distributing similar facts about *human* procreation? To bring home the point, Harman published an extract from the book. "As the result of kicks or blows," the quotation began, "the horse's penis may become the seat of effusion of blood from one or more ruptured blood-vessels. This gives rise to more or less extensive swelling, and the penis should be suspended in a sling." The postmaster in Topeka confiscated all copies of the issue of *Lucifer* containing the editorial, and the next issue screamed across page one: "Published under Government Censorship."[12]

Such controversial articles caused financial difficulties for *Lucifer*, as content so inimical to Victorian sensibilities meant that only the publishers of a few radical books were willing to advertise in it. Subscriptions did not produce much revenue either; circulation peaked at 1,500. Moses Harman sought a solution to his revenue problem in Edwin Walker, who agreed, in exchange for the title of co-editor, to travel around the country to raise money for *Lucifer* by giving speeches on free love.

Large crowds turning out for lectures did not mean, however, that *Lucifer* received positive appraisals in the mainstream Kansas press. The *Osawkee Times* called *Lucifer* a "rotten concern," and the *Winchester Argus* dubbed it a "fearfully demoralizing sheet"; both papers demanded that the sexual reform paper be suppressed. The influential *Kansas City Times* said *Lucifer* was an "abomination" and "a disgrace to the state of Kansas. Its permanent destruction will be a thing to be thankful for."[13]

ATTACKING THE SANCTITY OF MARRIAGE

The central issue propelling free love advocates was the unjust treatment of married women. According to the social mores of the nineteenth century, husbands were expected not merely to provide financial and physical security for their wives but also to dominate every aspect of their being. Free lovers adamantly opposed this concept. They did not believe a woman should be required to submit to her husband's every demand. In particular, they argued that sexual relations in a marriage should occur because of mutual attraction, not forced obligation. They envisioned an equal partnership in which neither participant would rule or be ruled.

Victoria Woodhull's opposition to marriage was rooted in her own life experience. As a young girl, she had dreamed of falling in love and marrying her Prince Charming. "I supposed that to marry was to be transported to a heaven not only of happiness but of purity and perfection," she wrote. By the age of sixteen, however, Victoria faced a very different reality. She was married to a drunkard who had lied to her about being a doctor and was incapable of supporting his wife, daughter, and retarded son—Woodhull was convinced that the boy's affliction was a result of his father's drinking.[14]

In the pages of *Woodhull & Claflin's Weekly*, Woodhull insisted—clearly informed by what she had seen of the world—that myriad social problems were rooted in bad marriages. Crime, poverty, intemperance, abortion, and disease all evolved from ill-fated matrimony, she argued, and her definition of personal freedom centered on the right to end a bad marriage without being condemned as a social pariah. "It is simply nobody's business what anybody eats, drinks, or wears," she wrote, "and just as little who anybody loves, or how he loves, if the two parties to it are satisfied." Her solution to the problem was nothing short of what most Americans—a century ago as well as today—considered heresy: the obliteration of the institution of marriage. "The old, worn-out, rotten social system will be torn down, plank by plank, timber after timber, until place is given to a new, true and beautiful structure, based upon freedom, equality and justice to all—to women as well as men."[15]

The other sexual reform editors also denounced marriage. The Heywoods wrote in *The Word* that the husband/wife relationship was like that of master/slave, saying, "As masters quoted law and gospel over their slaves, so husbands emphasize their claim to wedded chattels." *The Word* branded marriage "coerced consent" and insisted that people should not make love because of legal statute but only in response to their own desires. "The belief that our sexual relations can be better governed by the state than by personal choice is," Ezra Heywood wrote, "as barbarous and shocking as it is senseless."[16]

Moses Harman used the pages of *Lucifer* to document the sexual bondage that many wives had to endure. In 1886, Harman published a letter he had received from a Tennessee reader named W. G. Markland. When Harman printed the letter, he added an editor's note reading: "Prudes and statute moralists had better not read this letter." Then followed the item that would soon become legend: " 'About a year ago F—— gave birth to a babe, and was severely torn by the use of instruments in incompetent hands. She has gone through three operations and all failed. I brought her home and had Dr. —— operate on her, and she was getting along nicely until last night, when her husband forced himself into her bed, and the stitches were torn from her healing flesh, leaving her in a worse condition than ever.' " After relating the details of this disturbing example of a brutal husband, Markland went on to ask a volley of poignant questions: "Was the husband's conduct illegal? Can there be legal rape? Does the law protect married women? If a man stabs his wife to death with a knife, does not the law hold him for murder? If he murders her with his penis, what does the law do?"[17]

Never before in the history of American journalism had an editor had the audacity to publish such graphic testimony to the sexual abuse that husbands were legally allowed to commit against their wives. The Heywoods applauded Harman's decision to publish the letter as a powerful "protest against rape in marriage."[18]

But Moses Harman was not finished. In another defiant move, he printed a letter from New York physician Richard O'Neill. The angry doctor stated that he had witnessed many cases of injury and even death caused by abusive husbands—O'Neill compared such men to elephants—like the man Markland had described: "Thousands of women are killed every year by sexual excesses forced on them. I know of several women who slowly perished from this cause."[19]

The Heywoods again praised Harman's courage in publishing material that exposed marital abuse. They called Dr. O'Neill's letter "wise & timely," saying that it provided irrefutable proof that many marriages were nothing short of legalized "sex abuse." The Heywoods also reprinted the letter verbatim in *The Word*.[20]

EXPOSING THE HYPOCRISY
OF THE VICTORIAN MAN

Part of the reason the editors were so outraged by the sexual bondage that wives had to endure was that proper Victorian society ignored the duplicitous lives of upper-class married men. It was common knowledge that leading male citizens publicly stated that all respectable persons must adhere to a strict moral code of behavior, even though these same pillars of society were privately having sexual relations with either prostitutes or the wives of the same men who belonged to their elite men's clubs. When a larger-than-life leader of the free lovers—Mrs. Satan herself—decided to expose this hypocrisy, she ignited a national scandal.

The Rev. Henry Ward Beecher was, in the 1870s, the country's most celebrated clergyman. The brother of renowned author Harriet Beecher Stowe, Rev. Beecher was a superb orator who drew several thousand people to Brooklyn's Plymouth Church every Sunday morning. He was so popular, in fact, that special vessels known as "Beecher boats" ran across the East River to ferry his fans over from Manhattan. But Rev. Beecher was, at the same time that he was preaching morality, having an affair with the wife of his parishioner and close friend, Theodore Tilton. When Elizabeth Tilton became pregnant by her pastor, she was so tormented with guilt that she confessed to several female friends.

One of the women Elizabeth Tilton confided in was Elizabeth Cady Stanton, who passed the tale onto Victoria Woodhull. Still smarting from the accusations that had been leveled at her own domestic arrangements with her former and current husbands, Woodhull published the edition of *Woodhull & Claflin's Weekly* that ultimately became as notorious as Woodhull herself—no easy feat. The headline set the sensational tone: "The Beecher-Tilton Scandal Case." Woodhull then related the sordid details of the affair, including divulging that Elizabeth Tilton was by no means the first married woman to share the esteemed clergyman's bed: "Henry Ward Beecher preaches to at least twenty of his mistresses every Sunday."[21]

When the *Weekly* hit the streets of Manhattan on November 2, 1872, thousands of people clamored to get their hands on the paper that—they had heard but could hardly believe—had the temerity to accuse a distinguished clergyman of having multiple sex partners. Woodhull, knowing full well that her revelations would produce a maelstrom of public attention, printed 100,000 copies of the scandal issue, but still newsboys hawked them for as much as forty dollars each. Overnight, Mrs. Satan's sexual reform newspaper had become the publishing sensation of the day.

The scandal issue and its aftermath again thrust Victoria Woodhull onto the front pages of the nation's leading newspapers. Details of the exposé and her previous escapades made for spectacular stories. Among the headlines: "Spicy Developments" and "An Outrage Upon Public Decency."[22]

Ironically, coverage of the scandal coincided with the November 5, 1872, presidential election in which, for the first time in history, a woman sought the White House. It was hardly the kind of publicity, however, that Woodhull would have liked. Nor had other aspects of her campaign gone as well as she had hoped. Because she was a woman and, at age thirty-four, not legally old enough to run, her name did not appear on the official ballot, meaning that supporters had to write in her name. She received so few votes that no one even bothered to tally their exact number.

EXPANDING THE SEXUAL VOCABULARY

While Victoria Woodhull was the most adept of the sexual reform editors at making headlines, Moses Harman and the Heywoods were the most committed to revolutionizing the text of the American newspaper. Frank discussion of sexuality, they argued, required the use of explicit words, and, more important still, the First Amendment guaranteed free speech to all citizens.

Harman promised his readers that he would not reject any contribution they sent to *Lucifer* merely because of the words they used, and his free love followers needed no further invitation. Markland's letter included the terms "rape," "genitals," and "penis," and Dr. O'Neill's added "intercourse," "private organ," and "semen"—all terms that Victorian America condemned as unacceptable for publication.

Ezra Heywood campaigned for the use of explicit language as well. "The sex organs and their associative uses have fit, proper, explicit, expressive English names," he wrote. "Why not have character enough to use them and no longer be ashamed of your own creative use and destiny? Why giggle, mince, simper, skulk and dodge about?"[23]

But the writer who set the pace when it came to expanding the sexual vocabulary was Angela Heywood. With a disarming level of comfort, this Victorian wife and mother wrote in a tone that was open, bold, liberating—and graphic. Extolling the beauty of the male sex organ, Angela described the word "penis" as "a musical word" and celebrated the organ's singular function in the circle of life—"What mother can look in the face of her welcome child and not religiously respect the rigid, erect, ready-for-service, persistent male-organ that sired it?" She also insisted that the word "cock" should be fully accepted into the language as a synonym for penis. "In literature we have cocks as weathervanes, cocks as fowls, cockel hats, cocked rifles," she argued, so "Cock is a fowl but not a *foul* word."[24]

Nor did Angela bristle at the word that many people, still today, speak of only as "the F word." She argued that the phrasing "sexual intercourse" was too cumbersome to define an activity "commonly spoken of in one word of four letters that everybody knows the meaning of." So Angela casually used the word "fuck" in her articles, saying in her whimsical style: "Such graceful terms as hearing, seeing, smelling, tasting, fucking, throbbing, kissing, and kin words are telephone expressions, lighthouses of intercourse centrally immutable to the situation; it is as impossible and undesirable to put them out of pure use as it would be to take oxygen out of the air."[25]

CENSORING THE SEXUAL REFORM PRESS

Victoria Woodhull's scandalous revelations about a venerated man of the cloth combined with Moses Harman and the Heywoods' shocking ideas about sexual reform and explicit language provided the kindling that set ablaze the most savage crusade against pornography in the history of American publishing.

The knight errant who led the crusade was Anthony Comstock. The dry-goods salesman turned moral vigilante undertook his crusade to avenge the corruption of a friend who had been, in Comstock's words, "diseased by reading a filthy book." By the early 1870s, Comstock had founded the Society for the Suppression of Vice and had become a Christian warrior whose name would forever be linked to the crusade to repress what he considered obscene material.[26]

In 1872, Comstock was looking for a high-visibility case to expand his New York City crusade into a national one; at precisely his moment of need, like manna from Heaven, came Victoria Woodhull's scandal issue. Comstock gained so much free publicity from leading the moral charge against the "notorious Victoria" that he received sufficient financial backing from such wealthy men as financier J. Pierpont Morgan and soap magnate Samuel Colgate to create his very own censoring operation. They paid Comstock a salary to stamp out vice and strengthen anti-obscenity legislation nationwide.

In early 1873, "St. Anthony," as the free lovers called him, went to Washington to lobby for federal laws. The anti-obscenity bills were taken up during a frenzied all-night session that was made all the more chaotic when Comstock unveiled his traveling exhibit of pornography. At 2 a.m. on a Sunday morning, Congress passed legislation that quickly became known as the Comstock Acts. The statutes dramatically broadened previous laws, stipulating that anyone found guilty of mailing or receiving "obscene, lewd, or lascivious" material—Congress did not define any of the terms—would be sentenced to ten years in prison. Comstock ensured that the laws would be carried out by having the congressmen name him a special post office inspector charged with identifying and confiscating unmailable material.[27]

NO HOLDS BARRED

Despite the powerful forces of censorship that Comstock brought to bear, the sexual reform editors did not slow their campaign; they accelerated it. By the 1880s, it was clear that the dissident editors would allow no holds to be barred in their assault on sexual repression.

One of the most controversial topics the editors promoted was promiscuity. Victoria Woodhull expressed her support of multiple sex partners in the way she lived her own life. While married to Canning Woodhull, she worked as a prostitute and had an affair with James Blood; while married to Blood, she had affairs with Cornelius Vanderbilt and other men of wealth and prominence—including Theodore Tilton, the husband of the woman she exposed as the lover of Rev. Beecher. In 1874, Woodhull publicly endorsed multiple sex partners, announcing: "I am a very promiscuous free lover." Moses Harman and the Heywoods also defended promiscuity, but in less personal terms. Harman denounced laws against adultery as "unwarranted invasion of private and personal right," and the Heywoods argued that lust was such a grand and marvelous force that it was selfish for a person to reserve all of its gifts for only one other person.[28]

Moses Harman's most strident act of defiance against Victorian morality came when he advocated what he labeled "free marriage"—men and women living together as husband and wife without the sanction of church or state. In 1886, the editor orchestrated a ceremony between his golden-haired daughter, Lillian, who was sixteen, and *Lucifer* co-editor Edwin Walker, who was thirty-seven. During the ceremony, Lillian said, "I enter into this union with Mr. Walker of my own free will and choice." In the next issue of *The Word*, Ezra and Angela Heywood staunchly supported the bride and groom, calling them "brave exponents of Progress."[29]

The Heywoods adamantly believed that a woman's individual rights fully entitled her to abort a fetus. They wrote that a woman had to be "mistress of her own person" and, therefore, her justification for ending a pregnancy "is as unquestionable as her right to eat, breathe, or walk." This was a radical stand at the time, as having an abortion was a crime punishable by death.[30]

To a modern-day audience, one of the most shocking arguments put forth by the sexual reform editors evolved from their belief that conventional marriage was tantamount to sexual bondage. The fact that wives were forced to have sex with their husbands was so damaging, the editors argued, that babies born to unwed mothers were, in fact, *superior* to babies born to married women. Ezra Heywood first raised this radical idea in 1875, arguing that single women should be encouraged to have babies. "The marriage institution is a State Intrusion which destroys love, hinders intelligent reproduction, causes domestic discord, and corrupts and poisons the sources of life," resulting in babies who are ugly and of weak character. Moses Harman agreed, telling his readers that children born from a husband forcing himself upon his wife carried the psychological scar of being "born under protest" throughout their lives.[31]

Another controversial topic—today but far more so in the nineteenth century—supported by the radical papers was sex education. The Heywoods dramatized American children's need for straightforward information about sex by printing an anonymous letter from a New York mother. "The other day," the woman began, "my little girl, who is in her twelfth year, came to me and said, 'Mama, what does "fuck" mean?' " When the woman asked where her daughter had heard the word, the girl answered, " 'Today at school, Willie said to me, 'Mamie, won't you fuck me?' " The mother took this response as a cue that it was time to explain the facts of life to her daughter; she then provided the girl with a full description of intercourse and the sex organs, including comparing her breasts and genitals to those of her daughter. The mother also described how she and her daughter had examined a photograph of an erect penis. The mother went on to say that she had engaged in sexual intercourse for the first time at age twelve—"I was fascinated with it," she wrote.[32]

PAYING A HIGH PRICE

By the mid-1870s, Anthony Comstock's crusade against the editors of the sexual reform press had become relentless. He believed that God had chosen him to silence the men and women he described as "Satanic editors" who were "foul of speech, shameless in their lives and corrupting in their influences."[33]

Victoria Woodhull was his first target. After being indicted on obscenity charges for the Beecher story, Woodhull was in and out of jail for a year and a half between the publication of her scandal issue and the trial that decided her fate. There was no question that the details of the Beecher-Tilton affair violated the sweeping concept of obscenity as Comstock defined it. But as the trial began, Woodhull was visited by a group of Plymouth Church parishioners who were eager to put the scandal behind them. By the end of the visit, Woodhull had struck a deal; she would give up any evidence she had against Beecher—she had nothing but hearsay, but the parishioners didn't know that—in exchange for escaping punishment on the obscenity charges. Two days later, as if ordained by God Himself, the judge dismissed the case because of insufficient evidence.

In spite of the courtroom victory, Woodhull's life was in shambles. She estimated that the legal case had cost her, when personal losses were combined with business losses, $500,000. She also had been evicted from her mansion, had been forced to close her brokerage firm, and had been divorced by James Blood—not such a committed free lover after all, Blood took none too kindly to his wife's multiple affairs. Commodore Vanderbilt's declining health ended his financial support, so Woodhull's only source of income was the public lectures that she often had to cancel because of respiratory problems. In June 1876, she was finally forced to give up the enterprise that she had clung to the longest; *Woodhull & Claflin's Weekly* ceased publication.

But Victoria Woodhull was a woman of resilience. When Vanderbilt died in 1877, he left the bulk of his $100 million fortune to his son William while giving only small amounts to his other nine children. William was so terrified that Mrs. Satan might testify that the Commodore had been unduly influenced by spirits, and therefore of unsound mind when he signed his will, that the junior Vanderbilt paid her $100,000 to leave the country. She then settled in London and promptly married shy millionaire bachelor John Biddulph Martin. Victoria Claflin Woodhull Blood Martin then became the picture of domestic bliss, dedicating her life to her husband and her two grown children. When Martin died in 1897, he left his wife a million dollars, allowing her to live out her life in the comfort of the Martin family estate to the venerable age of eighty-eight.

Ezra Heywood's life was not so charmed. Comstock called the editor of *The Word* "the chief creature of this vile creed" of free love, and for three decades the censorship czar pursued Heywood with a vengeance. Comstock had Heywood arrested five times and convicted twice—leading to sentences of four years in prison. With Ezra in jail and Angela struggling to feed their four children, the Heywoods lost the Mountain Home resort to foreclosure and had to suspend publication of *The Word*. After Ezra completed his second prison term—this one at hard labor—he tried to revive his sexual reform journal. His body could no longer sustain the heavy workload, however, and he died a year after leaving jail, in 1893 at the age of sixty-four. *The Word* ceased publication with Ezra's death. During her old age, Angela—the woman who was once led the effort to expand the English language with regard to sexual terminology—worked as a cleaning woman.[34]

Moses Harman's final years were sadly reminiscent of Ezra Heywood's. *Lucifer*'s first clash with the law came the morning after Lillian Harman and Edwin Walker consummated their free marriage in 1886. The arrest warrant charged that they were living together "unlawfully and feloniously," and they were taken to jail to await trial. The case of the Lucifer lovers, as Lillian and Edwin became known, created front-page headlines in newspapers nationwide. The *Topeka Daily Capital* said the lovers were "fools" seeking "cheap notoriety," and the *Kansas City Times* stated that free marriage, free love, and *Lucifer* were all "absurd, subversive and untenable." Most far-reaching in its impact was the coverage that the Associated Press sent to the country's major dailies. The wire service routinely referred to *Lucifer* by the inflammatory labels "social vampire" and "national menace," while incorrectly telling the nation that Walker was married and had deserted his wife and five children—Walker, in reality, was legally divorced and continued to support his two children.[35]

The citizens of Kansas were so outraged by Moses Harman's ungodly acts that court officials moved the trial along at breakneck speed, the jury quickly found Edwin and Lillian guilty, and the judge sentenced Edwin to seventy-five days in jail and Lillian to forty-five. In addition, he said both defendants would remain in jail until they paid the court costs. After Edwin and Lillian served their full sentences, they stayed behind bars because they refused to pay the fees, saying that doing so would be admitting that their relationship was illicit. So they remained in jail for six months, finally agreeing to go home only when Moses Harman insisted that they were desperately needed to produce *Lucifer* because he was about to be carted off to jail himself.

Harman's 1887 arrest on obscenity charges led to a sentence of five years in the Kansas penitentiary. After he served his time, the censors still pursued the seventy-year-old editor. Harman was then sentenced to another year in jail, this one at hard labor; the elderly man who had walked with a limp since childhood broke rocks for nine hours a day. Lillian kept the journal alive until her father was released and returned as editor. But the years in jail had sapped his last reserve of energy, so he was forced to cease publishing *Lucifer* in 1907. He died in 1910. Lillian, who had lived separately from Edwin Walker for many years, then quietly wed another man and left the public arena for a life of domesticity as a wife and mother.

LIMITED LEGACY

It would be an overstatement to suggest that the sexual reform press of the late nineteenth century changed American society. Unlike *The Liberator*, these dissident journals were not a key factor in ending an institution as powerful as slavery; unlike *The Revolution*, they did not set an agenda for an unyielding crusade for social change such as the Women's Rights Movement. The sexual reform press, in fact, never even succeeded in spawning a social movement that was larger than itself; there never existed—in the sense of membership and ongoing activities—a sexual reform movement per se.

Most fundamentally, the sexual reform press failed utterly in its central goal of destroying the institution of marriage and replacing it with a system in which women and men were free to create and dissolve sexual unions at will. Nor were other proposals adopted—promiscuity continued to be condemned, proper society did not embrace explicit sexual language, and abortion remained illegal for another 100 years. In fact, the sexual reform press very well may have worsened the very situation it was trying to improve. By fueling Anthony Comstock's vitriolic censorship campaign, the dissident papers unleashed a savage attack on sexual expression; "St. Anthony" died in 1915, but the federal law that bore his name was not substantially revised until the 1930s—some states still had lingering Comstock laws in effect into the 1970s.[36]

And yet, the editors of the radical journals should not be dismissed, as some authors have done, as members of a "lunatic" or "infidel" fringe. Although the scale of the sexual reform press was small and its impact limited, its intensity and ambition were great. The scrappy journals flouted the Victorian code of respectability that condoned sexual activity only as a necessary but unspeakable means of reproducing the species. Likewise, the publications challenged the powerful and pervasive social consensus that enforced the code of silence in all things sexual.[37]

Challenged indeed. Like the dissident publications that preceded them, *Woodhull & Claflin's Weekly*, *The Word*, and *Lucifer, the Light-Bearer* provided a venue for a conversation that the mainstream press of their day refused to hear. Some of the topics the sexual reform papers discussed are still considered beyond the pale of polite discourse today—among them promiscuity and the superiority of babies born to unwed mothers. Other of the topics sound dauntingly contemporary—graphic language, sex education, abortion. Perhaps what is most curious about the list of topics is how few of them have progressed to the point of widespread acceptance; only the marriage contract no longer allowing wives to be subjugated and adults being allowed to live together without being married seem to fit into that category, and many Americans will disagree even with that limited assessment.

What can and should be credited to the sexual reform press is that it allowed many contentious conversations to begin. For the four decades between 1870 when *Woodhull & Claflin's Weekly* was founded and 1907 when *Lucifer* ceased publication, this intriguing genre of the dissident press offered a platform for the discussion of sexual reform that establishment journalism refused to grant. By the early decades of the twentieth century, general-circulation publications were beginning to make room for some of these topics—the need to rethink the legal limits of the marriage contract and to reform the nation's divorce laws— but that dialogue may not have commenced when it did had it not been for the efforts of Victoria Woodhull, Ezra and Angela Heywood, and Moses Harman.[38]

What also most certainly can be said is that these defiant women and men paid an exorbitant price for their dissidence. They dared Victorian society to rethink its view of sexual behavior despite censure, repression, denunciation, and the dark shadow of public disgrace. To a range of degrees and for various lengths of time, each sexual reform editor suffered public disrepute and personal deprivation, including being condemned as criminals and serving time behind bars. In the case of Ezra Heywood and Moses Harman, their confinement to jail extended for many years and ultimately destroyed their health and undoubtedly hastened their deaths. In the final analysis, then, the story of the sexual reform press is a story of ideas before their time and of social insurgents who dedicated their talents, their resources, and—in some cases—their very lives to a provocative brand of dissident journalism.

5 CRUSADING AGAINST THE BARBARISM OF LYNCHING

With the collapse of Reconstruction and the departure of federal troops from the former Confederacy, the defeated and demoralized South devised a new means, beginning in the 1870s, to maintain economic and political control over former slaves.

Lynching black men had the short-term purpose of terrifying and intimidating former slaves so they would remain docile and the long-term purpose of perpetuating the feudal system that reigned throughout the South. To rationalize the barbaric act, southern racists contrived the black man's mythical lust for the white woman. During the final two decades of the nineteenth century, lynching claimed the lives of at least 3,000 African American men. Many of the victims were not only hanged but also riddled with bullets, mutilated, castrated, and burned.[1]

Most mainstream newspapers, especially in the South, fully supported—even applauded—lynching as a necessary means of controlling blacks, who were portrayed in news stories as uncivilized and dangerous. When eighty white men in DeSoto, Louisiana, hanged Reeves Smith in 1886 after he was accused of, though never tried for, entering the bedroom of a white woman, the *New Orleans Daily Picayune* characterized the mob as "composed of the best people in the parish." The *Picayune* went on to "commend" the lynchers as civic-minded men who clearly had the well-being of their community in mind when they lynched Reeves. "As we have said before," the city's largest paper stated, "all such monsters should be disposed of in a summary manner."[2]

The first full-scale crusade against lynching came in the form of a social movement launched by a fiercely militant African American woman journalist. In 1892, Ida B. Wells told the readers of the Memphis newspaper she edited, aptly titled the *Free Speech*, that they should abandon a community that killed innocent men. A few months later, the sharp-tongued Wells dared to challenge the myth that the lynch mobs were hiding behind, stating point blank that some white women *willingly* engaged in sexual relations with black men. "Nobody in this section of the country believes the old thread-bare lie that Negro men rape white women," Wells wrote. "If southern white men are not careful, they will over-reach themselves, and public sentiment will have a reaction and a conclusion will be reached which will be very damaging to the moral reputation of their women."[3]

With those provocative words, the thirty-year-old Wells launched the Anti-Lynching Movement in this country, unleashing such outrage among southern manhood that she was forced to abandon Memphis and live in exile in the North. Death threats kept Wells from returning to her home, but they did not silence her. Indeed, her banishment imbued Wells with a sense of prophetic mission that propelled her to create a dissident journalistic campaign to arouse the conscience of all of America—and England as well—to the brutalities previously only whispered about in the rural South.[4]

EARLY CHALLENGES

Born into slavery in 1862 in Holly Springs, Mississippi, Ida Bell Wells was the oldest of eight children in a family headed by Jim Wells, a carpenter, and Lizzie Wells, a cook. Ida's life was turned upside down in 1878 when a yellow fever epidemic killed her parents and one of her brothers. Refusing to allow her siblings to be separated, the sixteen-year-old young woman assumed full responsibility for the family. Having already completed high school, she piled her hair on top of her head so she would look older and secured a teaching job in a rural school nearby.[5]

Wells began her life of activism during a train ride in 1884. After purchasing a first-class ticket, Wells sat in the ladies car among white women until a conductor told her that blacks were allowed only in the smoking car. When Wells refused to move and the conductor tried to force the petite woman from her seat, she bit his hand. Three men finally dragged Wells from the car, as white passengers stood on their seats and applauded. After the incident, Wells sued the Chesapeake & Ohio Railroad. The circuit court ruled in her favor and awarded her $500 in damages. Although the Tennessee Supreme Court later reversed the ruling, she nevertheless had established a reputation as an uncompromising woman who was willing to fight an unjust system, regardless of the odds against her.

When the mainstream press failed to report the train ride incident to her lik-

At the age of thirty, Ida Bell Wells—called the "Black Joan of Arc"—launched the anti-lynching press in America. (Reprinted from Alfreda M. Duster, *Crusade for Justice: The Autobiography of Ida B. Wells* [Chicago: University of Chicago Press, 1970])

ing, Wells entered the world of journalism, in 1885, and told the story herself. About the same time, Wells moved to the larger city of Memphis to a higher-paying teaching job. She then balanced full-time teaching with part-time newspaper writing, selling articles to numerous African American newspapers.

Wells received effusive praise from T. Thomas Fortune, editor of the *New York Age* and dean of black journalism. After meeting the diminutive Wells,

Fortune told his readers she was "girlish looking in physique" and "as smart as a steel trap." He also paid Wells a compliment that few American women— black or white—had ever heard before: "She handles a goose quill with a diamond point as handily as any of us men in newspaper work." Wells was soon dubbed, partly because of her beauty, the "Princess of the Black Press."[6]

RAISING A MILITANT VOICE

In 1889, Wells bought one-third interest in the *Memphis Free Speech*, a Baptist weekly. Her two male partners became business manager and sales manager, while Wells raised a militant editorial voice. Two years later, Wells criticized the city school system she worked for, saying the conditions in the black schools were disgraceful; after her article appeared, she was summarily fired from her teaching job.

Then Wells became a full-time editor with her livelihood depending on the circulation of the *Free Speech*. She traveled by herself through Mississippi, Tennessee, and Arkansas to secure new subscribers. A taste of Wells's ingenuity came when she learned that white news dealers, realizing that many illiterate blacks were buying the *Free Speech* to pass it on to literate friends who would read it aloud to them, were selling copies of white newspapers to blacks who asked for Wells's paper. So to prevent illiterate blacks from being duped, Wells began printing the *Free Speech* on pink paper. In less than a year, the circulation of her weekly jumped from 1,500 to 3,500 and became, for the first time, financially profitable.[7]

Although no copies of the *Free Speech* have survived, Wells's articles reprinted in other newspapers paint a portrait of a hard-hitting journalist. In one editorial, she lambasted African Americans who took advantage of others of their race to gain favor with whites, condemning them as "good niggers." In another, she responded to blacks being sent to prison for stealing five cents while whites thrived after absconding with thousands of dollars by saying of the black thief: "Let him steal big."[8]

FOUNDING A MOVEMENT

By 1891, Wells had transformed the *Free Speech* into a ferociously anti-lynching newspaper. In a typical article, she praised African Americans in Georgetown, Kentucky, who had protested the lynching of a local man by burning down every white-owned building in town. Calling their action a "true spark of manhood," Wells wrote: "So long as we permit ourselves to be trampled upon, so long we will have to endure it. Not until the Negro rises in his might and takes a hand in resenting such cold-blooded murders, if he has to burn up whole towns, will a halt be called in wholesale lynching."[9]

The signal event in Wells's personal experience with lynching exploded in the spring of 1892. Three of the editor's friends—she was godmother for the daughter of one of them—had established a grocery store in an African American section of Memphis. When the men's success jeopardized a white grocer's economic security, he began harassing his black business rivals. Events escalated to the point that the white grocer and twelve supporters, all armed, entered the back door of the black store and threatened to kill the customers and storekeepers alike. When the African American men fired toward the intruders, a mob of white men killed the three black grocers.

Wells denounced the crime, saying that Memphis was not a fit place for African Americans to live. "There is only one thing left that we can do; leave a town which will neither protect our lives and property, nor give us a fair trial in the courts, but takes us out and murders us in cold blood."[10]

Heeding the editor's call, some 2,000 Americans of African descent abandoned Memphis, severely damaging the local economy. The campaign was so successful, in fact, that the city's leading white businessmen pleaded with Wells to stop writing her editorials. She refused.[11]

Indeed, Wells was only warming up. Adopting the techniques of modern-day investigative journalism, she began examining the circumstances surrounding individual lynchings. Although she often was the only black person at the scene after a hanging, her risky pursuit—she carried a loaded pistol in her purse—paid off when she made a shocking discovery: Every case she scrutinized involved a white woman who had *willingly* become sexually intimate with a black man. It was only later, when the white woman's attraction for the black man became known and she grew desperate to protect her reputation, Wells discovered, that the woman had accused her African American lover of rape.

Wells then wrote the most incendiary editorial of her life, as she asserted that white women were often attracted to black men. "There are many white women in the South who would marry colored men if such an act would not place them beyond the pale of society," she defiantly stated. "White men lynch the offending Afro-American, not because he is a despoiler of virtue, but because he succumbs to the smiles of white women."[12]

The idea that white women of the Victorian Era might feel such a taboo sexual desire drove the white men of Memphis to hysteria. The city's mainstream press demanded that the "scurrilous" writer of the editorial either be lynched or branded with a hot iron and castrated—the paper assumed the writer was a man. Wells was at a church convention in Philadelphia when a mob destroyed her press and newspaper office, threatening to kill her and cause mass bloodshed if she returned to Memphis.[13]

GOING INTO EXILE

Although Wells's editorial drew hatred from white editors, T. Thomas Fortune admired her courage. He invited Wells to move to the North and write for his *New York Age*, giving her one-fourth interest in the nationally circulated African American paper, in exchange for her subscription list for the *Free Speech*.[14]

After joining the staff of the *Age*, Wells set out to awaken black readers throughout the United States to the reality of the lynchings that were taking place in the South. Wells turned the *Age*'s front page into the closest thing America had to an official record of the chilling acts of racial abuse, filling the paper with the details surrounding dozens of lynchings she had investigated first hand.

Her inaugural story in the *Age*, which covered the entire front page, described the events in Memphis and denounced the rape myth. Fortune touted the blockbuster as the "first inside story of Negro lynching" and sold 10,000 copies, far more than any other single publication in the seventy-five-year history of the African American press. "It created a veritable sensation," Fortune later said of the article, "and was referred to and discussed in hundreds of newspapers and thousands of homes. It was a historic document, full of the pathos of awful truth."[15]

The huge article told, for example, of a black man in Tuscumbia, Alabama, who was lynched even though the white woman he supposedly had raped had publicly stated that she and the man had been involved in a consensual sexual relationship of long duration. Wells also accused the white press in Indianola, Mississippi, of incorrectly stating that a black man had been lynched because he had raped the sheriff's eight-year-old daughter when, in reality, the girl was in her twenties and had gone to the man's room of her own free will.[16]

Knowing that northern readers unfamiliar with the abuses routinely taking place in the South would question the veracity of her reports, Wells not only named names but also blended concrete details and direct quotations into her stories to add to their credibility. Her item about the lynching of Ebenezer Fowler identified him as "the wealthiest colored man in Issaquena County,

Miss.," and reported that the "armed body of white men who filled his body with bullets" was composed entirely of local merchants whose incomes had declined because of Fowler's superior business acumen.[17]

Wells made her account of another case come alive by directly quoting the woman involved. The African American man, William Offett, had been convicted of raping the wife of a white minister, even though the woman had testified that Offett came to her home at her request. Wells quoted Mrs. J. S. Underwood as saying: "I invited him to call on me. He called, bringing chestnuts and candy for the children. By this means we got them to leave us alone in the room. Then I sat on his lap. He made a proposal to me and I readily consented. He visited me several times after that. I had no desire to resist."[18]

Like other dissident journalists before and after her, Wells was not satisfied merely to report the injustices but also wrote searing editorials against the South, saying: "Her white citizens are wedded to any method, however revolting, for the subjugation of the young manhood of the race. They have cheated him out of his ballot, deprived him of civil rights or redress in the civil courts, robbed him of the fruits of his labor, and are still murdering, burning and lynching him." Accusing black men of raping white women was "merely an excuse to get rid of Negroes who were acquiring wealth and property," Wells wrote, "and thus keep the race terrorized and 'keep the nigger down.' "[19]

As for how the violence could be ended, Wells's first proposal was the same one that she had recommended, and that had succeeded, in Memphis: economic reprisals. Specifically, Wells urged her readers to boycott any white businessman who condoned lynching. "The white man's dollar is his god," she wrote bitterly. "The appeal to the white man's pocket has ever been more effectual than all the appeals ever made to his conscience."[20]

Her second proposal was that oppressed African Americans demand that the nation's newspapers write editorials condemning lynching as barbaric. "The strong arm of the law must be brought to bear upon lynchers in severe punishment, but this cannot and will not be done unless a healthy public sentiment demands and sustains such action," she wrote. "The people must know before they can act, and there is no educator to compare with the press."[21]

Wells's third—and most controversial—proposal was one that militant leaders of her race would continue to make for generations to come: African Americans had to defend themselves against violence. "Of the many inhuman outrages of this present year, the only case where the proposed lynching did *not* occur was where the men armed themselves in Jacksonville, Fla., and prevented it. The only times an Afro-American who was assaulted got away has been when he had a gun and used it in self-defense."[22]

Wells followed this observation with one of the most radical statements that any African American leader of the nineteenth century would ever make: "A Winchester rifle should have a place of honor in every black home." She went on to justify her bold proposal by saying: "When the white man knows he runs a risk of biting the dust every time his Afro-American victim does, he will have greater respect for Afro-American life. The more the Afro-American yields and cringes and begs, the more he is insulted, outraged and lynched."[23]

EXPANDING THE CRUSADE

Although Wells criticized White America, she soon came to realize that the success of her movement depended on her ability to win the hearts and minds of white northerners to the anti-lynching cause, as they dominated all of the nation's political, social, and legal institutions. That the target audience for Wells's writing crossed the color line became clear late in 1892 when she expanded her dissident press crusade beyond African American newspapers to create her first publication that was marketed to whites as well as blacks.

Using the high sales volume of her debut article in the *New York Age* as a selling point, Wells persuaded T. Thomas Fortune to finance the reprinting of the best of her anti-lynching writing in a pamphlet titled "Southern Horrors: Lynch Law in All Its Phases." Fortune knew that white readers, in particular, would be curious to get a look at the comely African American spitfire who was defying the nation's pro-lynching establishment, so he hired an artist to fashion a flattering line drawing of his protégé that he placed on the cover of the pamphlet. Fortune then distributed copies of "Southern Horrors" to bookstores in both white and black shopping districts of numerous northern cities.

Wells did her part to promote sales by devoting several of the pamphlet's twenty-five pages to the contentious topic—then as well as now—of interracial marriage. "The miscegenation laws of the South only operate against the legitimate union of the races," she wrote, thereby challenging the long-standing legal ban against black/white couples. "Many white women in the South would marry colored men if such an act would not place them within the clutches of the law."[24]

Adding to the prestige of "Southern Horrors" was a letter of support from Frederick Douglass, the most respected African American leader of the nineteenth century, that Wells reprinted in the pamphlet. In the letter, Douglass admitted that he had accepted the rape myth until Wells had challenged it. "Let me give you thanks for your faithful work on the lynch abomination," Douglass wrote in the letter. "There has been no work equal to it in convincing power. I have spoken, but my word is feeble in comparison." Douglass ended his letter with words of exuberant praise for the anti-lynching pioneer: "Brave woman! You have done your people and mine a service which can neither be weighed nor measured."[25]

Similar words of support appeared in leading African American newspapers across the country. "Before the advent of Miss Wells and the consequent Anti-Lynching Movement," the *Indianapolis Freeman* wrote, "the Negro's case in equity had lingered comparatively unnoticed for years." The *Chicago Defender* expressed the same sentiment, saying: "If we only had a few men with the backbone of Miss Wells, lynching would soon come to a halt."[26]

African American women also supported their courageous sister. Some 250 upper-class black women organized a testimonial dinner for Wells at Lyric Hall in New York City. Later described as "the greatest demonstration ever attempted by race women for one of their own number," the dinner was a spectacle without peer. Wells's name was spelled out in electric lights across the dais, miniature versions of the *Free Speech* were used as programs, soul-stirring music was interspersed with uplifting speeches, and $500 was collected and donated to Wells's crusade. The climax of the event came when Wells gave an emotional account of her experiences while investigating lynchings.[27]

LECTURING FOR THE CAUSE AT HOME AND ABROAD

Wells's speech at that testimonial dinner launched her career as an orator. For the sympathy aroused by her heartfelt words and delivery were the catalyst for her, in 1893, to begin lecturing against lynching throughout the North.

Wells spoke to as many white audiences as she could and also made personal appeals to the editors of mainstream newspapers in the dozens of cities she visited. "A factual appeal to Christian conscience," she said in a typical speech, "will ultimately stop these crimes."[28]

After hearing one of her presentations, the editor of a British newspaper offered to sponsor Wells on a lecture tour in England. The politically savvy Wells eagerly accepted, knowing that Great Britain's role as the world's biggest importer of cotton gave English views considerable weight in the American South.

And, indeed, Wells's overseas tour advanced her campaign enormously. By the time she returned to the United States, the British Anti-Lynching Committee had been formed to oppose lynching in the American South, with its membership including such notables as the Duke of Argyll (Queen Victoria's son-in-law), the Archbishop of Canterbury, members of Parliament, and the editors of the *Manchester Guardian*.[29]

Wells's rising influence because of her English speaking tour—some people were now calling her the "Black Joan of Arc"—had direct impact on the Anti-Lynching Movement. The effect was particularly dramatic in Memphis, which exported more cotton than any other city in the world. When Wells gave British business and political leaders first-hand accounts of lynchings that had taken place in Memphis, she did serious damage to the image of her former home town. So, as a direct result of her efforts, the city fathers were forced to take an official stand against lynching, and for the next twenty years there was not another incident of vigilante violence there.[30]

In addition, numerous articles about Wells, her lectures, and the Anti-Lynching Movement had now begun to appear in such mainstream publications as the *Literary Digest, Atlanta Constitution, Washington* (D.C.) *City Post*, and *New York Sun*. Although the articles were uniformly critical of Wells—the *New York Times* denounced her as a "slanderous and nasty-minded mulatress" and a fraud: "She knows nothing about the colored problem in the South. A reputable or respectable negro has never been lynched, and never will be"—they nevertheless increased her visibility and communicated her message to White America.[31]

And, on rare occasion, the mainstream press even began to publish words of support for the Anti-Lynching Movement that Wells had founded. After Wells supplied the *Chicago Inter-Ocean* with documentation showing that the white woman a black man named Ed Coy allegedly had raped had, in fact, seduced the man, the white paper published an article supporting Wells's conclusion: "The woman was a willing partner in the victim's guilt." After that initial breakthrough, Wells persuaded the paper's editor to publish other supportive articles. "The real need is for a public sentiment in favor of enforcing the law and giving every man, white and black, a fair hearing before the lawful tribunals," the *Inter-Ocean* argued in the summer of 1893. "The Negro has as good a right to a fair trial as the white man."[32]

Wells's trip to England was such a triumph that she was invited back for another speaking tour in 1894. This time, she presented more than 100 lectures, was honored at a breakfast with members of Parliament, and wrote a weekly column titled "Ida B. Wells Abroad" for the *Inter-Ocean*—marking the first time the paper had ever published the work of an African American writer.[33]

Wells maintained the intensity of her crusade. She devoted an entire year to lecturing and organizing a network of local and statewide anti-lynching societies from New England to California, focusing in particular on white audiences. Her mantra during her presentations became: "It is the white people of this country who have to mold the public sentiment necessary to put a stop to lynching."[34]

It was also in 1894 that Wells entered the rough-and-tumble of political lobbying. Within a month after returning from her second triumphant British speaking tour, she persuaded Congressman Henry Blair of New Hampshire to introduce federal legislation calling for an investigation of all acts of mob violence committed as punitive measures—"by whipping, lynching, or otherwise"—against alleged criminals. Blair presented his fellow members of Congress with petitions from citizens of twelve states—Wells had collected a good portion of the names during her lecture tour. Blair's proposal eventually died in committee, but it marked the first time that the travesty of lynching had been debated in the U.S. Congress.[35]

Wells's lobbying efforts were far more effective on the state level. Between 1893 and 1897, she helped persuade the legislatures in five southern states to enact their first anti-lynching laws. The measures established penalties against sheriffs who failed to protect accused persons from mob violence and against private citizens who broke into jails or otherwise obstructed the legal process.[36]

Early in 1895, Wells began distributing another pamphlet, this one providing the nation's first comprehensive history of lynching, "A Red Record: Tabulated Statistics and Alleged Causes of Lynching in the United States." The most memorable single element of the 100-page work was one of the most haunting images ever printed in an American publication. The photo, taken at an Alabama lynching in 1891, showed a black victim hanging lifeless from a tree—his neck broken to the point that it was almost at a right angle to his head. Surrounding the dead man was a crowd of white men and boys posing proudly for the traveling photographer who had captured the moment, eager to show their unflagging support for law and order as practiced in the American South.[37]

The pamphlet listed the names, dates, locations, and charges for all of the lynchings that had taken place during the previous year, while also noting the progress of the Anti-Lynching Movement. "There is now an awakened conscience throughout the land," Wells could justly write, "and Lynch Law can not flourish in the future as it has in the past." To support her rose-colored assessment, Wells cited Ohio Governor William McKinley calling out the militia in October 1894 to protect a black prisoner from a lynch mob—the man was later found innocent of the charges and released.[38]

Meanwhile, statistics documented both Wells's optimism about the decline of lynching and her success as a dissident journalist. For in 1893, the number of

The most memorable element in Ida B. Wells-Barnett's 1895 pamphlet, "A Red Record," was the haunting image of an 1891 lynching in Alabama. (Reprinted from "A Red Record")

lynchings nationwide had decreased for the first time—dropping from 235 to 200.[39]

By the time Wells wrote "A Red Record" in 1895, she no longer needed T. Thomas Fortune's support as she was an internationally known activist and publishing entrepreneur in her own right. She paid to have the pamphlet printed and distributed to white as well as black bookstores throughout the North and, to the extent possible, the South.

Marketing the hefty booklet also launched the Central Anti-Lynching League, a national information clearing house for Wells's written work. "Anti-lynching societies and individuals can order copies from the league," she wrote at the end of the pamphlet. "The writer hereof assures prompt distribution according to order, and public acknowledgment of all orders through the public press."[40]

ENTERING A NEW PHASE OF LIFE

By this point, Chicago had become Wells's home base. She first went to the city in 1893, between her trips abroad, to take her anti-lynching crusade to the throngs of visitors who attended the historic World's Columbian Exposition.

She collaborated with Frederick Douglass and Ferdinand L. Barnett, editor of the *Chicago Conservator*, to write and publish an eighty-page pamphlet titled "The Reason Why the Colored American Is Not in the World's Columbian Exposition." Her section reproduced some of her anti-lynching writing, and she distributed 20,000 copies of the pamphlet at the fair, while also drawing a sizable crowd to the public lecture she gave at the Haitian Pavilion.[41]

Soon after arriving in Chicago, Wells began writing anti-lynching articles for the *Conservator*. Barnett, like Wells, had been born a slave. He went on to earn a law degree from Northwestern University and in 1878 founded the paper as the first African American publishing voice in the city. Tall, handsome, and with courtly manners that made him acceptable to prominent whites, Barnett was a strong advocate for racial equality.

As Wells and Barnett, whose wife had recently died, worked together on various projects, they came to recognize the compatibility of their shared commitments to activism and journalism. They married in July 1895, with the bride reaffirming her life-long independence by adopting a hyphenated last name in one of the earliest instances of that feminist practice.

After the marriage, Ida B. Wells-Barnett became owner and editor of the *Chicago Conservator* while her husband focused on his new position as the first

African American assistant state's attorney in the city's history. Barnett had two sons from his first marriage, and, within a year after their wedding, Wells-Barnett embraced motherhood with the same enthusiasm that characterized other aspects of her life. She gave birth to four children—including a daughter named Ida B. Wells Jr.—in eight years.[42]

Partly out of concern for her two stepsons who already had lost one mother and partly because of how the death of her own parents had disrupted her and her siblings' youth, Wells-Barnett announced in 1897 that she was relinquishing her position as editor of the *Conservator* and retiring from public life to devote all her time and energy to her family.

Her "retirement" lasted five months.

Wells-Barnett resumed her activism in response to the brutal lynching of a Lake City, South Carolina, man in 1898. She was outraged by the incident in which the man was hanged and he and his infant son were burned "to a crisp," according to the *Charleston News and Courier*, because "the good people of Lake City" were angry that federal officials had appointed the man to the prestigious position of town postmaster. After investigating the events, Wells-Barnett led a citizen delegation to the White House to ask President William McKinley to punish the offenders and, because the victim was a federal employee, to enact a national anti-lynching law. "Nowhere in the civilized world save the United States," she protested, "do men go out in bands to hunt down, shoot, hang or burn to death a single individual." McKinley assured Wells-Barnett that he was in "hearty accord" with her concerns and that the appropriate departments would look into the matter, although ultimately nothing came of those promises.[43]

That lack of action reinforced Wells-Barnett's adamant belief that White America had to be convinced of the barbarism of lynching. So she renewed her commitment to publishing her dissident words in pamphlets that were aimed at both black and white readers.

In 1900, she published "Mob Rule in New Orleans," a fifty-page booklet that focused on a series of race riots that erupted in Louisiana. Her detailed account of the tragedy included harsh critiques of the city's two mainstream dailies, the *Picayune* and the *Times-Democrat*. Both papers, Wells-Barnett wrote, routinely used the terms "ruffians," "fiends," and "monsters" as synonyms for African American men and consistently encouraged mob violence through statements such as one in the *Times-Democrat*: "The only way that you can teach these Niggers a lesson and put them in their place is to go out and lynch a few of them as an object lesson. String up a few of them, and the others will trouble you no more."[44]

The most far-reaching effort Wells-Barnett was involved in during this period was helping to found the National Association for the Advancement of Colored People. She was one of sixty persons, including only one other African American woman, who organized the 1909 gathering where the NAACP was formed.

Wells-Barnett stunned the crowd that had assembled for the historic meeting, as she told her fellow activists: "Agitation, though helpful, will not alone stop the crime of lynching." Despite her years of activism, she continued, it had become clear to her that the "only certain remedy" was to persuade the country's political community to designate lynching a federal crime. Wells-Barnett's speech helped set the course for the NAACP, as the founders accepted her proposal not to be aggressive in their opposition to whites but to include them in the organization's leadership positions.[45]

Her position vis-à-vis strategy carried considerable weight because of the success of the Anti-Lynching Movement; by 1909, the number of lynchings reported nationwide had dropped to eighty-seven.[46]

Throughout the early decades of the twentieth century, Wells-Barnett remained actively involved in dissident journalism through articles she wrote for the *Chicago Tribune* and several national magazines. Although the articles were aimed at white readers as well as black, the irrepressible activist pulled no punches. In a 1913 piece in *Survey* magazine, Wells-Barnett protested: "The nation cannot profess Christianity, which makes the golden rule its foundation stone, and continue to deny equal opportunity for life, liberty and the pursuit of happiness to the black race. When our Christian and moral influences not only concede these principles theoretically but work for them practically, lynching will become a thing of the past."[47]

Wells-Barnett's strong words were still very much needed, as many mainstream publications continued to denigrate Americans of African descent. "The Negroes, as a rule, are very ignorant, are very lazy, are very brutal, are very criminal," the *Atlantic Monthly* wrote in 1909. "They are creatures of brutal, untamed instincts, and uncontrollable feral passions, which give frequent expression of themselves in crimes of horrible ferocity. They are, in brief, an uncivilized and semi-savage people."[48]

The founder of the Anti-Lynching Movement remained committed to changing White America's perception of her people by uncovering and reporting the truth about the lynchings that continued to plague the country. Although she regretted having to spend time apart from her children, Wells-Barnett could not turn down the standing offer from the nation's leading newspapers and magazines that were eager to publish her compelling investigative articles. So whether the incident had taken place relatively near Chicago, such as in East St. Louis, Illinois, in 1918, or hundreds of miles away, such as in Elaine, Arkansas, in 1922, Wells-Barnett packed her bag—and her pistol—and traveled to the scene to probe the details that had led to the wrongful killing. The journey to Arkansas marked Wells-Barnett's return to the South for the first time since she had been banished from that section of the country thirty years earlier.[49]

Although Wells-Barnett went to many cities during the first two decades of the twentieth century, her most frequent destination was Washington, D.C., where she became a familiar presence in the halls of Congress. Some sixteen anti-lynching bills were introduced in committees of the Senate or the House of Representatives during those years, each one seeking to establish lynching as a federal crime. And by 1918, some of the proposals were considered with sufficient seriousness that they became the subjects of public hearings—with Wells-Barnett the most inveterate of the witnesses at the sessions.[50]

A major breakthrough finally came in 1922 when a federal anti-lynching bill moved out of committee and onto the House floor. Missouri Congressman Leonidas Dyer introduced the legislation, and hard lobbying by Wells-Barnett and other leaders of the NAACP succeeded in getting the bill passed in the lower house. Despite visits to the offices of dozens of senators, Wells-Barnett—by then sixty years old—had to stand by helpless and watch as a powerful southern filibuster blocked a vote in the Senate. After that disappointing defeat, the NAACP shifted its focus to campaigning for anti-lynching legislation on the state level.[51]

In sync with this strategy, Wells-Barnett decided, after four decades of relentless lobbying of lawmakers, to seek elected office herself. So in 1930, she campaigned for a seat in the Illinois State Senate, running as an independent. She held dozens of rallies, published hundreds of articles and editorials in the city's newspapers, and blanketed the city with thousands of flyers, but the outspoken woman received a mere eight percent of the vote.[52]

Within a year of her first bid for elected office, Ida B. Wells-Barnett contracted a kidney disease. After a brief illness, she died in 1931, at the age of sixty-nine.[53]

A LIMITED LEGACY

W.E.B. DuBois's eulogy read: "Ida Wells-Barnett was the pioneer of the anti-lynching crusade in the United States. She began the awakening of the conscience of the nation." DuBois, the leading African American intellectual of the early twentieth century, was wise to choose the verb *began*. For in 1892 when the

"Princess of the Black Press," then barely thirty years old, launched her social movement against the barbaric act of lynching, it was, in fact, only the beginning of a long and arduous journey.[54]

The white overlords who ruled the American South had no intention of abandoning the highly effective technique they had devised, as Wells put it, to "keep the nigger down." And yet, a single voice of dissidence did *begin* the slow process of wearing away the bigotry that was underpinning the heinous practice of lynching. After less than a year of challenging conventional thinking regarding black men raping white women, the dissident journalist could rightly claim progress; never again would the South commit as many lynchings as it had in the year that Wells launched her crusade in 1892.[55]

Other milestones of progress could be attributed to this agent of change as well. The anti-lynching legislation enacted by the various states beginning in 1893 provided several punitive measures. With hidebound law enforcement officials and vigilante citizens being punished for the first time, "Judge Lynch" clearly was on the run.

Journalists and historians alike placed the credit for that progress at the feet of the "Black Joan of Arc." T. Thomas Fortune, Wells-Barnett's long-time admirer, wrote, "No history of the Afro-American will be complete in which this woman's work has not a place." Others soon added to the chorus of praise. An early scholar of women journalists gushed, "No writer, the male fraternity not excepted, has struck harder blows at the wrongs against the race," and the first historian of the lynching phenomenon cited Wells-Barnett's hundreds of newspaper articles and numerous pamphlets—some of them distributed to as many as 20,000 readers—as the single most important catalyst for state legislatures enacting anti-lynching laws.[56]

And yet it would be an overstatement to assert that either Wells-Barnett or the Anti-Lynching Movement that she founded was successful in eradicating the crime of hanging innocent African American men. No federal law was passed, and southern racists continued their reign of terror via the rope well into the twentieth century. Indeed, it would not be until the year 1953 that, for the first time, not a single lynching occurred anywhere in the United States.[57]

Despite Ida B. Wells-Barnett's courage and fortitude, then, her anti-lynching press must be consigned to the category of the dissident press that helped initiate a conversation about a problem but ultimately failed to solve it.

6 EDUCATING AMERICA ON THE MERITS OF SOCIALISM

The end of the nineteenth century saw the emergence of a new genre of the dissident press created to drive a stake into the heart of what its founders considered a pernicious threat to the world's greatest democracy: capitalism.

According to these publications, the Industrial Revolution had elevated the lust for financial gain into the most powerful force in American life. This pervasive greed had, in fact, become so strong that it had spawned an elite class of economic aristocrats who wielded unlimited control and absolute authority on the scale of medieval kings. These robber barons—men such as Andrew Carnegie, John D. Rockefeller, and J. Pierpont Morgan—controlled the nation's banks, mills, railroads, mines, and the omnipresent factories that had become the very symbol of the nation; this small cadre of men had, in effect, transformed the United States into a nation "of" the corporation, "by" the corporation, and "for" the corporation.

In stubborn opposition to the rise of capitalism stood the fledgling concept that fueled the newest genre of journalistic dissidence: socialism.

The core of this widely misunderstood belief is support of government intervention on behalf of the working class. Further, socialists believe that laborers who produce goods also should control the means by which those goods are made and distributed, thereby allowing those same workers to reap the economic and political profit that are generated by their effort. Late-nineteenth- and early-twentieth-century socialists were convinced that the forces of capitalism had grown so insidious that, in order to preserve the democratic way of life, a new political power had to be put into place to restructure American society.

During the final years of the nineteenth century, socialists founded a third party that became a major player in American politics. Some 1,200 socialists were elected to local, state, and congressional offices, and in 1912—when the party was at its apex—Socialist Party presidential nominee Eugene V. Debs received almost a million votes, which amounted to six percent of all ballots cast.

This impressive showing did not erupt from nowhere; committed socialists had been building a grassroots base by articulating their anti-capitalist ideology through a network of publications far larger than any dissident press that had come before it. The socialist press numbered more than 300 newspapers with a combined circulation of two million. Many of the individual papers could boast that they had been published for several years and had substantial circulation, but one of them stood head and shoulders above all the rest.[1]

One historian has called the *Appeal to Reason* the most important publication in the history of the American Left, another has dubbed it "the most popular radical publication of any kind in American history," and a third has written: "No American newspaper has had the character, impact, and indignant fervor of the *Appeal to Reason*."[2]

There is ample evidence to support these dramatic assertions. From 1895 when the *Appeal* was founded (six years before the Socialist Party existed) until 1922 when it ceased publication (well after the party's influence had ebbed), this dissident weekly served as the national voice of the Socialist Movement. In addition, the paper's unique "Tell the *Appeal*" editorial policy expanded the paper's 100-person full-time staff into a network of thousands of writers from around the country who worked as volunteer correspondents. Further evidence of the *Appeal*'s strength came when its editor decided that the inhuman working conditions in Chicago's meat packing plants had to be reported; he hired novelist Upton Sinclair to write an exposé so gripping that it became, in book form, the classic of American literature that generations of students have read as *The Jungle*.[3]

Most remarkable of all was the *Appeal*'s circulation. This national weekly newspaper, based in the tiny community of Girard, Kansas (population 2,500), surpassed every dissident publication in American history—as well as a goodly number of mainstream ones—to build a paid subscription base of a stunning 760,000.[4]

And so, even though the socialist press ultimately failed in its effort to destroy capitalism, the *Appeal to Reason* deserves a chapter in the history of dissident journalism. For during the final years of the nineteenth century and the first years of the twentieth, it was a very real part of the American experience.

The paper provided the excitement, the vitality, and the continuity that the Socialist Movement needed in order to survive and to thrive. Week after week, the *Appeal* bridged the thousands of miles from the Atlantic to the Pacific to unify geographically dispersed socialists and pull them together into a single community. The paper's huge circulation and uninterrupted publication for an impressive twenty-seven years played a singular role in legitimizing and energizing the Socialist Movement. As founder J. A. Wayland frequently told his readers: "The *Appeal* is yours for the revolution."

J. A. WAYLAND, GUIDING SPIRIT

Julius Augustus Wayland was born in rural Indiana in 1854, the youngest of seven children, only four months before a cholera epidemic took the lives of his father and two siblings. Because the surviving members of the Wayland family were unable to hold onto the family grocery store, they were thrust into poverty and forced to live on the pittance that Julius's mother made by taking in laundry. As a penniless and largely uneducated teenager, Julius was apprenticed to the printer at a local newspaper. But by the age of twenty-three, the ambitious young man was well on his way to success; he married Etta Bevan, a woman from a prosperous local family, and purchased a newspaper of his own.[5]

As the youthful entrepreneur enjoyed the financial fruit of capitalism, however, he began reading about the downside of that system. Drawn deeper and deeper into the socialist philosophy, he gradually came to believe that his calling in life was to create a national socialist newspaper as an educational tool without peer. "I devoted my whole energies to the work of trying to get my neighbors to grasp the truths I had learned," Wayland wrote. "If we could put a socialist paper every week into the hands of every voter in the United States, we could capture the government." In 1895, Wayland, then in his early forties, moved to Kansas and founded the *Appeal to Reason*.[6]

Wayland neither looked nor comported himself like a political insurgent. With prematurely gray hair and always walking with his shoulders stooped, he was so painfully shy that he assiduously avoided giving the public lectures that other socialist propagandists depended on to attract converts into the fold. Even after Wayland's name grew in stature, he lived an ascetic life and even used an alias when attending Socialist Party events, opting to be an anonymous spectator who quietly observed and recorded the comments of others.

The founder of the flagship of the socialist press also suffered from chronic depression. "There have been many dark hours—days and months of them together," he later wrote of his early days of publishing the *Appeal*. "I have walked the floors many a night; I have walked the silent woods and lonely railroad tracks with feelings akin to suicide." He felt overwhelmed by the enormous mission before him—to publish a dissident paper to educate America on the

The pressures of editing a dissident publication to promote socialism ultimately became so great that J. A. Wayland committed suicide. (Courtesy of Leonard Axe Library, Pittsburg State University)

merits of socialism—and admitted that he often became despondent. When the dark feelings engulfed him, he wrote, "I would busy myself in work to forget the troubles and losses. I kept on."[7]

Publishing a socialist paper while supporting a wife and five children was a constant struggle. That task was compounded by the *Appeal*'s ideology; if he was to remain true to the anti-capitalist doctrine, Wayland knew he could accept none of the advertisements from businesses and corporations that provided the revenue for mainstream papers. When his wife died of cancer in 1897, Wayland was on the brink of closing down the *Appeal*. To keep the paper—and his life's mission—alive, he compromised his principles by accepting a few small ads and beginning to experiment with techniques to build circulation. By 1900, the advertising and subscription revenue—Wayland insisted on keeping the annual fee at a mere fifty cents so working-class readers could afford it—finally exceeded his printing and mailing costs.

It was also in 1900 that Wayland hired Fred D. Warren, twenty years his junior, to become the *Appeal*'s managing editor, with Wayland becoming publisher. Like Wayland, Warren was a Midwesterner with middlebrow tastes and values. During the first dozen years of the new century, the *Appeal* hit its stride, expanding from four pages to twelve, soaring in circulation, and becoming America's major venue for preaching the anti-capitalist/pro-socialist gospel.

CONDEMNING CAPITALISM

The mushrooming growth of industry and finance during the second half of the nineteenth century radically changed the American class structure. For while the nation's overall wealth soared, the quality of life for many working-class men and women plummeted. Unable to afford to buy the goods and services that they themselves were producing, many farmers and factory workers were trapped in grinding poverty, facing the harsh realities of economic and human survival on a daily basis.

The *Appeal to Reason* denounced that bleak situation—in the plain-spoken language of the American worker. Wayland, who had experienced hardship and deprivation firsthand during his youth and when struggling to keep his paper alive, wrote in a simple style and always spoke directly to his readers. Typical of his thousands of editorials was one that began: "In the midst of plenty, you are starving. The more you produce, the less you get. Why? Simply because that plenty of your own creation has been appropriated by the capitalistic class. That class, which you have enriched, keeps you in poverty."[8]

Wayland charged that the fault lay with the cold, callous, and malevolent nature of the robber barons who were keeping the common worker enslaved. "Every man capable of performing a fair day's labor can and does produce about three times the amount of wealth necessary to keep him and his family eating the best of food, dressed in the best of clothes, and housed in the best of houses. The American worker is robbed, through the private ownership of the means of production, of four-fifths of what he produces. The fault, my friend, is with the cursed economic system that robs him."[9]

While Wayland's prose form of choice was the essay, another signature element in the *Appeal*'s editorial mix was the kind of human anecdote that could bring a tear to the reader's eye. Many of those vignettes came from readers who worked in the bowels of American industry. In one such article, a textile worker described Roselie Randazzo, a young Italian woman who worked next to her in a New York City sweatshop. They were among the many "women with stooped shoulders and dead faces," she wrote, who stitched artificial flowers onto velvet and brocade ball gowns to be worn by the wives of wealthy capitalists. Roselie's fingers were the most deft in the shop and her "blue-black curls and velvety eyes" made her a rare beauty. The harsh winter and brutal working conditions took their toll on the girl, however, until the day that, according to the author of the story, "I turned in time to see Roselie fall forward among the flowers. As I lifted her up, the hot blood spurted from her lips, spattering the flowers as it fell." The next day, the writer went to Bellevue Hospital to visit her young coworker but found only an entry in the patient register: "Roselie Randazzo, seventeen; hemorrhage; died 12:30 p.m."[10]

CELEBRATING SOCIALISM

Standing in vivid contrast to such poignant depictions of the human cost of capitalism were portraits of socialism as the system that could rescue American workers from their misery.

For the *Appeal*, as for the Socialist Party, socialism was based on three key elements. First and foremost was public ownership of the means of production; all factories should be in the hands of national, state, or local governments so they could function like public schools or state universities—for the well-being of the people. The second element of a socialist system was that the primary purpose of the economy should be to make goods that could be used by the people, not so wealthy industrialists could amass huge profits. The third element was that America should be a classless society in which all citizens received full value for their labor.

Wayland believed there could be a smooth and tranquil transition from capitalism to socialism if all American citizens became educated about the two contrasting systems and then voted their conscience at the ballot box: "Books not bayonets, pamphlets not pistols, paper not powder, speeches not swords." In concert with this goal of a peaceful conversion, Wayland contended that socialism was totally in keeping with the bedrock concepts inherent in the democratic form of government, such as liberty, equality, individual rights, and the pursuit of happiness. Wayland insisted: "Socialism is merely more democracy."[11]

To describe the kind of society that would emerge if socialists were elected to office, the *Appeal* called upon long-time party leader Eugene V. Debs, who ran for President of the United States four times. "The badge of labor will no longer be the badge of servitude," Debs wrote of the America he envisioned. "Every man will gladly do his share of the world's useful work; every man can then honestly enjoy his share of the world's blessings."[12]

Debs went on to describe how the triumph of socialism would have positive implications beyond economics. "Life will no longer be a struggle for bread; then the children of men can begin the march to the highest type of civilization that this world has ever known." Because people would not have to devote every hour of the day to working merely to survive, Debs wrote, the higher-level human activities related to science, art, and literature would all flourish. "This earth for the first time since it was flung into space will be an habitable globe; it will be fit for good men and good women to live in."[13]

PROMOTING ORGANIZED LABOR

One of the pillars supporting the temple of socialism, according to the *Appeal*, was strong labor unions. "Labor wants the full result of its effort," the paper asserted, "and is entitled to it."[14]

A particularly strong voice on behalf of unions was that of folk hero Mary Harris "Mother" Jones, the charismatic leader who successfully organized the nation's miners, textile workers, and street car operators. Typical of Jones's writing was a 1908 investigative piece that exposed the unsafe working conditions in Alabama cotton mills. "The weavers are encircled by twenty-four terrifying looms in a steamed atmosphere which is worse than hell," she wrote. "At any moment a rebellious shuttle may shoot forth and knock an eye out. A loose skirt may be seized by a wheel or a strap, and then the horrors of the accident can better be imagined than told."[15]

Worst of all, Jones continued, were the harmful effects that the wretched conditions had on the health of the laborers. Every mill worker had to contend with constant chills and fevers, she wrote, and many also suffered from malaria. Most laborers endured chronic headaches and were, to a person, "pale, dyspeptic, hollow-chested," yet they couldn't quit their jobs because they looked so

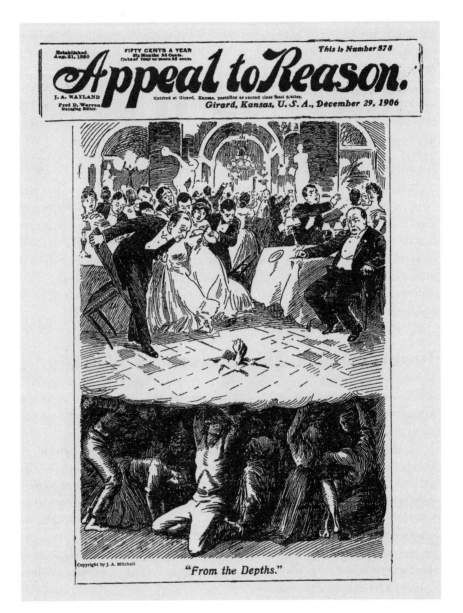

"From the Depths."

As the flagship of the socialist press, the *Appeal to Reason* often published front-page drawings encouraging American laborers to rise up against the robber barons.

unhealthy that no other employer would hire them. "One woman told me that her mother had gone into that mill and worked, and took her four children with her," Jones wrote. " 'I have been in the mill since I was four years old. I am now thirty-four,' she told me. She looked to me as if she was sixty."[16]

Mother Jones did not merely report; she also raised her voice in outrage. "I stand for the overthrow of the entire system," she wrote. "I stand for the teachings of Christ put into practice, not the teachings of capitalism and graft and murder."[17]

SERVING AS SOCIALISM'S NEWSPAPER OF RECORD

Because capitalism was accepted as an integral part of the American way of life while socialism was viewed by most people with a mixture of fear and hostility, mainstream newspapers covered events and issues from a resolutely procapitalist perspective.

That meant news articles as well as editorials in newspapers across the country were consistently disparaging of socialists, characterizing them as enemies of the state and threats to civilized society. A San Francisco paper routinely used the terms "incendiaries" and "assassins" as synonyms for socialists; a paper in Minneapolis called them "a public menace" and wrote that "Outbreaks of violence and disorder are largely traceable to this disturbing element"; and a paper in the nation's capital called all members of the Socialist Party "fiendish" and "wild-eyed" while also blithely characterizing them as "murderers."[18]

The *Appeal to Reason* adopted a dramatically different stance. Determined to develop a socialist consciousness among the American people, Wayland reported from a point of view that was reproachful not of socialists but of capitalists.

Typical was the *Appeal*'s coverage of the 1904 Colorado strike that pitted hard-rock miners and union men against the organized forces of capital—mine owners, state militia, and Governor James H. Peabody, who was militantly anti-labor. Nowhere was the class war more violent than during this bloody dispute: fifty men killed, 1,500 jailed. The coverage provided a textbook example of advocacy journalism. "Gov. Peabody's thugs and tin-horns are, at this hour, engaged in driving all the union men and their wives and children out of Teller County," one article began. "Every epithet and insult the blackguards can think of are hurled at the defenseless prisoners."[19]

The *Appeal* provided similarly pro-union and pro-socialist coverage wherever workers went out on strike for better pay and working conditions— textile workers in Massachusetts, rubber workers in Ohio, railroad workers in Mississippi.[20]

The paper supplied laborers with supportive coverage during other events as well. One story reported how African American tenant farmers who had protested their woefully inadequate living conditions had become the victims of wholesale shootings in Arkansas, and another described how convicts nation-wide were being forced to work without pay and under the most brutal of con-ditions well beyond their jail terms. Other articles illuminated the realities of urban and rural poverty, abusive treatment of recent immigrants, and legisla-tive and judicial corruption.[21]

When it came to positive coverage, the newspaper tenaciously documented the progress that the Socialist Movement was making in politics across the country. The detailed coverage of elections was consistent with the paper's insis-tence that the impending revolution could be achieved without resorting to vio-lence—the slogan "ballots not bullets" dotted hundreds of the *Appeal*'s pages. A news item from Alabama began with the exuberant statement: "Socialism in the South—in Dixie! Who would have thought such a thing possible?" The piece went on to boast that, between 1901 and 1903, the number of local Socialist Party political organizations had jumped from two to twenty.[22]

During the following decade, as socialist candidates won in municipal races from Berkeley, California, to New York City, articles did not merely trumpet the victories but described in painstaking detail the specific strategies that political leaders had employed—thereby providing guidelines for socialists hoping for similar successes in their respective cities. After voters in Butte, Montana, elected a socialist mayor, treasurer, judge, and five aldermen in 1911, the *Appeal* carried a lengthy story about what the Butte socialists considered their three most effective steps: founding their own newspaper, getting the jump on the rival parties by announcing their platform two weeks before the Democrats or Republicans did, and concentrating their recruitment efforts on wooing the working class.[23]

MUSTERING THE APPEAL ARMY

The *Appeal to Reason* could not have provided the comprehensive national coverage that became its hallmark without its legion of loyal volunteers whose ranks climbed to 80,000 by 1912—the same year that circulation reached its extraordinary zenith of almost ten times that number.

The names of some of the writers were familiar—Helen Keller and Jack London, both members of the Socialist Party, contributed articles—but such literati were far outnumbered by unknown writers. Martha Baker of Suffolk, Virginia, identified herself as a "poor, uneducated girl" who was "not worth the subscription price" but nevertheless wanted to share her praise for how well socialism treated women. William Babcock of Cleveland described the poverty conditions among Ohio laborers. Clarence E. Broom of Manitou, Oklahoma, wrote, "Of all the slaves with their different trades and occupations, we farmers feel and know that we are the worst oppressed."[24]

Perhaps the most heart-wrenching contribution the paper ever printed was an unsigned letter from an unemployed father of three. The Florida man wrote that he had become so distraught "that this beautiful, fertile nation is reeking and groaning under a huge load of ignorance, crime and misery" that he had decided to commit suicide. The *Appeal* enlisted the help of the post office to find the writer and return the $2.50 postal money order he had enclosed in his letter. By the time the paper located the man, however, he was already dead.[25]

CARRYING THE CRUSADE BEYOND THE PRINTED PAGE

The *Appeal to Reason* was more than a newspaper. It also was an activist institution that engaged in a plethora of community-building endeavors that had little or no connection to journalism.

The thousands of men and women who composed the *Appeal* Army and contributed articles were a major element of the activist strategy. Those writers-cum-agitators sold subscriptions and distributed bundles of the paper free of charge at public meetings, in barbershops and union halls, on trains and street corners, on porches and doorsteps—wherever they could find a potential convert.

Wayland often mobilized his "foot soldiers for socialism" into a potent grassroots political force to support candidates for office or defeat a potentially harmful legislative initiative. In 1908, a U.S. House of Representatives committee was considering a bill to deny second-class mailing privileges, which allowed publications to be sent at a reduced rate, to any newspaper or magazine that the local postmaster deemed to be "radical." Concerned that the restriction could seriously harm his paper, Wayland called on the army to flood the nation's capital with protests. The bill was summarily defeated in committee, with congressmen later acknowledging that the deluge of protests against the bill by *Appeal* readers—they came from every state in the union—had turned the tide.[26]

Buoyed by his success, Wayland conceived of other proactive techniques to educate America about the benefits of socialism. *Appeal* Study Clubs were organized in small towns and urban neighborhoods throughout the country; the editorial content of that week's *Appeal* was the subject of discussion. The *Appeal* Lecture Bureau dispatched members of the paper's staff on nationwide speaking tours; the price of admission to a speech was the purchase of a new subscription to the paper for either the person attending or for a friend or relative. The *Appeal* Agitation League promoted socialism; the group's most successful venture was sending sample copies of the paper to school teachers, union members, politicians, and members of state and federal legislatures.

Wayland recognized the benefits of diversifying his business beyond publishing, so he experimented with a variety of enterprises aimed at increasing profits. Wayland's Aerial Navigational Company attempted to manufacture airplanes; although only one of the fourteen prototypes ever actually lifted off the ground, Wayland took comfort in knowing that his was the first airplane company west of the Mississippi River. A more lucrative venture was his Girard Manufacturing Company, which produced vegetable oil, salad dressing, and a coffee substitute; Wayland promoted the company as an effort to wean the public away from goods being sold by the robber barons.[27]

In concert with the growing commercial emphasis in Wayland's enterprises, the pages of the *Appeal* gradually carried more and more advertisements. Rationalizing that the ad revenue was essential to his mission of creating a major socialist publishing voice, Wayland ran ads from companies that produced everything from rubber stamps to poultry feed, and from promoters of various get-rich-quick schemes—"Send us your address, and we will show you how to make $3 a day absolutely sure." As in mainstream publications of the era, ads in the *Appeal* for patent medicines promised cures for cancer, rheumatism, baldness, and male impotence (that last ad claimed that an electric belt would do the trick).[28]

Wayland developed a range of circulation-building techniques as well. The premiums the *Appeal* offered to readers who brought in new subscribers began with vases and gold watches, then escalated to motorcycles, a yacht, and a ten-acre fruit farm. The paper came up with another stroke of huckster genius by offering a complete brass band to the American city that boasted the largest number of *Appeal* subscribers. The promotional articles guaranteed that the seventeen instruments—including seven cornets, three basses, and a baritone—would be made of the finest French brass. After three months of white-hot competition, Los Angeles took home the band.[29]

CREATING THE LITERARY SENSATION OF THE AGE

Despite the number and breadth of Wayland's ventures, his biggest success story always remained the *Appeal to Reason*, and the most influential of the paper's myriad publishing blockbusters was the one still being read today.

It was in 1905 that editor Fred D. Warren approached Upton Sinclair, then a relatively unknown novelist who had recently converted to socialism, with the idea of exposing the slave-like conditions of immigrants working in Chicago meat packing plants. Sinclair accepted Warren's offer, as well as the $500 advance, and spent seven weeks living among the indigent workers.

Sinclair's series described, in riveting prose, the plight of the workers in all its chilling dimensions—the unsanitary conditions in the plants, the inhumanity of the tenements, and the unethical practices of the corrupt businessmen who took advantage of the newcomers to America's shores. Sinclair wrote the articles, which were titled "The Jungle," with the fire of a man who had witnessed human suffering at its most base level. And from the first installment that appeared in the *Appeal*, it was immediately clear that neither the food industry nor journalism would ever be the same.

In his powerful literary style, Sinclair described how the strapping and earnest Lithuanian immigrant Jurgis Rudkus came to the land of promise and threw all his manly strength into serving his adopted homeland. Then Sinclair forced the reader to witness, in excruciating detail, how capitalism savagely reduced Rudkus to a bitter, defeated shadow of his former self who found relief from his pain only by joining the Socialist Movement.

Sinclair's most shocking revelation was that exhausted workers occasionally collapsed into the huge vats where meat was prepared for canning, which meant that human flesh became destined for human consumption. "For the men who worked in tankrooms full of steam," Sinclair wrote, "their peculiar trouble was that they fell into the vats; and when they were fished out, there was never enough of them left to be worth exhibiting. Sometimes they would be overlooked for days, till all but the bones of them had gone out to the world."[30]

"The Jungle" had immediate impact. For among the multitude of persons who voraciously read every word of the series was Theodore Roosevelt. Sinclair's articles touched the President so profoundly that he demanded that Congress pass laws to regulate how meat was processed, leading to the Pure Food and Drug Act of 1907. From that time through the present, meat has been examined by federal authorities before it has been sold to consumers.

Prominent historians and such respected mainstream publications as the *New York Times* have called these protective measures a direct product of Sinclair's articles, thereby making "The Jungle," which was reprinted in book form a year later, one of the most influential pieces of journalism ever published. The standard history of investigative reporting at the turn of the century stated that there was no work with "a nearer approximation of what was generally thought of as 'genius.' 'The Jungle,' from the moment it began to appear in the *Appeal*, was recognizably the literary sensation of the time."[31]

A CAMPAIGN OF SUPPRESSION

The support that elected officials gave the *Appeal to Reason*'s campaign for sanitary meat processing was the exception rather than the rule. For the government tried relentlessly to suppress the dissident paper.

The opening salvo was aimed at the sizable share of the *Appeal*'s circulation that was derived not from paid subscriptions but from the bundles that supporters purchased and distributed free at public places and in their neighborhoods to attract new converts to socialism. In 1901, federal postal officials announced that only paid subscriptions could be mailed at the low second-class rate; unless Wayland could prove within ten days that the people who received the paper actually paid for it, the Post Office would cancel the *Appeal*'s second-class permit—for the bundles as well as for individual paid subscriptions.

Wayland called the *Appeal* Army into active duty. In less than a week, he produced 68,000 subscriber signatures, saved his permit, and proved he could rely on his readers in an emergency. That final lesson was important because the paper's war against government suppression had only just begun.

The next major battle came in 1906 when "Big Bill" Haywood and two other leaders of a miners' union were arrested for the murder of former Idaho Governor Frank Steunenberg. Wayland not only insisted that the union leaders were innocent but accused law enforcement officials of having acted illegally by extraditing—the *Appeal* said "kidnapping"—Haywood and his associates by arresting them in Colorado and taking them to Idaho to be tried.[32]

These circumstances led to the publication of a legendary editorial by Eugene V. Debs—often described as the most militant statement the *Appeal* ever published—titled "Arouse, Ye Slaves!" Departing from the paper's long-standing opposition to violence, the article threatened that if the government officials succeeded in having the union leaders convicted, "a million revolutionists" would "meet them with guns."[33]

Debs's shrill editorial prompted angry responses from the highest levels. President Roosevelt, despite his earlier praise for the *Appeal*'s exposé of the meat packing industry, assailed the paper as a "vituperative organ of pornography, anarchy and bloodshed" that "encourages every form of brutal wrongdoing." Canadian officials refused to mail the issue containing Debs's editorial, labeling the paper "seditious"; only Wayland's plea for help from the *Appeal* Army succeeded in creating a torrent of mail so huge that Canadian officials reversed their initial ruling and allowed the paper to be mailed.[34]

Although the *Appeal* won each battle and also claimed victory when Haywood and the other union men were found not guilty, the fees charged by its defense attorneys were a major financial drain. What's more, each battle diverted time and resources from Wayland's primary mission of trying to educate the country about the merits of socialism.

Meanwhile, the dissident journalist was also suffering severe setbacks in his personal life. His second wife, Pearl Hunt, was killed in a motorcar accident, and Wayland himself was diagnosed with cancer. Federal agents and mainstream reporters hostile to socialism added to the embattled publisher's sorrows. The *Appeal* office was broken into several times, an attempt to assassinate Wayland failed only because a gun misfired, and anti-socialist newspapers fabricated stories about Wayland having sexual relations with a fourteen-year-old girl who later died, according to the stories, while attempting to abort Wayland's child.[35]

For a man who shunned the public eye and struggled with depression throughout his life, the accumulation of attacks—legal, physical, emotional, journalistic, moral—were more than he could bear. On the final of many sleepless nights, Wayland walked up the stairs into his bedroom, put a pistol into his mouth, and pulled the trigger. Before killing himself, the bone-weary publisher had written a brief note saying: "The struggle under the competitive system is not worth the effort; let it pass."[36]

The death in November 1912 brought the *Appeal*'s glory days to an end. Walter Wayland assumed the role of publisher, but he lacked his father's single-minded commitment to the advancement of socialism. In one particularly foolhardy act, the youthful Wayland was so threatened by Fred D. Warren's long-time association with the *Appeal* that he fired the man who had, for a dozen years, made the day-to-day editorial decisions for the paper. Subscriptions immediately dropped into free fall.

World War I also took its toll on the paper. The *Appeal* initially opposed the war as a senseless loss of life waged purely for the benefit of the capitalist elite. But two months after the United States entered the conflict in April 1917, Congress passed the Espionage Act that made it illegal—punishment was a $10,000 fine and twenty years in jail—to publish material that encouraged disloyalty to the government. The act further allowed postal officials to prevent the mailing of any publication that violated the law. Walter Wayland was told the *Appeal* could either switch to a pro-war stance or, like some eighty other anti-war publications of the period, stop printing. He opted to support the war, going so far as to rename his father's paper the *New Appeal* to accentuate its shift to a voice of moderation.[37]

The paper never recovered from the combination of the death of its founder, the removal of its long-time editor, and the restrictions that came with the war, although it continued to appear—and lose circulation—until November 1922.

SETTING A HIGH WATER MARK

The *Appeal to Reason* may be the only publication in American history that attracted enough readers to qualify as a member not only of the dissident media, but also of the *mass* media. Its weekly circulation of 760,000 established a benchmark that no other dissident publication before or since has achieved. The paper's mission was an imposing one as well. Even though capitalism was firmly ensconced as America's economic system of choice, the *Appeal* challenged that concept. Confronting the conventional wisdom that dominated American society at the time, the paper insisted, "Socialism vs. Capitalism—Freedom vs. Slavery—that's the real issue for the workers."[38]

But the *Appeal* and its guiding spirit J. A. Wayland also can be criticized. First, they failed in their mission to destroy capitalism. The Socialist Movement that the *Appeal* championed did not remain a significant player in American politics beyond the first two decades of the twentieth century. The Socialist Party's last major hurrah came in 1920 when Eugene V. Debs, in jail because of his opposition to the war, garnered almost one million votes in the presidential election, as he had in 1912. As the 1920s unfolded, the party faded from the political landscape because of a lethal combination of internal ideological disagreements and external repression from the government. So, in short, the *Appeal* promoted a cause that was not only unpopular at the time but that—

unlike initiatives such as the Abolition and Women's Rights Movements—never gained acceptance into the mainstream of American thought.[39]

Second, Wayland can be faulted for the price he was willing to pay in order to increase his paper's influence. The paper's founder was so determined to achieve his mission that he adopted policies that were decidedly inconsistent with the anti-capitalist ideology the paper espoused. Most obvious was accepting advertisements; although they began as a small part of the *Appeal*'s editorial content, they grew into a much larger presence. Also incongruous with the paper's core principles were the circulation-building techniques that Wayland employed; offering products as rewards, from gold watches to a brass band, for readers who brought in new subscriptions was a tribute to the consumerism that the paper denounced editorially. These practices clearly contradicted the newspaper's anti-capitalist credo. The *Appeal*'s experience provides strong evidence that it may not be possible for a dissident publication to achieve a mass circulation while also remaining true to its ideological convictions.

These shortcomings do not, however, negate the paper's importance. The *Appeal to Reason* educated millions of Americans about socialism, portraying the concept in such positive hues that readers flocked to the Socialist Party—drawn to the paper's alluring vision of a new social, political, and economic Eden. For twenty-seven years, the *Appeal* played a singular role in building a vibrant Socialist Movement. As one historian has written, "The history of this wondrous paper *is* the history of American socialism."[40]

Political historians also credit the *Appeal*'s numerous exposés with increasing the pace of Progressive Era reform at the turn of the last century. "The Jungle" series and its key role in attempting to ensure that American meat was—and continues to be—safe to consume are the most obvious example. But other investigative pieces published in the *Appeal* also helped propel numerous reform efforts—including reducing white slavery, breaking the tight grip that trusts and monopolies had on the nation, and improving the working conditions in American mines and factories.[41]

Thousands of dissident publications have emerged since the demise of the socialist weekly, and they have supported all manner of political and social causes. Yet none of them has attracted the sheer number of readers that Wayland's paper did. Because of the combination of its huge circulation and its commitment to social change, the *Appeal* has achieved legendary status within the American Left.

In the 1980s when the ultra-liberal newspaper *In These Times* was searching for a historical model for American publications with a social conscience to follow, it turned not to the legions of dissident publications that had been founded in the twentieth century, but to one that began publishing from rural Kansas more than a century ago. Focusing specifically on the 80,000 "foot soldiers for socialism" that Wayland inspired to sell, write for, and otherwise support the *Appeal to Reason*, *In These Times* wrote: "Their methods were simple but brought startling results."[42]

7 FOLLOWING ANARCHY TOWARD A NEW SOCIAL ORDER

Of the many social movements that have helped shape this nation, none has been more misunderstood than the one advocating anarchism. Despite the widespread connotation that this concept is supported only by wild-eyed and demented monsters whose single goal is to destroy civilized society, the men and women who introduced the anarchist philosophy to America during the late nineteenth and early twentieth centuries were, in fact, committed and courageous defenders of the poor and the powerless.

Following an ideology much like that of the Founding Fathers, the anarchists shared a unifying belief in the absolute supremacy of individual liberty. A person who embraced this philosophy opposed any citizen being controlled by forces other than his or her own decision making. So in the late 1800s when the robber barons were rapidly transforming America into a land of Haves and Have Nots, the anarchists spoke up on behalf of common laborers and the poorest of the poor. Like the socialists, the anarchists wanted to end capitalism, but in addition they also wanted to abolish the government as it existed, arguing that the politicians were conspiring with the industrialists to line their own pockets. So rather than capture state power through elections, as socialists tried to do, the anarchists wanted to eliminate the state and replace it with self-management by each individual citizen. The major difference between anarchists and other progressive thinkers, then, was that they were convinced that capitalism had such a powerful vice grip on the United States—and that those same capitalists would refuse to give up their power—that the nation's most pernicious ills could not be eliminated at the ballot box but only through the profound and fundamental change obtainable through a full-fledged revolution brought about by an armed insurrection.

Because anarchism was such a radical notion, supporters never expected the mainstream press to discuss it with any degree of fairness. So one of the first steps the founders of the Anarchist Movement took was to establish their own press to articulate their unique ideology. More than 100 anarchist newspapers and magazines have been published at one time or another in the history of this country; during the movement's heyday at the turn of the last century, several dozen publications were established to spread the anarchist credo.[1]

In the 1880s, the most important of the publications was *The Alarm*, a Chicago-based weekly newspaper edited by Albert R. Parsons and distributed throughout the country. After Parsons was hanged in 1887 for his alleged role in the deadly Haymarket incident, the Anarchist Movement was without a national voice for some twenty years. In 1906, the largest and most influential of all anarchist publications was founded in New York City by a Russian immigrant whose name ultimately would become synonymous with anarchy in America: Emma Goldman. Reflecting the larger-than-life personality of its editor, *Mother Earth* dominated this genre of the dissident press until 1917 when the monthly magazine was banned from the mails and Goldman was imprisoned and then deported.[2]

Although *The Alarm* and *Mother Earth* were separated by two decades, they communicated many of the same messages. They both prided themselves on being voices of the people and on seeking the end of capitalism as well as the state. Most important of all, *The Alarm* and *Mother Earth* both insisted that the country had become so corrupted by ruthless industrialists and dissolute politicians that the situation called for nothing short of a mass uprising—similar to the American Revolution—that would clear the way for a new social order.

ALBERT R. PARSONS: PIONEERING ANARCHIST

The leading editor during the early years of the Anarchist Movement grew from the most American of roots. Albert Richard Parsons was born in 1848 into a family that could trace its lineage to colonial times—five Parsons brothers had been passengers on the *Mayflower*. Young Albert grew up in Waco, Texas, and when he was thirteen years old and the Civil War erupted, his patriotic heritage propelled him to enlist and fight under the command of his older brother, a Confederate general. When the war ended, however, Albert chose a path less traveled.

Parsons—much like Ida B. Wells-Barnett—was deeply concerned about the racial injustice that Americans of African descent were forced to endure. "They were now 'freemen,'" Parsons wrote, "without an inch of soil, a cent of money,

Albert R. Parsons's handsome facial features and personal charisma helped swell the ranks of the Anarchist Movement during the final decades of the nineteenth century.

a stitch of clothes or a morsel of food." In addition, Parsons was disturbed that the vast majority of blacks were not allowed to vote and were terrorized by Ku Klux Klan vigilantes who committed atrocities of every kind—robberies, beatings, rapes, murders.[3]

Determined to improve the racial situation, Parsons secured a job in the district clerk's office and during local election campaigns took to the stump to encourage African Americans to vote and whites to accept blacks as their equal. Parsons was charming as well as strikingly handsome, passionate about the issues he believed in, and impeccable in his dress and grooming, with clear-cut features, fine dark eyes, jet-black hair, and a jaunty moustache. With his resonant tenor voice and manifest sincerity, he held the attention of his listeners and became widely known as a champion of Black America.

His stand was not popular. White southerners branded Parsons a heretic and a traitor. Waco society grew even more outraged when he married a beautiful young woman whose mother was Mexican and whose father was Native American. After Albert and Lucy Parsons married in 1872, Waco was so hostile to the interracial couple that they moved to the less racially charged city of Chicago.

On a personal level, Albert and Lucy Parsons fared well in their new environs, as he secured steady work as a typesetter. On a broader level, though, they now witnessed the sufferings not only of blacks but also of whites and recent immigrants who toiled at the mercy of factory owners. There existed, Albert Parsons would later write, "a great fundamental wrong at work in society."[4]

So Parsons became a labor agitator who spoke and organized local factory workers to unite in an effort to secure higher wages and better working conditions. The city's establishment society reacted to him much as Waco's had, with the *Chicago Tribune* calling Parsons and other labor organizers "blatant Communist demagogues."[5]

Beginning in 1877, Parsons attempted to change society through politics by running for city alderman on a platform of fair wages for city employees. Although he lost, Parsons made a respectable showing by polling a sixth of the vote. So during the next five years, Chicago laborers repeatedly turned to him as their nominee; he ran for alderman three times, for state assemblyman twice, and once each for sheriff and county clerk—losing every race. The Socialist Party even tried to nominate Parsons for President of the United States, but he declined.[6]

By the early 1880s, Parsons had become disillusioned with the political process as an effective avenue of reform. He then began reading the radical ideas being put forth by a handful of New York dissidents. These men of militant temperament pinned their hopes not on the ballot but on direct action and armed mutiny, believing that true equality would be achieved only by destroying the existing system—root and branch. The power of the capitalist rested on force, they insisted, and therefore would have to be conquered by force as well.

Those political rebels formed the embryo of the Anarchist Movement. Parsons first created a chapter in Chicago and then made his home city the epicenter of the entire movement. In 1884, he used his printing skills to found and edit *The Alarm*, the weekly newspaper that immediately became the leading voice of anarchism.

SOUNDING *THE ALARM*

Mid-1880s America was fertile ground for revolution because of a nation-wide economic depression that resulted in masses of idle and destitute laborers. Immigration remained heavy, compounding the number of unemployed. New arrivals crowded into the cities, where conspicuous wealth rubbed shoulders with grinding poverty.

The Alarm announced that the nation's misery was the work of a single villain: capitalism. Parsons filled his pages with charges that industrialists and financiers had accumulated their riches by turning common workers into "wage slaves" who remained constantly "on the verge of starvation." Capitalists had concentrated the nation's wealth in the greedy hands of five percent of the population, making them nothing less than "usurpers, thieves, and murderers." Government officials were enemies of the working class as well, Parsons wrote, because they had conspired with the robber barons to enact laws that favored the Brahmins of American society while paying no heed whatsoever to the workers.[7]

Parsons did not stop with accusations but described exactly how the anarchists planned to end the exploitation of the poor. "We are revolutionists. We fight for the destruction of the system of wage-slavery," he wrote. "Statute law, constitutions and government are at war with nature and the inalienable rights of man, and social revolution is the effort of nature to restore its equilibrium." The time for rebellion was now, Parsons insisted. "The social war has come, and those who are not with us are against us."[8]

Nor did Parsons leave any doubt that the revolution would, by necessity, be a violent one. Peaceful methods were of no avail, he argued, because "the privileged are not in the least disturbed by argument, protest or petitions. They have but one answer to all appeals—force." The "wealth aristocracy" had gained its power by the sword, he wrote, and therefore would have to be dethroned by the sword as well. "Let robbers and pirates meet the fate they deserve! Against them there is but one recourse, force! Agitate, organize, revolt! Proletarians of the world unite! We have nothing to lose but our chains; we have a world to win! Lead on to liberty or death!"[9]

Like many dissident journalists before and after him, Parsons did not rely on printed words alone but took his ideas to the people through public addresses. Fellow anarchists gathered twice a week to hear Parsons speak on topics identical to the fiery headlines in *The Alarm*—such as "How the Working People Are Being Robbed" and "The Poverty of the Masses." Parsons had tapped into a deep-rooted discontent, and his audience often swelled to several thousand.

When the number of people grew so large that no meeting hall in all of Chicago could accommodate them, Parsons moved outside to a grassy area on the shore of Lake Michigan.[10]

As Albert Parsons held the crowd spellbound by his commanding oratory, Lucy Parsons moved among the enthralled listeners to sell subscriptions to *The Alarm*. By the end of 1885, weekly circulation had climbed to more than 3,000. In addition, particularly bold articles from the newspaper were reprinted and distributed as circulars in quantities as large as 25,000.[11]

But like many dissident papers, *The Alarm* teetered on the brink of financial collapse. Early issues of the four-page paper contained a page and a half of advertisements for clothing and furniture, restaurants and beer gardens. When business owners became aware of the controversial nature of the paper's editorial content, however, the advertising revenue dwindled; by mid-1885, ads filled less than a quarter of a page. Besides struggling to find businesses willing to be connected with the paper's insurgent ideas, Parsons faced the fact that his target audience had, by definition, few pennies to spare.

Albert Parsons fully understood the plight of his readers, as by the mid-1880s he had to feed not only himself and his wife but also a son and daughter. Blacklisted because of his radical activities, he could no longer find work as a typesetter, and the income from *The Alarm* was so meager that he and Lucy both took on additional jobs. He earned money by going on exhausting speaking tours; she opened a small tailor shop, specializing in making women's cloaks. Their combined income kept the paper in print—but just barely.

The Alarm focused on one specific solution to the myriad problems facing the politically and economically disenfranchised: dynamite. Parsons saw the explosive as the great equalizer that would allow ordinary workers to stand up against police and the armed guards that the factory owners hired. "One man armed with a dynamite bomb is equal to one regiment of militia," he wrote. By the spring of 1886, every issue carried a spirited editorial heralding an imminent armed conflict with the capitalists. In late April, Parsons wrote: "WORKINGMEN TO ARMS! The wage system is the only cause of the world's misery. It is supported by the rich classes, and to destroy it, they must be either made to work or DIE. One pound of DYNAMITE is better than a bushel of BALLOTS!"[12]

THE HAYMARKET TRAGEDY

On May 4, 1886, the anarchists held the latest of their ongoing protest meetings in Haymarket Square, an open space in downtown Chicago. The crowd was at its largest—some 3,000 strong—when Parsons spoke, denouncing the inequities that capitalism wrought. After he finished, the passionate editor left the platform to join Lucy and their children in a cafe a block north of the square.

Although the crowd—by this point numbering fewer than 300—remained calm and orderly, a company of police officers suddenly marched into the square and ordered the meeting to end. The speaker who had followed Parsons was surprised by the arrival of the police, but he agreed to stop and began to step down from the speaker's platform. At that precise moment, something sputtered over the heads of the audience and fell into the center of the police. A terrific explosion shook the street, making a thunderous noise and shattering windows for blocks around. After the bomb exploded, several officers fell wounded, and the rest began firing randomly into the crowd. When the sound and smoke of the gunfire stopped a few minutes later, the streets were littered with bodies.

The fatalities included eight policemen and at least as many protesters—the exact number was never determined because the families of civilian casualties did not want the reputations of their dead loved ones smeared by being connected with anarchism. An important detail the newspapers of the day did not highlight was that only one of the officers and none of the civilians was killed by the bomb—the rest by police bullets.[13]

Details be damned, news of the Haymarket riot spread like wildfire, provoking a nationwide convulsion of hysteria. Violent speech had led to violent deed. Dynamite had been intentionally used, for the first time in U.S. history, to destroy human life.

Cities across the country seethed with fear and hatred. People gathered on street corners, excited and feverish, to talk about the awful event. Wild rumors filled the air—the anarchists were planning to kill all police, blow up public buildings, plunder stores and warehouses; the bomb was the first strike in a nationwide uprising; the anarchists were scheming to seize control of the entire country.

The nation's newspapers fanned the flames. The day after the Haymarket incident, a page-one *New York Times* story headlined "Anarchy's Red Hand" began: "The villainous teachings of the Anarchists bore bloody fruit in Chicago." The papers demanded revenge, insisting that the bomb was part of an organized plot to destroy America. The *Philadelphia Inquirer* described Parsons and the other anarchists as "cutthroats and thieves" who were "crazed with a frenetic desire for blood"; the paper called for their immediate execution. The *St. Louis Globe-Democrat* wanted prompt action as well: "There are no good Anarchists except dead Anarchists."[14]

Although the bomb thrower was never apprehended and no evidence linked any specific person to detonating the explosive device, eight anarchists were brought to trial and convicted of murder. One of the men committed suicide while in jail, three received long jail terms, and four—including Parsons—were publicly hanged.[15]

The Haymarket tragedy had a severe chilling effect on the Anarchist Movement. Public opinion had been deeply aroused, and a fear of subversion engulfed the entire country. For years the nation remained in the grip of panic. Indignation against not only anarchists but against all progressive thinkers became a fixture in the American culture well into the new century.

EMMA GOLDMAN: MOST DANGEROUS WOMAN IN AMERICA

At the same point that "anarchism" was becoming known as the most heinous word in the English language, a spirited young woman was coming into her own in New York City.

Emma Goldman had been born into a poor Jewish family in Russia in 1869. When Emma turned sixteen, her father demanded that she submit to an arranged marriage. The headstrong Emma rebelled and emigrated to America. She settled in Rochester, New York, and began working in a clothing factory. Visions of the American dream soon faded, however, as she found herself laboring sixty hours a week for a mere two dollars and fifty cents.

When Emma met a handsome textile worker named Jacob Kershner who spoke of a secret plan to travel in order to escape the oppressive drudgery of factory work, she accepted his marriage proposal in a heartbeat. But on her wedding night in 1887, Emma confronted a new disappointment; she discovered that Kershner was impotent.

It was at this point that Goldman—disillusioned with both her work and her personal life—came into contact with the Anarchist Movement by reading a copy of *The Alarm*. "The next morning I woke as from a long illness," she later wrote. "Something new and wonderful had been born in my soul." The inspirational words of Albert Parsons swept Goldman out of her depression and propelled her to abandon her husband and move to New York City and a job in a factory where workers enjoyed better conditions because they had formed a union. She also joined a group of young immigrants who gathered after work to discuss the new social order that anarchism promised.[16]

This began a period of liberation in Goldman's thinking. One of her decisions was that the responsibilities of motherhood would encumber her, so she

The entire nation came to know Emma Goldman by epithets ranging from "Red Emma" to "the Queen of the Anarchists" to "the most dangerous woman in America." (Photo by *Chicago Daily News*; Courtesy Chicago Historical Society)

made the conscious choice never to bear children. By no means, however, was Goldman willing to forego the pleasures of sex. By the late 1880s, she was the central figure in a *ménage à trois* with two fellow anarchists, Alexander Berkman and Modest Stein—even though she was still married to Kershner.

Goldman, Berkman, and Stein became involved in radical activities outside the bedroom as well. The most significant of their endeavors began in 1892 when workers at the Carnegie Steel plant in Homestead, Pennsylvania, went on strike to protest the company's low wages. The company then hired 300 armed guards to keep the factory open; the conflict between the laborers and the outsiders escalated into violence and the killing of ten workers.

The deaths so outraged Goldman and Berkman that they devised a plot to assassinate Henry Clay Frick, chairman of Carnegie's board. The radical couple believed that the murder of the powerful industrialist would spur workers across the country to seize the nation's factories—and a revolution would take fire. According to the plan, Berkman would kill Frick while Goldman, who had matured into a powerful speaker on behalf of the Anarchist Movement, would explain the purpose of the deed to the public.

Berkman succeeded in forcing his way into Frick's office and firing three bullets that knocked the steel baron to the floor—but did not kill him. The terrorist act resulted in Berkman being sentenced to fourteen years in prison and Goldman to one.

Goldman ultimately considered her year behind bars to be time well spent because by 1894 when she was released, she emerged as a national celebrity— "Red Emma" was now known far and wide as the most dangerous woman in America. During the next few years, the charismatic speaker gave thousands of public lectures in this country and abroad.

Emma Goldman was a short, full-figured woman with wavy dark hair, clear blue eyes and a *joie de vivre* that was captivating to members of the opposite sex. "If your revolution doesn't allow me to dance," she often said, "I don't want any part of it." Eager to break the chains of societal convention, Goldman enjoyed a series of lovers—a tall blond named Ed Brady, a Midwesterner named Max Baginsky, hobo-turned-physician Ben Reitman, Czech anarchist Hippolyte Havel, a nineteen-year-old she knew only as Dan.[17]

Goldman's public notoriety soared to new heights in 1901 after a Buffalo, New York, factory worker named Leon Czolgosz shot and killed President William McKinley. For the assassin told police that he was an anarchist and that, a year earlier, he had heard a speech by Emma Goldman—that final detail causing police to infer that Goldman was, in fact, responsible for the President's murder.

When a police search for "the High Priestess of Anarchy" spread nationwide, she escaped underground. Only after a frantic four-month dragnet did police finally arrest and jail her. When questioned, Goldman did not take the easy route of distancing herself from Czolgosz—she had never met him and he was not a member of any anarchist organization—but, instead, chose to defend him. Goldman compared Czolgosz to Jesus Christ and said he had been driven to murder by the unbearable living and working conditions that all laborers had to endure. Despite Goldman's vehement defense, Czolgosz died in the electric chair.[18]

Goldman was never charged in relation to the McKinley assassination, but that fact did not prevent the country's leading newspapers from attacking her— and relentlessly so. Typical was the *New York World*'s description of Goldman as "a wrinkled, ugly Russian woman" whose goal was to "kill all rulers." Partly in reaction to such scathing representations of her, Goldman launched her own magazine in 1906. She chose the title *Mother Earth* to evoke an image of regenerative natural powers that could prepare the ground for the growth of a new anarchist world.[19]

MOTHER EARTH SPREADS THE ANARCHIST GOSPEL

The magazine quickly became the leading forum for discussions of the most controversial issues of the era. Varying in length from thirty to sixty pages, the hefty monthly discussed politics and art, reported on radical activities, and articulated Emma Goldman's personal philosophy.

Mother Earth's circulation soon soared to more than 10,000. What's more, the magazine served as the inspiration and focus for the revitalized Anarchist Movement that had been all but destroyed by the hysteria that followed the Haymarket tragedy. A large part of the magazine's success evolved from the fact that its substantive editorial content expanded the movement beyond its working-class origins of the 1880s by attracting middle-class professionals—doctors and professors, lawyers and journalists.[20]

After Alexander Berkman was released from prison, he assumed many of the editorial duties at *Mother Earth* while Goldman toured the country raising money through her speaking fees. For despite the magazine's popularity, "the Queen of the Anarchists' " unyielding positions—she dedicated one issue to the memory of presidential assassin Leon Czolgosz—kept advertising revenue to a minimum.

Goldman was much in demand as a speaker. In just the first half of 1910, she gave 120 speeches in twenty-five states, even though the cities she visited often greeted her with venomous attacks. The *Chicago Tribune* announced her arrival with its lead story on page one: "Bold Priestess of Reds Appears; Emma Goldman Arrives in Chicago with Sneers for the Police."[21]

Such comments often presaged—and helped foment—unpleasant incidents. Typical was the police response to one of Goldman's arrivals in Boston.

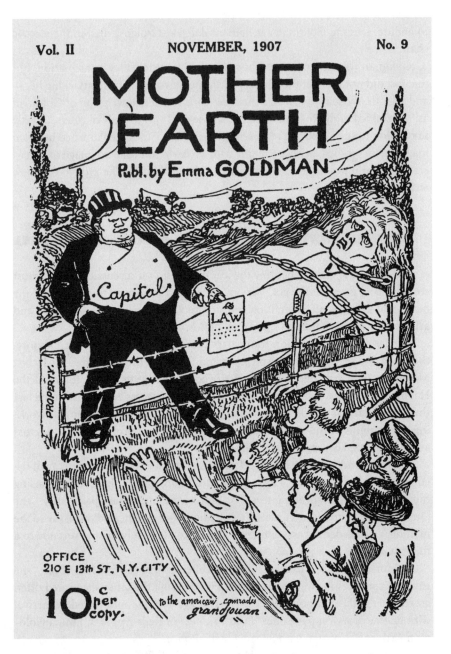

As illustrated by this cover, *Mother Earth* saw the millionaire capitalists as ruthless men who had succeeded in crafting laws that allowed them to oppress American workers.

Mother Earth reported that "Captain Mahoney, a great, big, pig-faced Irishman, weighing about two hundred and fifty pounds, rushed to the stage and without the slightest provocation dragged Miss Goldman from the platform, and pulled and hauled her through the hall like a sack of flour, cursing and shoving her all the way." Goldman was arrested and jailed dozens of times.[22]

The number of such incidents escalated with the approach of world war. For as global tension intensified, it brought a steady erosion of civil liberties; the vast majority of Americans agreed to the suspension of constitutional rights on the grounds of a national emergency.

Not so Goldman.

In April 1917, *Mother Earth* published an article titled "Why You Shouldn't Go to War—Refuse to Kill or Be Killed" that explicitly opposed all armed conflicts, and particularly the one the United States had entered into earlier that month. In May, Goldman and three friends founded the No-Conscription League to encourage and aid conscientious objectors and, according to *Mother Earth*, to oppose "all wars waged by capitalist governments."[23]

In June 1917, a U.S. marshal and twelve other officers arrested Goldman and Berkman for conspiring against the draft under the Espionage Act—the same law that led to the *Appeal to Reason* reversing its position vis-à-vis World War I. While the editors were in jail, Justice Department officials and the police ransacked the *Mother Earth* office and seized letters, mailing lists, and manuscripts.

During her and Berkman's trial, Goldman told the jury that in order for America to justify its entry into the war, as President Woodrow Wilson claimed, "to make the world safe for democracy," its leaders "must first make democracy safe for America." If free press rights were denied, she asked, how could America claim to be a democracy? Her impassioned speech fell on deaf ears, as Goldman and Berkman were found guilty and sentenced to the maximum penalty of two years in prison and a fine of $10,000.[24]

With *Mother Earth* declared "unmailable" and its driving spirit behind bars, Goldman's followers began publishing a somewhat more moderate newsletter titled *Mother Earth Bulletin*. In short order, that publication was suppressed in May 1918.

In 1919, the U.S. government began efforts to deport Goldman and Berkman. Twenty-four-year-old J. Edgar Hoover, an assistant to the Attorney General, took special interest in the matter, writing a memo that stated, "Emma Goldman and Alexander Berkman are, beyond doubt, two of the most dangerous anarchists in the country and if permitted to return to the community will result in undue harm."[25]

On a chilly early morning in December 1919, Goldman and Berkman were shunted into a dilapidated military ship and cast off from American soil—Goldman cradled her typewriter in her lap. Hoover was among the officials on hand to observe the deportation. As she sailed away, "Red Emma" committed her final act of defiance against the state: She made an obscene gesture at Hoover.

Emma Goldman then lived in exile, first in the Soviet Union and then in France and England, continuing to write, lecture, and agitate. She was in Canada helping refugees from fascist Spain and Italy when she died in 1940, at the age of seventy-one.

SPEAKING UP FOR THE POOR AND THE POWERLESS

With regard to the common editorial themes that appeared in the pages of *The Alarm* and *Mother Earth*, the publications both prided themselves on serving as voices for the country's laborers—a segment of the population whose concerns the mainstream press of the day consistently ignored.

Albert Parsons made the point in the first issue of *The Alarm* in October 1884, stating that he was founding the newspaper to speak "on behalf of the wage slaves of this country." The theme remained prominent in every issue, which referred to its target audience as "Les Misérables." In a typical article, Parsons wrote, "To the despised, destitute, disinherited of the earth, anarchy offers love, peace and plenty." In one of the articles that was reprinted as a circular, he said that he spoke for the 40,000 men and women in Chicago and the two million nationwide who were freezing to death because they did not have overcoats or proper shoes "while mountains of good clothing, which you made, sits in the store houses!" Through cold nights, the poor and homeless slept on stone streets, Parsons wrote, often eating only a bowl of soup or slice of bread for an entire day.[26]

When Emma Goldman founded *Mother Earth*, she also expressed her commitment to providing a publishing voice for the downtrodden of society. "The poor have never yet had equal rights," Goldman wrote in her blunt, no-nonsense style. "Justice can result only from equality, and equality will be established only when poverty is abolished." Many of Goldman's bare-knuckled essays denounced how factory owners were abusing their employees. "From North to South and East to West, the country re-echoes with the numberless brutalities and cold-blooded outrages perpetrated against labor," she wrote, insisting that workers "should no longer submit meekly to the indignity, injustice, and crimes heaped upon them."[27]

Unlike Parsons, however, Goldman did not limit the audience of *Mother*

Earth to common laborers but argued that her magazine also spoke to, and on behalf of, office workers and members of the professions. She urged these members of the middle class to come down off their pedestals and realize that they, too, were being exploited by the American aristocracy of wealth. Only through the cooperation of the middle and working class would the people of America "establish a real unity," the dissident journalist wrote, and "wage a successful war against present society."[28]

CONDEMNING CAPITALISM

The two leading anarchist publications also shared common ground with regard to their position on the capitalistic system that had come to dominate the American economy, with *The Alarm* and *Mother Earth*—like the *Appeal to Reason*—repeatedly condemning that system as the source of America's social ills.

Albert Parsons summarized the problem in one of his earliest issues, saying, "We have lost sight of the pleasure in work." Laborers no longer felt any pride of workmanship or even understood where they stood in the production process, Parsons argued, so working men and women were increasingly estranged from their labor, from themselves, and from their fellow Americans. The anarchist editor pointed the finger of blame at capitalism. The sumptuous dinners the factory owners and financiers feasted upon, Parsons wrote, had been "wrung from the blood of our wives and children, and the champagne thus obtained ought to strangle them."[29]

Particularly damaging, in Parsons's eyes, was the growing specialization of labor, with its corrosive effects on the human spirit. Constant repetition of the same minute task benefited only the employer, he wrote, while promoting boredom and frustration among the workers, accentuating the master-slave relationship. Under the capitalist system, he raged, the workers were merely hired hands, cogs in an intricate machine, receiving little satisfaction from the monotonous, mind-numbing drudgery they performed. Because of capitalism, *The Alarm* screamed, millions of dignified human beings had been "degraded" and "used each day for ten hours as appendages of the lifeless machines!"[30]

Emma Goldman's position on capitalism was perhaps best summarized in a piece titled "White Slave Traffic," which was published in the January 1910 issue of *Mother Earth*—an issue that postal officials suppressed because of the essay. In the item, Goldman took the blame for prostitution away from the women who sold their bodies and placed it squarely on the shoulders of capitalists. "Not merely white women, but yellow and black women as well" became women of the night, the defiant editor argued, because of the "exploitation of capitalism that fattens on underpaid labor, thus driving thousands of women and girls into prostitution" because the women asked themselves, " 'Why waste your life working for a few shillings a week in scullery, eighteen hours a day?' " The only way to stanch the burgeoning increase in prostitution, Goldman continued, was to abolish the institution of capitalism.[31]

DENOUNCING GOVERNMENT

A central tenet of the anarchist philosophy was that government in all its varied forms had to be destroyed, partly because such authoritarian rule denied individual liberty and partly because past experience showed that people who were elected or appointed to public office inevitably served the wealthy while ignoring the poor.

The Alarm communicated its opposition to government through a torrent of statements that began in the premier issue: "The more we are governed, the less we are free," "The true science of government is the science of getting rid of government," and "In the name of law, authority and government, the human race is enslaved." To support its anti-government stand, *The Alarm* repeatedly exposed instances of brutality and corruption among government workers. Typical was an article, written by Lucy Parsons, that accused a Chicago police sergeant of assaulting a sixteen-year-old working-class girl in the station house, nearly killing her.[32]

"Red Emma," as the world came to know her, also denounced the state. Labeling government a "curse" upon America, Goldman described the system of federal, state, and local authorities as a "pyramid of lies, fraud, exploitation, and suppression." She went on to say that "to destroy this body- and soul-killing foundation of robbery" would be the first step toward creating a true "human civilization." The *Mother Earth* editor reprinted an essay by revered man of letters Ralph Waldo Emerson that appeared to echo her anti-government position. "Every State is corrupt," Emerson had written. "The less government we have, the better."[33]

CALLING FOR ARMED REBELLION

Fundamental to the anarchist philosophy was the insistence that the nation's ills could be corrected only through a full-fledged social revolution. *The Alarm* and *Mother Earth* both supported this belief, as well as the fact that the grip of the capitalists and their governmental hirelings was so tight that the open rebellion would, by necessity, be a violent one.

Parsons, arguing that the Anarchist Movement's central mission of emancipating the workers could be accomplished only by eliminating capitalism and reorganizing society on new foundations, filled his paper with calls for insurrection. "Be men, you young Americans. Come out, unite with us, and with your help the tyrant's reign shall end," barked one editorial. Another stated defiantly: "A revolution is a sudden upheaval—a convulsion of the feverish body of society. We are only preparing society for it and insist that the laborers should arm themselves and keep themselves ready for action. The better the latter are armed, the easier the struggle will be ended and the less there will be of bloodshed."[34]

Dozens of *Alarm* articles spoke of the violent nature of the impending revolution. An editorial labeled "July 4, 1776" told readers: "Remember that against tyrants and tyranny all means are not only justifiable but necessary! Prepare for action; the conflict is even now upon us." Another warned American capitalists: "Tremble! oppressors of the world! Not far beyond your purblind sight there dawns the scarlet and sable lights of the Judgment Day!" Dozens of *Alarm* articles praised the power of explosives: "Dynamite! of all the good stuff, this is the stuff. Stuff several pounds of this sublime stuff into a gas or water pipe, plug up both ends, insert a cap with fuse attached, place this in the immediate neighborhood of a lot of rich loafers who live by the sweat of other people's brows, and light the fuse. A most cheerful and gratifying result will follow. A pound of this good stuff beats a bushel of ballots all hollow, and don't you forget it."[35]

Mother Earth talked repeatedly of the coming revolution, too, with many essays arguing that the middle class ultimately would ignite the rebellion. "The pioneers of every new thought rarely come from the ranks of the workers," Goldman argued, but from "the so-called respectable classes." It was not material poverty but "spiritual hunger and unrest," she wrote, that were "the most lasting incentives" that drove people to radicalism. So her vision of the revolution was one in which "doctors, lawyers, and judges rubbed elbows with procurers and dive-keepers."[36]

Although *Mother Earth*, founded two decades after the Haymarket incident, did not specifically advocate the use of dynamite as frequently as *The Alarm* had before that momentous event, Goldman's magazine fully supported violence. "Yes, we believe in violence," one essay began. "We will use violence whenever it is necessary to use it." Speaking directly to American capitalists, the piece continued, "When you train your machine guns on us, we will retaliate with dynamite." Another essay restated the same point, saying, "Violence is justified, aye, necessary in the defensive and offensive struggle of labor against capital," and "Labor's success will be hastened and its courage strengthened, by tempering oppression with dynamite."[37]

ENVISIONING A NEW WORLD

A final theme on which the two anarchist publications coincided was their lack of precise detail regarding the future society that would exist in the United States after the twin evils of capitalism and government were destroyed. This shortage of specifics was not a failure of the editors, but a conscious decision. If Parsons and Goldman had described how post-revolutionary America should look, they argued, they would have been as guilty of dictatorship as were the autocratic rulers they were trying to destroy.

Parsons did, however, specify two concrete points. First, under the new social order that he envisioned, private property would be eliminated. No longer would one individual own more than another, Parsons said, as all property would be jointly held by all Americans. Second, the pioneering anarchist said that, under the system that he dreamed of, labor would be organized on a cooperative basis. People would work only at the jobs they freely chose; the traditionally least attractive jobs—a sewer worker, for example—would be made more appealing by being the most highly compensated in terms of fewer hours of labor per day.[38]

Although Goldman, like Parsons, said it was not her place to describe post-revolutionary America, *Mother Earth*, like *The Alarm*, provided some details about the new society the magazine's guiding spirit visualized. According to Goldman, anarchism's primary commitment vis-à-vis building a new society was to ensure that every individual could reach his or her fullest level of expression. She said there should be no institutions of authority or man-made laws, thereby allowing people to follow "natural law," which she defined as "that factor in man which asserts itself freely and spontaneously without any external force." When critics said that eliminating authority would lead to chaos, the lusty anarchist disagreed, insisting that the people would cooperate and provide each other with mutual aid—free of violent tendencies, greed, and jealousy.[39]

Goldman further stated that the anarchist society's "economic arrangements must consist of voluntary productive and distributive associations." In contrast to the capitalist society in which man was robbed "not merely of the products of his labor, but of the power of free initiative and originality," Goldman said society under anarchism would leave the individual free to do meaningful work. The average worker would closely resemble the artist: "one to whom the making of a table, the building of a house, or the tilling of the soil is what the painting is to the artist and the discovery to the scientist—the result of inspiration, of intense longing, and deep interest in work as a creative force."[40]

Goldman's outline of a utopian society was not sufficiently detailed to satisfy the mainstream press. After a number of newspaper editors chided her for failing to provide more specifics about the society she foresaw, Goldman spoke to them via an essay in *Mother Earth*. "You call a society based on anarchy a dream, gentlemen; well, I plead guilty. But when we can't dream any longer, we die. That's what is the matter with you. You've lost your dreams!"[41]

A DREAM UNFULFILLED

When attempting to assess the impact of the anarchist press that emerged in the late nineteenth century, it initially may seem that this particular genre of the dissident press was a complete and utter failure. Albert R. Parsons was hanged; Emma Goldman was imprisoned and then deported. Neither the full-fledged revolution nor the new social order that were envisioned by *The Alarm* and *Mother Earth* ever progressed from paper to reality. And today the mere mention of the word "anarchist" sends a shudder up the spine of even the most tolerant of Americans.

Approached from a different perspective, however, the legacy of the anarchist press appears far less bleak. For the two forces that the radical publications identified as most perilous to the well-being of the United States—capitalism and government—both went through major transformations, just as the publications had hoped, during the early years of the twentieth century.

Regarding capitalism, numerous measures were taken to impose constraints on this seemingly out-of-control economic system. In the most celebrated action, the U.S. Supreme Court ruled in 1911 that the Standard Oil Company, which controlled ninety percent of the oil needed to light American homes and power American factories, was acting in violation of the Sherman Anti-Trust Act; that decision forced the mammoth monopoly to dissolve into thirty-eight smaller companies. In another high-profile series of actions, Congress passed the Meat Inspection Act and the Pure Food and Drug Act, which placed new restrictions on the meat packing and patent medicine industries. The power wielded by a long list of other titans of capitalism was limited as well—including the railroads, telephone and telegraph companies, and the trusts that dominated American mining and the production of sugar, liquor, and beef.[42]

Major changes also occurred in government. On the national level, the practice of U.S. senators being hand picked by state legislatures ended with a constitutional amendment stipulating that senators would thereafter be elected directly by the American people. On the local level, politics was pushed a considerable distance away from the operation of cities and counties because of the widespread adoption of the city-manager form of government, which meant that professional administrators rather than career politicians began heading local governments. And these men and women, in turn, began to reduce the political spoils system by requiring that job applicants possess formal credentials and pass standardized employment tests.[43]

Although these metamorphoses in capitalism and government certainly cannot be attributed solely to the anarchist press, the vociferous editorial attacks that The Alarm and Mother Earth published, coupled with the constant agitation by the editors of the two publications, may have helped—at least to a limited degree—raise public awareness of numerous issues facing the masses of Americans that capitalism had pushed to the margins of society, thereby adding to the momentum for reform that ultimately took place.

Despite these changes and the ancillary role the anarchist press played in bringing them about, there is still no question that this particular genre of the dissident press fell far short of its primary goal of igniting a social revolution. Unlike the early labor newspapers in their success at helping to empower the American worker or The Revolution in its role in establishing a far-sighted agenda for women's rights, The Alarm and Mother Earth did not change America in any fundamental way. This shortcoming resulted partly from the setbacks that occurred because of the Haymarket tragedy, the McKinley assassination, and World War I. But far more than any of these individual incidents or even their combined force, the Anarchist Movement did not have a significant impact on this nation because some concepts—as well as the presses that support them—are simply too radical for a critical mass of the American people to embrace. Destroying capitalism, eradicating all forms of government, and using dynamite to lead this nation toward an ill-defined utopian society clearly were beyond the pale.

The genres of the dissident press that emerged during the final years of the nineteenth century suggest several more overarching characteristics that apply to many of the publications that were "voices of revolution." Some of the traits evolved from themes that originated in dissident voices that were published earlier in the century, and others had been at least hinted at by that first generation—and then came into full bloom during the second.

THE FINANCIAL STRUGGLE THAT IS ENDEMIC IN THE DISSIDENT PRESS SOMETIMES LEADS TO DECISIONS THAT ARE MORALLY OR IDEOLOGICALLY QUESTIONABLE

Because the radical nature of the causes that dissident publications champion often denies them the advertising and circulation revenue that sustains mainstream media, editors sometimes experiment with creative ways to achieve financial solvency.

Elizabeth Cady Stanton defended her decision to accept capital from a millionaire who also was perceived to be a racist, saying she would "accept aid from the devil himself" as long as he did not influence *The Revolution*'s editorial content. Stanton's unyielding position was strengthened by her decision to stake out the high ground on other financial issues, refusing to accept ads for patent medicines because she believed they were dangerous.

Victoria Woodhull had no such high ground on which to defend her eagerness to accept money from millionaire industrialist Cornelius Vanderbilt, who financed *Woodhull & Claflin's Weekly* in exchange for sexual favors from her voluptuous sister Tennessee Claflin.

Numerous of the fiscal decisions that socialist publisher J. A. Wayland made were questionable not on moral grounds, but ideological ones. *Appeal to Rea-*

son published ads from companies that produced a variety of manufactured items and from promoters of various get-rich-quick schemes—hardly consistent with the *Appeal*'s anti-capitalist philosophy. Wayland's circulation-building techniques, although they succeeded in creating the largest newspaper in the history of the dissident press, also were incongruous with the paper's ideology, with readers being encouraged to bring in new subscribers by being offered incentives such as gold watches, motorcycles, and a yacht. Finally, Wayland's decision to diversify his business operation by manufacturing items ranging from salad dressing to airplanes flew directly in the face of his campaign to eradicate capitalism.

THE AMERICAN GOVERNMENT IS NO FRIEND OF THE DISSIDENT PRESS

Although encouraging a free press and celebrating diverse opinions are purported to be hallmarks of a democratic society, the U.S. government used its myriad powers, with unyielding impunity, to silence the voices of journalistic dissent that emerged during the final decades of the nineteenth century.

The sexual reform press so offended the puritanical mores of the Victorian Age that the federal government engineered a comprehensive attack on sexual expression, led by "St. Anthony" Comstock and the eponymous obscenity acts that he propelled into law.

The federal government's campaign to shut down the *Appeal to Reason* was even more relentless, beginning in 1901 with postal officials in Washington threatening to cancel the socialist weekly's second-class mailing permit and continuing for the next fifteen years with ongoing harassment of publisher W. A. Wayland. The government's assault on the leading voice of socialism climaxed after the country entered World War I and Congress passed the Espionage Act that made it illegal to publish material that encouraged disloyalty. Postal authorities then finally succeeded in preventing the *Appeal* from being mailed—until Wayland's son, in complete betrayal of his dead father's legacy, agreed to support the war.

The federal government's offensive against the anarchist press was absolutely ruthless. The U.S. Post Office suppressed various issues of Emma Goldman's *Mother Earth* and then, in 1917, Goldman and editor Alexander Berkman were found guilty, under the Espionage Act, of conspiring against the draft and were sentenced to the maximum penalty of two years in prison. The Justice Department was called in to strike the fatal blow against the beleaguered dissidents by deporting two of American history's most cacophonous editorial voices.

**DISSIDENT JOURNALISTS PAY A HIGH PRICE FOR THEIR EFFORTS
TO PROVOKE SOCIAL CHANGE**

Although the first generation of editors suffered public humiliation ranging from William Lloyd Garrison being pelted with rotten eggs to Susan Brownell Anthony being verbally attacked more harshly than any other woman of her time, the level of punishment meted out to dissident journalists escalated as the nineteenth century moved toward its end.

After daring to challenge the myth that lustful black men in the South were raping white women by the thousand, anti-lynching editor Ida B. Wells was physically threatened to the point that she was forced into exile in the North, not daring to set foot in her native South for three decades.

Sexual reform editors Moses Harman of *Lucifer, the Light-Bearer* and Ezra Heywood of *The Word* were convicted on multiple obscenity charges, under the Comstock laws, and then served many years in prison, several of them at hard labor that ultimately destroyed the two aged men's health and undoubtedly hastened their deaths.

Pioneering anarchist editor Albert R. Parsons was hanged and his later counterparts Emma Goldman and Alexander Berkman were first jailed and then deported. All three of these editors clearly possessed a variety of qualities as journalists, provocateurs, and visionaries that could have guaranteed them all the benefits of conventional success—had they not been determined to effect social change.

Socialist editor J. A. Wayland, like Parsons, paid the supreme price for his journalistic dissidence, becoming so depressed because of the various forms of persecution he suffered—legal, physical, and emotional attacks by law enforcement officials combined with attacks on his morals by the mainstream press— that he took his own life.

**SOME DISSIDENT PRESS TOPICS ARE SO INIMICAL TO SOCIETAL VALUES
THAT THEY ARE NEVER EMBRACED BY THE AMERICAN PUBLIC**

Although many dissident publications champion unpopular concepts that eventually filter into the mainstream of American thought, others are so contrary to the nation's mores and core principles that they fail utterly in gaining the support of more than a small minority of the population.

Some of the beliefs promulgated by the sexual reform press—that the institution of marriage should be eliminated and that babies born to unwed mothers are superior to babies born to married women—are seen today, as they were during the Victorian Age, as the ravings of a lunatic fringe; the handful of publications that advanced such ideas never even succeeded, in fact, in building a social movement in support of its ideas.

Dissident newspapers such as the *Appeal to Reason* helped the Socialist Movement become a political force to be reckoned with at the end of the nineteenth century and the beginning of the twentieth, but capitalism ultimately proved to be so entrenched in the U.S. economy that socialist precepts remain beyond the pale of most citizens of this country—indeed, are seen as patently *un*-American.

Anarchism, to an even greater extent and despite the support of such determined publications as *The Alarm* and *Mother Earth*, also failed to have any significant influence on the national consciousness; today very few Americans have even a rudimentary understanding of—much less any support for—the anarchist philosophy.

THE DISSIDENT PRESS PROVIDES A PUBLISHING VENUE FOR WOMEN JOURNALISTS

Throughout most of the history of mainstream American journalism, the vast majority of the men who have traditionally dominated the field have opposed women either entering or advancing in this bastion of testosterone. Until the late twentieth century, therefore, the number of women who succeeded in editing establishment newspapers was minuscule. From the earliest years of dissident journalism, by contrast, women have played prominent roles.

After Elizabeth Cady Stanton, Susan Brownell Anthony, and their legendary newspaper *The Revolution* took their place among the pioneers in the field, the second generation witnessed a veritable explosion of female dissident journalists.

Victoria Woodhull and her *Woodhull & Claflin's Weekly* were the leading forces in creating the sexual reform press, paving the way for Angela Heywood and her groundbreaking work in *The Word*.

Ida B. Wells-Barnett, during a time when women of color were largely barred from public life, became synonymous with the anti-lynching press, as well as the social movement surrounding it, through her singular work in the *Memphis Free Speech*, the *New York Age*, the *Chicago Conservator*, and the series of pamphlets she published.

Emma Goldman created an indelible mark, through her work as founder and editor of the leading voice of the Anarchist Movement, as one of the quintessential—as well as most memorable—figures in the history of the American dissident press.

PART 3
RISING FROM A LONE VOICE TO A MASS MOVEMENT

The general lack of success that the dissident press experienced at the end of the nineteenth century did not dissuade an unlikely pair of early twentieth-century editors—different not only in their crusade of choice but also in their race, their gender, and their class—from embarking, virtually single-handedly, on campaigns that all sense of reason dictated were doomed to unmitigated failure.

Nevertheless, these two visionary activists-cum-journalists raced full throttle into the dark abyss of uncertainty. The first attempted to mobilize the millions of Americans of African descent who were confined to poverty and deprivation in the rural South; the second set out on the equally daunting task of empowering the throngs of poor immigrant women who had recently been drawn to America's shores.

Driven by an extraordinary storehouse of courage, will, ability, and "spirit of revolt," the pair of fearless editors showed—in a textbook example of the power of the dissident press—that a single individual truly can inspire social change of titanic proportion.

8 PROPELLING BLACK AMERICANS INTO THE PROMISED LAND

Throughout the nineteenth century and well into the twentieth, the vast majority of black Americans remained second-class citizens. Ninety percent of them lived in the South, prohibited from voting or holding public office and denied political and economic control over their own lives. Most black men and women worked from dawn to dusk as field hands, paid whatever paltry sum their white employers chose to give them. Enduring a virtual feudal system in which even the most basic of human rights did not exist, women and girls were forced into sexual servitude by white overlords who kept black men demoralized and in a constant state of intimidation.

Not until the second decade of the twentieth century did the peonage system that defined the lives of disenfranchised blacks finally begin to fade from the American experience. During World War I, huge numbers of men, women, and children abandoned the oppressive social order in the South to create the first mass migration of African Americans and to take advantage of unprecedented opportunities in the manufacturing centers of the North. The wartime build-up opened new job possibilities to black workers because the global conflict raised the demand for industrial products while simultaneously stemming the flow of European immigrants who in earlier decades had been the major source of the urban workforce. The exodus from the South was so significant that it ultimately rivaled emancipation as a liberating experience, as Americans of African descent came to see the North as nothing less than the storied Promised Land.

The mass movement grew to staggering proportions between 1916 and 1919 as cities, towns, and backwater farming communities below the Mason-Dixon Line watched the throngs of defectors swell larger and larger. During a time when the entire black population of the United States totaled only ten million, the Great Migration saw the number of African Americans moving from the South to the North climb to 500,000.[1]

The historic demographic shift had major effects on the North as well, with the African American population of New York, Detroit, and Philadelphia mushrooming as never before. But the urban center that drew more southern blacks than any other was Chicago. Various factors contributed to the city's pre-eminence as a racial magnet—industrial jobs abounded and the tracks of the Illinois Central Railroad stretched from Tennessee, Mississippi, and Louisiana straight to the terminal in downtown Chicago. But as historians have studied the Great Migration, they have repeatedly identified one more force as key to the city becoming the focal point of this unprecedented mass movement: the *Chicago Defender*.[2]

Carl Sandburg was among the many historians who credited the dissident newspaper with sparking the migration, writing, "The *Defender*, more than any other one agency, was the big cause of the 'northern fever' and the big exodus from the South." A second scholar stated that "Chicago's image as a northern mecca can be attributed mainly to the *Chicago Defender*," and a third wrote, "The *Defender* became one of the most potent factors in a phenomenal Hegira that began to change the character and pattern of race relations in the United States."[3]

Robert S. Abbott, the paper's founder, also was lauded for his role in the mass movement. One scholar wrote that Abbott "set the migration in motion," and another crowned Abbott, because he urged blacks to leave the South, "the greatest single force" in the history of black journalism. Though it would be an overstatement to credit Abbott with single-handedly *causing* the remarkable phenomenon, he clearly was a man of vision who used the means available to him as a newspaper editor to synchronize the northern migration with the flow of history. "We advocate migration," Abbott said in one of the hundreds of editorials he wrote on the subject. "On account of the war demands, economic conditions in our industrial life afford us an opportunity to better our condition by leaving the South."[4]

In the early 1900s, the *Chicago Defender* was the largest black newspaper in the country, boasting a circulation of 230,000. Of even more importance to the mass movement, the weekly was distributed nationally, with two-thirds of its copies sent outside of Chicago—most of them into the South.[5]

While these statistics are impressive in their own right, they do not take into account two modes of informal circulation. The *Defender* was routinely passed among relatives, friends, neighbors, and church members who could not afford the $1.50 a year subscription. As one man wrote, "Copies were passed around until worn out." In addition, large numbers of illiterate southern blacks gathered in churches and barbershops to hear one person read the paper out loud.

Such communal reading was so pervasive that scholars estimate that each copy of the *Defender* was read by five to seven people. Therefore, during the height of the migration, the number of African Americans reading the paper, or hearing it read aloud, soared well beyond the one million mark.[6]

In many towns across the South, the *Defender*'s arrival became a weekly event of major proportion. A Louisiana woman wrote that the paper was "a God sent blessing to the Race" and that she would "rather read it than to eat when Saturday comes," and another reader marveled that "Negroes grab the *Defender* like a hungry mule grabs fodder." In Mississippi, "a man was regarded as 'intelligent' if he read the *Defender*," and even illiterate men bought the paper "because it was regarded as precious." In short, the *Chicago Defender* achieved a mass appeal far beyond anything Black America had ever known. "With the exception of the Bible," one scholar said, "no publication was more influential among the Negro masses."[7]

And the primary message, delivered week after week, was simple and direct: Go North!

RISE OF THE "WORLD'S GREATEST WEEKLY"

Robert Sengstacke Abbott was born in 1868 to former slaves living in rural Georgia. A young man of remarkable will and fortitude, Abbott earned a bachelor's degree from Hampton Institute in Virginia and a law degree from Kent College in Illinois. His dream of practicing law evaporated, however, when Chicago's leading African American attorney told Abbott his skin was "a little too dark" to make a positive impression in the country's white-dominated courtrooms. Abbott vowed that if he could not effect social change through law, he would do so through journalism.[8]

The *Chicago Defender* appeared in the spring of 1905. Abbott had no money to pay anyone to help him with the various duties involved in publishing a newspaper, so he became the sole writer, editor, printer, ad salesman, accountant, and newsboy. For the next four years, he struggled to keep the paper afloat, failing to increase his weekly circulation beyond a scant 300 copies.

On the brink of abandoning the newspaper business, Abbott changed his tactics. Instead of filling his pages with the tepid community news—religious items mixed with announcements of local births, weddings, and deaths—that was the staple of black journalism of the era, he began serving up spicier fare. Political cartoons lampooned racist government officials, and shrill editorials denounced black oppression. Most noteworthy of all were the front-page ban-

The first African American journalist to become a millionaire, Robert S. Abbott routinely wore double-breasted suits, spats, and gloves, while carrying a walking stick topped with a gold handle. (Courtesy Regnery Publishing Company)

ner headlines, many of them printed in bright red ink and each one larger than the one before—"White Man Rapes Colored Girl," "Aged Man Is Burned to Death by Whites." Critics called Abbott's approach to the news sensationalistic, but circulation and advertising revenue soared.[9]

Reveling in his success, Abbott—never a modest man—set his sights on creating an African American paper that lived up to the boastful motto he placed at the top of page one: "The World's Greatest Weekly." To achieve this lofty ambition, Abbott focused on two goals. First, he had to circulate his paper in the South, the area of the country that was home to the vast majority of African Americans. Second, he had to prove to his readers that the *Defender* was willing to speak boldly on behalf of Black America.

To expand into the South, Abbott curried the favor of the thousands of black men who worked as sleeping-car porters. He began in 1910 by inaugurating a weekly column called "Railroad Rumblings," filling it with bits of news and personal items about railroad workers. The editor also vigorously supported the efforts of railroad workers, playing a major role in securing a ten-percent wage hike for them. This strategy was prelude to the brilliant step Abbott took in 1916:

This 1916 *Chicago Defender* editorial cartoon depicted a terrorized black laborer escaping from the South by racing toward the industrializing North that welcomed him. (Courtesy Chicago Defender)

He began giving bundles of the hot-off-the-press *Defender* to black porters just before they left Chicago, asking the men to deliver the papers to newsboys waiting for them in the hundreds of towns and cities the trains passed through as they headed south. It was a circulation-building concept inspired both in its simplicity and its success. During Abbott's campaign for the mass movement to the North, his paper was distributed not only in large southern cities such as New Orleans—where readers could buy it on city buses or from any of three news dealers who sold 1,000 copies a week—but also in tiny communities from Yoakum, Texas, to Palataka, Florida.[10]

With regard to showing black readers that the *Defender* was agitating for them, Abbott refused to cower to White America. After a vigilante mob killed a black man in North Carolina, the editor called for retaliation: "An Eye for an Eye, a Tooth for a Tooth." Other page-one headlines carried the same rebellious message—"Lynching Must Be Stopped by Shotgun," "When the Mob Comes and You Must Die, Take at Least One with You," and "Call the White Fiends to the Door and Shoot them Down." The *Defender*'s strident editorial content convinced southern readers not only that the World's Greatest Weekly truly was the "defender" of the race but that the North must be far freer than the South if an editor was allowed to print such statements—and live to read them.[11]

VILIFYING THE SOUTH

Although racism was rampant in the South in the early 1900s, most African Americans knew of the widespread abuse only through word of mouth or personal observation because white papers below the Mason-Dixon Line *would not* report it and southern black papers *dared not* report it.

Not so the *Defender*. The outspoken weekly—in a continuation of the model that Ida B. Wells-Barnett had pioneered in her anti-lynching publications of the late 1800s—was committed to documenting the acts of persecution wherever they occurred. So Abbott drafted the army of railroad porters who distributed the *Defender* to double as correspondents who ensured that an incident that took place anywhere in the South found its way into the paper and, consequently, was reported nationwide.

One front-page article listed dozens of southern towns where any black man who was on the street after 8:30 p.m. was automatically arrested—then beaten. Another item reported that white residents of Clarksville, Tennessee, were so angry when blacks built a church in a middle-class section of the city that they burned the building to the ground. Still another item told Black America that when a white patrolman in Memphis told an African American woman walking on the street to halt but she kept walking, the officer shot her and then left her to bleed to death rather than take her to a hospital, saying she would have gotten blood on the upholstery of his brand new police car.[12]

In none of these instances was there a single arrest.

Abbott also published uncompromising editorial cartoons. In one drawing, an African American man fleeing from a white man with a gun was running toward a waiting automobile labeled "Northern Industries." In another, a black man was hanging from a tree while, in the background, a cluster of black men, women, and children marched northward; the cartoon was labeled "The Exodus."[13]

Beside many of the drawings appeared fiery editorials spewing forth Abbott's venom toward the South. One raged that sixteen black men had been lynched in Georgia during the previous month, "a record even for this state of backward civilization where violence triumphs over law." Abbott ended the piece with a statement and a question: "We have this same hideous story every year. Are we ever going to do anything about it?" In another editorial, the dissident editor insisted, "Anywhere in God's country is far better than the southland. Come join the ranks of the free. Cast the yoke from around your neck. See the light. When you have crossed the Ohio river, breathe the fresh air and say, 'Why didn't I come before?' "[14]

More than willing to place blame, Abbott waged rhetorical warfare against southern racists, filling his columns with invective far too dangerous for any black editor to express openly in the South. He routinely called white people "crackers" and referred to white politicians as "pigeon-livered." In one angry editorial, Abbott labeled white leaders "wage thieves," "ignorant asses," and "murderers"; in another, he called southern whites "no-accounts," "persecutors," "ravishers of Negro women," and "killers of Negro men."[15]

But more compelling even than the editorial cartoons or the angry oratory were the gruesome details contained in the news stories. For when reporting violence in the South, the *Defender* spared nothing, adopting a far more sensationalistic tone in its coverage than had Ida B. Wells-Barnett's publications before it. Indeed, some scholars have suggested that Abbott may even have embellished the stories for maximum effect. Regardless of how much of the final product was reality and how much was the creation of an editor committed to moving his readers to action, the articles were shocking.[16]

- A story from Temple, Texas, described how a black man named Will Stanley, while waiting to be tried on a murder charge, "was taken from jail at midnight and burned on the public square in the presence of hundreds of men, women, boys and girls, who cheered as the victim went up in smoke."[17]

- Another estimated that between 15,000 and 20,000 whites in Waco, Texas, watched as eighteen-year-old Jesse Washington, another black man awaiting trial, was tied to a tree and set on fire, "with the horror of flames rising around the flesh of the squirming boy and as tears rolled out of his eyes." But the crowd was still not satisfied. "After the fire subsided, the mob hacked with pen-knifes the fingers, the toes and pieces of flesh from the body, carrying them as souvenirs to their automobiles."[18]

- From Dyersburg, Tennessee, came the story of the final hours of Lation Scott, a prisoner who was bound to an iron post while men heated pokers and irons until they were "white with heat" and thereby prepared for their dastardly task—boring out the prisoner's eyes. When this occurred, "Scott moaned," the *Defender* reported, before continuing in riveting detail. "The pokers were worked like an auger, that is, they were twisted round and round. The smell of burning flesh permeated the atmosphere, a pungent, sickening odor telling those who failed to get good vantage points what their eyes could not see: Irons were searing the flesh." Scott was still alive when the townspeople, including women and children, piled wood and rubbish around him and continued to feed the fire until he became "a heap of charred ashes and bones."[19]

GLORIFYING THE NORTH

Abbott's depiction of the appalling realities of life in the South stood in glaring contrast to his exaltations about the benefits of moving to the North. Week after week, the *Defender* used advertisements, editorials, and news and feature stories to tell readers of the Black American Dream awaiting them at the northern end of the railroad tracks. Abbott even negotiated with the Illinois Central Railroad for reduced fares for groups of ten or more migrants traveling together and printed, free of charge, the train schedule—one way from south to north.

If any single word captured the reason, according to Robert S. Abbott, that African Americans should relocate to the Promised Land, that word was spelled J-O-B-S. The *Defender* published thousands of employment ads such as: "Wanted—Men for laborers and semi-skilled occupations. Address or apply to the employment department, Westinghouse Electric Co." Many of the ads specifically mentioned that "Negroes" were urged to apply, and the jobs themselves targeted that same audience, asking for "warehouse workers," "cement mixers," and "laborers for steel mill" who did not have to have specific skills, only a willingness to work. The wages in the ads appealed to blacks as well; southern farm workers typically were paid seventy-five cents a day, while northern factory wages started at $4 a day and climbed as high as $10.[20]

Abbott reinforced the job opportunities through a stream of statements on his editorial page that insisted the integrated employment that blacks had dreamed of for so long had finally arrived—in the North. "The bars are being let down in the industrial world as never before," he asserted. "We have talked and argued and sat up late at night planning what we would do if we only had an opportunity. Now that it is here, how many are going to grasp it?" The powerful editor often challenged his readers, insisting that it was not only in their best interest individually to take advantage of the new opportunities provided by the wartime build-up but also their duty to the race. "We must fill the new positions offered us; by so doing we will secure a stable position in the world's work," Abbott thundered. "Our chance is right now."[21]

In addition to glorifying Chicago as offering unlimited jobs, Abbott beat his northern migration drum by portraying his adopted city as a wonderland of leisure-time activities. For a southern black field worker who spent from dawn to dusk looking at the back end of a mule, opening the *Defender* was comparable to discovering a whole new world.

The film "Trooper of Company K" was "easily the greatest production ever attempted by our people," the *Defender* gushed. Complete with an "all colored cast" of 350 and featuring heartthrob Noble Johnson as a military hero, the paper continued, "It depicts in gripping scenes the unflinching bravery of the troopers under fire and how they, greatly outnumbered, sacrificed their blood and life for their country. Interposed in the picture are scenes of romantic love, comedy and human interest. Don't fail to attend the Washington Theater during the run of this wonderful picture." Although the paper's praise of "Trooper" was unrestrained, the film was only one of forty available to African American Chicagoans the first week of October 1916—forty more than were available to blacks living anywhere in the South.[22]

The *Defender's* hefty entertainment section reported that amusement options extended well beyond the silver screen. "Remarkable dramatic actress" Dorothy Donnelly played the lead in the stage play "Madame X" at States Theater, William and Salem Tutt starred in a musical extravaganza at The Grand, the Drake-Walker Players drew packed houses nightly for their musicale at The Monogram, Joe Sheftel and his Black Dots regaled audiences with "real harmony, real dancing, and a riot of fun" at The Orpheum, and Clabrun Jones and his Yama Yama Players, complete with their own orchestra and chorus of fifteen voices, presented a musical review at the New Monogram.[23]

In the opinion of the *Defender*'s music critic, though, the best show to hit Black Chicago—"Entertainment Extraordinary!"—was Clarence Jones performing "first class vaudeville" at the "everything up to the minute" Owl Theater—"with 1,200 roomy seats, $10,000 Kimball pipe organ, 8 piece orchestra, and perfect ventilation."[24]

The *Defender* also promoted the cornucopia of activities that African Americans could enjoy during the day. The paper bragged about the city's well-equipped playgrounds and the open access, regardless of race, to the beaches along Lake Michigan. Sports fans were told of the triumphs of black Chicago's own boxing champion, Jack Johnson, and were reminded that games between African American baseball teams took place nearly every day and that the Chicago-based American Giants were the greatest black sluggers in the country.[25]

By 1918, a Mississippi man spoke for thousands of his race when he wrote that, after reading the *Defender*, he was quite sure that Chicago was nothing short of "heaven itself."[26]

CREATING "MIGRATION FEVER"

Abbott did not stop with vilifying the South and glorifying the North but also took it upon himself to engineer what became known as "migration fever."

The crusading editor believed that southern blacks were more likely to leave their homes if they saw themselves not as isolated migrants but as members of a mass movement. So he methodically communicated to his readers that a widespread exodus was, in fact, taking place. As one scholar put it, Abbott constructed "an atmosphere of hysteria. The more people who left, inspired by *Defender* propaganda, the more who wanted to go, so the migration fed on itself until in some places it turned into a wild stampede"—all choreographed by the dissident editor.[27]

Abbott launched his campaign in the fall of 1916 by spreading a photograph across his front page and labeling it, in inch-high capital letters: "THE EXODUS." The huge image showed the railroad yard in Savannah, Georgia, literally covered with hundreds upon hundreds of African Americans—so many people that the train tracks were barely visible—waiting to board the next north-bound train. The caption told readers: "Men, tired of being kicked and cursed, are leaving by the thousands as the above picture shows."[28]

In the months that followed, Abbott raised momentum for migration to a fever pitch by blanketing his pages with dozens of headlines—"Leaving for the North," "Farewell, Dixie Land," "300 Leave for North"—and by filling rivers of type with news items crafted to inspire still more departures. From Meridian, Mississippi: "Members of the Race have left for Chicago. They are going where better wages and schooling conditions exist." From Selma, Alabama: "Over 200 left here on the railroad for the north." From Talladega, Alabama: "The great exodus has struck Talladega County." From Summit, Mississippi: "Twenty-four carloads passed through here last week." From Waycross, Georgia: "There are so many leaving here that Waycross will be desolate soon." From Aberdeen, Mississippi: "The migration to the north seems to be an epidemic that breaks out every Saturday when the latest *Chicago Defender* arrives."[29]

Abbott eagerly highlighted his paper's role in propelling African Americans into the Promised Land. "The *Defender* propaganda to leave the south where they find conditions intolerable is receiving a hearty response," read one item, while others highlighted the observations of the hundreds of men and women who contributed news items to the proactive paper. One correspondent wrote of seeing 2,000 black men and women gathered at the Memphis train station. "Number 4, due to leave for Chicago at 8:00 o'clock, was held up twenty minutes so that those people who hadn't purchased tickets might be taken aboard," the man wrote. "It was necessary to add two additional eighty-foot steel coaches to the Chicago train in order to accommodate the Race people, and at the lowest estimation there were more than 1,200 taken on board."[30]

After the migration impulse took hold, one of the ways Abbott kept reader enthusiasm at a high level was by juxtaposing images of the South and the North. A typical pictorial item consisted of two photos, one on top of the other. The lower image, which filled only two columns, was of the Freetown School in Abbeville, Louisiana, a one-room shack that barely managed to remain standing and was labeled "Jim Crow school"; above it appeared a five-column image of Chicago's integrated Robert Lindblom High School with a row of stately pillars standing tall in front of the modern building. The caption: "One of the many reasons why members of the Race are leaving the south. They are seeking better education for their children, as well as getting away from slavery, Jim Crow laws and concubinage."[31]

Another way the dissident editor kept migration mania at a white-hot level was by tying specific acts of racial violence to the escalating pace of the movement. After Eli Persons was burned to death in Tennessee in 1917, Abbott show-cased the incident on page one under the exaggerated headline: "Millions Pre-pare to Leave the South Following Brutal Burning of Human." Abbott further emphasized his message in the news article that followed, calling Persons's mur-der the "last straw" and informing his readers that "thousands are leaving Mem-phis" in the wake of the heartless crime. Abbott used the same technique after an angry Abbeville, South Carolina, mob killed Anthony Crawford. The head-line read "Lynching of Crawford Causes Thousands to Leave the South," and the story raged, "Respectable people are leaving daily. The cry now is—Go North! where there is some humanity."[32]

In other pleas that were part of Abbott's relentless advocacy of what he called the "Flight out of Egypt," he appealed to the manhood of his readers. "Every black man, for the sake of his wife and daughters especially, should leave the south where his worth is not appreciated enough to give him the standing of a man." Other times, the journalistic provocateur urged his readers to see their decision to leave the South as part of history-in-the-making. With this theme, Abbott argued that migration to northern cities would reduce racial prejudice. "Only by a commingling with other races will the black man take his place in the limelight beside his white brother. Contact means everything."[33]

Abbott, like other dissident journalists before him, extended his effort to effect social change far beyond publishing. To persuade white employers to hire blacks, the editor gave hundreds of speeches to church and civic organizations in Chicago and other northern cities. Abbott knew these audiences would pay close attention to his appearance and how he comported himself, as he was one of the few middle-class African Americans the white businessmen would come into contact with. So partly to impress those men and partly because he was fas-tidious by nature, Abbott took great care to dress in expensive suits and hats—finishing off his outfit with gloves, spats, a diamond stick pin, and a gold-headed walking stick.[34]

By 1919, historian Carl Sandburg was praising Abbott's leading role in creat-ing the fever for northern migration. Calling the *Defender* the "single promo-tional agency" responsible for the historic mass movement, Sandburg wrote in the *Chicago Daily News*, "There has been built here a propaganda machine that carries on an agitation that every week reaches hundreds of thousands of peo-ple of the colored race in the southern states."[35]

Historians were not the only ones who connected Abbott with the Great Migration. For in the minds of hundreds of thousands of black Americans, the editor was the messiah who was miraculously raising the quality of their lives. Many of the envelopes being sent from the South did not even mention the

Chicago Defender but were addressed simply: "Robert S. Abbott, Chicago, Illinois." W. A. McCloud of Wadley, Georgia, began his letter by describing Abbott as "a great and grand man and a lover of his race," while another writer told Abbott, "I feel I know you personally." Thousands of readers sought Abbott's counsel—"your paper is all we have to go by," read one, "so we are depending on you for advise [sic]." Others went well beyond asking for mere words of wisdom. Throngs of African Americans with little knowledge about the world beyond the rural South assumed the "Help Wanted" notices in Abbott's paper meant that the editor himself was looking for workers; he was besieged with a flood of letters asking him for a job—"I garntee [sic] you good and reglar [sic] service," a Florida man promised. Hundreds of letters came with requests for Abbott's recommendation as to where the readers could find suitable housing once they moved to Chicago; some even asked if Abbott himself had a spare room in his own house.[36]

REAPING THE PERSONAL REWARDS

At the same time that the mass exodus filled the editor's mailbox and changed America's demographic landscape, it also transformed the fortunes of Robert S. Abbott. The ambitious editor became one of Black America's first millionaires, filling his pages with advertisements not only for jobs but also for a wide range of products that appealed to Chicago's swelling ranks of African American consumers—stylish hats and hair-straightening products for women, suits and sporting goods for men.

As Abbott became one of the nation's richest and most powerful men of African descent, he made a public spectacle of his wealth and status. He not only dressed ostentatiously but also lived in a massive red brick mansion filled with Hepplewhite antiques and an ebony-finished living room set imported from China. Abbott also took grand tours of Europe and hired a chauffeur to drive him around Chicago in a Rolls Royce limousine. Some people criticized the editor for flaunting his wealth; others praised him for providing a symbol of what a visionary and hard-working black man could achieve in modern-day America—if he lived in the North.

Critics and admirers alike whispered about the details of Abbott's personal life. His 1918 marriage to Helen Morrison shocked Black America—Abbott was fifty and dark skinned, his wife was twenty and so fair that many people thought she was white. Hoping that his beautiful young bride would produce an heir, Abbott lavished Helen with furs, diamonds, and the latest Paris fashions. But after fifteen years of marriage and no children, Abbott divorced his first wife and quickly married his second. Edna Brown Denison was twenty-five years younger than Abbott and also had light skin—Abbott's biographer described her as being "as completely white as any Caucasian." Unlike Helen, however, Edna was a widow with a ready-made family of four children that Abbott treated as his own. At least one detail about Abbott's personal life cast the dissident editor into the category of "quirky"; he was so formal in his comportment that he never allowed either of his wives to address him, even in the privacy of their own bedroom, as anything but "Mr. Abbott."[37]

RESISTING THE BACKLASH

While the migration of half a million African Americans was cause for celebration among Abbott and his followers, it created a crisis for another segment of the population: southern white employers who relied on cheap black labor. Amid predictions of crops rotting in the fields without black workers to harvest them, Alabama's *Montgomery Advertiser* spoke for much of the South when it angrily protested: "Our very solvency is being sucked out from underneath us."[38]

Unwilling to allow the advancement of African Americans to disrupt their lives and livelihoods, white southerners fought back. The state of Georgia began requiring anyone who recruited southern laborers to purchase a license for the hefty sum of $25,000, and Alabama officials passed a law against "enticing Negroes" to leave the state. Illegal means were used as well, with north-bound trains being sidetracked and African Americans who talked of moving to the North being threatened, beaten, and snatched from railroad stations and arrested as vagrants.[39]

The *Defender* did not allow the backlash to go unnoticed. A banner headline on page one announced: "Emigration Worries South; Arrests Made to Keep Labor from Going North." The Georgia-based story said, "The whites here are up in arms against the members of the Race leaving the south." The article went on to report that the "bully police" in Savannah were refusing to allow African Americans to enter the local railroad station. "They used their clubs to beat some people bodily," while arresting others merely for carrying suitcases in the vicinity of the station.[40]

Much of the white response was aimed at the *Defender*. In Tennessee, a law made it illegal to read "any black newspaper from Chicago," and, in Arkansas, the governor charged that the *Defender* "fomented racial unrest," prompting a judge to issue an injunction restraining circulation of the paper. Two black men in Georgia were jailed for thirty days merely for having articles from the *Defender* in their pockets, and at least a dozen African American men were run out of their respective hometowns for trying to sell copies of the paper. When a Texas woman was accused of sending Abbott an article about a lynching, whites burned several black homes and publicly flogged the principal of the town's black school. In the most serious of the violent incidents, two African American men who sold subscriptions to the *Defender* in Alabama were attacked and killed by a white mob.[41]

Abbott received threatening letters such as one from an Arkansas racist who wrote: "You are agitating a proposition through your paper which is causing some of your Burr heads to be killed. You could be of assistance to your people if you would advise them to be real niggers instead of fools." Southern politicians joined the chorus of criticism. Senator John Sharp Williams of Mississippi called the *Defender* "a tissue of lies, all intended to create race disturbance and trouble," Congressman M. D. Upshaw of Georgia denounced the paper as "inflammatory in stirring up race prejudice" and "publishing wild and exaggerated statements about white crimes," and Senator Edward Gay of Louisiana charged that Abbott was the sole cause of the "unrest at present evident among the negroes of the South."[42]

The U.S. government also grew increasingly concerned about Abbott's paper. Officials in the nation's capital established a special surveillance operation that combined the forces of the military, postal service, and Justice Department. Because their mutual goal was to maintain national security during World War I and the *Defender* was a self-declared voice of dissent, the paper was declared "subversive" and emerged as a primary target for federal investigation.[43]

The efforts to inhibit distribution of the *Defender* coupled with criticism of it by white southerners, however, also served to assure African Americans of the paper's courage. When southern leaders forced distribution underground, blacks responded by going to great lengths to obtain the paper. Storekeepers passed copies to customers by hiding them in other merchandise or passing them along surreptitiously. "We have to slip the paper into the hands of our friends," one distributor wrote. "Every school teacher is closely watched, also the preacher." Sleeping-car porters played their part, too. When white officials no longer allowed bundles of the *Defender* to be delivered to railroad stations downtown, the porters began tossing the bundles to agents waiting beside the tracks in rural areas just outside of town.[44]

Unflinching, the dissident editor fought back from the pages of his paper. With even more ferocity than before, Abbott stridently urged African Americans to come North. "If there ever was a time to strike for freedom in its broadest sense, that time is right now," he wrote. "If we fail to reap the benefits of this golden opportunity, we have but ourselves to blame." In another challenge to readers who questioned if they should defy the white southern power structure, Abbott insisted: "Your neck has been in the yoke. Will you continue to keep it there? The *Defender* says come North."[45]

Abbott also countered the backlash with a flow of articles about how blacks who already had joined the Great Migration were prospering in their new environs. One item assured readers that "every one is getting work in the north"; another told of fifteen black families who were thriving in their industrial jobs that paid "sixty to seventy dollars per month, against fifteen and twenty" they had been paid while working longer hours in the South.[46]

Abbott also continued to report the exodus. A story headlined "Determined To Go North" stated that in Jackson, Mississippi, "Although the white police and sheriff and others are using every effort to intimidate the citizens from going North, this has not deterred our people from leaving. Many have walked miles to take the train for the North. There is a determination to leave and there is no hand save death to keep them from it."[47]

A MIXED LEGACY

Robert S. Abbott and the *Chicago Defender* successfully overcame the antimigration backlash, and the number of southern blacks moving north eventually reached the half million mark.

In 1919, however, Abbott brought his historic campaign to an abrupt halt. He made the decision because of several factors. First, as the influx of African Americans swelled the population of Chicago and other northern cities, those urban metropolises began to strain at the seams. The rapid increase in population created many problems related to crime, health, housing, and education. The large number of blacks suddenly entering American industry during the war also led to difficulty, as organized labor did not fully embrace non-white workers.

The biggest problem of all came, ironically, with the American victory in World War I. That success meant that millions of white soldiers returned home to Chicago and other northern cities to find that the jobs and neighborhoods they had left behind had been appropriated by hundreds of thousands of African Americans. The ebullient young white men were anxious to reaffirm the old caste system; the newly empowered blacks were in no mood to be pushed around. Tension exploded in July 1919 with a four-day race riot in Chicago—the single event that forever changed the tenor of the *Defender*. The paper's headlines told the story: "Riot Sweeps Chicago," "Gun Battles and Fighting in Streets Keep the City in an Uproar," "Scores are Killed." When the smoke cleared, fifteen whites and twenty-three blacks lay dead, with 500 others wounded. Although Chicago was hit the hardest, other northern cities felt the crisis as well, with the "Red Summer" witnessing some twenty race riots nationwide.[48]

So Abbott could no longer, in good conscience, portray his adopted city as the Promised Land. Like the rest of his race, the editor came to see that many of the same problems that existed in the South would persist in the North. Chicago and other industrial cities became yet another location where the Black American Dream was ultimately deferred.

By the fall of 1919, Abbott had lowered the decibel level of his dissidence. From the time of the race riots until his death in 1940, the visionary editor continued to provide a voice for Black America, but that voice no longer defied White America as it had during the height of the Great Migration. Indeed, the paper has continued—becoming a daily in 1956—to be one of the most widely respected black newspapers in the country today.

The historic journalistic crusade the *Defender* undertook should, by no means, be viewed as a failure. For the mass exodus that the dissident newspaper spearheaded from 1916 to 1919 was a glorious triumph that permanently altered the face of the United States. During a time when the vast majority of Americans of African descent were suffering lives defined by subjugation and terror, the *Defender* offered its readers a concrete alternative. The nationally circulated black paper inspired hundreds of thousands of men and women to take advantage of a unique opportunity, thereby helping to propel the first major migration in African American history.

And a magnificent migration it was. The flight out of the South did not merely mark a demographic shift. It also signaled the death knell for the feudal existence that most African Americans had been forced to endure, thereby giving them a glimpse, for the first time, of a modern and civilized way of life that was defined by personal as well as racial freedom.

For three remarkable years, the "World's Greatest Weekly" committed its ample resources to advancing the unprecedented exodus. The courageous newspaper provided, as no other publication in the country, dramatic evidence of the inhumane treatment meted out to southern blacks. The *Defender* published hard-driving headlines, news stories, editorials, and editorial cartoons, as well as advertisements and feature stories that showcased the employment and leisure-time activities awaiting African Americans who relocated to Chicago.

And, finally, the paper harnessed the power of the press to create a migration fever that spread to virtually every city, town, and farming community in the South. The African American men and women who heeded Abbott's call created new black urban centers in the North that have remained firmly in place, while continuing to grow both in size and impact, since that time.

Robert S. Abbott's successful effort to transform the lives of half a million people—not to mention the lives of their children and their children's children—was so remarkable that his leadership of the mass movement has assumed legendary status. Scholars who have studied the 3,000 African American newspapers that have been published during the last 200 years have repeatedly singled out the *Chicago Defender*'s role in the Great Migration as the most extraordinary achievement in the entire history of this most prolific of advocacy presses.[49]

9 DEMANDING WIDER ACCESS TO BIRTH CONTROL INFORMATION

In the early years of the twentieth century, most abortions were not only illegal but also extremely dangerous, as they often were performed by unlicensed "doctors" under unsafe and unsanitary conditions. But giving birth to numerous children was also a concern because of the physical toll that multiple pregnancies took on the mother and the fact that many parents—especially immigrants who worked in low-paying jobs—could not afford to feed and clothe a large number of children. And yet, despite the dual problems with abortions and unrestricted childbirth, for a woman to prevent herself from becoming pregnant was considered a violation of the laws of both God and nature. Printed information about sex education was branded filthy and obscene, and anyone who dared to send such material through the U.S. mail faced a $5,000 fine and five years in prison.[1]

It was in this repressive climate that a petite and delicately feminine mother with three small children and all the comforts of the upper class—her husband was an architect, and they lived in an affluent suburban community—founded a dissident magazine dedicated to enlightening its readers about a term that the editor herself coined when she used it in her first issue: birth control.[2]

In 1914 when Margaret Sanger began publishing *Woman Rebel*, she was arrested and denounced as a menace to society. Although law enforcement officials suppressed the magazine and she was compelled to flee from the United States and live apart from her family, Sanger was not deterred from her mission. When she returned from exile, she founded a second magazine, *Birth Control Review*, to resume her campaign of social insurgency. Indeed, despite opposition from pulpits, courtrooms, newsrooms, and a whole phalanx of fears, myths, pruderies, and dragons of morality that purported to speak for civilized America, Sanger succeeded in publishing her birth control magazines for a quarter of a century while simultaneously founding and leading the Birth Control Movement.

In the inaugural issue of *Woman Rebel*, Sanger wrote that she was creating the radical monthly because she believed that women were enslaved by motherhood, by childbearing, "by middle-class morality, by customs, laws and superstitions." To liberate women from that slavery, Sanger wrote, "It will be the aim of the *Woman Rebel* to advocate the prevention of conception."[3]

But Sanger did not stop there.

She demanded that women be allowed to control both their bodies and their minds. "I believe that deep down in woman's nature lies slumbering the spirit of revolt," she wrote. "Woman's freedom depends upon awakening that spirit of revolt within her against these things which enslave her." In a dramatic front-page manifesto that ran just below her magazine's bare-knuckled editorial motto "No Gods No Masters," Sanger boldly stated, "The aim of this journal will be to stimulate working women to think for themselves and to build up a conscious fighting character." Sanger challenged women "to look the whole world in the face with a go-to-hell look in the eyes" and "to speak and act in defiance of convention."[4]

With those mutinous words, Margaret Sanger—a woman who was so meek in appearance that observers said she seemed "about as dangerous as a little brown wren"—set out on the odyssey that transformed her into an icon among feminists and humanitarians alike. Throughout her journey, the core of Sanger's message would remain the same: Women need information about birth control.[5]

To a degree reminiscent of the abolitionist press being synonymous with William Lloyd Garrison and the anti-lynching press being synonymous with Ida B. Wells-Barnett, the story of the birth control press is the story of Margaret Sanger.

EMERGENCE OF A WOMAN REBEL

Margaret Higgins was born in 1879 into a devout Catholic family headed by Michael Higgins, a stonecutter who operated his own business, and Anne Higgins, a homemaker who cared for the family's Corning, New York, home.[6]

Although Margaret initially studied at a private boarding school, her mother's chronic tuberculosis grew so severe that the girl was brought home to care for her younger siblings. Margaret's earliest childhood memory was of a mother wasting away because constant pregnancies—she gave birth to eleven children and lost seven more to miscarriages—prevented her from gaining the physical strength necessary to resist the disease that afflicted her. "My mother died in her forties," Margaret later said with a sense of bitterness, "but my father enjoyed life till he was in his eighties."[7]

At age nineteen, Margaret enrolled in nursing school. Her soft brown eyes and abundance of charm and wit, however, attracted so many young men that she struggled to remain focused on her studies. Six months after meeting William Sanger, the most persistent of her suitors, she dropped out of school and married him. For the next eight years, the Sangers lived in a spacious home in fashionable Hastings-on-Hudson just up the river from New York City. William worked the long hours that were expected of a young architect in the prestigious firm of McKim, Mead & White; Margaret assumed the role of supportive wife and mother, producing and caring for two sons and a daughter.

By 1910, the four walls of the Sanger home had become too confining for

This photo from the falsified passport issued to "Bertha Watson" allowed Margaret Sanger to travel under an alias during her year of exile in Europe. (Courtesy Sophia Smith Collection, Smith College)

Margaret, so she began working for the Visiting Nurses Association. The job took her into the immigrant tenements on New York's Lower East Side, revealing a pathos of poverty and human deprivation previously unknown to her.

Working-class women, Sanger quickly learned, often had no idea how to avoid becoming pregnant, even though upper-class women such as herself were fully aware of several options. Pharmacies sold rubber condoms that could be placed over a man's penis and rubber shields that could be placed in a woman's vagina. Doctors and nurses also could fit women with diaphragms, and women themselves could use sponges and spermicidal douches, powders, and jellies. More basic methods included a man withdrawing his penis before ejaculation and couples practicing the rhythm method of avoiding intercourse during fertile phases of the woman's menstrual cycle—and yet many working-class women were totally unaware of these precautions against pregnancy.

Soon after Sanger began her job as a visiting nurse, she met Sadie Sachs. The young Jewish immigrant had three children and was dangerously ill from blood poisoning brought on by an illegal abortion. By giving Sachs around-the-clock attention for three weeks solid, Sanger nursed her back to health. When Sachs had regained her health, she begged her doctor to tell her how to avoid another pregnancy, but he refused; to provide information about contraception was against the law—even for a doctor. Three months later, Sanger returned to find Sachs weakened by yet another abortion. Sadie Sachs's subsequent death, at the age of thirty, propelled Sanger to abandon nursing in pursuit of fundamental social change. "A moving picture rolled before my eyes," she later recalled. "Women writhing in travail to bring forth babies, the babies themselves naked and hungry, wrapped in newspapers to keep them from the cold. I could bear it no longer." Sanger then made the pledge that charted the course that would dominate the rest of her life: "Women should have knowledge of contraception. I will strike out—I will scream from the housetops."[8]

Sanger began screaming by writing about sex education for the *New York Call*, a socialist newspaper. In her "What Every Girl Should Know" column, Sanger tackled taboo topics—from pregnancy and abortion to menstruation and masturbation—with a candor totally at odds with the conservative mores of proper society.

A piece on venereal disease attracted the most attention, as it provoked a response from Anthony Comstock. During his forty years as U.S. Post Office Inspector, the country's most notorious public censor had convicted some 3,000 men and women on obscenity charges. Comstock banned Sanger's February 1913 column, prompting the *Call* to publish an empty box below the headline "What Every Girl Should Know—Nothing: by order of the U.S. Post

Office." It took several weeks of legal wrangling before the column finally made it into print.[9]

Sanger's confrontation with Comstock catapulted her into the public spotlight while at the same time strengthening her resolve to make sex-education information available to the poor women who so desperately needed it. After several months of talking with the various voices of political and cultural ferment who were living in bohemian New York City, Sanger founded the magazine that would win her a place in the history of the dissident press.

The first issue of *Woman Rebel* appeared in March 1914, and it was immediately evident that Sanger had succeeded in her stated goal of making her publication "red and flaming." The eight-page magazine berated the criminal sanctions imposed on contraception and attacked the institutions of marriage and motherhood as negative forces that limited women's opportunities. Sanger looked beyond economic and political arguments to promote an autonomy for women that required wholesale change in attitude and behavior.[10]

Sanger's rebellious tone ensured that at least the outlines of her message would be heard beyond the few hundred people who subscribed to *Woman Rebel* because a spate of sensational news stories in the mainstream press expressed outrage at her journalistic venture. Establishment papers called Sanger a "vile menace" and "raving maniac" who was "determined to explode dynamite under the American home," while they declared her campaign for wider access to birth control information "brazen heresy." The archetype comment in the daily press appeared in a *Pittsburgh Sun* editorial about *Woman Rebel*: "The thing is nauseating."[11]

The most significant response came from Comstock. He confiscated the first issue and notified Sanger that he would prosecute her if she continued to publish her magazine. She defied the ruling by editing more issues of *Woman Rebel*, surreptitiously dropping copies into mailboxes throughout the city in an effort to avoid detection. In August 1914, police arrested her on felony counts for publishing nine specific articles deemed to be indecent. The charges carried a combined sentence of forty-five years in prison.

As Sanger's October trial date approached and her erstwhile supporters— doctors, socialists, feminists—all abandoned her, she decided to flee from the authorities and live abroad until the political climate at home improved, even though that meant allowing *Woman Rebel* to die. It was not surprising that she was willing to separate from her husband, as their love had faded and she had begun an affair with Walter Roberts, a poet and journalist, in 1913. More difficult to understand was Sangert's decision to leave New York without even saying goodbye to her three small children—Stuart was ten, Grant six, Peggy four.[12]

THE WOMAN REBEL

NO GODS NO MASTERS

VOL I.   MARCH 1914   NO. 1.

THE AIM

This paper will not be the champion of any "ism."

All rebel women are invited to contribute to its columns.

The majority of papers usually adjust themselves to the ideas of their readers but the WOMAN REBEL will obstinately refuse to be adjusted.

The aim of this paper will be to stimulate working women to think for themselves and to build up a conscious fighting character.

An early feature will be a series of articles written by the editor for girls from fourteen to eighteen years of age. In this present chaos of sex atmosphere it is difficult for the girl of this uncertain age to know just what to do or really what constitutes clean living without prudishness. All this slushy talk about white slavery, the man painted and described as a hideous vulture pouncing down upon the young, pure and innocent girl, drugging her through the medium of grape juice and lemonade and then dragging her off to his foul den for other men equally as vicious to feed and fatten on her enforced slavery — surely this picture is enough to sicken and disgust every thinking woman and man, who has lived even a few years past the adolescent age. Could any more repulsive and foul conception of sex be given to adolescent girls as a preparation for life than this picture that is being perpetuated by the stupidly ignorant in the name of "sex education"?

If it were possible to get the truth from girls who work in prostitution to-day, I believe most of them would tell you that the first sex experience was with a sweetheart or through the desire for a sweetheart or something impelling within themselves, the nature of which they knew not, neither could they control. Society does not forgive this act when it is based upon the natural impulses and feelings of a young girl. It prefers the other story of the grape juice procurer which makes it easy to shift the blame from its own shoulders, to cast the stone and to evade the unpleasant facts that it alone is responsible for. It sheds sympathetic tears over white slavery, holds the often mythical procurer up as a target, while in reality it is supported by the misery it engenders.

If, as reported, there are approximately 35,000 women working as prostitutes in New York City alone, is it not sane to conclude that some force, some living, powerful, social force is at play to compel these women to work at a trade which involves police persecution, social ostracism and the constant danger of exposure to venereal diseases. From my own knowledge of adolescent girls and from sincere expressions of women working as prostitutes inspired by mutual understanding and confidence I claim that the first sexual act of these so-called wayward girls is partly given, partly desired yet reluctantly so because of the fear of the consequences together with the dread of lost respect of the man. These fears interfere with mutuality of expression —the man becomes conscious of the responsibility of the act and often refuses to see her again, sometimes leaving the town and usually denouncing her as having been with "other fel-

lows." His sole aim is to throw off responsibility. The same uncertainty in these emotions is experienced by girls in marriage in as great a proportion as in the unmarried. After the first experience the life of a girl varies. All these girls do not necessarily go into prostitution. They have had an experience which has not "ruined" them, but rather given them a larger vision of life, stronger feelings and a broader understanding of human nature. The adolescent girl does not understand herself. She is full of contradictions, whims, emotions. For her emotional nature longs for caresses, to touch, to kiss. She is often as well satisfied to hold hands or to go arm in arm with a girl as in the companionship of a boy.

It is these and kindred facts upon which the WOMAN REBEL will dwell from time to time and from which it is hoped the young girl will derive some knowledge of her nature, and conduct her life upon such knowledge.

It will also be the aim of the WOMAN REBEL to advocate the prevention of conception and to impart such knowledge in the columns of this paper.

Other subjects, including the slavery through motherhood; through things, the home, public opinion and so forth, will be dealt with.

It is also the aim of this paper to circulate among those women who work in prostitution; to voice their wrongs; to expose the police persecution which hovers over them and to give free expression to their thoughts, hopes and opinions.

And at all times the WOMAN REBEL will strenuously advocate economic emancipation.

THE NEW FEMINISTS

That apologetic tone of the new American feminists which plainly says "Really, Madam Public Opinion, we are all quite harmless and perfectly respectable" was the keynote of the first and second mass meetings held at Cooper Union on the 17th and 20th of February last.

The ideas advanced were very old and time-worn even to the ordinary church-going woman who reads the magazines and comes in contact with current thought. The "right to work," the "right to ignore fashions," the "right to keep her own name," the "right to organize," the "right of the mother to work"; all these so-called rights fail to arouse enthusiasm because to-day they are all recognized by society and there exist neither laws nor strong opposition to any of them.

It is evident they represent a middle class woman's movement; an echo, but a very weak echo, of the English constitutional suffragists. Consideration of the working woman's freedom was ignored. The problems which affect the

Although the format was conventional, the name *Woman Rebel* and the editorial motto "No Gods No Masters" clearly defined Margaret Sanger's first magazine as a member of the dissident press.

During 1915, Sanger lived in Europe under the *nom de guerre* "Bertha Watson." She devoted her days to research at health institutions in France and England, which were more enlightened about contraception than was the United States. At night, the winsome "Bertha" enjoyed a carefree life with one or the other of her two lovers. The first was a Spanish radical named Lorenzo Portet, the second the distinguished British psychologist Havelock Ellis—both men were married at the time, as was Sanger.[13]

After a year abroad, she returned to New York partly because she had premonitions about her daughter suffering from poor health. The mother's instincts proved all too prescient when Peggy contracted pneumonia a month after her mother came back to the United States. Peggy's death late that year had major impact on Sanger's personal life, as her two young sons both blamed their sister's death on their mother's prolonged absence. Sanger placed both boys in boarding school.

Sanger's legal problems evolved more satisfactorily. After she returned to America, the beautiful and articulate woman became the toast of the country's social and intellectual elite. With such prominent supporters as authors Pearl S. Buck and H. G. Wells, philanthropist Juliet Rublee, society matrons Frances Tracy Morgan and Alva Smith Vanderbilt Belmont, and suffragist Harriet Stanton Blatch (Elizabeth Cady Stanton's daughter), Sanger took on the aura of a celebrity whose every legal maneuver produced a flurry of news stories. Government prosecutors became concerned that Sanger would become a popular martyr, so they dropped all charges.

Buoyed by that victory and her growing public profile, Sanger orchestrated a massive campaign to make contraceptive material available to all women. The diminutive Sanger—she stood only five feet tall and weighed barely 100 pounds—led mass rallies on the streets of New York and then set off on a national speaking tour that included some 120 lectures.

In October 1916, Sanger rented a building in the Brownsville section of Brooklyn to establish the country's first birth control clinic. This defiant act led to her immediate arrest, as she had broken the law by disseminating birth control information. Found guilty under the Comstock laws, Sanger spent thirty days in the Queens County Penitentiary.

Sanger's time in jail was not in vain. The judge who ruled that she had broken the law wrote in his decision that, while laypersons such as Sanger did not have the legal right to dispense contraceptive advice, licensed physicians did. Sanger had, in short, succeeded in opening the door that previously had been securely barred. No longer would doctors have to fear being sent to jail for responding to pleas such as the one by Sadie Sachs.

In February 1917, Sanger founded her second monthly magazine. "Birth control is the most vital issue before the country today," she wrote in the inaugural issue. "The men and women of America are demanding that this vitally needed knowledge be no longer withheld from them, that the doors to health, happiness, and liberty be thrown open and they be allowed to mould their lives, not at the arbitrary command of church or state, but as conscience and judgment may dictate."[14]

Birth Control Review was a continuation of *Woman Rebel*, although solid financial and political support from Sanger's well-heeled benefactors ensured that the second publication would survive far longer than the first, ultimately being published without interruption for twenty-three years. The combined content of the two magazines articulated the themes that defined the social movement she had ignited.

PROVIDING VITAL INFORMATION TO WORKING-CLASS WOMEN

During Sanger's many years as a dissident journalist, she would repeat the central premise of her movement hundreds of times. The first of those instances came in the lead editorial of the first issue of *Woman Rebel* in 1914. The headline read "The Prevention of Conception," and the editorial itself began with Sanger asking the disarmingly simple question: "Is there any reason why woman should not receive clean, harmless, scientific knowledge on how to prevent conception?" Sanger then continued, "The woman of the upper class has all available knowledge and implements to prevent conception, but the woman of the people is left in ignorance of this information." The intrepid editor went on to tell how only upper-class women had access to the subrosa grapevine of information about birth control, forcing working-class women to turn to "bloodsucking men with M.D. after their names" who performed abortions in shadowy back alleys with "no semblance of privacy or sanitation."[15]

Sanger concluded her editorial by exposing the real reason, in her mind, that the financiers and industrialists who ran the United States conspired to deny birth control information to the underclass: Capitalism would survive only as long as poor women continued to produce masses of children who did not receive proper educations and were thereby doomed to become the next generation of laborers to grind away their lives in the nation's factories. "No plagues, famines or wars could ever frighten the capitalist class," Sanger wrote, "so much as the universal practice of the prevention of conception."[16]

The "little brown wren" did not mellow as the years passed. Indeed, Sanger became even more vehement in her demand that women on the lowest rungs of the socioeconomic ladder be told how to prevent pregnancy. In a 1920 *Birth Control Review* editorial titled "A Birth Strike To Avert World Famine," she took one of the most radical steps in a career paved with many of them, calling for every woman in America to pledge that not a single baby would be born anywhere in the country for the next five years. "Each woman who is awake to the true situation," Sanger insisted, "should make it her first task to encourage and to assist her sisters in avoiding child bearing until the world has had an opportunity to readjust itself."[17]

The impassioned editor did not limit her campaign to her own words only but also opened the pages of her magazines to her readers. "The following letters are published to illustrate the deep interest in and widespread demand among women of the working class for knowledge concerning birth control," Sanger said in a note above a typical batch of letters. A California woman wrote: "Enclosed find ten cents, for information of how to prevent conception. I am nearly crazy with worry from month to month." An Illinois woman made the same request: "I am the mother of six children. I am not well enough to have any more. Will you please send me information so I can prevent me having another child."[18]

Sanger responded to the plaintive cries in two ways. *Woman Rebel* and *Birth Control Review* continually denounced the laws that made it illegal to provide women with birth control information. The founder of the Birth Control Movement wrote that her magazine did not print contraceptive information because, "It is illegal in this country to give such information. This law is obsolete, pernicious, and injurious to the individual, the community and the race. The law must be changed."[19]

Sanger's second form of response was direct and immediate. When a reader requested contraceptive information, Sanger sent back a personal letter advising the woman where she could find the answers she needed. In most cases, that meant providing the name and address of the nearest physician willing to provide birth control material. If the woman was isolated from all sympathetic doctors, Sanger herself sent the requested information—thereby breaking the law.

CONTRIBUTING TO THE ILLS OF SOCIETY

Supplying working-class women with birth control information would not only ease the difficulties that individual women faced, Sanger contended, but also would help alleviate a long list of social ills that plagued American society.

DECEMBER, 1922   20 CENTS

BIRTH CONTROL
REVIEW

Edited by Margaret Sanger

Official Organ of
THE AMERICAN BIRTH CONTROL LEAGUE, Inc., 104 Fifth Avenue, New York City

One of the fundamental messages of the birth control press was that ignorance of contraceptive methods condemns a mother to the deprivation of a family larger than she can reasonably support.

Paramount among those problems was poverty. As long as poor women remained ignorant of how to prevent pregnancy, Sanger insisted, they would continue to give birth to more children than they could afford to raise and therefore would have to endure lives of hardship and desperation—as would their children. Typical was an article Sanger wrote for *Woman Rebel*, titled "A

Little Lesson for Those Who Ought to Know Better," that used an easy-to-follow format consisting of brief questions and correspondingly brief answers. The piece asked: "Why should people only have small families?" And then answered: "In order to be able to feed, clothe, house and educate their children properly." Sanger sprinkled such simple and succinct statements throughout her magazines. A piece titled "Can You Afford to Have a Large Family?" included the sentence: "Science teaches us that there are innocent but safe methods by which parents can control the size of their family," and an article titled "Into the Valley of Death—for What?" included the sentence: "As long as the working class bears children, this fact alone will keep it in poverty."[20]

Closely related to economic deprivation was the problem of prostitution. Young women still in their teens or early twenties who found themselves with two or three tiny mouths to feed, Sanger wrote, still longed to wear the "pretty colored ribbons, fluffy lace, bangles, beads and bracelets" that were the trappings of single girls of the same age. Many young women who struggled to balance their responsibilities as mothers against their desires as young women, Sanger continued, eventually sold their bodies as prostitutes, thereby becoming more victims of capitalism's "cruel system of ignorance and greed."[21]

The most dire item on Sanger's list of shameful social ills was abortion. For while the guiding spirit of the Birth Control Movement encouraged women to prevent unwanted births, she adamantly opposed ending human life after the point of conception. Sanger's objection evolved not from moral concerns but from fear about the physical well-being of women who aborted their unborn babies. Of the 150,000 abortions that occurred in the United States annually during the early years of the twentieth century, one in six ended in the woman's death. "Abortions, with their horrible consequences, would be quite needless and unnecessary if the subject of preventive means were open to all to discuss and use," Sanger wrote. "What a wholesale lot of misery, expense, unhappiness and worry will be avoided when women shall possess the knowledge of prevention of conception!"[22]

ACCESS TO BIRTH CONTROL AS A FEMINIST ISSUE

Throughout her quarter century as a dissident journalist, Sanger relentlessly championed a proposition that is still controversial today but in the early twentieth century was nothing short of heresy: A woman should have the right to control her own body.

In a statement that could just as easily appear in a women's liberation publication today, Sanger wrote on the front page of *Woman Rebel* almost a century ago: "A woman's body belongs to herself alone. It is her body. It does not belong to the United States of America." Relating the issue to a woman's right to have access to birth control, Sanger continued, "Enforced motherhood is the most complete denial of a woman's right to life and liberty."[23]

Not surprisingly, Sanger's ahead-of-her-time position on the issue of reproductive rights was at odds with the Catholic Church that she had grown up in but had later abandoned. "The Catholic Church is one of the greatest enemies against the achievement of woman's economic, intellectual and sexual independence," she wrote. "The Church denies personal liberty to women." In one article, Sanger even went so far as to accuse Catholic priests of opposing birth control solely to counteract their own "impotency anxiety."[24]

The most frustrating of the conflicts that grew out of Sanger's unyielding support of a woman's right to control her own body was with most feminists. Sanger derided the Women's Rights Movement as "sadly lacking in vitality, force, and conviction" because its platform was limited to what she considered to be the "frivolous" concerns of middle- and upper-class women, such as winning "the right to ignore fashions." Sanger supported a much more militant agenda, insisting that "women's organizations will never make much progress until they recognize the fact that women cannot be on an equal footing with men until they have full and complete control of their reproductive functions."[25]

DEFYING OBSCENITY LAWS

Sanger knew when she entered the rough-and-tumble world of advocacy journalism that her publishing effort would provoke legal action against her. The lead editorial of the premier issue of *Woman Rebel* in March 1914 ended with Sanger acknowledging that discussing contraception in print was illegal, followed by a pair of rhetorical questions that virtually dared post office officials to arrest her: "Is it not time to defy this law? And what fitter place could be found than in the pages of the WOMAN REBEL?"[26]

The second issue contained equally brazen references to *Woman Rebel*'s intentional flouting of obscenity laws, with Sanger beginning the lead story with several mocking statements: "The Postmaster did not like the first number of the *Woman Rebel*. He is empowered by the federal government to stop the circulation of any printed expression of honest convictions. It is a crime to have honest convictions in these United States." Sanger's rhetorical burlesque continued: "The *Woman Rebel* realizes that the Post Office is always 'right,' since it has the monopolized power to enforce that 'right.' Therefore the *Woman Rebel*, humbled and repentant, curtseys coyly to the Postmaster and apologizes for the expression of any opinion that is unmailable."[27]

Neither the subsequent suppression of *Woman Rebel* nor Sanger's arrest on obscenity charges diminished the editor's defiance. The July issue contained more jeering. "If you fail to receive any number of this magazine," Sanger told her readers, "you may conclude that the United States Post Office has decided that it is not fit for you to read. We suggest that all readers write to the Postmaster General and express appreciation for the kindly interest taken by the Post Office in keeping you pure and virtuous by prohibiting you from reading any matter that is adulterated with the truth. Our benign Government is certain that the truth is not only poisonous but obscene."[28]

In the final issue of *Woman Rebel* that Sanger edited before fleeing to Europe, she again attacked the inanity of birth control information being censored. A front-page story told how Sanger had been arrested and was scheduled to be tried. The mocking tone was now absent, but Sanger's insolence remained very much intact. "We are witnessing the arch-hypocrisy of the United States flattering itself upon its 'civilization' yet stamping out every glimmer of intelligence, and stifling any honest expression of thought."[29]

"THE OUTSTANDING SOCIAL WARRIOR OF THE CENTURY"

At the same time that Sanger was promoting her cause through her magazines, she was continuing to lead the social movement that she had founded. She was the driving force behind a series of national birth control conferences, and in 1922 she incorporated the American Birth Control League as a non-profit charitable institution that provided services to individual women and also encompassed public education, legislative reform, and medical research related to contraception. Within a decade, the league had grown to include scores of clinics nationwide.[30]

Sanger's personal life continued to be as nonconformist as the social movement she led. During her early years of editing *Birth Control Review*, she had an affair with Billy Williams, a former reporter who helped her raise money. In 1920, she had sexual liaisons with Hugh de Selincourt, a handsome and debonair novelist, and H. G. Wells, the novelist and essayist who had reached the pinnacle of his career as one of the best known writers in the world.[31]

Sanger's personal life settled down—up to a point—in 1921 after she met Noah Slee, a millionaire businessman who owned the company that manufactured Three-in-One household oil. Although Slee had been married for thirty years, he was instantly beguiled by Sanger. Slee and Sanger then divorced their spouses, married each other, and began a new life together in a long, rambling stone house overlooking a lake in upstate New York.

Sanger and Slee made an improbable couple. She tended to be irreverent and fun-loving, he staid and sober. She was an atheist, he a pillar of the Episcopal Church. She was a member of the Socialist Party, he a Republican. Although she bewildered and often exasperated him, he found her irresistible. She gave him satisfaction in love, and he provided her with ample funds to pour into her magazine. Slee also was generous with Sanger's two sons, helping finance their college educations.[32]

On their wedding day, Slee signed an agreement that his wife would, in all respects, maintain her personal freedom as well as her own name. Throughout more than twenty years of marriage, which ended only with Slee's death in 1943, he held to this contract. The extent to which Slee was aware of his wife's affairs with numerous men during their marriage—including Wells, de Selincourt, journalist Harold Child, and businessman Angus Sneed MacDonald—is not clear.[33]

Sanger's infidelity was not widely known at the time, and New York's high society continued to support her. Indeed, the Birth Control Movement's most beneficent patrons were the wealthy socialites who had been entranced by the charming and diminutive woman who wore simple and classic little black dresses—"The more radical the ideas," Sanger believed, "the more conservative you must be in your dress."[34]

By the mid-1920s, the dissident editor was being lionized in the national press as a brave clarion of social progress. "She is, by far, now and from the beginning, the ablest and the most effective friend that the cause of Birth Control has ever had," gushed the tony *New Yorker* magazine in a 1925 profile. "To see her, one is astounded at her youth, at her prettiness, her gentleness, her mild, soft voice." Even more important than the praise of Sanger was the positive treatment that the subject of birth control had begun to receive in the mainstream press—largely because of its founder. The *New Yorker* led the way, saying, "She has carried her crusade for birth control through from the time when simply to mention it was to invite imprisonment to the time when, ten years later, it has every contour of calm respectability." Other publications followed suit. In 1926, the *New York Times* wrote facetiously that "the terrible Margaret Sanger whom thousands of the pious have been taught to regard as the female

Antichrist" was, in reality, "engaged in no more iniquitous enterprise than the effort to help people be happy."[35]

This flattering press coverage helped establish Sanger as a popular lecturer. Billed by her booking agent as "The Outstanding Social Warrior of the Century," she crisscrossed the country addressing civic and women's groups while simultaneously helping to create dozens of local birth control clinics. Passage of the Nineteenth Amendment giving women the right to vote, in 1920, added to the momentum of her cause; having finally cleared the suffrage hurdle, even moderate feminists were then willing to adopt winning a woman's right to control her own body as their next goal.

But still, Sanger continued to pay a high price for the headway she was making. On numerous occasions, she made advance arrangements to speak in a particular city but then discovered, shortly before the appointed hour, that local law enforcement officials had canceled the reservation she had made at the designated auditorium. In each case, she fought the efforts to muzzle her by facing down the authorities, often by speaking from the steps of city hall or the police station. Although her audacity netted her an arrest on charges of disorderly conduct, she accepted the citation gladly. For she ultimately succeeded in drawing an even larger crowd than she would have had she been allowed to speak at the auditorium she had initially reserved.

And the progress continued.

By the early 1930s and as *Birth Control Review*'s circulation topped 30,000, both Sanger and her cause were being embraced by large segments of the public. In 1931, the American Woman's Association awarded Sanger its prestigious medal of honor in recognition of her "vision, integrity and valor." The accompanying citation read: "Margaret Sanger has devoted her life to the highest of all pursuits, the betterment of social welfare. She has opened the door of knowledge and thereby given light, freedom, and happiness to thousands caught in the tragic meshes of ignorance. She is re-making the world." The *New York Herald Tribune* promptly ran an editorial labeled "She Deserves It" that read: "Mrs. Sanger has carved, almost single-handed and in the face of every variety of persecution, a trail through the densest jungle of human ignorance and helplessness. Her victory is not by any means complete, but the dragons are on the run."[36]

This support from the public and the media propelled birth control onto the national agenda. Once placed in that spotlight and with Sanger's loud and dogged advocacy, the triumphs began. In 1930, the Anglican Church reversed its long-standing position and officially sanctioned the use of contraception, and a year later the Church of Christ did the same. In 1935, the General Federation of

Women's Clubs gave its support, as did the Young Women's Christian Association. And then came the watershed year of 1936. First a national poll found that seventy percent of Americans supported the use of birth control, and then a landmark legal decision by a New York Appeals Court reinterpreted the Comstock laws to establish that birth control information was not obscene and, therefore, could be distributed through the mail.

Each time mainstream news organizations recorded one of these victories, they gave due credit to Sanger—and then competed to see which of them could sing her praises loudest. *Time* magazine dubbed Sanger "tireless," and *The Nation* weighed in with "valiant." *Life* magazine ran a four-page photo essay chronicling Sanger's life and bubbling, "That there are today 320 birth control clinics in the U.S. is due largely to this single-minded woman's ceaseless efforts." The *New York World-Telegram* applauded Sanger's "fiery belligerence" that had successfully transformed a "frail, sweet-faced" mother into the "general" at the vanguard of the Birth Control Movement.[37]

A LEGEND IN HER OWN LIFETIME

Many dissident journalists do not live long enough to witness how their revolutionary ideas filter into the mainstream of American thought. Margaret Sanger did.

By the time the editor of *Woman Rebel* and *Birth Control Review* died of arteriosclerosis in 1966, at the age of eighty-seven, birth control had become an accepted element in modern-day life. One out of every three non-Catholic American women of child-bearing age was routinely using an oral contraceptive, and an untold number of others were using diaphragms or interuterine devices. What's more, the American Birth Control League that Sanger had founded in 1922 and had transformed into Planned Parenthood in 1946 was operating hundreds of centers nationwide—plus ninety projects outside the United States.

Sanger was also instrumental in the development of the birth control pill. At a masterfully orchestrated dinner party in 1951, she introduced Katharine McCormick, the wealthy daughter-in-law of the inventor of the mechanical reaper, to Gregory Pincus, a fertility expert who ran a small and underfunded research institute. By evening's end, McCormick wrote Pincus the first of many hefty checks bearing her signature. And nine years later, Pincus brought the Sanger-inspired dream of the "perfect" contraceptive to fruition.

Although it would be an exaggeration to attribute all of these successes and the complete sea change in America's attitude toward contraception to the "little brown wren," the *New York Times* came close to doing exactly that in the front-page obituary that it ran to record the activist editor's death. "As the originator of the phrase 'birth control' and its best-known advocate, Margaret Sanger survived federal indictment, a jail term, numerous lawsuits, and hundreds of raids on her clinics to live to see much of the world accept her view that family planning is a basic human right."[38]

It would have been difficult for someone reading those laudatory comments to reconcile them with the statements that the nation's leading newspapers had made about Sanger half a century earlier—that she was a "vile menace" and "raving maniac" whose magazine was nothing short of "nauseating."

Beginning in 1914 with the founding of *Woman Rebel* and continuing with an indomitable sense of purpose for the next several decades without retreating a single inch, Sanger used the power of the printed word to give voice to the voiceless and to spearhead her triumphant campaign to convince a recalcitrant America that a woman's right to control conception, her body, and her very self is a right that must be available not only to the upper-class woman who commands wealth and power, such as Margaret Sanger, but also to her poor and powerless working-class sister, such as Sadie Sachs.

DISSIDENT VOICES/COMMON THREADS III

Although the generation of dissident publications that emerged during the early years of the twentieth century consisted of only two genres, that small contingent nevertheless added several more intriguing items to the list of overarching characteristics that define the "voices of revolution."

DISSIDENT JOURNALISTS WHO ARE UNCONVENTIONAL IN THEIR THOUGHTS ALSO TEND TO BE UNCONVENTIONAL IN HOW THEY CONDUCT THEIR PERSONAL LIVES

An editor of a nineteenth-century publication occasionally broke societal taboos—Moses Harman orchestrating the "free marriage" of his sixteen-year-old daughter to his thirty-seven-year-old co-editor of *Lucifer, the Light-Bearer* comes to mind. During the early 1900s, however, such maverick practices moved toward becoming the rule rather than the exception. Both of the journalists who led the dissident press boldly into the twentieth century made personal decisions that defined them as unique individuals—one eccentric, the other notorious.

While Robert S. Abbott was using the *Chicago Defender* to better the lives of oppressed African Americans living in the South, his own personal life was one of conspicuous consumption—grand tours of Europe, a chauffeur-driven Rolls Royce limousine, a mansion filled with expensive antiques. In addition, while Abbott's decision to divorce his first wife to marry his second was unusual, his insistence that both women address him, even in the most intimate of settings, as "Mr. Abbott" was at the very least quirky, and some could justly say *bizarre*. Finally, the dark-skinned Abbott's marriage to women half his age and with skin so light that they could have passed for white also broke social proscriptions that were firmly in place during the early years of the twentieth century—as well as the twenty-first.

Margaret Sanger carried societal rule-breaking to even greater heights, making several decisions that established her as the epitome of the name she gave her first dissident magazine: *Woman Rebel*. Keeping the name "Sanger" when she remarried broke from a long-standing tradition, as did requiring her second husband to agree—in writing—that his wife would maintain her personal freedom during their marriage. These somewhat unusual activities paled in comparison to her decision to engage in multiple sexual affairs during both of her marriages—sometimes juggling two lovers, in addition to her husband, at the same time. Perhaps the decision that arbiters of proper behavior find the most disturbing involved Sanger's children; for a woman to travel to Europe for a year without even saying goodbye to her three children—aged ten, six, and four—was not so much a break with convention as a betrayal of the responsibilities of parenthood.

DISSIDENT JOURNALISTS ON THE VANGUARD OF SOCIAL CHANGE SOMETIMES BECOME SYNONYMOUS WITH THEIR MOVEMENTS

The nineteenth-century dissident press provided two examples of editors who were so committed to eradicating particular evils that they came to personify, in the public mind, those campaigns. William Lloyd Garrison and Ida B. Wells-Barnett were widely known as the chief prophets of, respectively, the anti-slavery and anti-lynching crusades. In the early twentieth century, the two leading dissident editors both assumed—and willingly so—the roles as the very embodiments of the movements they founded.

When African American men and women of the early 1900s thought of the Great Migration, they immediately thought of Robert S. Abbott. Indeed, during the height of the massive demographic shift, southern blacks often sent their letters directly to Abbott, asking not only for his general advice but also for a job and a place to stay when they came to Chicago. Critics of the migration connected it to Abbott as well, making him the target of threatening letters written by hate mongers and of public denunciations by southern politicians—including a U.S. senator from Louisiana who accused Abbott of being the sole cause for blacks abandoning the South. Likewise, when scholars of African American history mention the migration, they immediately cite the dissident editor's catalytic role in it, one writing that Abbott "set the migration in motion" and another identifying him, because of his role in the phenomenon, as "the greatest single force" in the entire 200-year history of African American journalism.

Margaret Sanger is perhaps even more widely connected with the Birth Control Movement. Literally thousands of women addressed their inquiries about contraception not to *Woman Rebel* or *Birth Control Review* but specifically to Sanger. It was not surprising, then, that when Sanger died fifty years after founding the movement, the *New York Times* published her obituary on the front page and labeled the dissident editor the "best-known advocate" of birth control, who had lived long enough "to see much of the world accept her view that family planning is a basic human right." That the names Margaret Sanger and the Birth Control Movement are synonymous has remained securely intact since her death. Any book, article, or encyclopedia entry about birth control—and there have been thousands of them—would be utterly incomplete if it did not describe the central role of the founder of that crusade and the woman who fully deserved the apt appellation: "The Outstanding Social Warrior of the Century."

THE MOST SUCCESSFUL DISSIDENT EDITORS ARE ACCOMPLISHED NOT ONLY AT JOURNALISM AND ACTIVISM BUT ALSO AT DEVELOPING STRATEGY

One stringent gauge of the success of a particular editor's efforts to effect social change is to consider whether he or she witnessed a radical transformation not only in society's thoughts but also in its actions, vis-à-vis the issue at hand, *in his or her own lifetime.* This is such a rigorous standard that perhaps the only dissident editor from the nineteenth century who cleared the bar was William Lloyd Garrison. Further analysis suggests that one of the reasons why the abolitionist editor triumphed so remarkably may have been that he was a masterful provocateur—gaining attention for his cause by, among a long list of techniques, creating media events such as publicly burning the Constitution.

In the early twentieth century, two more editors joined Garrison in this elite category of exceptional dissidents. Abbott and Sanger both saw dramatic change, largely because they also proved their mettle as extraordinarily gifted strategists.

When Abbott's *Chicago Defender* was on the brink of failure, he had the vision to change his tactics and replace the tepid community news that African Americans were accustomed to reading with more spirited content; although the techniques were both untried and controversial, Abbott began lampooning racist government officials, denouncing black oppression, and sensationalizing the news with front-page banner headlines—many of them in bright red ink and huge letters—in keeping with his audacious promise to create "The World's Greatest Weekly." Abbott further demonstrated his talents as a strategist by recruiting black sleeping-car porters to distribute the *Defender* throughout the

South and by producing the militant editorial content that made his paper the country's largest black publishing venture. Spurred on by his success, the dissident editor next developed the successful formula—vilifying the South, glorifying the North, creating "migration fever"—that helped propel hundreds of thousands of African Americans to abandon their homeland and that made Robert S. Abbott a black press legend, as well as a millionaire.

The elements in Margaret Sanger's visionary strategy were also incredibly effective. An early enrollee in the all-publicity-is-good-publicity school of media relations, Sanger readily admitted that she made the content of *Woman Rebel* "red and flaming" to attract comment from the mainstream press; on cue, leading papers across the country responded with a flurry of sensational stories maligning her as a "vile menace" and "raving maniac." Pleased that the stories and editorials had moved birth control into the national spotlight, Sanger continued to play the commercial press like a violin. Writing articles that dared postal officials to arrest her on obscenity charges, giving lectures on the steps of local police stations to ensure that she would be arrested and jailed on disorderly conduct charges, calling for every woman in America to pledge that not a single baby would be born anywhere in the country for five years—they were all examples of Sanger's genius at attracting publicity. Other of her tactics were equally successful. Using her pretty face and diminutive size to full advantage, she donned a simple and classic little black dress when she took her message to members of America's social and intellectual elite, coming away with major financial donations as well as the necessary clout to make birth control an accepted practice.

PART 4
CHANGING THE WORLD IN A
SINGLE GENERATION

Synergy is powerful.

The opposition to U.S. military involvement in Vietnam began in the mid-1950s and steadily grew during the 1960s. That anti-war sentiment was soon joined by a rising momentum to create a counterculture that, in turn, helped impel a generation of defiant young rebels to develop agendas and strategies for securing civil rights for African Americans, for gay men and lesbians, and for women.

All five of these social movements—fueled by the establishment's repression and bigotry—were potent forces in their own right; they represented a remarkable quintet of parallel initiatives of immense import and impact. But, in addition, each of the efforts seeking fundamental change was influenced by the era's palpable sense of uncertainty because of the ominous threat of nuclear holocaust and the back-to-back assassinations of three of the nation's most promising young political leaders.

Also crucial to the strength of these various movements was the energy they drew from each other. Any one of them could have stood as the defining social revolution of the middle to late twentieth century. So when their passion and intensity were combined, they ignited the most explosive period in the entire history of the dissident press in America.

10 OPPOSING AMERICA'S "DIRTY WAR" IN VIETNAM

The self-assurance won so dearly by the victory in World War II began to fade from the American consciousness during the late 1940s, replaced by fear and anxiety. The pervasive Cold War mentality took hold as Eastern Europe came under the grip of communism and the Soviet Union flexed its muscles by detonating an atomic bomb. The most disturbing event of all was the fall of China in 1949. For despite huge infusions of American aid, the Nationalist forces of Chiang Kai-shek withdrew to the island of Taiwan, sacrificing mainland China to communist leader Mao Zedong. A few months later, the United States was again engaged in battle on foreign soil, this time in an effort to prevent Korea from joining the Communist Bloc. The Korean War lasted three years and claimed the lives of 54,000 American soldiers.

A military undertaking that ultimately would create an even darker chapter in American history—indeed, one of the bleakest on record—began to unfold in the early 1950s when President Truman, hoping to establish a democratic beachhead in Southeast Asia, sent military aid to a tiny French colony, 7,000 miles from the United States, known as Vietnam. By 1954, the French had withdrawn and Vietnam was divided in half—a communist government under Ho Chi Minh controlled the North; a purportedly pro-democracy government under Ngo Dinh Diem controlled the South. The American commitment continued, with President Eisenhower sending military personnel—the government called them advisers, critics called them imperialists in uniform. President Kennedy increased the U.S. military presence in Indochina, and President Johnson upped the stakes still higher in 1965 by committing massive American ground troops—within two years, the total exceeded 500,000.

Throughout these various stages of escalating involvement, mainstream American journalists supported the effort, serving as exuberant cheerleaders for the military. This devotion continued, according to scholars who have studied this highly controversial phenomenon, until January 1968 when the North Vietnamese orchestrated the Tet Offensive. Named for the lunar New Year holiday that coincided with it, this well-planned attack resulted in simultaneous assaults on more than 100 sites—virtually every city, town, and military base in South Vietnam. Most noteworthy was the enemy's successful capture of the U.S. Embassy compound in Saigon.[1]

After Tet, the news media criticized U.S. involvement in Vietnam with a vengeance. The climactic moment came in late February when avuncular CBS news anchor Walter Cronkite counseled the viewing public that it was time for Americans to withdraw from Vietnam "not as victors, but as an honorable people who lived up to their pledge to defend democracy, and did the best they could."[2]

Although the Tet Offensive and mainstream news coverage of it unquestionably signaled a pivotal change in public opinion regarding the war, not all journalistic voices had been singing the praises of U.S. involvement before that point. A vociferous anti-war press had begun denouncing the war as early as 1954, with the chorus of criticism growing both in size and decibel level during the early and mid-1960s. Those dissident publications, which ultimately numbered several hundred, not only laid the groundwork for the seismic shift against the Vietnam War in early 1968 but also were a vital force in igniting and then fueling the massive Anti-War Movement that created a second major battlefield in the fighting: the homefront.[3]

Some of the earliest opposition to the war came in the mid-1950s from the pages of the *Catholic Worker*, the voice of pacifist Dorothy Day. The *Worker* was soon joined by *I.F. Stone's Weekly*, the Washington-based newsletter penned by its iconoclastic namesake. Anti-war coverage received a major boost in early 1964 when the *National Guardian* began offering its readers the riveting immediacy of first-hand accounts reported by battlefield correspondent Wilfred Burchett. In the mid-1960s, the movement to end the war gained more momentum still when *Ramparts* magazine provided eye-popping investigative coverage—including the shocking revelations of a disillusioned American soldier and wrenching photographs of suffering Vietnamese children—showing that the fighting really was, as the anti-war press had been insisting for more than a decade, "The Dirty War."[4]

THE *CATHOLIC WORKER* SOUNDS
AN EARLY ALARM

One of the first journalists to question American military involvement in Southeast Asia was Dorothy Day, the legendary radical who still today is remembered as an archetype of political and social dissidence.

Born in Brooklyn in 1897, Day was a beautiful and charismatic young woman whose early life defined hedonism—promiscuity, abortion, attempted suicide, a child born out of wedlock. But then, when Day turned thirty and with her infant daughter's well-being to consider, she changed the course of her life by converting to Roman Catholicism and founding, in 1933, the *Catholic Worker* newspaper.

Committed to social justice in many forms, the New York City monthly became the centerpiece of a social movement that quickly grew to include some 100 "houses of hospitality" that provided—and still provide today—free food and beds to the poor and the homeless in dozens of American cities. The Catholic Worker movement was grounded in the principles of racial equality, individual responsibility, and commitment to the teachings of God and the Catholic Church.

Throughout its long lifespan, the *Catholic Worker*—which continues to be published today—has always sold for one cent. The paper has never carried paid advertising, relying on the kindness and generosity of its supporters. "When we need money," Dorothy Day explained, "we pray for it."[5]

In 1954 and with a national circulation of 60,000, the *Worker* launched its pacifist crusade against the Vietnam War with a front-page editorial. Day had, for many years, expressed her displeasure with the U.S. government spending too much tax revenue on the military and not enough on social programs, and this criticism was the thrust of her pioneering article. "It is not Christianity and freedom we are defending, in the jungles of Vietnam," Day wrote, "but our possessions." Specifically, a third of the rubber coming from Indochina eventually wound up in the United States, Day argued, and America's powerful military-industrial complex was determined that the supply would not be disrupted. It was rubber production rather than humanitarian concern, Day wrote, that had propelled the U.S. military into the obscure nation of Vietnam.[6]

As had been the case since Day had founded the *Catholic Worker* twenty years earlier, she was concerned primarily with the poor and the powerless. In this instance, that placed her focus on the Vietnamese workers and their exploitation by "the Godlessness of our Western materialism." Every peasant—man, woman, and child alike—collected the sap from 200 to 400 rubber trees a day and received a mere forty cents for the back-breaking labor, the venerable editor wrote, and American industrialists had no intention of allowing that situation to change. Day possessed an unshakable belief that God watches out for the most vulnerable of His children, however, and was convinced that the peasants ultimately would triumph over the Western military invaders. "It is the poor of the world, it is the exploited, it is the dominated," she wrote, "that will conquer."[7]

The article was the first of a steady stream of anti-Vietnam War essays that dotted the pages of the *Catholic Worker*. One of the most powerful, titled "The Root of War," denounced the "war-madness that is spreading with a furious contagion all over the world," before going on to say that "of all the countries that are sick," the United States was "the most grievously afflicted." Repeating Day's earlier indictment of the military operation in Vietnam as an example of America "exploiting other people," the article contained such incendiary phrases as "immoral act," "obsession with evil," and "enormous act of murderous destruction." The piece did not stop with name calling, however, but spelled out exactly what the United States had to do. "The first real step toward peace would be a realistic acceptance of the fact that our political ideals are perhaps to a great extent illusions and fictions to which we cling out of motives that are not always perfectly honest."[8]

Besides accusing the nation's leaders of duplicity, the *Catholic Worker* presaged a theme that would become a mainstay of the Anti-War Movement by pointing the finger not just at the generals but also at American politicians. "We will never get anywhere unless we can accept the fact that politics is an inextricable tangle of good and evil motives in which," the paper stated point blank, "the evil predominate."[9]

I. F. STONE'S WEEKLY JOINS THE CAMPAIGN

By the early 1960s, Dorothy Day was not the only aging renegade editor who was using a publication to speak out in opposition to the American military operation in Indochina; she had been joined by another dissident journalist of wide reputation.

Isidor Feinstein "Izzy" Stone, born in Philadelphia in 1907, worked for the *Philadelphia Record* and *New York Post* before gaining national attention as an investigative reporter for the liberal journal *The Nation* in the 1930s and 1940s. The impish Stone—he stood five-foot-seven and had a mischievous grin that seemed more like that of a boy than a man—was never satisfied merely to quote official sources, preferring instead to comb through public documents and then challenge the government's version of the truth.

In 1953, he launched his anti-establishment *I. F. Stone's Weekly* from his Washington, D.C., home. Stone was sometimes criticized for his sizable ego— symbolized by the gall of giving the newsletter his own name—but was far more often praised for his success at ferreting out the facts that the establishment press had missed.

Typical of the *Weekly*'s scoops was a 1958 story that accused the Atomic Energy Commission of lying when it said that underground tests had no effect beyond a very limited range. Stone then mobilized his mainstream journalistic contacts and forced the agency to admit that, in fact, the nuclear tests had wide impact far beyond the detonation site. That incident and others like it boosted the *Weekly*'s circulation above the 70,000 mark, transformed I. F. Stone into a folk hero for the American Left, and guaranteed that his newsletter would be read by the nation's leading shapers of news and public policy.[10]

In the early 1960s, Stone turned his biting editorial commentary on American involvement in Indochina. At the same time that establishment news organizations were vilifying North Vietnam—the *New York Times* referred to the North Vietnamese army as "the encroaching Communist menace," and the major television networks characterized them as "cruel, ruthless, and fanatical"—the *Weekly* filled its pages with criticism of the United States. Stone made reference to the country's "swollen military budget," "perilous delusions," and "threats of destruction."[11]

Many essays in the *Weekly* broke new ground. One of the most significant came when Stone predicted that the U.S. military could not defeat the North Vietnamese, a startling and contentious statement in the wake of World War II and the Korean War. The *Weekly* called the war "a quicksand which could absorb a major share of our youth" and—in a statement that would reverberate for years to come—"a war that cannot be won."[12]

Stone broke from the mainstream journalism pack on other points as well. In 1963, he made the observation—one that myriad journalists would repeat after the Tet Offensive five years later—that the U.S. military's conventional tactics were futile in the unfamiliar terrain of Southeast Asia. Every time American fighters thought they had trapped a group of North Vietnamese soldiers, Stone wrote, the enemy guerrillas would suddenly "melt" into the jungle. "The greatest military power on earth is ineffective," Stone wrote. "Never have so many armed with so much been able to do so little. Super power seems to have become super impotence."[13]

Stone's most stunning allegation came in 1963 and ultimately was confirmed by the release of the controversial Pentagon Papers in 1971: Leaders at the highest level of the U.S. government were sending young American men to their deaths in Southeast Asia not for humanitarian reasons, but for political ones. "Kennedy cannot afford to go into the campaign next year and face a Republican cry that under the Democrats we 'lost' Vietnam," Stone wrote. "The national interest is to be subordinated to the convenience of the political leadership."[14]

On a visual level, the most astonishing element of the war coverage in *I. F. Stone's Weekly* during the early 1960s was the photographs of Vietnamese civilians. One unforgettable image showed a Vietnamese man cradling his young son in his arms. The boy, who was no more than a toddler, stared forlornly into the camera, pieces of skin dangling from his legs, arms, back, and face. Stone wrote that the boy had been burned by napalm, a deadly incendiary that American military leaders swore was used solely to destroy military sites and never was allowed to harm civilians. "We think it [the photo] tells a story every decent American should heed," Stone said. "This is what we are doing to the innocent in Vietnam and Cambodia. We hope you find it revolting."[15]

In early 1962, *I. F. Stone's Weekly* called—in another statement that would be long remembered—for the withdrawal of all U.S. military personnel from Vietnam. After that initial demand, Stone repeatedly and with increasing ferocity urged American officials to negotiate an end to the war as soon as possible, with many of his pronouncements sounding almost identical to the words that Walter Cronkite would use—and that would shake the nation—in 1968. "It is becoming increasingly evident," Stone wrote, "that the undeclared war in Vietnam can and will ultimately be settled only at the conference table."[16]

NATIONAL GUARDIAN PROVIDES ON-SITE REPORTS

Another influential anti-Vietnam War publication originally had been launched in 1948 to support the short-lived Progressive Party, which offered a far-left alternative to the Democrats and Republicans. *National Guardian* founder James Aronson was a disenchanted *New York Times* veteran eager to focus on issues of importance, regardless of their popularity. In the 1950s, the

By publishing this poignant photograph in 1964, *I. F. Stone's Weekly* provided early documentation of the effects that napalm bombing was having on Vietnamese children.

Guardian made a name for itself by spearheading a doomed campaign to save convicted spies Julius and Ethel Rosenberg from execution and by reporting the early stages of the Civil Rights Movement.

By 1963, Aronson had transformed his New York-based weekly into a militant voice in opposition to the war in Southeast Asia. Even though the U.S. government claimed only to be providing the South Vietnamese with "a few" military advisers, the newsweekly reported that the American forces had, in reality, swollen to more than 12,000 soldiers whose "advisory role" included leading daily strafing and napalm bombing missions. The *Guardian* also disclosed that at least sixty-six of the U.S. "advisers" had been killed.[17]

The single most salient point the *National Guardian* made, beginning in early 1963, was one that *I. F. Stone's Weekly* had already made—but that the mandarins of the American press refused to admit for another five years—by stating, without so much as a hint of equivocation, that the United States would never win the war in Indochina. The *Guardian* did not make this weighty pronouncement quietly or subtly, but loudly and repeatedly. "The U.S. cannot win the war," stated one piece; "Victory for the U.S. force is out of the question," said another; "The end of the road in Vietnam will be military defeat," insisted a third.[18]

In a piece labeled "Our 'Dirty War,'" the *Guardian* articulated two reasons for its pessimistic stance vis-à-vis the war. First, as I. F. Stone also had pointed out, American soldiers were unable to fight the kind of guerrilla warfare that the North Vietnamese and rebel Viet Cong waged in the tropical jungles of their homeland. Second, U.S. forces lacked the support of the South Vietnamese people; rather than wanting the United States to help them become a democracy, the majority of the South Vietnamese wanted the Americans to leave—though Washington politicians claimed otherwise.[19]

On a broader scale, the most important contribution the *National Guardian* made was to provide its 25,000 subscribers with breaking news written by the only correspondent reporting from behind the battlelines for an American news organization. Wilfred Burchett was an Australian-born journalist whose articles made some of the most compelling war reporting ever written. Indeed, by early 1964, the *Guardian* was considered essential to the diet not only of the country's leading activists but also of establishment politicians and military leaders.[20]

For while the mainstream American media were characterizing North Vietnam as a backward country whose military was inept and ineffective against the mighty U.S. forces with their sophisticated tactics and advanced technology, Burchett painted a strikingly contradictory picture.

Particularly significant was his account of the North Vietnamese army's 1964 assault on the U.S. airfield at Bien Hoa in South Vietnam. Mainstream American news media had pooh-poohed rumors that the enemy had triumphed, but Burchett provided concrete details that showed the reports were based on incontrovertible fact: The North Vietnamese killed three dozen American "advisers" and destroyed twenty-one B-57 jet bombers worth $25 million— without losing a single man or plane. The *Guardian* correspondent also documented that the North Vietnamese soldiers had received "great help from the local people," thereby reinforcing the paper's editorial stance that the South Vietnamese did not support the U.S. military operation in their country.[21]

Burchett reported similar American defeats at Loc Ninh, at Binh Gia, and in numerous hamlets along the Mekong Delta, while *Guardian* editor James Aronson highlighted the stories with such provocative headlines as "The U.S. myth about Vietnam" and "U.S. debacle in South Vietnam."[22]

So, by mid-February 1964, Aronson had ample support for the bold headline he stripped across the top of the *National Guardian*'s editorial page: "Get out of Vietnam!" In that stunning editorial, the paper used words virtually identical to those that the country's most prestigious newspapers, news magazines, and television networks would begin using four and five years later. "The writing is on the wall for this U.S. mis-adventure in South Vietnam," the *Guardian* wrote. "This is a war the U.S. cannot win. America will spill more blood, destroy more villages, wipe out more rice fields and buffalo, but that is about all." The editorial ended with the statement that was fast becoming the mantra of the anti-war press: "The U.S. must get out and stay out of Vietnam."[23]

Throughout 1965, the *Guardian* continued its drumbeat of dissidence by exposing lies and deceptions that it laid at the feet of America's military and political leaders. The list was long and reprehensible. One article reported that bloodthirsty U.S. pilots went unpunished after purposely aiming their bombs at North Vietnamese schools and hospitals—even though officials continued to insist that air attacks targeted military sites only. Another piece revealed that U.S. military brass had adopted a new strategy to bring the enemy to their knees; American planes were dropping bombs on North Vietnamese sanitariums for lepers and other persons with mental and physical disabilities. Still other stories reported that U.S. bombing targets in North Vietnam had been expanded to farms, markets, and residential districts and to irrigation dams and flood control dikes in the countryside—actions that, according to the *Guardian*, "could cost literally millions of lives."[24]

RAMPARTS TAKES THE CASE TO A MASS AUDIENCE

By 1965, dissident publications opposed to U.S. involvement in Southeast Asia had been raising their objections for more than a decade, and yet the American commitment to the war continued to escalate, with President Johnson sending 175,000 ground troops to Vietnam by year's end. That was also the year that another anti-war publication, this one with a huge circulation, entered the picture.

Ramparts had been a lackluster intellectual Catholic journal that its youthful new editor, Warren Hinckle, was determined to transform into a high-profile muckraking magazine. Hinckle saw taking a stand against the Vietnam War as the perfect vehicle for gaining the national attention that could propel his San Francisco-based monthly, which at the time already had a circulation of 100,000, into the must-read publication he had in mind.

Hinckle launched his campaign against the Indochinese war in July 1965 with a devastating critique titled "The Vietnam Lobby." The ten-page investigative piece offered the first detailed documentation that American involvement in Vietnam was not an impulsive response to communist aggression, as government officials claimed, but a deliberate and long-planned act of American imperialism. The article described how conservative Roman Catholic Cardinal Francis Spellman had groomed the future dictator of South Vietnam, Ngo Dinh Diem, at a New York seminary in the early 1950s and then had lined up support for him in U.S. government and intellectual circles. The *Ramparts* exposé also targeted mainstream press puffery that assured Americans that Diem's regime was an Asian "miracle" and model of democracy—even though Diem was, in reality, totally corrupt. (Diem was involved in so much criminal activity that the United States eventually had to change course and oust him; he was assassinated, on CIA orders, in November 1963.)[25]

Ramparts followed its opening anti-Vietnam War salvo with an even bigger blockbuster, this one a first-person perspective on the war from one of the American military's own. On the cover of the February 1966 issue was emblazoned a photo of a formidable-looking Green Beret with his chest displaying a dazzling collection of medals and ribbons testifying to his bravery and patriotism. In the twelve-page piece that followed, former Master Sergeant Donald Duncan gave an insider's view of the U.S. military in Southeast Asia that was both enlightening and bloodcurdling: American soldiers routinely tortured and killed civilians they suspected of helping North Vietnamese soldiers, white GIs treated African American soldiers with abuse and derision, the United States operated assassination squads to kill leaders in neutral Cambodia, and military officials consistently exaggerated the number of enemy soldiers they had killed—Duncan told of one incident that he was involved in that resulted in the deaths of six Viet Cong, which his superiors inflated to 250. Most shocking of all was Duncan's revelation that the ranks of the Viet Cong that continually attacked American troops consisted primarily not of rebels from North Vietnam, but from South Vietnam—the very people U.S. forces were supposedly defending.[26]

Many of the direct quotations in Duncan's article, which *Ramparts* ballyhooed with full-page ads in major American papers, were nothing short of devastating. "Little by little, as all the facts made their impact on me," Duncan wrote of his experience in uniform, "I had to accept that the position, 'We are in Vietnam because we are in sympathy with the aspirations and desires of the Vietnamese people,' was a lie." Of his eighteen months of active duty in Southeast Asia, Duncan said, "We weren't preserving freedom in South Vietnam. The whole thing was a lie."[27]

The January 1967 issue of *Ramparts* carried another gripping piece in which Dr. Benjamin Spock, the world's most famous baby doctor and an outspoken critic of the war, talked about the one million Vietnamese children who had been killed or wounded. "Not many of them even get to hospitals, which are few and far between," Spock wrote. "Materials for the adequate treatment of burns—gauze, ointments, antibiotics and plasma—are usually non-existent. Flies are in the wounds." Even more heart-wrenching than the words were the sixteen pages of photos that ran with the article. Printed on glossy paper and in full color, the magazine brought the realities of the fighting home to readers as words could not. Pictures of children with burnt flesh and others with bandaged stumps where arms and legs should have been were silent witnesses to the grisly effects of napalm. One little girl had lost an eye, and another had so many open wounds on her face, the product of American shrapnel, that they obscured her other features. A young boy was so grotesque—his eyelids had been burned away and his chin somehow had become grafted to his chest so the boy had no neck whatsoever—that a reader instinctively turned the page quickly.[28]

The stories and photos that *Ramparts* published between 1965 and early 1967 succeeded in providing editor Warren Hinckle with both the attention and the readership that he had hoped. Two years after Hinckle launched his anti-Vietnam War campaign, the magazine's circulation reached 250,000, making it far and away the largest dissident publication in the country at the time—and simultaneously carrying the realities of the war to a significant slice of the American people.

PROMOTING THE CREATION OF AN ANTI-WAR MOVEMENT

During much of the time that the four dissident publications were reporting and denouncing the murder and mayhem that had become standard practice in Indochina, they were simultaneously helping to establish and to fuel the largest and most effective anti-war movement in U.S. history.

One early call for creating a movement to bring the war to an end came in *I. F. Stone's Weekly* in 1962. In the piece, Stone proposed that such a movement be formed and then went on to stipulate that its first action be to investigate the war and thereby discover what Stone was sure would be incriminating documentation to pave the way for withdrawing American forces. The provocateur went on to stipulate exactly who the leaders of the embryonic movement should talk to. "There are plenty of returned Americans, military and civilian, to testify," Stone insisted. "It is time the full truth about the war were told."[29]

Like the generations of dissident journalists who had preceded him, Stone was not satisfied merely to use the printed word to call for a new social movement, as he also became one of the first critics featured at what ultimately swelled into a gigantic wave of anti-war rallies that swept across the American landscape.

Stone was a featured speaker at the march that scholars now consider the first major public demonstration against the Vietnam War. That event in the spring of 1965 drew 25,000 protesters who encircled the White House and then walked to the grounds of the Washington Monument to listen to Stone. In his historic oration, the militant editor compared the anti-Vietnam War activists to the leaders of the American Revolution, telling them it was their patriotic duty to denounce their country's military and political establishments, which Stone labeled "monstrous institutions." Stone urged the demonstrators—about three-fourths of them were college students—to "go home and talk about these things." Later that year, Stone devoted an entire issue of the *Weekly* to celebrating the rapid growth of the Anti-War Movement.[30]

News reports written about that first demonstration made it abundantly clear that dissident publications would cover anti-war protests very differently than mainstream publications would. *I. F. Stone's Weekly* and the other anti-Vietnam War voices promoted upcoming rallies in advance and then provided saturation coverage after the fact, including verbatim transcripts of the speeches that activists had made. Mainstream publications, on the other hand, preferred to focus on more superficial details. Several papers spent space squabbling about the exact number of people who participated in the first rally; even though the police had announced at a press briefing that the crowd numbered 25,000, the *Washington Post* and *Washington Evening Star* argued that the correct figure was 16,000, the *New York Herald Tribune* said 15,000, and the *New York Times* reduced the number to 10,000. But the most important detail, according to the titans of American journalism, was one that *I. F. Stone's Weekly* never even mentioned: how the protesters were dressed and groomed. The *Washington Evening Star* reported a profusion of "tight pants" and "long hair," the *Herald Tribune* thought it important to chronicle an abundance of "dark glasses," "overalls," and " 'beatnik' outfits of oddly cut clothing," and the *Times*, the nation's newspaper of record, weighed in with the observation that the protesters sported an abundance of "blue jeans" and "beards." The *Washington Post* felt compelled to report that, at one point during the rally, one of the 100 counter demonstrators yelled out: " 'Why don't you take baths?' "[31]

By this point in the mid-1960s, *I. F. Stone's Weekly* was no longer alone among dissident journalistic voices in supporting the creation and growth of an Anti-War Movement.

Like Izzy Stone, Dorothy Day was so widely respected by the American Left that she was in demand as a speaker at early anti-Vietnam War rallies. Also like her fellow maverick, Day often reprinted the texts of her speeches in the publication she edited. "The word of God is clear in the New Testament and the Old," Day told 30,000 listeners who gathered at Manhattan's Union Square in late 1965. "Thou shalt not kill, Love your enemies, Overcome evil with good. To love others as He loved us, to lay down our lives for our brothers throughout the world, not to take the lives of men, women, and children, young and old, by bombs and napalm and all the other instruments of war." Despite Day's advanced age—she turned sixty-eight that year—and wide reputation as a pacifist, counter demonstrators heckled her by screaming "Moscow Mary! Moscow Mary!"[32]

It was also in 1965 that Day made headlines nationwide when she, in an editorial in the *Worker*, urged every young man in America to refuse to serve in the armed forces. Making such a statement was highly risky because it was a direct violation of the federal law prohibiting any citizen from encouraging persons facing the draft to refuse service. Conviction would have meant a five-year prison sentence and a $5,000 fine, although Day was never prosecuted.[33]

One of the *National Guardian*'s first statements on behalf of the nascent Anti-War Movement came in early 1964 when editor James Aronson stripped the headline "It's time for a broad U.S. peace movement" across the front page. "There are many thousands of Americans," Aronson wrote in the editorial that followed, "who are deeply committed and eager to act against the war." After throwing his full support behind such a movement, Aronson went on to define its mission and activities, saying that anti-war activists should fight for disarmament, reduced military spending, and an end to the draft. The movement must, Aronson wrote, "oppose the military-industrial network profiting from arms production."[34]

Other *Guardian* pieces reinforced the importance of the Anti-War Movement. "The time is now for every concerned American to demand that the U.S.

government withdraw its forces from South Vietnam," one argued; "Unless we all unite in a great outcry of horror," demanded another, "we shall not waken from the nightmare in time." Many of the essays prescribed specific actions that would be necessary if the movement were to take fire. A typical directive told readers: "Write your representatives in Congress, speak out in your community and your organizations, urge your peace and civic groups, union locals, churches, schoolmates and friends to join your call. You can spark the organization of public meetings of protest, of letter-writing campaigns to your local newspapers, of delegations to your congressmen home for weekends."[35]

Because *Ramparts* published only in-depth investigative pieces, its editorial format was not conducive to promoting the Anti-War Movement—at least not directly. The muckraking magazine's support, however, came blazing through in statements within its articles. The 1966 exposé about Sergeant Donald Duncan's perspective on the Vietnam War, for example, included his thoughts about youthful demonstrators protesting the war even though they had never worn military uniforms. "I think they should be commended," *Ramparts* quoted Duncan as saying. "I had to wait until I was 35 years old, after spending 10 years in the army and 18 months personally witnessing the stupidity of the war before I could figure it out. That these young people were able to figure it out so quickly and so accurately is not only a credit to their intelligence, but a great personal triumph over a lifetime of conditioning and indoctrination."[36]

The men and women involved in the anti-Vietnam War press paid a high price to pursue their crusade. Three of the nation's most powerful communities—politicians, military leaders, and industrialists—all were determined to continue to reap the personal and financial benefits they received from the international conflict. In addition, the elected officials and top generals had no intention of becoming the first men in history to allow the United States to withdraw from a foreign war without full and complete victory. The country's power elite, therefore, brought pressure on the dissidents to cease their journalistic campaign.

National Guardian editor James Aronson later spoke of some of the ways he and his co-workers suffered. Because few businesses were willing to buy advertisements in an anti-war newspaper, the staff members had to live on the same painfully low salaries that persons writing for previous generations of the dissident press had experienced. "Payless paydays" were frequent, Aronson recalled, and the only way most members of the staff were able to survive financially was by having supportive wives or husbands who made decent salaries in their jobs. Other problems were more difficult to overcome. Not only staff members but also their friends and relatives were repeatedly interrogated by

FBI agents, and on many nights those same targeted individuals received phone calls at regular intervals for hours on end—when they answered the phone, the caller hung up. A friend at the telephone company confirmed that government officials tapped the *Guardian*'s telephones, and several reporters and editors had to endure annual audits by the Internal Revenue Service. Hate mail poured into the office, and the local postmaster supplied the federal government with the names of *Guardian* subscribers who then received intimidating phone calls and visits from FBI agents, resulting in hundreds of canceled subscriptions. On several occasions, metal scraps and tools mysteriously appeared in the presses at the plant that printed the paper, forcing costly repairs and production delays.[37]

CHANGING THE CONSCIOUSNESS OF THE AMERICAN PEOPLE

The Tet Offensive in late January 1968 was unquestionably the most significant military action in the war. The pivotal moment in the well-orchestrated assault came when a suicide squad captured the grounds of the supposedly impregnable new U.S. Embassy in Saigon, killing five American soldiers. That action ended after six hours, but heavy fighting continued for ten more days.

Tet's repercussions were huge. Although U.S. forces soon reclaimed the ground taken during the offensive, the reaction on the homefront gave the enemy a psychological victory of monumental importance. Before Tet, U.S. officials had consistently told the American people that victory in Vietnam was imminent. In a major speech in Washington, D.C., two months before the attack, General William C. Westmoreland, commander of U.S. forces, had insisted, "We have reached an important point when the end begins to come into view." The mainstream media had blindly echoed the same upbeat tune, with not a single major newspaper or television network calling for an end to the war. The *Washington Evening Star*'s coverage was typical, assuring its readers in November 1967, "The military war in Vietnam is nearly won."[38]

Tet changed all that. Dramatic televised images of the enemy's takeover of the U.S. Embassy compound shocked both the American public and the mainstream media, which finally realized that they had been duped. Overnight, news organizations that previously had been happy to serve as handmaidens to the government suddenly became harsh critics. Before Tet, editorial commentary by television journalists had run four to one in favor of U.S. policy; after Tet, comments ran two to one against.[39]

The American people quickly followed suit. In one of the most abrupt shifts in public opinion ever recorded, within six weeks after the Tet Offensive, one American in five switched from supporting the war to opposing it. So for the first time in the twenty years of U.S. involvement, a majority of Americans opposed the war. The surge of opposition led President Johnson not to seek re-election and to begin withdrawing troops, leaving a death toll of more than 58,000 Americans and some three to five million Southeast Asians.[40]

While there is no question that the mainstream news media—particularly television—played an enormous role in hastening the end of the most controversial war in American history, by no means did negative coverage of U.S. involvement in Vietnam begin with Tet. For fourteen years before that climactic event, the anti-war press had been criticizing the war—loudly and relentlessly. What's more, those dissident journalistic voices had played a leading role in igniting and then continuing to kindle an Anti-War Movement that became so robust and so widespread that it encompassed a powerful majority of the American public that the political elite could not ignore.

Week after week, month after month, year after year from 1954 until the last American soldier was helicoptered out of Indochina in 1975, the anti-war press devoted its energies to convincing the American people that the war was unconscionable. That effort began with the single pacifist voice of the *Catholic Worker* but gradually, during the early and mid-1960s, gained momentum as *I. F. Stone's Weekly*, the *National Guardian*, and *Ramparts* joined the crusade and lifted the combined circulation of just the four publications discussed here to some 400,000—not to mention the several hundred other dissident voices spawned by this dauntless quartet.

The anti-Vietnam War press became an influence on American thought not solely because of its growing circulation but because of other factors as well. The earliest publications to oppose the war were edited by a pair of radicals who already had strong followings among American intellectuals, Dorothy Day and Izzy Stone. In addition, the courage that it took for the first publications to oppose U.S. involvement in Indochina—no small act in a nation that prided itself on never having lost a foreign war—attracted legions of independent-minded readers. It was also significant that the anti-war press, through the on-the-spot battlefield reports by Wilfred Burchett in the *Guardian*, provided information not available in other publications, including such breaking stories as the North Vietnamese victories at Bien Hoa, Loc Ninh, and Binh Gia, and the fact that the Viet Cong rebels included many South Vietnamese—the people the United States was supposedly fighting *for*, not against. Further, the anti-war press went beyond merely restating the government's statistical body counts;

the dissident publications looked at the human cost of the war through the suffering being inflicted on the Vietnamese people. Finally, the sensational articles in *Ramparts*, especially Sergeant Donald Duncan's first-person exposé, made for reading that was both illuminating and riveting.

Perhaps the most remarkable legacy of the dissident anti-Vietnam War press is the degree to which the accusations and revelations that originally appeared in its pages ultimately were adopted by the mainstream American media. For after the Tet Offensive, it was as if the country's leading journalists had simply combed through the back files of the anti-war press and then repeated the statements that had been published there five, six, and seven years earlier. It was not until February 1968, for example, that the *Wall Street Journal* told its readers that "the whole Vietnam effort may be doomed; it may be falling apart beneath our feet" and that "everyone had better be prepared for the bitter taste of a defeat"— revelations that *I. F. Stone's Weekly* had been making since 1963. It was also in February 1968 that ABC television first reported that the reality of the fighting in Vietnam was "the exact opposite of what American leaders have been leading us to believe" and that CBS first stated that "the Viet Cong proved they could take and hold almost any area they chose"—revelations that the *Catholic Worker* had first made in 1961 and the *National Guardian* had made in 1964. Likewise, it was in February 1968 that *Time*, the country's most prestigious news magazine, suggested that the South Vietnamese political leaders did not deserve the support the United States had been giving them—a position *Ramparts* had staked out in 1965. Finally, it was in late February 1968 that CBS, after anchor Walter Cronkite had returned from a trip to Vietnam, first called for the American military to withdraw from Southeast Asia—an editorial plea that *I. F. Stone's Weekly* had been making since 1962.[41]

11 DEFINING A COUNTERCULTURE OF SEX, DRUGS, ROCK 'N' ROLL ... AND SOCIAL JUSTICE

The Vietnam War was by no means the only force challenging the established order during the 1960s. Race, gender, class, personal freedom, the work ethic, recreational drugs, the nature of consciousness—they were all on the table as social turbulence fueled a zeal for self-expression, a disdain for authority, and a mistrust of conventional wisdom that came crashing together to form the Counterculture Movement.

Some of the young rebels belonged to organizations, such as the Students for a Democratic Society, that sought to build a New Left constructed on a desire for fairer, more equitable political relationships in the larger society. Others found their identities as hippies, focusing on changing themselves via chemicals, meditation, and alternative lifestyles. At the core of both camps stood committed activism, a robust spirit, passion for change, and three concepts that the counterculture celebrated and the dominant culture condemned: sex, drugs, and rock 'n' roll.

Despite the significance of the infectious rebellion, the mainstream media were slow to recognize it as a newsworthy phenomenon. The country's leading journalistic outlets ridiculed the young activists and ignored the injustices the movement was attempting to correct. Owned by corporations that were part and parcel of the establishment, many major media voices inherently favored the status quo and, therefore, opposed the social change the Counterculture Movement advocated.

So, some 500 brash and boisterous newspapers came on the scene for the twin purposes of recording the activities of the movement and playing a central role in creating the vibrant new culture that was utterly at odds with many conventional American values.[1]

One of the largest, most influential, and longest lasting of the papers was the *Berkeley Barb*, founded in 1965 near the campus of the University of California at Berkeley. Another strong voice that emerged from a major campus community was *The Paper*, which began publishing in 1965 in East Lansing, home of Michigan State University. A third member of this lively genre of the dissident press was *The Kudzu*, founded in 1968 in Jackson, Mississippi, to provide a counterculture voice in the Deep South.

These publications—all tabloids—represent three distinct types of papers. Some, like the *Barb*, were financially independent publications that relied on advertising revenue and demonstrated strong commitments to the communities that surrounded them. Others, like *The Paper*, received university funding, for at least part of their histories, and devoted much of their editorial attention to issues on their particular campus. Still others, like *The Kudzu*, were hippie papers that struggled to survive with scant advertising, no university funding, and a small readership confined to a tiny slice of the population.

The counterculture papers were often amateurish or rag-tag in appearance, with many words misspelled or misused, as well as headlines and graphics frequently drawn by hands that lacked artistic talent. The late-night deadlines and liberal drug use also meant that various details, such as numbering the pages, slipped through the cracks. Other creative touches, such as articles being placed upside down or sideways on the page, were not accidents but deliberate expressions of an anti-establishment approach to journalism.

"Wild-and-woolly" was another apt description for the papers. Slang and coarse language were sprinkled liberally into news stories as well as the personal essays that dominated the papers. Drawings and photographs of naked women added gratuitous titillation; between the staff box and an editorial cartoon on page two of *The Paper*, the editors frequently placed a photo of a voluptuous young woman, her breasts and genitalia fully exposed. Demeaning references to women—such as "broads" and "babes"—were also strewn through the publications, which were edited almost exclusively by men.[2]

In keeping with the Counterculture Movement's emphasis on self-expression, the papers lifted personalized journalism to a new high. After discussing several of the songs on a new Beatles album, an exhausted music reviewer on the staff of *The Kudzu* who identified himself only as "Allan" wrote: "I'm not going to continue like this since its [sic] almost 2:30 am Saturday morning. I've got 3 big tests next week, 2 papers, and an infant puppy. Buy the goddamn album and form your own opinions."[3]

Technological advances threw open the floodgates for a new wave of media activism. Since the mid-nineteenth century, newspaper copy had been set in hot lead type on a Linotype machine and then printed on a huge press, a system that required technical training and a major financial investment. But the introduction of cold-type printing in the early 1960s made newspapers quick, easy, and cheap to produce. Anyone with a typewriter could prepare copy and paste it onto flat sheets of paper that could then be photographed and duplicated for only a few dollars.

BERKELEY BARB: IGNITING THE REVOLUTION

Considering that "Don't trust anybody over thirty" was the mantra of the Counterculture Movement, it is ironic that the founder of the best known of the papers was a balding, fifty-year-old family man. Throughout the early 1960s, Max Scherr had joined the youthful patrons at his Steppenwolf Bar in complaining about the conservative policies that defined not only the nearby University of California but also local, state, and federal politics. In addition, Scherr had become increasingly frustrated with the widening gap that separated the era's newspapers from the readers they claimed to be serving.

So in August 1965, Scherr sold his bar for $10,000 and used the money to start a weekly paper aimed at young people. He dubbed his publishing enterprise the *Berkeley Barb*, choosing the second word in the name carefully; like the sharply pointed projection on an arrow, he wrote, the *Barb* would "nettle that amorphous but thickhided [Scherr later said that he had meant 'thick-headed'] establishment that so often nettles us."[4]

Hundreds of other voices of the counterculture would soon emulate the editorial mix that Scherr had pioneered. News coverage was dominated by sympathetic articles about anti-Vietnam War rallies and exposés of brutality by the local "fuzz." An abundance of music reviews alongside eye-catching photos and psychedelic drawings added considerable spice. But the defining editorial element in the *Barb* was the plethora of personal essays written from a decidedly and unapologetically anti-establishment point of view.

The *Barb*'s size and reputation skyrocketed in May 1969 because of a controversy that focused national attention on Berkeley. The incident began when hippies and street people planted trees and flowers in a university-owned vacant lot that had been slated to be used for a soccer field and dormitories. Scherr catapulted the local conflict into the national news spotlight by promoting it as the quintessential David-versus-Goliath story, while clearly siding with the underdog through blatantly biased comments such as: "The creators of our Park wanted nothing more than to extend their spirits into a gracious green meandering plaything. They wanted to make beauty more than an empty word in a Spray Net commercial."[5]

The *Barb*'s rhetoric contrasted sharply with that of the stodgy *Berkeley Gazette*, which focused its coverage on what the paper considered appalling behavior by the hippies: "Several persons openly smoked pot, nearby residents reacted with shock and dismay."[6]

Police and National Guard troops were called in to get rid of the "riff-raff," prompting 20,000 students to gather for a peaceful protest. When police intervened and killed one demonstrator and injured several others, public opinion joined the *Barb* in the hippie camp. By the end of the volatile thirteen-day siege, Governor Ronald Reagan finally sent the troops home, the university revised its plans and turned the property into a park, and the *Berkeley Barb* had a worldwide reputation as a triumphant journalistic defender of the people.

That incident and the paper's lively editorial mix were a winning combination. By late 1969, the paper was being distributed nationwide with a circulation of 93,000, and Scherr was employing a staff of forty. The *Barb* was on firm financial ground as well, with a wealth of retail ads from local merchants and major national companies eager to reach well-heeled college students. An abundance of classified ads also offered a wide range of items and services—many of them sexual.

THE PAPER: SPREADING THE MOVEMENT INTO THE MIDWEST

A counterculture paper founded only a few months later than the *Barb* was edited by a very different type of person and in an equally distinct part of the country.

Michael Kindman had left his home on Long Island to study journalism at Michigan State University, one of 200 National Merit Scholars the huge land-grant institution had aggressively recruited to upgrade the MSU academic reputation and, it hoped, shed the disparaging nickname "Moo U." But after arriving in East Lansing, Kindman decided he'd been hoodwinked. A dearth of cultural and intellectual stimulation combined with a stodgy journalism curriculum and student newspaper made Kindman restless to become part of the counterculture that he heard was beginning to catch fire on other campuses around the country.[7]

So in December 1965, Kindman resigned from the *Michigan State News* and founded *The Paper*. He fashioned his debut editorial after Max Scherr's first statement about the *Barb*: "We hope unabashedly to be a forum for ideas, a

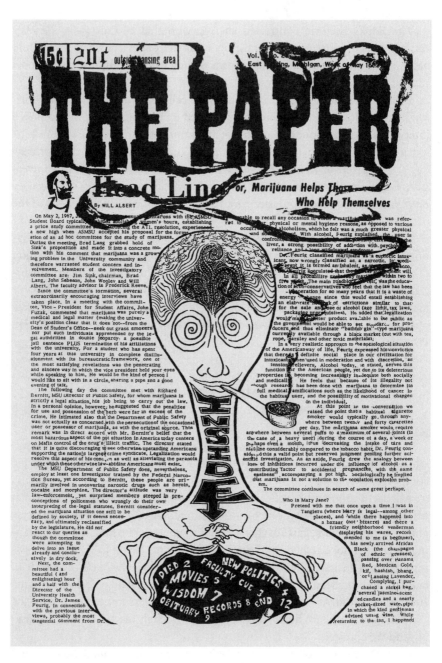

The Paper in East Lansing, Michigan, was one of many counterculture publications that eagerly celebrated the rise of the drug culture during the 1960s.

center for debate, a champion of the common man, a thorn in the side of the powerful."[8]

Michigan State helped fund *The Paper* because it was a student endeavor, as all staff members were enrolled at the university. Editorial content reflected the weekly's strong interest in campus affairs, making *The Paper* an early champion of students having a say in how their institutions functioned. Alongside the stories and editorials supporting student rights, *The Paper* published a spirited mélange of articles, reviews, and artwork much like that of the *Barb* and other counterculture papers—by 1966, *Time* magazine was derisively comparing the publications to a blight of pesky "weeds" and criticizing their editors as "political zealots."[9]

The Paper's journey into the counterculture coincided with Michael Kindman's personal odyssey into the drug culture. He took his first LSD trip and began using acid within a year of becoming a dissident journalist and was soon spending more time tripping than studying. "More and more of us were exploring taking drugs and being stoned together," Kindman later wrote of the staff. "We just got off on all the fun we were having, exploring the corners of our minds and finding new meanings in everything we looked at."[10]

In 1966, *The Paper* published a high-profile article that cogently combined its anti-university and anti-Vietnam War positions. The story evolved from a *Ramparts* piece, the magazine's latest blockbuster about the roots of the war, that exposed a secret alliance between Michigan State and South Vietnamese dictator Ngo Dinh Diem. According to *Ramparts*, MSU professors had trained Diem's police, drawn up his budget, and written his constitution—all with U.S. money funneled through the CIA. The magazine reprinted an MSU inventory that included tear gas projectiles, .50-calibre guns, grenades, and mortars. The withering nine-page indictment ended with the poignant question: "What the hell is a university doing buying guns, anyway?"[11]

When Michael Kindman saw the *Ramparts* exposé, he knew he had the makings of a major story. So he summarized the national magazine's accusations juxtaposed against the milquetoast defense that the university published in the *Michigan State News*. And along with the huge story blanketing page one, *The Paper* printed a full-page caricature of a Vietnamese woman as a buxom MSU cheerleader beside the statement: "The story of a sellout. The April issue of *Ramparts* chronicles how and why Michigan State University abdicated its integrity in a calculated search for gold and glory in Vietnam."[12]

It surprised no one when MSU axed *The Paper*'s university funding. The publication's finances remained stable, however, because the staff agreed to work for free and the printing costs were covered by the revenue from the paper's 5,000 paid subscriptions and the bountiful advertising from local and national companies that, like those in Berkeley, were eager to reach the highly desirable college-student market.

THE KUDZU: CREATING A BEACHHEAD IN THE DEEP SOUTH

One of the ways a third member of the counterculture press differed from the *Barb* and *The Paper* was its location in the most conservative region of the country. In describing 1960s Mississippi, the paper's founder wrote: "Most whites openly professed white supremacy, right-wing militaristic patriotism, and fundamentalist Christianity. They also had repressive, Victorian sexual attitudes and were oppressively anti-intellectual."[13]

David Doggett was intimately familiar with the realities of his native state, having grown up in small Mississippi towns where his father had served as a Methodist minister. In 1964, Doggett entered Millsaps College in Jackson, a tiny liberal arts school, and promptly joined a fraternity, began dating a cheerleader, and started spending his free time in local jazz clubs.

In Doggett's sophomore year, his life changed. Eager to become involved in both the Civil Rights and Counterculture Movements, Doggett replaced the fraternity, cheerleader, and jazz with active membership in the Southern Student Organizing Committee—SSOC was to the Deep South what Students for a Democratic Society was to the country as a whole.

Doggett then became the archetypal hippie; he grew a beard and shoulder-length hair, wore love beads and a peace medallion, and indulged in lots of sex and lots of drugs. After graduating in 1968, he worked as a full-time organizer for SSOC with a subsistence salary of fifteen dollars a week, deciding that his primary mission as a professional agitator would be to found a hippie paper in Jackson.

The Kudzu's name referred to the tenacious vine that grows over old sheds, trees, and telephone poles throughout the South, with Doggett hoping his publication would spread in a similar fashion. An editorial titled "Generational Revolt" in the first issue described what Doggett saw as the scope of the youth rebellion. "We do not seek a narrow, violent, political revolution. We seek a much more profoound [sic] revolution, a revolution of a whole culture."[14]

The paper functioned as a collective with no one on the staff having specific titles or responsibilities. The young volunteers lived in a small apartment that doubled as a newspaper office. Because *The Kudzu* was the only visible institution in the Deep South that advocated radicalism, the office soon became the center of the Counterculture Movement for that part of the country.

The paper appeared irregularly once or twice a month and varied dramatically in size—eight pages one issue, thirty the next. It carried few ads, and revenue from circulation, which peaked at 1,200, came nowhere near paying the printing costs. A handful of loyal supporters made sporadic financial contributions, all of them small, to keep the paper afloat. "If it hadn't been for periodic

From its home in Jackson, Mississippi, *The Kudzu* provided a hippie voice from the Deep South.

donations from my parents," Doggett later said, "I would have starved to death."[15]

The staff's major nemesis was not money, however, but the local police. Outraged by *The Kudzu*'s very existence, officers arrested the dozen staff members when they attempted to sell copies of the first issue. When Doggett asked what the charges were, an officer picked him up and threw him into the back of the sheriff's car. During the questioning that followed, Doggett and the other students were clubbed and kicked.[16]

That was the first of many encounters with police in which staff members were charged with obscenity, had their cameras and notes confiscated, and were evicted from a series of apartments. After each arrest—Doggett estimated the total reached at least forty—and subsequent round of beatings, the police would drop the charges. "After all, we weren't doing anything illegal," Doggett said. "We were just trying to publish a newspaper."[17]

No easy task. "We worked sixteen hours a day," Doggett recalled. "We finished the layout [on production days] at 5 o'clock in the morning, then piled in some clap-trap car or VW bus and rushed to New Orleans to make the printer's 9 o'clock deadline."[18]

Despite the many travails involving finances, police harassment, and long hours, the youthful staff members found creative ways to keep up their spirit. They added the names of their cats and dogs to the staff box published in the paper and turned their apartment/office into a safe house for runaway teenagers and other hippies passing through town. The staff also relaxed every Sunday by listening to rock music in a local park or retiring to the banks of the Pearl River. "We all stripped off our clothes and went swimming," Doggett recalled fondly, "and sat nude around a campfire."[19]

OBLITERATING SEXUAL TABOOS

A liberated attitude toward sex was a hallmark of the counterculture press, in both editorial and advertising content. The papers were determined to make America loosen up and enjoy the new freedoms that the 1960s offered through free love—defined as sexual activity of virtually any type with anyone, anytime, any gender, any number.

The *Berkeley Barb* set the standard. The paper's major venue for sexual discourse was a first-of-its-kind medical advice column titled "Dr. HIPpocrates." Berkeley physician Eugene Schoenfeld, who wrote the column, answered questions from readers not in arcane medical jargon but in street language—and often with his tongue firmly implanted in his cheek. Many young people across the country, in fact, bought the *Barb* solely to hear what Dr. HIPpocrates had to say, his information being equally relevant to people living in Berkeley, Boston, Baton Rouge, or, for that matter, Bangkok.

"Question: Can infectious hepatitis be contracted through cunnilingus? Answer: This is an excellent way—if the recipient of your affection has the disease." "Question: Is it possible to get a venereal disease in the bathroom? Answer: It is certainly *possible*, but the floors are usually cold and hard. In other words, only in the very rarest of circumstances could one contract a venereal disease other than by direct and intimate physical contact with another person."[20]

Hearing candid words from Dr. HIPpocrates was not the only reason that people with active libidos were buying the *Barb*. By the late 1960s, the tabloid was printing rivers of erotic classified ads. They offered plenty of intriguing adventures for men ("Groovy blond chick, semi-hip, seeks interesting male 30–40") as well as women ("Two young males, 21–24, seek a nympho woman or girl to live in"), with a sprinkling of possibilities for gay men, too ("Gay guy, 26, seeks guy, 26–29, for sincere lasting relationship. Prefer a blonde").[21]

Half a continent away, *The Paper*'s sexual content was only slightly more restrained. The Michigan paper illustrated one issue with six pages of erotic photos of nude couples engaging in foreplay and intercourse—the paper's regular printer refused to print the photos, forcing the editors to scour the Midwest to find one who would. In the various essays wedged between the titillating images, *The Paper* called for "free birth control pills for all coeds" and for the elimination of all sexual taboos—"The more restrictive the moral codes of conduct, the less emotionally responsive the sexual practices will be." Other bold statements included: "We are all searching for the Ultimate Orgasm. Why should we let petty considerations sway us from this grand desire?"[22]

The Kudzu's location in the Deep South didn't stop the hippie paper from joining the effort to liberate readers from their sexual hang-ups. Many of the messages were communicated through the personal advice column "Heavy Hog." When an eighteen-year-old young woman wrote that she had a crush on a member of a local band and needed help dealing with her feelings of jealousy toward the musician's other female fans, the columnist wrote that the young woman's real problem was not jealousy—but fidelity. "Don't get so hung-up on one guy," came the response. "Groove with a bunch of them. Get naked and smoke. Come and go. Take a trip to Paradise and free your body and soul. You'll be happier."[23]

CELEBRATING RECREATIONAL DRUGS

As shown by the "Heavy Hog" response, the counterculture press saw the drug-induced psychedelic experience as an instant way to step outside the prevailing culture and look on society from an estranged perspective—the activity that was, after all, the central goal of the *counter*culture. Because of this benefit, using drugs was well worth the risk of being arrested and sent to jail.

Much of the *Berkeley Barb*'s coverage of drugs, like that of sexual topics, came from the oracular Dr. HIPpocrates. By providing factual responses to questions about the effects of various drugs, the popular doctor destroyed many of the myths that wafted through the American youth culture. "Question: I have heard that marijuana usage causes vitamin deficiencies. Can you tell me if this is so? Answer: There are no known harmful effects from the use of marijuana." In addition to giving such straightforward answers, Dr. HIPpocrates was sometimes proactive, letting his readers know about new recreational drugs that had become available. "It is time that some straight information be given about the new hallucinogen STP," he wrote in one column. "STP produces a 12 to 30 hour psychedelic experience similar to LSD."[24]

The Paper's pro-drug stance began with such supportive statements as: "The harm resulting from drug use, if any, affects only the user, and the government has no right to deny an individual his freedom of action if his action endangers no one but himself." And then, in late 1969, *The Paper* took a huge proactive step by publishing information that helped drug users evade narcotics agents. In a feature story titled "NARCS," the paper reported the name and physical description of an undercover agent who had succeeded in infiltrating the local hippie community to the point that she was responsible for several arrests. The article described how Barbara Bencsik was masquerading as a hippie but was, in fact, "the lowest form of animal life imaginagle [sic]." After *The Paper* identified Bencsik, local drug users avoided her, forcing police officials to reassign the woman who had been one of its most effective officers.[25]

Despite its location in the most conservative region of the country, *The Kudzu* also campaigned to liberalize drug laws. In a typical article, the paper asserted that "scientific evidence shows that marijuana is harmless both to the individual and to society." The piece went on to accuse politicians of making the possession of marijuana illegal solely as a means of social control, rather than out of any concern for the well-being of the users. "It is a common practice for police or other law enforcement officials to use marijuana charges (real or trumped up) to jail radicals who prove to be a threat to the status quo." The paper did not stop with abstractions but went on to accuse the local police in

Fayetteville, Arkansas, of planting marijuana on several young people who had organized a Students for a Democratic Society chapter in that city. "These SDS members will have to spend a good bit of there [sic] time that could have been used for organizing in fighting the phony charges instead."[26]

PROMOTING A REVOLUTION
THROUGH ROCK 'N' ROLL

In 1954, a nineteen-year-old musician from Mississippi named Elvis Presley compressed the red clay of the Pentecostal Church and the rhythms of Black America until they exploded to create rock 'n' roll. A dozen years later when the Counterculture Movement was at full tilt, rock music had gained an urgency and a defiance that radiated a sense of what life could feel like if people would cast off their inhibitions. "Satisfaction," "Purple Haze," "Lucy in the Skies with Diamonds," "Hey, Jude," "Why Don't We Do It in the Road," "Happiness Is a Warm Gun," "Street Fighting Man," "Revolution"—they were all vinyl diary entries marking a listener's first demonstration, first one-night stand, first trip, first brush with teargas, first night in jail.

Despite rock 'n' roll's evolution into a potent cultural force, the established media largely ignored it. When mainstream newspapers and magazines mentioned the new musical form at all, they did so with anthropological detachment; it was a passing fad worthy of no more than a one-time feature story written in the snide tone of superiority that the graybeards of American journalism reserved for articles about children.

So the emergence of rock 'n' roll into a phenomenon of unparalleled cultural dimension was left to the counterculture press to chronicle. The *Barb* and its imitators, therefore, treated rock 'n' roll as both music and an agent of change. The papers put rock at the journalistic center of the odyssey they were sharing with their readers, knowing that music had become the main touchstone for many young people who had become alienated from society. The Baby Boomers were taking over—first the music, then every other facet of American life.

The musical prophet for the counterculture generation was Bob Dylan. "He progresses and breaks ground for his fellow travellers," one piece said. "There are times when you HAVE to listen to 'Like a Rolling Stone' and nights when you HAVE to hear 'Sad-Eyed Lady [of the Lowlands]' before you can stop your mind. There are moments when 'Tambourine Man' sifts to consciousness. That's all there is." The writer then made a valiant effort at articulating exactly *why* Dylan was the leading musician of the era. "When you listen closely to

Dylan, you feel the words. It's using words to appeal to the senses, not to the rational mind. You feel it through your eyes or ears or skin."[27]

Among the decade's numerous musical groups, the Beatles were the most important. Sensing the seismic influence that the British imports would have on the United States, a counterculture paper often devoted a page or more to reviewing the latest Beatles release. After *Time* and *Newsweek* had both pooh-poohed what became known as the legendary "White Album," for example, *The Kudzu* published a song-by-song analysis. "The new double album is a difficult and complex work which deserves a great deal of careful consideration," the piece began. The author was particularly taken with "Rocky Raccoon," which music historians ultimately would identify as the epitome of John Lennon's dark wit. "The theme seems to be confused identity crises and (I know you want to believe it) the need of modern man to see the paltriness of his life with a heroic vision, and his inability to do so. In the end the song turns in upon itself, becoming a bitterly farcical commentery [sic] on the human condition. Listen to this one yourself."[28]

It didn't take long for the music industry to realize that the counterculture press had developed an intimate relationship with a new generation of consumers. So the major record companies began pouring advertising money into the alternative papers. Typical was a two-page ad—it ran in the *Barb*, *The Paper*, and numerous other publications—that read "Underground . . . Overground. All that matters is that you dig the sound" above images of two dozen album covers from Columbia Records. Such ads were a major boon to the papers, most of which had been shoestring operations until the influx of ads from Columbia—the General Motors of the music industry—and other record companies.[29]

FIGHTING FOR SOCIAL JUSTICE

The lifestyle themes that were so pronounced in the counterculture press—it would be difficult to name three more tantalizing topics than sex, drugs, and rock 'n' roll—should not obscure the demands for social justice that also played a prominent role in the various papers.

The emphasis the publications placed on ending the Vietnam War came bursting off the front page of the premier issue of the *Berkeley Barb*. The event at hand was a group of activists blocking a troop train that was transporting soldiers through Berkeley. The *Barb* expressed its sympathy with the demonstrators by reporting that GIs aboard the train supported the civilian protest. When the soldiers saw the demonstrators, the *Barb* said, they quickly hand lettered signs that they then pressed against the windows so the protesters could read them. "Keep up the good work. We're with you," read one; "I don't want to go," pleaded another. Mainstream newspapers that covered the demonstration made no mention of the signs.[30]

The *Barb* story also illustrated the paper's commitment to local issues. Just below the lead story about the protest, the paper ran an article focusing on how the local police had physically abused the demonstrators. The *Barb* story began: "Thursday, August 12, 1965—a day of brutality in Berkeley," reporting that the police had clubbed several protesters and had left one woman on the railroad tracks with a train approaching, adding that friends of the woman had to pull her to safety "at the last instant."[31]

The paper's intention to be proactive—it would not only report the news but also make events happen—was clear from the suggestive nature of the final paragraph of the police brutality story: "Two more troop trains are due in Berkeley next week. Suppose a thousand or more Berkleyans have a first hand look?" That activist orientation became a signature element of the paper's highly interpretive approach to the news. When San Francisco police halted a peace march through the Haight-Ashbury district, the *Barb* made the event its lead story of the week, under the anti-police headline "Slug-Happy Cops Wreak Havoc in the Haight," and when Los Angeles officers broke up a peace demonstration, the *Barb* shrieked "BLOOD PURGE! Cops Ambush LA Protesters."[32]

The Paper's anti-Vietnam War content also reflected that publication's activist stripe, in this case a focus on Michigan State issues. Coverage that fit the bill perfectly evolved after Jim Thomas, a former MSU student then fighting in Vietnam, began sending poems and creative-writing pieces to *The Paper*. In one item, Thomas wrote: "Here we are aboard an assault ship bound to do battle against the powers of evil. We'll hit the beach tomorrow. Time to practice being hard." In early 1967, Thomas's dispatches abruptly ended when the twenty-year-old corporal was killed in action. In a black-bordered tribute on page one, *The Paper* lamented: "America has lost a soldier, and America can afford that. But it has also lost a poet, and no nation can afford that."[33]

Other editorial crusades waged in *The Paper* included trying to eliminate MSU's Reserve Officer Training Corps and the National Merit Scholar program that had brought editor Michael Kindman to the university, and seeking to reduce the cost of textbooks by creating a student co-op. Kindman and his staff generally became involved in national issues of the Counterculture Movement only when there was a local angle; when two national SDS leaders came to campus, *The Paper* printed verbatim texts of their speeches.[34]

Although *The Kudzu* joined its counterculture press colleagues in opposing the Vietnam War, the paper's major editorial thrust was to seek social, political, and economic equality for Americans of African descent. David Doggett, as both a hippie and a civil rights activist, was determined that the paper would advance the cause of black men and women, even though it was published in the depths of the segregated South. So when African Americans working for the city of Jackson—the only jobs open to blacks were as garbage collectors—formed their own union and attempted to secure collective bargaining rights, Doggett turned the effort into a major news story. After the City Council voted not to recognize the union, *The Kudzu* reported the defeat under the headline "City Dumps on Garbage Men" and threw its editorial support behind the black workers, writing that the action "left laborers with no vacation and no grievance prosedure [sic] when they were fired."[35]

Doggett saturated his paper with articles about the myriad incidents throughout the South in which young African Americans were attempting to secure their civil rights. Typical was a story about 1,800 black high school students in Leland, Mississippi, boycotting classes to protest the poor quality of their education; the final sentence of the story pointed out that the school district had been cut off from federal funding because it refused to comply with court orders to desegregate. Other stories told of students at Mississippi's Tougaloo College holding a mass teach-in to demand that black studies courses be added to the curriculum, and of students at Bluefield State College in West Virginia bombing a campus building to protest the lack of black cultural events on campus.[36]

FALLING VICTIM TO THE GOVERNMENT'S SECRET WAR

By late 1968, the counterculture press had become the central force in defining the dynamic youth rebellion. Editors were proudly calling their press, in the vernacular of the era, a "magic mushroom" that was exploding both in size and impact.[37]

The editors were not alone in recognizing the significance of their publications. On the very day that Richard Nixon was elected President, FBI Director J. Edgar Hoover sent a memo to his offices coast to coast. The subject of the communiqué was a plan Hoover had developed to halt what his lieutenants were characterizing, with considerable panic, as the "vast growth" of counterculture papers. Hoover ordered every agent in the country to begin an immediate

"detailed survey concerning New Left-type publications being printed and circulated in your territories," instructing the agents to send him detailed information on each paper's staff, printer, and advertisers.[38]

That memo was the opening round in a Secret War the FBI and other federal
and local agencies waged against the counterculture press. In an extension of the
Counter Intelligence Program (COINTELPRO) that the FBI had launched
against communism in the 1950s, Hoover told his agents to do whatever was
necessary to force the papers to "fold and cease publication" and thereby eliminate what he considered the movement's most important means of developing
and spreading its anti-establishment ideology. That offensive—which would
not come to light until more than a decade later when Freedom of Information
Act requests forced the FBI to open its files to the public—included an alarm-
ing array of illegal activities.[39]

One way the FBI consistently broke the law was through forgery. Agents in
Texas created phony letters in which they posed as parents complaining about
how counterculture papers were harming their children, prompting university
officials to prevent the papers from being distributed on their campuses; such
letters resulted in outlawing *The Rag* at the University of Texas and *Dallas Notes*
at Southern Methodist University, among others. Agents also falsified letters to
University of Alabama administrators threatening to make life difficult for the
school if it did not stop two instructors from donating money to a student
paper—the two teachers were subsequently placed on probation.[40]

Obscenity laws gave the police a tool that appealed to citizens disturbed by
the turbulent changes in America's sexual mores. One nefarious campaign was
against *Miami Daily Planet* editor Jerry Powers, who was arrested twenty-eight
times on charges of selling obscene material. He was acquitted each time, but he
still had to pay a phalanx of bail bondsmen $93,000. The *Daily Planet's* experi-
ence was by no means unique. Although the counterculture papers generally
won their obscenity battles, it often took years for judgments to be handed
down. The expenses required for a publication to defend itself, therefore, meant
that the financially vulnerable operations often did not survive. *NOLA Express*
in New Orleans triumphed in two obscenity cases the government filed against
it, and yet the paper was forced out of business because of the legal fees it had to
pay its lawyers. Likewise, *Open City* in Los Angeles had to pay legal fees related
to an obscenity conviction; the paper was later vindicated by a higher court, but,
by that time, the lawyer bills had forced *Open City* to cease publication.[41]

Local police and politicians were also fond of using drug laws to silence
counterculture papers. FBI and CIA agents—even though federal law prohibits
the Central Intelligence Agency from conducting activities *inside* the United

States, the agency was very active in the Secret War—increased the effectiveness of their drug raids by infiltrating the staffs so narcotics squads would know exactly when drugs were likely to be used, such as immediately after a weekly deadline had been met.

The very real threat of drug arrests created a state-of-siege atmosphere on many staffs. After the *Daily Flash* printed a series of articles critical of St. Louis Police Chief Walter Zinn, an undercover policeman was assigned to infiltrate the paper; a short time later, the officer arrested editor Peter Rothchild for possession of marijuana. When the entire staff of the *Argus* in Ann Arbor, Michigan, was arrested on drug charges, the paper immediately ceased publication. Perhaps the best-known drug case was that of John Sinclair, editor of Detroit's *Sun*; arrested and tried solely on the testimony of two undercover narcotics agents who had infiltrated the staff, Sinclair was sentenced to ten years in prison for possessing two marijuana cigarettes.[42]

In some instances, the motivating factor for punishing a counterculture paper was pure revenge. When the *Philadelphia Free Press* published damaging information about Police Commissioner Frank Rizzo, he vowed to destroy the paper. During the next six months, police officers waged a relentless vendetta against *Free Press* staff members—physical assaults, searches of homes and offices without warrants, breaking into the locked cars of several staff members, opening the mail sent to and from the newspaper. The most disheartening event occurred when the mainstream *Philadelphia Evening Bulletin* published a major story on the *Free Press* that described staff members as "violent" and revealed confidential financial, family, and employment information about staff members—material that could only have come from Philadelphia police and FBI files. By the time Rizzo and his co-conspirators had finished with the counterculture paper, its long-time printer and numerous advertisers had abandoned it, forcing the paper to cease publication later that year.[43]

The most frightening of all the battles in the Secret War were those involving violence that was so severe that the perpetrating law enforcement officials could justifiably be labeled "domestic terrorists." The office of the *Washington Free Press* in the nation's capital was ransacked just before the 1969 presidential inauguration; four years later, the *New York Times* printed FBI documents proving that the raid had been the work of agents from the FBI and U.S. Army. Other FBI files now available link agents to firebombings of the offices of the *Helix* in Seattle, *Space City* in Houston, *Orpheus* in Phoenix, *Great Speckled Bird* in Atlanta, and *Free Press* in Los Angeles. The most sustained campaign of violence may have been against Milwaukee *Kaleidoscope* editor John Kois; his car was firebombed and shot at, and the windows in his newspaper office where he was working were shattered by gunfire.[44]

SPIRALING DOWNWARD

The rapid growth in the number of counterculture papers during the late 1960s was mirrored by a rapid decline in the early 1970s. Of the 500 papers being published in 1968, only forty still existed a decade later.[45]

That dramatic drop can be attributed to many factors. The gradual withdrawal of U.S. troops from Vietnam was one critical element, as were the inexperience, self-indulgence, political naiveté, heavy drug use, and fatigue of the youthful editors and staff members. But overwhelming these various factors was the Secret War by federal and local government agencies. Operating with pragmatic immorality, FBI agents and other law enforcement officials waged a take-no-prisoners assault on the counterculture press.

The Paper felt the impact of the Secret War primarily through its pocket book. After the university cut off the paper's funding, it became almost entirely dependent on local and national advertising. That situation was fine—until the Secret War began. Michigan FBI agents targeted *The Paper*'s local advertisers by forging letters signed "Disgusted Patron" and sending them to East Lansing merchants, objecting to the counterculture paper's often ribald content. Local advertising immediately plummeted. The even more serious attack involved the paper's biggest advertisers: national record companies. In January 1969, a memo from the FBI's San Francisco office to the headquarters in Washington asserted that Columbia Records "appears to be giving active aid and comfort to enemies of the United States" by advertising in counterculture publications such as *The Paper*. The memo went on to urge top FBI officials to use their high-level contacts to persuade Columbia and other major record companies to sever their relationships with the counterculture press. The double-page ads that had become the major source of income for the defiant Michigan weekly soon disappeared, followed by the one-page ads by smaller record companies.[46]

The Paper ceased publication in November 1969.

The Kudzu, as a hippie paper, never depended on advertising for its sustenance, relying instead on the youthful energy of its staff. So the secret warriors had to employ other tactics to take down the Mississippi paper. They were happy to do so, as the paper's office was seen, and rightly so, as the hub of the Counterculture Movement in the Deep South and yet, despite relentless harassment by Jackson police for two years, the paper had continued to function. So in 1970 the FBI placed *The Kudzu* and its staff under intense surveillance. Agents began searching the office at least once each and every day—always without warrants—claiming to be looking for SDS leaders. On several occasions, the uninvited visitors threatened to kill certain staff members, and once they held eight of the young people at gunpoint for several hours. The FBI's terrorizing tactics were highly effective in driving away the hippies who composed *The Kudzu* staff, as they were pacifists who had dropped out of the dominant culture to embrace a contemplative life of yoga and meditation—not guns and ammo.[47]

The Kudzu ceased publication in December 1972.

The Berkeley Barb survived far longer than most counterculture papers, but its destiny also was determined by the Secret War. The commercial paper that Max Scherr and his family depended on for their livelihood had, by 1969, grown into one of the largest dissident publications in the country, with a circulation approaching 100,000, editorial content that was less politically radical than that of *The Paper* or *The Kudzu,* and an abundance of the one- and two-page ads that the country's leading record companies were eager to place in a paper that circulated heavily among University of California students. When the titans of the music industry pulled their ads, therefore, Scherr was desperate to find a new source of revenue. He struck the mother lode through classified sex ads, with the ads soon filling as many as fifteen of his twenty-eight weekly pages. The ads gradually shifted from the statements of sexual freedom they originally had been, however, to blatant pornography—such as "Outcall services to your hotel or motel in Eastbay area" and "Lovie Craves It is back and showing her beaver up close to gents"—that was in total conflict with the Women's Liberation Movement that had emerged alongside of the Counterculture Movement. Ads for prostitutes and massage parlors were not sexually liberating; they perpetuated the oppressive concept of women being sex objects who could be bought and sold as a commodity. By the mid-1970s, the *Barb* was known not as a counterculture paper but as a vulgar and sexist one.[48]

The Berkeley Barb ceased publication in July 1980.

CREATING A GOLDEN AGE OF AMERICAN YOUTH

Like many genres of the dissident press, the counterculture papers did not have a lengthy lifespan, with most of the publications surviving no more than half a decade. Despite its brief history, however, the printed voice of the Counterculture Movement retains a certain "magic" that many other forms of the dissident press do not. When today's college students are asked to name an example of non-mainstream journalism, the most frequent response is a reference to those rag-tag, wild-and-woolly, highly personalized publications that spoke for that golden age in the history of American youth: The Sixties.

Further evidence of the unique stature of counterculture papers comes from noting the large quantity of material that has been written about this particular genre of the dissident press. Scholars have paid scant attention to many alternative journalistic endeavors that have sought to change society—no books have been written about the nineteenth-century sexual reform press, the anarchist press, or the birth control press. Scholars have, by contrast, published half a dozen books specifically about the 1960s counterculture press.[49]

But this press is of historical significance for more reasons than the interest it generates among students and scholars. Looking at the major themes that dominated this genre of journalistic dissidence shows that it ultimately had enormous impact on society. The publications certainly succeeded in helping America become more liberated about sexual activities and recreational drugs—although it can be debated whether the country is better for it. Likewise, the counterculture press played a singular role in legitimizing rock 'n' roll; after publications such as the *Berkeley Barb* and *The Kudzu* began writing about this new musical genre in the mid-1960s, such middle-of-the-road publications as *Time* and *Newsweek* added, by the early 1970s, rock 'n' roll columns. And with regard to social justice, the counterculture press clearly helped the anti-war press hasten the end of the Vietnam War, assisted in expanding the Civil Rights Movement to college campuses, and became a catalyst for many of the rights now enjoyed by American college students—such as university curricula being shaped by student demands and university policy-setting boards and committees no longer being considered complete without student representation.[50]

Acknowledging the impressive legacy that the short-lived counterculture press left in its wake begs a "what if" question that can be asked as the final thought about this category of the dissident press: What might the *Berkeley Barb*, *The Paper*, *The Kudzu*, and the hundreds of newspapers like them have been able to accomplish *if* the nation's law enforcement officials had not harassed, intimidated, and beaten the staff members or committed acts of domestic terrorism—such as ransacking and fire-bombing the offices of this memorable generation of committed and high-spirited journalists?

12 STANDING TALL AND TOUGH AGAINST RACIAL OPPRESSION

Although J. Edgar Hoover and his agents-turned-domestic-terrorists disliked every aspect of the Counterculture Movement, at the very top of their list were the Black Panthers. Like many white Americans, the FBI director and his lieutenants saw the young black men—with their leather jackets and military berets, their clenched jaws and the guns gripped tight in their fists as they marched defiantly through city streets—as the most dangerous element in society, destined to destroy everything that was good about America. The Panthers represented "the greatest threat to the internal security of the country," Hoover said in 1969, and directed his men to do everything humanly possible, both legal and illegal, to "destroy" them.[1]

In the minds of very few people living in the 1960s or the decades that followed, on the other hand, did mention of the words "Black Panthers" evoke the image of a cluster of passionate, forward-thinking young journalists bending over their typewriters into the wee hours of the morning to articulate a political ideology that would guide Black America into the new millennium.

And yet, the same militant activists who led the Black Panther Party into legendary status as one of the most fearsome organizations in the history of the United States, in fact, also produced a weekly newspaper that developed a remarkably far-reaching vision for Americans of African descent. Indeed, many of the concepts introduced in the pages of the *Black Panther* newspaper continue to reverberate through this nation today.

During the paper's initial four years, from 1967 to 1971 when the party was at its peak, the editorial content was dominated by five major topics: police brutality, violence as self-defense, economics as the most serious form of oppression, Black American genocide by the federal government, and the need to resurrect black manhood. The enduring quality of these themes and the power and poignancy with which they were originally articulated combine to document that the racial activists who wrote for the paper—most notably Huey P. Newton, Bobby Seale, Eldridge Cleaver, David Hilliard, and Fred Hampton—were accomplished and far-sighted dissident journalists.

Because of the strength, insight, and pure effrontery of the editorial content of the *Black Panther*, it exploded into the largest African American newspaper in the country, with its 100,000 weekly circulation surpassing that of any of its competitors threefold. The paper was a truly grassroots publishing endeavor that provided a venue in which even the most powerless members of an oppressed minority found a voice. It is not surprising, then, that a publication with such a huge reach and vast potential to effect social change also soon attracted the wrath of the FBI and its Secret War.[2]

RAISING A REVOLUTIONARY VOICE

Huey P. Newton and Bobby Seale created the Black Panther Party in Oakland, California, in the fall of 1966 because, as Newton wrote at the time, "We want freedom. We want power to determine the destiny of our Black Community."[3]

The two young men—Newton was twenty-four, Seale twenty-nine—belonged to families that had migrated west during World War II in search of jobs in the naval shipyards and munitions factories that had flowered on the West Coast during the country's wartime build-up. While the families successfully escaped the rigid segregation of the South, however, they still suffered discrimination in employment, housing, and education—forces that thrust the Newton and Seale families into poverty.

Young Huey and Bobby both spent their childhoods in Oakland and met while studying at Merritt College. Taking advantage of one of the victories achieved by the counterculture press, the two young men joined forces and succeeded in having classes in black history added to the curriculum. Encouraged by their campus victory, they next set out to improve life in Oakland's black ghettos. They began by knocking on doors and asking what the residents felt they needed most in order to improve the quality of their lives. Then Newton and Seale translated those answers into the programs at the center of the Black Panther Party—free health clinics, free breakfasts for school children, and free workshops in the political process.

But it was another of the party's community-based activities that caught the attention of the public: armed patrol cars.

Newton, Seale, and the other young African American men they recruited into the party would climb into their cars—a gun in one hand, a law book in the other—and trail police cruisers around Oakland. So whenever police stopped black suspects, the armed Panthers made sure the officers did not violate the constitutional rights of the men and women they detained. The police were outraged that armed black men had the audacity to monitor them, even though it was fully legal for Californians to carry loaded guns, as long as the weapons were not concealed. The African American community had a very different reaction; blacks were impressed that the young men were committing their time and energy to protecting the rights of their fellow citizens. Even more important, the harassment and brutality that the Oakland police previously had directed against black men and women began to decline.

The white power structure, however, was less concerned about the ill treatment of black citizens than about armed black men cruising the streets of Oakland—a sight that most white people found terrifying. So in early 1967, a white East Bay legislator drafted a bill that would disarm the Panthers by making it illegal to carry a loaded gun in public, whether concealed or not. When twenty Panthers stormed into a chamber of the California Assembly brandishing loaded rifles, pistols, and shotguns to protest the proposed legislation, newspapers across the country captured the moment in photos—and the Black Panthers were instantly known nationwide. Although the black activists failed to block the bill, the publicity boosted party membership—virtually overnight—to more than 10,000.[4]

The catalyst for founding a Panther newspaper was a local incident that took place in early April 1967. According to the report filed by a white deputy sheriff of the Richmond, California, police department, when the officer tried to arrest Denzil Dowell on suspicion of stealing a car, the young man fled. The deputy sheriff then shot and killed the black twenty-two-year-old, and the authorities ruled the death justifiable homicide. Dowell's family charged, however, that the officer had threatened to kill Dowell long before the incident. When the mainstream news media failed to give the case the attention that Newton and Seale thought it deserved, they started their own paper.

The premier issue of the *Black Panther* appeared in late April 1967 as two mimeographed sheets stapled together and distributed to some 3,000 residents of Oakland's black neighborhoods. The weekly paper quickly expanded to twenty-four tabloid pages and its circulation increased manyfold, sold nationwide for twenty-five cents via the network of local Black Panther Party chapters that had erupted in thirty cities.

The *Panther*'s editorial content was dominated by strident essays insisting that African Americans would never secure true freedom unless they waged a social and political revolution. References to the United States being a fascist nation were frequent, as were shrill demands for drastic change. "People are not going for all the bullshit America preaches," one article screamed. "Oppressed peoples are forming a proletarian force that will rise and crush the pig power structure. All Power to the People!!" In another essay, Newton wrote, "The only way that we're going to be free is to wipe out once and for all the oppressive structure of America."[5]

News stories also fulfilled a crucial function. For the *Panther* was often the only source of information about events occurring in America's black communities that were being ignored by the establishment press. When African American high school students in High Point, North Carolina, went politely through the proper channels to request that the local school board add black studies to the curriculum but then were summarily suspended, the story appeared in the *Panther*; the mainstream press did not report the incident. Likewise, when Los Angeles police responded to a white landlord's complaint against his black women tenants operating a day care center in his building by herding the teachers and children onto the lawn and holding them at gunpoint, the *Panther* reported the story in all its bizarre detail; the mainstream press did no so much as mention it.[6]

These and hundreds of other news articles were written by people who were not official members either of the *Panther* staff or the party. But by printing the stories, the paper gave poor and politically dispossessed African Americans a venue for community news they had never had before. Bobby Seale said that giving common people a voice was one of the *Panther*'s most significant contributions because the stories "come from the hard core of the black community, the grassroots." Fred Hampton, chairman of the party's Illinois chapter and a contributor to the paper, made the point in more colorful terms: "If you don't read the *Black Panther* paper, fuck it right there—you ain't read shit."[7]

Artwork was integral to the editorial mix. Images of pistols, shotguns, machine guns, hand grenades, and clenched fists dotted every issue. Among the other compelling graphics were dozens of cartoons featuring pigs dressed in police uniforms. Some of them depicted the officers as inept and foolish—one showed a cluster of pigs in police uniforms firing pistols into the air while dancing and swigging down alcohol, another had a pig sleeping in the driver's seat of his police car as black youths surrounded the vehicle and aimed their weapons at the hapless officer's head. Other of the images were even more sinister. One showed an angry black man preparing to thrust a huge knife into a crying pig/policeman; another depicted a black man holding a shotgun that he had just used to kill the pig/policeman lying lifeless at his feet.[8]

In Defense Of
Self Defense

The *Black Panther* newspaper is credited with establishing "pig" as a derogatory synonym for "policeman"—both in print and in visual depictions.

Absent from the *Panther*'s pages were the mainstay of establishment journalism: advertisements. No major businesses were willing to be associated with the paper's militant ideology—no matter how large the circulation—and very few of the small, black-owned enterprises in sympathy with the *Panther* could afford to buy ads. So the dissident journalists depended on circulation revenue to pay their printing and mailing costs. Sales grew so rapidly in the late 1960s that profits from the paper were used to support the party's other activities, such as the health clinics and breakfasts for school children. The Panthers who wrote, edited, and distributed the paper received no payment.

Eldridge Cleaver served as the *Panther*'s first editor, but Huey P. Newton emerged as the strongest and most articulate voice. Newton's image was a strong visual presence in the paper as well; photos of the handsome mulatto man—tall, muscular, and unsmiling in black leather jacket and beret, with a pump shotgun and bandolier of shells strapped across his chest—often filled an entire page. Men dominated the top positions on the paper, as they did in the party, with women largely confined to typing stories and laying out the pages.

The *Black Panther* rejected the strict language requirements observed by conventional American journalism. The paper has been credited with originating the term "pig" as a derogatory synonym for "policeman," and the slogan "Off the Pigs!" was sprinkled with regularity throughout the paper. Expletives such as "shit," "fuck," and "motherfucker" appeared frequently as well. Seale wrote, "The language of the ghetto is a language of its own, and as the party—whose members for the most part come from the ghetto—seeks to talk to the people, it must speak the people's language."[9]

STOPPING POLICE BRUTALITY

The prominent role that police brutality would play in the editorial content of the *Black Panther* became clear in how the Denzil Dowell incident dominated the first issue. A large photo of the young man ran under the headline "Why Was Denzil Dowell Killed?" Sharing page one was a boxed statement that announced a community meeting about the Dowell shooting and ended by saying, "Every black brother must unite for real political action." The rest of the issue was filled with a list of unanswered questions related to the killing and an essay raging against rampant police brutality.[10]

The essay provided a preview of the battery-acid prose style that would become a hallmark of the militant paper. "In the past, Black People have been at the mercy of cops who feel that their badges are a license to shoot, maim, and out-right murder any black man, woman, or child who crosses their gunsights," the essay read. "But there are now strong Black men and women on the scene who are willing to step out front and do what is necessary to bring peace, security, and justice to a people who have been denied all of these for four hundred years. The Black Panther Party takes action."[11]

In later issues, Newton argued that only police officers who had been raised in the black ghetto should be allowed to patrol there. When law enforcement officials sent white police into black neighborhoods, he wrote, they could be compared to the United States sending its "occupying army" of American soldiers into Vietnam. "The racist dog policemen must withdraw immediately from our communities, cease their wanton murder and brutality and torture of black people," Newton wrote, "or face the wrath of the armed people." In another essay, he articulated exactly how that rage would be manifested. First arguing that the peaceful demonstrations used in the Civil Rights Movement were ineffective and should be replaced by "guerrilla methods," Newton went on to endorse the murder of racist police officers. "When the masses hear that a gestapo policeman has been executed while sipping coffee at a counter," he wrote, "the masses will see the validity of this type of approach."[12]

Editorial efforts to stop police brutality extended beyond angry essays. Residents of black neighborhoods across the country contributed a steady stream of fact-based news stories reporting instances of African Americans being mistreated by officers in Chicago and Detroit, Boston and Philadelphia, New Haven and Winston-Salem. Many of the stories were illustrated by drawings that showed pigs dressed in police uniforms as they beat, tortured, and humiliated helpless black men and women. Eldridge Cleaver wrote of the paper's ubiquitous symbol of police brutality: "A dead pig is the most desirable, but a paralyzed pig is preferable to a mobile pig."[13]

EMBRACING SELF-DEFENSE CUM VIOLENCE

As illustrated by Newton's and Cleaver's open advocacy of killing racist police officers, the *Black Panther* did not embrace the nonviolent credo that was central to the Civil Rights Movement of the 1950s and 1960s. While the movement's Rev. Martin Luther King Jr. unequivocally opposed violence, Panther leaders opted for the approach that their fellow dissident journalist Ida B. Wells had pioneered the previous century and that their contemporary Black Power leader Malcolm X revived when he insisted that blacks should secure freedom "by any means necessary." Like the Black Power leader, the militant men who led the party believed that the nonviolent tactics used in the rural South would be ineffective in the urban North. The Panthers often quoted Malcolm X's mantra: "The time has come to fight back in self-defense whenever and wherever the black man is being unjustly and unlawfully attacked. If the government thinks I am wrong for saying this, then let the government start doing its job."[14]

The important role that self-defense would play in the Black Panther Party was immediately evident when Newton and Seale selected a name for their organization. They chose the panther as their namesake because, Seale said, "It is not in the panther's nature to attack anyone first. But when he is attacked and backed into a corner, he will respond viciously and wipe out the aggressor." A drawing of a panther, with its claws extended and teeth bared, appeared on the top of page one of the *Black Panther* each week, and additional drawings of the fierce animal appeared on inside pages as well.[15]

Various writers reinforced the importance of African Americans defending themselves. Newton wrote, "Black people can develop Self-Defense Power by arming themselves from house to house, block to block, and community to community throughout the nation." David Hilliard upped the level of militancy by insisting that self-defense extended to killing the enemy, including police officers: "We only advocate killing those that kill us. And if we designate our enemy as pigs, then it would be justified to kill them." Eldridge Cleaver echoed the same point—with an equal dose of defiance—by speaking directly to White America: "From now on, when you murder a black person in this Babylon of Babylons, you may as well give it up because we will get your ass. Black people, this day, this time, say halt in the name of humanity!"[16]

The most vehement endorsements of self-defense published in the *Panther* were tantamount to calls for violence. In a 1969 essay, David Hilliard singled out President Nixon as the man ultimately responsible for Black America's oppression. Hilliard's tone grew angrier and angrier as the essay progressed, and his final words sounded like those of a warrior poised to attack his enemy: "We will kill Richard Nixon. We will kill any motherfucker that stands in the way of our freedom. We ain't here for no goddamned peace, because we know that we can't have no peace because this country was built on war. And if you want peace you got to fight for it. All Power to the People."[17]

COMBATING ECONOMIC OPPRESSION

While the *Black Panther*'s essays raging against police brutality and promoting violence as a form of self-defense stirred the most public attention, essays on those topics were, in reality, far fewer in number than editorial statements that focused on economic oppression as the root problem facing African Americans. Every issue of the paper included at least one lengthy treatise focusing on economics.

The specific economic theme discussed most frequently was Huey P. Newton's demand that White America provide financial reparations to Black America for the debt that had been created by the institution of slavery. The cofounder of the party argued that the heinous practice of human bondage had doomed African Americans to their current subservient social, economic, and political position, and, therefore, the government should right that wrong by directing massive tax revenue into poor black neighborhoods. "The racist government has robbed us, and now we are demanding the overdue debt," Newton wrote. "We will accept the payment in currency which will be distributed to our many communities. We feel that this is a modest demand."[18]

Other writers echoed Newton's call. "We want land, bread, housing, education, clothing, justice, and peace," Seale began one manifesto. "The exploited,

Many of the editorial cartoons published in the *Black Panther* newspaper celebrated African-American men who committed violent acts against racist law enforcement officers.

laboring masses and poor, oppressed peoples throughout the world want and need these demands for basic human survival." Seale labeled the economic oppression against African Americans "domestic imperialism," which he defined as "black people being corralled in wretched ghettos."[19]

Economic repression was one of the few topics that women were allowed to write about. Connie Matthews focused on how the technological advances of an industrialized nation threatened black Americans. "Most of you will become redundant," she told *Panther* readers. "You in the middle, who think you have something, who have those bills and those $20,000 houses, you are the ones who are going to find out that the mortgage you are going to have to pay back is about twice what you thought originally. Get yourself hip to all this, get with it and educate your people because the Black Panther Party is out there in the front but we can't stay out there in the front forever. We will stay until everyone of us is killed or imprisoned by the racist pigs, but then someone will have to take over. So don't let us all die in vain. Power to the People."[20]

PREVENTING BLACK AMERICAN GENOCIDE

When Newton and Seale canvassed Oakland's black neighborhoods, providing health care emerged as a top priority for the Panthers, with local chapters founding free clinics in such far-flung cities as Kansas City and Boston, Seattle and Brooklyn, Houston and Chicago. The health-care initiative gained even more momentum after the party's dissident newspaper began a full-throttle assault on a medical crisis of such enormous dimension that it threatened to destroy Black America.

A black doctor launched the campaign against sickle cell anemia with a page-one article explaining the origins of the deadly disease. To develop immunity to malaria, Dr. Tolbert Small wrote, the bodies of people living in Africa centuries ago transformed their red blood cells from the original donut shape into a form resembling a sickle. But medical complications arose, he explained, when the men and women were captured by slave traders and transported to the United States where the modified cells proved to be a disadvantage in the new environment, resulting in sickle cell anemia.[21]

The disease—ninety-eight percent of American victims were black—blocked blood vessels and damaged numerous body organs, so victims suffered wracking pain in their joints, stomach, chest, and head. People afflicted with the disease also were highly vulnerable to infection and developed various brain and lung ailments, often dying before they reached the age of thirty.[22]

Although there was no known cure for sickle cell anemia, the doctor continued, it was possible to reduce the incidence of such a hereditary disease. Individuals carrying the trait—one in every twelve Americans of African descent—often exhibited no signs of the disease and could lead normal lives, Dr. Small wrote, but if a male and female carrier had children, there was one chance in four that those offspring would develop the full-blown disease.[23]

Dr. Small concluded by stating that testing and warning people that they were carriers would dramatically reduce the number of cases, and yet the U.S. government had not initiated a testing program. "Sickle cell anemia kills as often as muscular dystrophy or cystic fibrosis," he reported. "Yet it has received little public attention and none of the large scale government funding that those other two diseases have, both of which usually affect White victims."[24]

The editorial note accompanying the doctor's article made that same final point; it was not written in the same calm tone, however, but in the highly volatile one that characterized so much of the *Black Panther*'s content. "Black People are being eliminated in such great numbers," the note bluntly stated, "that the only conclusion that can be drawn is that a concentrated, malicious plan of genocide is being enacted upon us."[25]

That blockbuster article and editorial note were the opening salvo in the *Panther*'s campaign to alert Black America of the medical danger lurking in its midst. "As a people, we must become conscious of this genocidal plan and its many faces," read a typical piece, "so that we can fight the hard, long struggle— we must survive. If we do not become aware of the situation, we will be duped into the death of our entire People. Power to the People."[26]

The *Panther* also demanded that research to find a cure for the disease be increased. During 1970, the paper reported, the number of new cases of sickle cell anemia surpassed 1,600, compared to 1,200 new cases of cystic fibrosis and 800 of muscular dystrophy. Yet the government had committed only $100,000 to sickle cell research, compared to $7.9 million and $1.9 million for the other two diseases. "This racist government has no intention of ceasing the genocide," the paper raged. "Research on sickle cell anemia would hinder their plan of Genocide upon Black people."[27]

The most important aspect of the Black Panther Party's effort to eradicate sickle cell anemia—both through its newspaper and its network of free clinics— was that the campaign was accompanied by such compelling logic that the public health establishment could not ignore it. And after the American medical community took up the cause, Congress finally passed, in 1972, the National Sickle Cell Anemia Control Act, adopting the exact same priorities that the Panthers had called for years earlier—testing, warning, and funding research for a cure. Although there is no way to determine exactly how many lives and how much human suffering the Panther campaign saved, there is no question that they were substantial.

RESURRECTING BLACK MANHOOD

While slavery had been a devastating experience for African Americans of both sexes, the *Black Panther* believed that the abhorrent institution had its most long-lasting effects on black men because they had been denied the position of power and respect that white men traditionally held in relation to white women. Further, this reduced status was exacerbated by the economic deprivation that continued to define the Black American experience throughout the nineteenth and twentieth centuries. In Huey P. Newton's words: "The Black man feels that he is something less than a man. Often his wife (who is able to secure a job as a maid, cleaning for White people) is the breadwinner. He is, therefore, viewed as quite worthless by his wife and children. He is ineffectual both in and out of the home. Society will not acknowledge him as a man."[28]

The *Black Panther*, therefore, crusaded to resurrect black manhood to a position of respect and power in the African American as well as the white community.

Although an occasional article made reference to women being part of the revolutionary force that was standing tall against racial oppression, the vast majority of the paper's editorial content made it clear that men—and men only—should be at the vanguard. Newton wrote the seminal statement on the subject when he said that it was essential for the black man to "recapture his mind, recapture his balls. The Black Panther Party along with all revolutionary Black groups have regained our mind and our manhood."[29]

Rank-and-file members of the party often communicated the *Panther*'s position on the need to reclaim black manhood not by praising men but by demeaning women. Typical of the writers was an unnamed man who criticized African American women as uniformly "selfish" and imbued with a misplaced "feeling of superiority." The article went on to blame the endemic lack of stability in African American families on the black woman: "To a great extent, her attitude explains the high rate of divorce among Panthers and other revolutionaries." Other articles reiterated the proper—and limited—role for black women; one stated point blank: "It is what the Black woman can contribute to the Black man that is important."[30]

Male voices were not alone in placing tight restrictions on black womanhood, as numerous female writers in the *Panther* also defined the feminine role as one limited to supporting her masculine superior. A woman "must be the Black Man's everything," wrote one woman. "She must be what her man needs her to be." The writer went on to urge her fellow "Pantherettes" to be "warm, feminine, loving, and kind"—characteristics far different from those applauded in male revolutionaries—and to devote the bulk of their time to the domestic duties that would provide their men with a safe and calm haven at home.[31]

The African American woman playing a central part in resurrecting black manhood by adopting the traditional female role of nurturer and supporter came through even more clearly in an article titled "A Black Woman's Thoughts." The author began by asking the rhetorical question: "What is a Black woman's chief function, if it is not to live for her man?" She then continued by criticizing the white-dominated Women's Liberation Movement of the era, insisting, "Black women must drop the White ways of trying to be equal to the Black man. The woman's place is to stand *behind* the Black man." Later in the piece, the author made the same blunt assertion by telling her African American sisters: "Stop playing the role of a man."[32]

SILENCING THE DISSENTERS

FBI documents show that J. Edgar Hoover's illegal activities against the counterculture press extended to the *Black Panther*. Indeed, it was against the militant African American paper that Hoover's assault on the dissident press reached its most frightening level. Four months after the paper was founded, Hoover directed his field offices to "disrupt, misdirect, discredit, or otherwise neutralize the activities" of the staff. FBI memos that were made public through Freedom of Information Act requests show that, in response to the director's order, agents placed wiretaps on the telephones at the paper's office, strong-armed the man who distributed the *Panther* to triple the fees he charged the paper, and planted informants on the staff to provoke internal dissension.[33]

Staff members suspected, but could not prove, that the FBI also was behind a series of catastrophes that seemed more than coincidental: A warehouse filled with back issues burned to the ground. The *Panther*'s circulation manager in Southern California, Walter Pope, and then the national circulation manager, Sam Napier, were both murdered.[34]

Another instance involved much more than suspicion, as the American legal system ultimately ruled that the FBI and the Chicago police had conspired to murder Fred Hampton, who wrote for the paper. The FBI considered the nineteen-year-old Hampton a rising power figure in the party. So agents hired a petty criminal to infiltrate the Chicago operation; in exchange for information, law enforcement officers dropped auto theft charges pending against the man and gave him a monthly salary. The informant then became one of Hampton's assistants so he could provide the FBI with detailed descriptions of the charismatic leader's activities, including the specific firearms that were in his home. In December 1969, Chicago police obtained a warrant to search Hampton's apartment for illegal weapons. Fourteen officers burst through the front door in the middle of the night and fired forty-two rounds from a submachinegun into the bed where Hampton was sleeping.[35]

Although the law enforcement officials killed Fred Hampton, they were less successful against his mother, who filed a civil lawsuit against the local state's attorney who had orchestrated the raid—Hoover was also named as a co-conspirator. After a series of trials and appeals that extended for fourteen years, Iberia Hampton ultimately triumphed when a judge awarded her $1.85 million and ruled that there had, indeed, been a governmental conspiracy to deny her son his civil rights.[36]

Fred Hampton was by no means the FBI's only target. By 1970, agents had succeeded in having more than 700 Panthers arrested, thereby forcing the party to spend upwards of $5 million and much of its energy not agitating for racial equality but defending its beleaguered members.[37]

A mind-numbing series of arrests, trials, convictions, imprisonments, mistrials, overturned convictions, escapes to foreign countries, and violent deaths took a devastating toll on the paper and the party. In October 1967, Newton was arrested and charged with killing an Oakland police officer, leading to the *Panther*'s most ardent voice being jailed and tried—and making "Free Huey!" a pervasive plea in the paper. In September 1968, Newton was convicted of manslaughter, but in August 1970 the conviction was overturned and Newton was released. In April 1968, party treasurer Bobby Hutton was shot to death as he attempted to surrender to Oakland police; Eldridge Cleaver and David Hilliard were among seven Panthers who were then arrested on murder charges in connection with Hutton's death. Cleaver, who already had spent time in prison and refused to be jailed again, fled to Cuba and then Algeria. In May 1969, Seale was charged with killing party member Alex Rackley (Seale suspected Rackley of being an FBI informer); Seale spent two years in prison until a mistrial was declared. Also in 1969, Seale was sentenced to four years in prison for contempt of court because he had disrupted his trial on charges of conspiracy to incite a riot during the 1968 Democratic National Convention in Chicago—Seale and other defendants became known as the "Chicago Eight." Meanwhile, Hilliard was indicted for threatening President Nixon during a rally in Chicago—the same threat he made in the *Panther*. In 1974, police charged Newton with killing a prostitute, prompting the Panther leader to flee to Cuba. When Newton returned to the United States three years later, he withstood three costly trials before charges were finally dropped.[38]

By 1971, the FBI's strategy had succeeded, and the Black Panther Party had been reduced to a shell of its former self. And as the party diminished in strength, so did its journalistic voice. The editorship changed hands many times, and essays crafted by such dynamic leaders as Newton and Cleaver appeared only rarely. During the 1970s, the *Panther* included little of the editorial fire that had defined its early years. The weekly was reduced to a bi-weekly in the late 1970s and then a monthly in early 1980. It ceased publication in October 1980.

DISGRACING THE CAUSE?

At the same time that the *Black Panther* was speaking up on behalf of oppressed Americans of African descent, the Black Panther Party was rapidly gaining the negative reputation that ultimately would come to dominate White America's perception of it. With a loose structure that allowed considerable autonomy to local chapters as well as to individual members, there is no question that men affiliated with the party committed an untold number of abusive acts and inexcusable crimes. It is impossible, however, to know how many of the incidents were undertaken by Panthers of their own free will and how many were either instigated or fabricated by the FBI and its Secret War.

Drug abuse was one pervasive problem, as numerous members of the party—including Newton—became so dependent on cocaine that their lives reeled out of control; some members turned to drug dealing to support their habits. Sexual abuse was a concern, too, with party members taking their efforts to resurrect black manhood to extremes by raping and otherwise assaulting white as well as black women. Another disturbing activity involved rogue Panthers threatening and extorting money from struggling African American business owners, sometimes beating or maiming the very men and women they purported to be protecting. The long list of criminal acts attributed to the black revolutionary thugs is shocking, with the items ranging from harassment, robbery, and embezzlement to arson, prostitution, and murder.[39]

When the various negatives aspects of the African American revolutionaries were added together, according to some critics, the Panthers did far more to harm Black America than to help it. The author of a book devoted entirely to criticizing the party—titled *The Black Panther Menace: America's Neo-Nazis*—wrote, "The Black Panthers are, in fact, the worst enemy the black man has in America—on a par with his implacable, ignorant, bigoted foes in the Southern United States."[40]

A LASTING LEGACY

The *Black Panther* charted a unique journalistic course. By transforming the angry messages of black revolutionary icons into printed words, the newspaper performed a singular service for the Black Panther Party, as well as for Black America writ large. This dissident voice discussed topics that the American news establishment considered inimical to the well-being of the country. The impressive size of the audience that the *Panther* reached—100,000 at its peak—speaks to the eagerness with which readers embraced the paper's ideology.

Dwarfing the role that the *Black Panther* played during its years of publication, however, is the impact that the paper's editorial content has had since that time. For the primary themes raised in the pages of that revolutionary journalistic voice did not disappear when the paper ceased publication. Indeed, the issues that dominated the *Panther*'s pages still play important roles in the sociopolitical movement that continues to seek racial equality in this country today.

The most concrete example is the pig becoming a symbol for police officers. The *Panther* was the first publication to use this derogatory reference, in written form through editorials and graphic form through cartoons that depicted pigs wearing police uniforms—one of the newspaper's signature elements. This symbol was immediately embraced by the Counterculture Movement and then gradually became an accepted entry in the mainstream vocabulary as well.

Another powerful concept that grew its roots in the pages of the *Panther* was Huey P. Newton's demand that the U.S. government make restitution to African Americans for the sins of slavery by committing large quantities of tax money to poverty-stricken black neighborhoods. Although such proposed compensation was scoffed at by all but a handful of radical Americans in the late 1960s and is still far from becoming official public policy, the exact same proposal as the one articulated in the *Panther* has been debated in the halls of the U.S. Congress every year for more than a decade.[41]

The subjects of various other *Panther* essays are also still very much alive. The enormous public response to the videotaped beating of Rodney King by Los Angeles policemen in 1991 and the massive riots that were sparked by the acquittal of those officers are vivid reminders that police brutality remains a salient racial issue in this country. Likewise, the economic disparity between black Americans and white Americans—the median income of a black family is less than sixty percent of that of a white family—provides dramatic evidence that economic oppression of African Americans is another major problem. Although this country's medical community eventually responded to the sickle cell anemia crisis by initiating a testing program, the disease is still a concern of major dimension in Black America. Finally, resurrecting African American manhood from its historic struggle for respect and dignity remains a concern, as demonstrated by the efforts of 1995's Million Man March in Washington, D.C.[42]

A primary reason why the concepts that were communicated in the pages of the *Black Panther* did not fade from the American consciousness is that, when the newsprint began to yellow, the original essays and artwork were preserved in other forms. The activities of the Black Panther Party took on legendary proportions, historians theorize, because they represented the first nationwide black political phenomenon—as distinguished from religion-based undertakings such as the Civil Rights Movement—that stood tall and stood firm, the party leadership unequivocally and steadfastly refusing to back down, even when attacked by such powerful forces as the FBI.[43]

So the revolutionary rhetoric and artwork that originally appeared in the *Panther* was reproduced in other forms. During the 1970s, three books reprinted hundreds of the newspaper's essays and editorial cartoons, and by 1990 several dozen additional books—including some published by such major houses as Random House and Simon & Schuster—had reproduced lengthy excerpts from the paper. The hunger for the ideology espoused in the *Black Panther* still did not abate. In the 1990s, a dozen more books were added to the holdings of American libraries and book stores, and several of the earlier books were reprinted. Finally, by the turn of the new century, the only surviving high-profile voice from the long-deceased newspaper was keeping the words of the publication alive by quoting from it on his own Website—www.bobbyseale.com.[44]

And so, despite the passage of time, despite White America's overwhelmingly negative visceral reaction to the words "Black Panthers," and despite the many covert and illegal acts the FBI committed in an effort to destroy the *Black Panther*, the radical concepts that were initially voiced in the paper in the late

1960s and early 1970s have experienced a vibrant life of their own. Not only have those ideas outlived most of the youthful revolutionaries who originated them, but those same concepts that were shunned by establishment journalism during the years that the *Black Panther* was being published have now been either embraced as accepted political doctrine or, at the very least, are now being seriously debated in the larger society and, therefore, are most definitely having impact on the mainstream of American thought.

13 CREATING AN AGENDA FOR GAY AND LESBIAN RIGHTS

The Counterculture Movement helped lay the groundwork for gay men and lesbians to demand equal rights. With the liberated attitude toward free love and sexual exploration celebrating male-to-male and female-to-female sexual activity as never before, the time clearly had arrived for homosexuals to come out of the closet and march boldly to center stage.

Gay people have never been content to follow meekly in the paths of others, however, so it took their own seismic event to ignite a true social revolution, and then their own dissident press to transform that historic moment into a full-fledged social movement. The event was the Stonewall Rebellion in New York City in June 1969, and the press was a network of lesbian and gay publications that fanned the spark of defiance into a raging forest fire that ultimately would engulf the entire country through the Gay and Lesbian Liberation Movement.

Stonewall spawned the in-your-face gay newspapers that voiced outrage, demanded justice, and shrieked at the top of their lungs. The upstart tabloids fed on each other, pushing the envelope of good taste further and further—and then further still. Screaming headlines, titillating images, revolutionary concepts, and primal-scream language often designed more to create heat than light—they all contributed to the fervor of journalistic dissidence.

Merely listing the names of the papers that burst onto the streets of New York communicates a palpable sense of what they stood for: *GAY*, *Gay Times*, *Come Out!* The shockwaves reached other parts of the country as well, producing such colorful voices as *Gay Sunshine* and the *San Francisco Gay Free Press* on the West Coast and *Killer Dyke* in Chicago. The number of gay and lesbian publications being produced in 1970 surpassed 150, with a combined circulation of at least 250,000.[1]

The most important achievement of the publications was not amassing large numbers—although the figures were, indeed, impressive—but creating an arena in which lesbians and gay men could discuss what their social movement hoped to be. Editors and writers stood on the front lines of the ideological warfare, introducing the themes that would define this highly controversial social revolution for decades to come.

Martha Shelley, who participated in the Stonewall Rebellion and then became one of the most powerful voices of the era through her essays in *Come Out!* and *Killer Dyke*, later recalled: "It was that marvelous moment at the very beginning of a new adventure when everything—absolutely *every*thing—seems possible. Every topic was on the table. We didn't agree a lot, but we always gave each other respect. We'd all been involved in other movements where gay people were second class. No more. Now we had our own movement, and we were primed to debate just where that movement would take us."[2]

THE STONEWALL REBELLION LIGHTS THE FUSE

The Stonewall Inn was the epitome of the grim realities of the gay bar scene in 1960s America. It was operated by three Mafia figures—Mario, Zucchi, and Fat Tony—who routinely referred to their clientele as "faggot scumbags." Paying only $300 a month rent and raking in $5,000 every weekend, the trio turned a tidy profit, even after paying off the officers from the Sixth Precinct to keep the police raids to a minimum.[3]

The club lacked many amenities, including running water behind the bar. After a customer used a glass, the bartender merely dipped it into a vat of stale water and then refilled it again for the next customer. Despite the health hazards, people flocked to the nightspot because it had the only gay dance floor in the city and bartender Maggie Jiggs dealt acid and uppers with aplomb. Drag queens and chino-clad young men in their early twenties dominated the crowd; a few lesbians and a sprinkling of older men—known in gay parlance as "chicken hawks"—who lusted after the underage boys completed the nightly mélange.

June 27, 1969, was the day New York buried music legend Judy Garland, a favorite among gay men. Some 20,000 people had waited up to four hours in the blistering heat to view the icon's body, with many of her admirers hitting the bars that night to unwind. Except for Garland's funeral, that Friday night at the Stonewall seemed like most every other one. Then, at 1:20 a.m., eight policemen stormed through the front door—and all Hell broke loose.

After the officers herded everyone into the street, the patrons and bystanders began jeering at the police. If a single individual inspired the crowd's resistance, it was a lesbian—she has never been publicly identified—who, when an officer shoved her into the street, pushed back. Emotions flared as the angry gays turned steely and began tossing beer cans, rocks, and even a couple parking meters that someone had ripped out of the sidewalk. When the officers retreated to inside the bar, the building suddenly burst into flames. The police somehow escaped the fire that night, but the social insurgents rioted every night for the next week, with their pent-up energy escalating into a full-scale rebellion involving 300 police officers struggling to control 2,000 newly empowered gay men and lesbians.

The mainstream press covered the riots much as it had covered previous events involving gay people—with scorn and ridicule. The headline "Hostile Crowd Dispersed Near Sheridan Square" above the *New York Times* story sent the message that gays were enemies of civilized society. The *New York Daily News*, for its part, portrayed the rioters as laughable: "Homo Nest Raided; Queen Bees Are Stinging Mad." The disdainful tone permeating the coverage in the *Village Voice* was the most disheartening of all because the tabloid billed itself as an alternative to the establishment press, and yet its stories overflowed with mocking references—"prancing," "fag follies," "wrists were limp, hair was primped."[4]

The only gay journalistic voice in New York at the time of the rebellion told a very different story. The "Homosexual Citizen" column in the sex tabloid *Screw* expressed unbridled enthusiasm by saying it was "thrilled by the violent uprising." The column went on to place the pivotal event in historical context. "A new generation is angered by raids and harassment of gay bars, and the riots in Greenwich Village have set standards for the rest of the nation's homosexuals to follow. The Sheridan Square Riot showed the world that homosexuals will no longer take a beating without a good fight. The police were scared shitless and the massive crowds of angry protesters chased them for blocks screaming, 'Catch them! Fuck them!' There was a shrill, righteous indignation in the air. Homosexuals had endured such raids and harassment long enough. It was time to take a stand."[5]

GAY SETS A LIVELY PACE

Although that column ensconced its two authors as journalistic prophets of the post-Stonewall era, they were already firmly established as gay press veterans.

Jack Nichols and Lige (short for Elijah) Clarke met in Washington, D.C., in 1964. A year later, Nichols organized the first public demonstration to protest unfair treatment of homosexuals, leading a brave little band of ten activists who formed a picket line in front of the White House. Clarke, who had been drafted and was working at the Pentagon, did not march but lettered the signs that his lover and the other protesters carried in the historic event.

Like many leaders of the 1960s dissident press, Lige Clarke (left) and Jack Nichols grew their hair long as a symbol of their liberated attitude and lifestyle. (Photo by Eric Stephen Jacobs; courtesy of Jack Nichols)

Nichols and Clarke entered gay journalism in 1966, writing—both under pseudonyms—for a Washington-based monthly titled the *Homosexual Citizen*. A year later, they transformed themselves into children of the counterculture, abandoning the starchy nation's capital and moving to the lower east side of Manhattan. Nichols stood six-foot-three and carried his million-dollar smile atop an athletic physique. Clarke was blond, lithe, and so strikingly handsome that he turned heads even at the trendiest of bars—gay or straight. In the new environs and intoxicated by the fumes of gay liberation, the attractive and gregarious couple began living large. Both men let their hair grow to their shoulders, wore bell bottom jeans and tie-dyed T-shirts, and experimented with the wide variety of drugs and sexual pleasures the bohemian neighborhood offered.

Nichols and Clarke then began writing their "Homosexual Citizen" column for *Screw*, which arguably was—and still is—the most vulgar newspaper in the history of publishing. Its debut edition in 1968 included a personal ads section called "Cocks & Cunts," spicy reviews of X-rated films, and lots of nude photos. The raunchy tabloid soared to a circulation of 150,000.[6]

The "Homosexual Citizen" simultaneously achieved its own notoriety, as each column offered something that straight readers had never seen before: a positive portrayal of homosexuality. Whether Nichols and Clarke were talking about contributions that gay people had made to world history or the opening of the country's first gay bookstore, the tone was invariably upbeat. In one column, they recalled their animated response when asked if they regretted not being straight. "The only answer we've got to this question is based on our present life together," they wrote. "We're having a ball!"[7]

Five months after the Stonewall Rebellion, Nichols and Clarke began editing their own newspaper, while also continuing to write their weekly column for *Screw*. GAY quickly became the newspaper of record for Gay America. The first anthology of gay nonfiction, *The Gay Insider: USA*, captured the essence of the spirited tabloid and its editors, writing: "Jack and Lige write a no-nonsense, unapologetic, vibrant, sexy, and liberated weekly message that is gobbled up by thousands like me, rendering the authors the most celebrated homosexuals in America. They are witty, wise, straightforward, and *pretty*."[8]

Each issue of GAY featured a full-page photo of a handsome man on the cover—Lige Clarke appeared on the first one—and a plethora of homoerotic images inside. To illustrate a three-inch article about arrests at a pornographic bookstore, the editors chose a photo of Studio Bookshop employee Rick Nielsen. This was not, however, the standard one-column headshot. The five-inch-by-twelve-inch photo featured a full-body shot of Nielsen, from the front, wearing nothing but a seductive smile—his genitalia dangling freely.[9]

GAY was financed by Al Goldstein. Having established *Screw* as a successful enterprise a year earlier, the straight entrepreneur invested $25,000 in *GAY* in hopes of earning still more profits. Goldstein distributed the paper and found advertising to support it; Nichols and Clarke supplied the editorial content.

The new sense of gay liberation that exploded in Greenwich Village after the Stonewall Rebellion gave the weekly paper a ready audience. Within a month, some 25,000 people were plunking down forty cents for the paper, giving it the largest circulation in the twenty-year history of the lesbian and gay press.[10]

As a commercial enterprise, *GAY* eagerly accommodated to its advertisers. So as the number of Mafia-owned gay bars and bathhouses burgeoned in the largest urban center in the country, an increasing proportion of the pages were filled with graphic ads that gloried in full frontal nudity.

COME OUT! RAISES A RADICAL VOICE

The archetype of the revolutionary journals that erupted after Stonewall shrieked onto the streets of Greenwich Village in November 1969. In that inaugural issue, *Come Out!* demonstrated the combative stands it would take by demanding that gay and lesbian consumers boycott any business that was aimed at gays but owned by straights—such as *GAY*.[11]

Come Out! did not aspire to journalistic fairness but blatantly rejected the conventions of the established social and political order, including those of the Fourth Estate. The first issue called readers to action: "Power to the people! Gay power to gay people! Come out of the closet before the door is nailed shut! *Come Out!* has COME OUT to fight for the freedom of the homosexual; to provide a public forum for the discussion and clarification of methods and actions nexessary [sic] to end our oppression."[12]

Come Out! was the printed voice of the Gay Liberation Front, born in New York City a month after Stonewall and quickly spreading across the country. The organization was composed of young gay men and lesbians whose revolutionary vigor had been inflamed by U.S. involvement in Vietnam, becoming to the Gay and Lesbian Liberation Movement what the Black Panthers had become to the Civil Rights Movement. The leftists demanded not only gay rights but the complete overthrow of American society.[13]

come out! 25c

a liberation forum for the gay community

GAY LIBERATION FRONT

VOL.1 NO 5   NEW YORK SEPT OCT 1970   35c OUTSIDE NYC

Come Out! was one of several radical newspapers that supported violence as a means of ending the oppression of gay men and lesbians.

The bi-monthly paper violated many journalistic standards. Pages often carried no numbers, and articles were riddled with typos and grammatical errors. Language was also more colorful and explicit than in most newspapers. Police were referred to as "pigs," "fascists," and "swine." "America" became "Amerika." The words "fuck" and "cunt" appeared with regularity.

Personal essays dominated the editorial content, along with a goodly number of letters from readers and reviews of books, records, and films. Illustrations consisted mostly of homoerotic drawings and photos. News articles were sprin-

kled throughout the twenty pages. Typical items praised gay activists for dis-
rupting an appearance by New York City mayoral candidates and denounced
the *Village Voice* for censoring a classified ad *Come Out!* had placed to solicit
articles—the *Voice* had deleted "Gay Power to Gay People" from the copy for
the paid ad, saying the word "gay" was obscene.[14]

In keeping with their nonconformist leanings, *Come Out!* staff members
eschewed hierarchical structure. The paper was published collectively by members of the front, with no one holding the title of editor. During a gay press
panel discussion, a staff member explained the philosophy behind the lack
of structure: "We have a definite view that the society is what's fucking us up.
That a capitalistic, heterosexual society is the root of all our problems. We
think compitition [sic] and producing to earn money is the root of a lot of our
problems."[15]

The paper contained no advertising, and staff members received no salaries.
Indeed, the very idea of paying journalists conflicted with the paper's anti-cap-
italism credo. In a letter to potential contributors, the staff wrote: "*Come Out!*
will not insult you by offering you payment." Most of the paper's 6,000 copies
were sold on the streets of Manhattan; members of Gay Liberation Front chapters in Chicago, San Francisco, and Los Angeles sold the rest, at two bits a pop,
in their home cities.[16]

EMBRACING VIOLENCE?

One issue that attracted considerable ink in the papers was whether activists
were justified in using violence in their effort to achieve equality. *GAY*, the
voice of moderation, opposed violence; *Come Out!* and other radical papers
endorsed it.

Jack Nichols and Lige Clarke were convinced that the major force impeding
the movement was ignorance. Straight people would grant gay people full
equality, the editors believed, as soon as they became familiar with gay issues. So
the editors supported acts of civil disobedience that raised the gay and lesbian
profile. *GAY* endorsed "kiss-ins" and "dance-ins," during which same-sex couples engaged in public displays of affection, by devoting front-page news stories
and editorials to the events. The paper also gave extensive coverage to the first
Gay Pride Parade up Sixth Avenue in 1970 to commemorate the anniversary of
the Stonewall Rebellion. *GAY* drew the line, however, at confrontations that
resulted in physical harm or property damage. Nichols and Clarke wrote point
blank: "We abhor violence in any form."[17]

Gay Sunshine was one of the several voices taking the opposite stand. "We as homosexuals must learn to be 'Violent Fairies' and shake off the silly passiveness idea that straights have handed us," the Berkeley tabloid insisted. "We are Revolutionaries and not 'Passive Pansies.'" Nor did *Gay Sunshine* pull any punches in identifying who should be the target of gay violence: "The enemy is straight society." Pat Brown, a hippie with his blond hair hanging well below his shoulders, was one of the eight men in the collective that created the paper. He later recalled: "When you've been pushing for a very long time and you don't see any progress, you do what you need to do to raise the visibility of your plight. We were willing to smash a few windows here and there. Cadillacs make wonderful barricades, and those big, huge gas tanks burn for a very, very long time."[18]

The radical papers demonstrated their support of violence through the images that dotted their pages. Drawings of machine guns, rifles, hand grenades, bombs, and clenched fists were common, and occasionally a pig dressed as a police officer—inspired by the *Black Panther*—could be found wandering across a page as well. The central role that violence should play in the movement was also communicated by photos showing crowds of gay revolutionaries marauding through the streets, leaving overturned cars in their wake. The papers made the same defiant statement when they enlarged photos—sometimes filling an entire page—of the signs that demonstrators carried during mass rallies: "Seize Your Community," "We Will Smash Your Hetero-Sexist Culture," "Fuck This Shit!"[19]

Come Out! initiated violent rhetoric in its first issue: "We're involved in a war—a people's war against those who opress [sic] the people. Power to the People!" A year later when gays rioted after a police raid on a Village bar, *Come Out!* encouraged further violence by echoing the chants the demonstrators had shouted at the police—"You better start shakin' 'cause today's pig is tomorrow's bacon!"—and crafting its own strident calls for violent action—such as "Destroy The Empire!" and "Babylon has forced us to commit ourselves to revolution!" The paper also urged readers to join the Gay Liberation Front's rifle club to prepare for the armed combat that was on the horizon. *Come Out!*'s most pro-violence stand came when it proposed burning the buildings on the City College of New York campus because the school promoted "establishment thinking."[20]

Gay Times, which consisted of one sheet of typing paper that editor John O'Brien glued to trees and utility poles, endorsed violence through the logo it carried at the top of the front page of every issue; the drawing showed a hand grasping a rifle, encircled with the words "To Love We Must Fight." The paper clearly reflected the values of its editor. Today O'Brien speaks with pride of burning a record shop to the ground during the Stonewall riots because the store discriminated against gays. He also boasts that destroying the shop led to the owner's heart attack and death. "I'm very proud of that," O'Brien said. "He was a total bastard. Some people deserve to die."[21]

Killer Dyke lived up to its militant name through both its artwork and its rhetoric. The members of the lesbian collective who founded the Chicago tabloid created one of their most memorable images by reproducing a likeness of Whistler's mother sitting sedately in her rocking chair—with a machine gun in her hand. In its first issue, the paper warned: "Sexist pig oppressors . . . beware! Those motorcycles roaring in the night . . . is that the Killer Dykes foaming at the mouth? zooming to get you?!"[22]

The *San Francisco Gay Free Press* also insisted that gays would achieve equality only by wrenching it forcibly from straights. The tabloid peppered its pages with terms such as "gay genocide" and drawings of bullets exploding in the faces of police officers. Editor Charles Thorp promoted violence, he told his readers, because he had repeatedly been physically attacked while distributing gay papers. On one occasion, Thorp's face had been slashed and on another he had been struck in the head with a baseball bat. A *Free Press* open letter to straight men stated: "I'll not be your slave. I demand of you my complete freedom, and if that displeases you, I'll take what is mine, by any and all means necessary. I've got my gun loaded. I'm rising up gay to smash your cock-power, understand?"[23]

The *Free Press* reported that gay revolutionaries were already preparing for violent action: "Guns are being loaded. Knives are being sharpened. Bombs are being made. We declare war on our oppressors." The tabloid said that large numbers of gays were training hard for guerrilla warfare: "All are committed to violent Gay revolution."[24]

FORMING A SEPARATE GAY NATION?

While many gay men and lesbians of all generations have enjoyed surrounding themselves with other gay people, post-Stonewall radicals went a giant step further. Buoyed by the sense of possibility that was wafting in the air, this militant minority insisted that contempt for homosexuality was so ingrained into the fabric of American life that gay people had no choice but to create their own society totally separate from straights. The issue of gay nationalism created another fault line that divided gay and lesbian publications into two distinct camps.

Among the most ardent champions of creating a gay state were the members of the Gay Sunshine collective. "We tried to isolate ourselves totally from straight society," recalled Pat Brown. "All of us wanted to eat, drink, and sleep—especially sleep—gay. So separatism definitely was injected into our editorial content." The Berkeley tabloid gave gay nationalism its blessing, saying: "It's time for us to take full charge of our lives, to seize control of our own world and make it fit to live in. Homosexual separatism is essential."[25]

A concrete proposal to create a gay nation emerged six months after the Stonewall Rebellion. In December 1969, members of the Gay Liberation Front in Los Angeles announced a plan to take over nearby Alpine County, centering on the town with the irresistible name of Paradise. They proposed turning the tiny resort community—population 367—into the first all-gay city in the world, complete with a gay civil service system and a museum of gay arts and history. Under California law, new residents of a county were required to wait only ninety days before becoming eligible to vote and removing current county officials from their jobs.[26]

The *San Francisco Gay Free Press* threw its support behind the proposal, surveying readers and finding that fully eighty-three percent of them supported the idea of a separate nation. "Gay people have given the Alpine Liberation Front a mandate to go on," the paper wrote. The *Free Press* further suggested the county be renamed "Stonewall Nation" and encouraged wealthy gays to buy the nine major businesses in the county. The paper went on to propose that gay and lesbian welfare recipients move to the county so it could be declared "impoverished" and become eligible for millions of dollars in public assistance to finance gay public housing and free social services.[27]

Other dissident gay journalists, both radical and moderate, were less enthusiastic about Stonewall Nation. Martha Shelley of *Come Out!* and *Killer Dyke* recalled: "A lot of us said, 'OK, let's get real.' I mean, blacks outnumbered us ten times over, and they made no headway at getting their own separate piece of land. It made no sense for us to waste our energy on gay nationalism."[28]

Jack Nichols of *GAY* agreed. "I never really thought of it as a serious proposal," Nichols said. "Sure, a lot of gays wanted to live in an all-gay world—that's why the Village in New York City and the Castro in San Francisco became gay meccas. That was fine by us. But creating an entirely new all-gay society with no connections to the dominant straight society whatsoever? That just wasn't going to happen. Why spend your time on some screwball idea like that when you could be working toward truly meaningful social change? Pick your battles, man, pick your battles."[29]

By early 1971 when a Christian right organization threatened to respond to the gay initiative by moving its own members into Alpine County, it was clear

ute his paper to their patrons. "The bars were hostile to the gay press. The concept of liberation was very threatening to them," O'Brien said. "They wanted us to remain frightened and in the closet. As long as we were scared, they had a lock on us and our money. They knew that if gays became stronger, that lock would end. We would start operating our own bars, and they'd be out of business. They thwarted our every effort."[46]

The radical papers did not rely solely on the impact of verbal assaults but also worked with their parent organization, the Gay Liberation Front, to create an alternative to the Mafia-owned bars. In the spring of 1970, the front sponsored dances at Alternate University, a progressive institution on Sixth Avenue. *Come Out!* promoted and covered the dances, stating: "The purposes which we set out for the dances are to provide an alternate to the exploititive [sic] gay bars in the city."[47]

THE REVOLUTION SUBSIDES

Like many dissident presses, the radical gay publications that erupted in the late 1960s were short-lived. By the end of 1972, lesbian and gay radicalism had faded from the political landscape. The demise was due at least partly to a resounding lack of tangible progress in securing equal rights. Although the 1969 Stonewall Rebellion had energized the Gay and Lesbian Liberation Movement, that historic moment had failed to produce substantive changes in the status of the American homosexual. Only the states of Connecticut and Illinois legalized sex between consenting adults of the same gender. In early 1972, the New York City Council—at the very epicenter of the revolution—rejected a proposal that would have banned discrimination against gay people in employment, housing, and public accommodation. Later that year, Democratic presidential candidate George McGovern promised reform in federal employment and military policies for gay men and lesbians—and then was summarily trounced by Richard Nixon.

Also relevant was the disintegration of the Gay Liberation Front, home to the most radical and visible activists. The front fell victim primarily to internal unraveling because of a handful of members expressing grievances and sub-grievances and sub-sub-grievances, most of them involving the front's structure. Many activists later suspected—although they could never prove—that the discontented voices were infiltrators the FBI had paid to join the front in order to destroy it.[48]

The full extent to which the FBI's Secret War contributed to the decline of gay radicalism in the early 1970s is unclear, although there is no question that agents investigated gay press editors.

John O'Brien of *Gay Times* was a favorite. The agents believed that O'Brien had to be a straight communist who had infiltrated the Gay Liberation Movement—which they called the "Fag" Liberation Movement—because the twenty-year-old young man's rugged appearance did not fit the FBI's profile of a gay man. In their reports, agents routinely referred to gay men as "sissies" and "pansies." So the agents thought O'Brien was a communist agitator who had joined the movement because such a virile young man would easily lead the weak-willed gay men into anti-American activities. After observing O'Brien distributing his paper, the agents conducted an intense investigation into the editor's personal life, which became part of the 2,800 pages of material the FBI collected on post-Stonewall editors and other activists.[49]

Gay Times was not the only gay and lesbian publication that well-informed FBI agents were reading. They also collected copies of *GAY* and *Come Out!*, sending them directly to J. Edgar Hoover in Washington. Referring to the historians who disclosed after Hoover's death that he was a closeted homosexual, John O'Brien quipped: "J. Edgar jacked off while reading our papers. I just know it."[50]

Regardless of exactly how the director interacted with the papers on a sexual level, Freedom of Information Act requests have not revealed the same number of FBI terrorist acts against the gay and lesbian press as against the counterculture and Black Panther presses. One possible explanation is that the homophobic director and agents considered lesbians and gay men to be too ineffectual to be seriously concerned about.

From the historical distance of three decades, it is clear that Hoover and his lieutenants were wrong, however, as gay journalism played a central role in nourishing the Gay and Lesbian Liberation Movement during the three years that the revolutionary impulse held sway. For it was in the pages of the various papers that the movement's bedrock ideological issues took root.

The publications succeeded in moving some issues to resolution. With regard to whether Gay and Lesbian America would redefine sexual mores for itself, the content of the publications—both editorial and graphic—showed that the answer was very much in the affirmative. Likewise, the issue of whether lesbians and gay men would create their own nation was resolved just as clearly—but in the negative.

Other questions were asked but not answered, with many of the issues still being debated today. The role that fringe groups, particularly drag queens, should play in the movement continues to divide the community. At the end of 1972, it also remained unclear which of the many reform efforts would be primary or if the battle would be fought simultaneously on many fronts—to gain legal rights, increase political clout, and break the Mafia stranglehold on the bars.

The question of whether violence should be a central tactic in the fight against homophobia was resolved by default; the issue evaporated as a major topic of discussion when the radical publications that supported it were extinguished in the early 1970s. *Come Out!* was buried in the same coffin as the New York Gay Liberation Front it spoke for. Others papers that were produced by individuals or collectives—*Gay Times, Gay Sunshine, Killer Dyke,* and the *San Francisco Gay Free Press*—did not have a sufficient financial base or workforce to sustain them.[51]

The single publication that survived the aftershocks of Stonewall was the only one with a combination of relatively calm voices and stable finances: *GAY.* The stances of the editorially moderate publication generally carried the day in the debates, and it was this commercial enterprise that possessed the fiscal stamina that would allow it to influence the next phase of gay and lesbian liberation, surviving into the mid-1970s.[52]

Joining *GAY* would be a reincarnation of one of the radical publications. Financial problems and splintering of energy among members of the Gay Sunshine collective ended the Berkeley-based tabloid in early 1971, but it reappeared a few months later as a commercial enterprise that communicated its message through substantive literary works and in-depth interviews with gay artists into the 1980s. Collective member Pat Brown recalled: "The gay press had been born and, like the movement, wasn't going to die. Not ever. Those were heady days when we liked to allude to mythology. I'm sure we saw *Gay Sunshine* rising from its ashes like the phoenix. Well, actually, I'm not sure we said it that way then. But if we didn't—what the Hell?—we should have."[53]

Although members of both sexes actively participated in the social movements that erupted during the tumultuous 1960s, none of those various efforts placed a high priority on securing equal rights for American women. In fact, the men who opposed the Vietnam War, created a counterculture, and fought racial oppression were every bit as sexist as other men. Gay males were somewhat more sensitive to women's concerns—but not enough so to satisfy many feminists. "We have met the enemy and he's our friend," a female staff member wrote in one counterculture paper. "And that's what I want to write about—the friends, brothers, lovers in the counterfeit male-dominated Left."[1]

And write she did.

The author was Robin Morgan, and the paper she wrote for was *Rat*. In February 1970, Morgan was part of an all-woman cabal that seized the New York City bi-weekly and transformed it into one of the leading voices of the Women's Liberation Movement.

"*Rat* must be taken over permanently by women—or *Rat* must be destroyed," Morgan wrote in the article, titled "Goodbye to All That," that became a manifesto for women revolutionaries. "We are rising, powerful, wild hair flying, wild eyes staring, wild voices keening, undaunted by blood—we who hemorrhage every twenty-eight days. We are rising with a fury older and potentially greater than any force in history, and this time we will be free or no one will survive."[2]

Morgan's angry pronouncement struck a chord. During the early 1970s, women created some 230 feminist publications that demanded an end to gender-based oppression. Four months after the women of *Rat* commandeered that paper, like-minded women in Iowa City, Iowa, founded *Ain't I a Woman?* as an equally militant voice in the Midwest. The network of papers quickly spanned the entire country—from *It Ain't Me Babe* in Berkeley, California, to *off our backs* in Washington, D.C.[3]

Although the four publications differed in the stridency of their ideological positions, they shared several fundamental traits: All four were published by women's collectives—some residential, others not—that eschewed the traditional hierarchy of mainstream publications by refusing to designate any staff member the "editor." They all printed an abundance of material submitted by readers. All four papers refused to adhere to a regimented publication schedule—sometimes only a week passed between one issue and the next; other times that gap stretched to several months. They kept their cover prices low—usually twenty-five cents—and limited their advertising to feminist enterprises, such as other women's liberation papers, so individual donations from members and friends of the collectives ended up covering most of the printing and mailing costs. In addition, none of the staff members received salaries, none of the papers made a profit, and none of the collectives was willing to divulge circulation figures for its publication—rejecting the concept as capitalistic and patriarchal.

The publications diverged significantly not only from the mainstream press and the male-dominated New Left presses that flourished during the era but also from the reform-oriented newspapers, magazines, and newsletters produced by local chapters of the National Organization for Women, founded in 1966 by Betty Friedan and other moderate feminists. For the women of *Rat* and their sisters at the various radical papers around the country would not be placated with a gradual increase in women's rights; they demanded complete gender equity, and they demanded it immediately.

Historical context seemed to justify their militant call. Despite the Suffrage Movement gaining women the right to vote and the Birth Control Movement making contraceptive information widely available, a huge gap still separated American women from true equality. One way to gauge the lack of progress was to revisit the agenda that Elizabeth Cady Stanton and Susan Brownell Anthony had articulated in the pages of *The Revolution* beginning in 1868. A century had passed, but women in 1970 still faced the same problems that the pioneering publication had sought to erase: Job discrimination. Unequal pay. Sexual harassment. Inadequate political representation. Domestic violence. A legal system that continued to define abortion as an illegal act.

All of these issues had, however, at least moved into the mainstream of debate, thereby becoming too tepid for the new generation of female journalistic insurgents. So the leaders of the women's liberation press defined a whole new agenda. The only issue that *The Revolution* had raised that was still prominent in the 1970s dissident women's press was the one that, more than any other, would define feminist debate during both that decade and in the ones to follow: abortion.

FINDING A VOICE

Robin Morgan's early adulthood took her through the same stages that many young women of her generation followed. First came her life as a devoted housewife. Morgan married a writer named Kenneth Pitchford in 1962, when she was twenty, and sought fulfillment by mastering the art of domesticity. "I felt legitimized by a successful crown roast," she later wrote.[4]

Next came Morgan's years in the New Left. While earning her living as an editor and proofreader for a publishing house, she committed her activist energies first to the *Guardian*, then to *Rat*. But she gradually came to realize that the male editors suppressed women by relegating them to typing and preparing food for the men—the true revolutionaries. Being limited to monotonous tasks, Morgan said, frustrated many of the women. "We were used to such an approach from the Establishment, but here, too? In a context which was supposed to be different, to be fighting for all human freedom?"[5]

An early indication of Morgan's emerging radicalism came when she covered the protest against the 1968 Miss America Pageant. In the article she wrote for *Rat*, which was reprinted in numerous other counterculture papers, Morgan reported that 200 activists crowned a live sheep the real beauty queen and then "twenty brave sisters disrupted the live telecast of the pageant it-self, shouting 'Freedom for Women!' and hanging a huge banner reading 'Women's Liberation' from the balcony rail." Morgan's coverage of the demonstration, which she had helped organize, was by no means objective. Her article called for "two *thousand* of us liberating women" to protest future pageants and ended by saying, "A sisterhood of free women is giving birth to a new life-style, and the throes of its labor are authentic stages in the Revolution."[6]

So by February 1970 when the women of *Rat* seized the paper from its male editors, Robin Morgan—then the mother of a six-month-old baby boy—was at the vanguard. Although the women shared the various clerical, editorial, production, and distribution responsibilities in a rotating fashion, no one questioned that Morgan's "Goodbye to All That" essay in the first issue of the new

Rat was the most powerful piece in the paper, immediately establishing her as the movement's leading oracle.

One of Morgan's most controversial points was that the multifaceted social revolution that was underway could not, if it hoped to be effective, be led by white men. They were unacceptable leaders, Morgan insisted, because they were not victims of the society they were trying to overthrow but were, in fact, privileged and tyrannical. "A legitimate revolution must be led by those who have been most oppressed," Morgan wrote, which meant "black, brown, and white *women*."[7]

Morgan's primary target was liberal men. First she summarized the low regard male leaders of the American Left had for women activists by quoting a racist joke: "Know what they call a black man with a Ph.D.? A nigger." And then, without taking a breath, Morgan produced the sexist variation that had recently become popular among white men: "Know what they call a radical militant feminist? A crazy cunt."[8]

Morgan then lambasted male activists in a litany of rhetorical condemnations. She chastised the men for listing women among the objects they wanted available to them after winning the revolution, quoting the leaders as demanding "free grass, free food, and free *women*." Morgan also denounced the male leaders for telling aspiring young male revolutionaries to "fuck your women till they can't stand up." Morgan ended her searing attack with an eloquently simple statement she made on behalf of all feminists: "Not my brother, no. Not my revolution."[9]

Overnight, "Goodbye to All That" became the guiding credo of the Women's Liberation Movement. The widely reprinted essay was quoted, debated, cried over, and fought about—Morgan received death threats from numerous men. Words and phrases from the seminal statement were excerpted and printed on posters and banners, used for slogans, and read aloud during hundreds of the feminist consciousness-raising sessions that swept the country. When women in San Diego founded a radical feminist paper, they named it *Goodbye To All That*, and in the months and years that followed, women bidding farewell to male-dominated groups—such as lesbians who abandoned gay male revolutionaries to join their straight sisters in the battle for women's liberation—referred to their pronouncements as "daughters" of Morgan's clarion call.[10]

The powerful words published in *Rat* had simultaneously launched three mighty forces—the Women's Liberation Movement, the network of newspapers that fueled that movement, and a torrent of radical feminist issues.

As one of the most strident of the women's liberation publications, *Ain't I a Woman?* fully endorsed women taking up arms to fight sexism.

CALLING FOR THE REVOLUTION

Robin Morgan, as the leading spokeswoman of the movement, made it clear from the outset that she and her followers would not be satisfied with a few half-hearted reforms. "Sexism," she wrote, "is the root oppression, the one which, until and unless we *up*root it, will continue to put forth the branches of racism, class hatred, ageism, competition, ecological disaster, and economic exploitation." Previous efforts to improve American society had failed, she wrote, because they had been undertaken by men "for the sake of preserving their own male privileges."[11]

In contrast, Morgan called for a feminist revolution that would affect every citizen—male as well as female. The movement would begin with "each individual woman gaining self-respect and, yes, power, over her own body and soul first, then within her family, on her block, in her town, state, and so on out from the center, overlapping with similar changes other women are experiencing, the circles rippling more widely and inclusively as they go."[12]

As the printed voice of a social, political, and economic insurrection of vast scope and ambition, the women's liberation press pulled no punches. The most militant of the feminist voices—like the *Black Panther* and the radical gay and lesbian publications of the era—exploded with images of rifles, pistols, bombs, hand grenades, and clenched fists, while shrill headlines reinforced the belief that American women were on the brink of armed rebellion: "Women Are Rising Up—They Are Angry," "Seize the Land," "Kick Ass," "Death to All Honkies!"[13]

Like the violent-oriented images and headlines, the most extreme editorial statements were concentrated in the most militant of the papers. "Our struggle is against the male power system which is a system of war and death," *Rat* defiantly stated in en early issue. "If in the process of that struggle we are forced to mutilate, murder and massacre those men, then so it must be." *Ain't I a Woman?* adopted an equally extreme position. "I want a revolution of women really castrating their men," one essay read. "I want to eliminate men because they are murderers and destructive and fucked up."[14]

The less militant voices called for change but stopped short of condoning murder or mutilation. *It Ain't Me Babe* established a nonviolent stance by stating in its first issue that the members of the collective founded the paper "to *defend* our right to be treated as human beings"—not to do intentional harm to anyone. *off our backs* made the point in its inaugural editorial as well, saying, "Our position is not anti-men but pro-women."[15]

EXPLORING FEMALE SEXUALITY

Throughout the first two centuries of American history, society had viewed sexuality almost exclusively in terms of bringing pleasure to men. So one of the major themes in the women's liberation press of the early 1970s was acknowledging that sex could—and most definitely *should*—be enjoyable for women as well. Indeed, this theme provides a vivid illustration of how the various dissident papers approached issues.

off our backs, the least radical of the papers, encouraged women to enjoy sexual activity but not to be reckless. The Washington, D.C., paper counseled its readers to avoid unwanted pregnancies by practicing birth control. Still cautious about the long-term effects of the pill, *oob* advised its readers to use a diaphragm. "The contraceptive preparation is not harmful to the vaginal canal nor harmful if ingested orally," one article reassured readers. The story then went on to describe step by step how to insert, lubricate, and remove the soft rubber device from the vagina.[16]

It Ain't Me Babe was next on the ideological continuum, adopting an editorial stance only slightly more radical than *off our backs*. Typical of the sex-related items in the Berkeley paper was one submitted by a reader and titled "Sex: An Open Letter from a Sister." The author described how she had felt like a failure for many years because she could not reach orgasm during intercourse with her husband, even though she easily did so by rubbing her hand against her clitoris. Only with the advent of the Women's Liberation Movement, the woman wrote, did she begin talking with other women and discover that she was not a "freak" but that many women were unable to achieve vaginal orgasm. "I am no longer ashamed of my clitoral orgasm, but I am so embarrassed about my ignorance and how I let this go on for years and years, and tears and fears."[17]

Ain't I a Woman? adopted a much more radical stance than either *off our backs* or *It Ain't Me Babe*, on female sexuality as well as other issues. One article, titled "Vaginal Politics," argued that the first two steps women had to take if they were to embrace the pleasures of sex were to explore their bodies and to reject any sense of shame attached to bodily functions. Readers could accomplish both goals, the paper suggested, by observing their bodies closely through a complete menstrual cycle. The article then walked readers through the various stages, ending with the observation that, "just before menstruation, the vaginal walls will be swollen and tender, the cervix swollen and blue with veins seeming to pop out on it." The most memorable element of the *Ain't I a Woman?* story was not the words, however, but the photographs that accompanied them. The images showed a naked woman positioned so that neither her face nor her upper body was visible, the entire photo being filled with her exposed genitalia. To complete the picture, arrows had been drawn in to indicate the most intimate of the woman's body parts—including the vagina and clitoris.[18]

Rat joined *Ain't I a Woman?* at the radical end of the ideological spectrum. In keeping with that position, the New York paper's content included a sexually explicit piece describing how a woman could bring herself to sexual climax. "It is time for all of us to learn how to make love to ourselves," the article began. With an unprecedented degree of journalistic explicitness, the piece then described how a woman could masturbate by moving her hand in "a downward stroke beginning just above the root of the clitoris, passing over the clitoris and on down the mid-line, into the vaginal entrance, following the front wall of the passage and ending a little way inside." Although the how-to description was the most memorable aspect of the article, which was accompanied by a drawing of a naked woman caressing her genitals, the story also carried a strong feminist message about female independence: "Masturbation is different from, not inferior to, sex for two. Also, with masturbation you don't have to worry about someone else's needs or opinions of you." That message was reinforced by the article's title—"Very Pleasurable Politics."[19]

CELEBRATING LESBIANISM

One of the issues that drew an indelible fault line between the radical women's liberation press and the moderate women's rights publications was the concept of women loving women—not only emotionally but also physically.

National Organization for Women founder Betty Friedan and other reform-minded feminists of the early 1970s preferred to sideline lesbians, arguing that homosexuality was so controversial that supporting it would impede progress on what they considered more important issues, such as electing more women to political office. Friedan publicly accused "men-hating lesbians" of trying to dominate NOW, prompting some lesbians to dub her "the Joe McCarthy of the women's movement."[20]

Radical women, on the other hand, insisted that fully embracing lesbianism was absolutely fundamental to their movement. The various women's liberation publications, whatever their level of stridency, were solidly positioned in this camp. Indeed, all of the publishing collectives included at least a few lesbians, with the number sometimes growing to a majority. In early 1972, the entire staff of *Ain't I a Woman?* was composed of gay women, prompting the paper to announce that it was being published by "a collective of 16 women functioning as a world-wide conspiracy of Radical Lesbians—and don't you forget it!"[21]

The single most frequent byline to appear above articles about lesbians was that of Rita Mae Brown, who wrote for *Rat* as well as *off our backs*. Brown often criticized the reform-minded feminists such as Friedan who said the only les-

It Ain't Me Babe, like other feminist voices, celebrated the importance of matriarchy as the lifeblood in the evolution of humankind.

bians who encountered problems because of their sexuality were those who "wear a neon sign." Brown began her response with a single word: "Bullshit." She then continued, "One doesn't get liberated by hiding. A black person doesn't possess integrity by passing for white."[22]

Much of Brown's writing was committed to analyzing exactly why so many people—especially men—hated lesbians. Part of the reason, Brown believed, was that "if we [women] all wound up loving each other, it would mean each man would lose his personal 'nigger'—a real and great loss if you are a man." She also argued that lesbianism threatened the male ego. "Men always explain lesbianism as a woman turning to another woman because either she can't get a man or because she has been treated badly by men. They can't seem to cope with the fact that it is a positive response to another human being. To love another woman is an acceptance of sex which is a severe violation of the male culture (sex as exploitation) and therefore carries severe penalties."[23]

Brown felt the sting of homophobia on a personal level. After she began writing and speaking openly about her sexuality, she was verbally attacked. On a typical occasion, a man telephoned her at home and said, "I hear you don't like men, you're a dyke, a cunt lapper. I've put a bomb under your stairway." Although the man then hung up and no bomb ever appeared, such comments still took their toll. Brown wrote, "I wish I could say that it didn't hurt."[24]

Another frequent byline in the various women's liberation papers was that of Martha Shelley, who was simultaneously writing for the gay and lesbian press. In one piece that appeared in *Ain't I a Woman?*, Shelley argued that feminists should not shun lesbians but revere them as models of women's liberation. "The lesbian, through her ability to obtain love and sexual satisfaction from other women, is freed of dependence on men for love, sex and money. She doesn't have to do menial chores for them (at least at home), nor cater to their egos, nor submit to hasty and inept sexual encounters."[25]

The bylines "Rita Mae Brown" and "Martha Shelley" were joined by hundreds of others, as an army of readers who were not yet ready to publicly identify themselves as lesbians nevertheless had strong opinions that they were eager to express through the anonymity of their first names. *It Ain't Me Babe* was particularly open to providing a venue for these women. "Mary" wrote, "As homosexuals, we must burst through our own alienation and jump the fences we set up in our own minds and in other people's minds about who we are and whether or not we matter to the world," and "Judy" echoed the same theme, saying, "The accusation of being a movement of lesbians will always be powerful if we cannot say, 'Being a lesbian is good.' Nothing short of that will suffice."[26]

DEMANDING EQUALITY FOR WOMEN OF COLOR

Lesbians were not the only group that the leaders of the moderate wing of the women's rights effort largely excluded from their movement. Betty Friedan and her nonrevolutionary cohorts focused their reform agenda on improving the quality of life for middle-class white women. Members of the collectives that produced the women's liberation press, by contrast, insisted upon broadening the agenda to include women of color, most of whom were members of the working class.

The Iowa City women who founded their own newspaper in the summer of 1970 made their commitment to African Americans clear when they chose *Ain't I a Woman?* as the name of their paper. Legendary former slave Sojourner Truth had first asked the poignant question in 1851 at a women's rights convention. "The man over there says women need to be helped into carriages and lifted over ditches," Truth said. "Nobody ever helps me into carriages or over puddles—and ain't I a woman? Look at my arm! I have ploughed and planted and gathered into barns and no man could head me—and ain't I a woman? I have born thirteen children and seen most of 'em sold into slavery and when I cried out with my mother's grief, none but Jesus heard me—and ain't I a woman?" Truth's defiant words were an early instance of a black woman calling for definitions of female gender not only to extend to African American women but also to include women's strength and suffering. *Ain't I a Woman?* echoed those demands by quoting Truth's words on the cover of its first issue, next to a drawing of the revered abolitionist with her clenched fist raised powerfully upward.[27]

off our backs, as a less radical women's liberation paper, reached out to women of color by making sure a series of question-and-answer interviews with women in the local Washington, D.C., area included several African American women. The paper's interview with a professional-level woman working in the U.S. Department of Health, Education and Welfare focused on why she had chosen *not* to join the National Organization for Women. "It's difficult for me to empathize with some of the things they talk about," the woman said. "If I were to define my priorities in order of importance to me in terms of my personal development, being female would not be first. What would be first is the fact that I am black." The *oob* interview also included how the woman perceived NOW and other women's organizations. "The groups that I'm familiar with," she said point blank, "have been primarily white."[28]

It Ain't Me Babe's editorial content related to women of color also criticized nonrevolutionary feminists. A piece titled "An Open Letter to Betty Friedan" read, "We relate to the black women in the south and the Chicano women in the southwest and the Indian women on the reservations who still can't even read," and then shifted to a question posed directly to Friedan, "Do you even know these women exist?" In a proactive step toward encouraging feminist consciousness-raising groups to include race in their discussions, *It Ain't Me Babe* published a list of questions that it hoped would spur substantive conversations; first on the list was, "Are you more afraid of being raped by a white man or a black man? Why?"[29]

Rat was not content merely to interview women of color or to suggest questions for discussion but insisted upon racing full throttle into the tension between black women and black men. An article titled "From Black Sisters to Black Brothers" began, "Now here's how it is. Poor black men won't support their families, won't stick by their women—all they think about is the street, dope and liquor, women, a piece of ass, and their cars." The angry piece continued, "Black women have always been told by black men that we were black, ugly, evil bitches and whores—in other words, we were the real niggers in this society—oppressed by whites, male and female, and the black man, too."[30]

FIGHTING BACK AGAINST PHYSICAL ABUSE

In addition to discussing the emotional and psychological pain that women were forced to endure, the publications also focused a great deal of their attention on the physical abuse of women—especially the rising number of rapes.

Robin Morgan raised this topic in an early issue of *Rat*. "Every day newspapers carry stories of atrocities committed against women: murder, rape, beatings, mutilations," Morgan wrote. The rate of sex crimes had increased so dramatically, she continued, that the situation amounted to the "attempted genocide of a people on the basis of sex." Neither Morgan, *Rat*, nor the other publications were satisfied merely to identify the problem of physical attacks on women, however, but also demanded an end to the abuse. "Women must defend our lives and bodies and minds against male violence, by any means necessary," Morgan wrote. "We must learn and practice self- and sister-defense."[31]

The other papers joined *Rat* in encouraging women to fight back against physical abuse, although their specific approaches to the topic varied.

off our backs, with a strong news orientation reflected in its subtitle "a women's news journal," concentrated on reporting instances of rape and other physical attacks. On occasion, though, the paper's editorial stand came blaring through in its selection of what stories to report and how to present them. When a male police officer on the District of Columbia's vice squad attributed the increase of rape cases to the Women's Liberation Movement—"These liberated women," he said, "have the attitude that they can walk the streets like a man"— *oob* headlined the item: "Sick Sick Sick."[32]

Ain't I a Woman?'s treatment of the physical abuse issue was consistent with its radical stripe. When the paper listed the specific needs of American women on its cover, an end to physical abuse was at the top. "We demand that women be given free self-defense and physical training," the members of the Iowa collective wrote. "Their physical development has been stifled by their socialization into being 'ladies.' They must be trained, beginning at a young age, to be strong and capable of defending themselves. The rape and beating of women will end only when it becomes just as dangerous to attack a woman as a man." *Ain't I a Woman?* made the same point, perhaps even more dramatically, through its images. One early cover showed a young woman standing tall with her arm raised over her head holding a rifle—a feminist warrior poised for battle.[33]

But the women's liberation publication that, more than any other, embraced the theme of women defending themselves against physical attack was *It Ain't Me Babe.* The Berkeley paper began its campaign on the cover of its premier issue, filling the page with a story headlined "Self Defense for Women" and a photo of a young woman in a karate stance. "We have depended on males to protect us too long," the article began. "It is time that all females learn to defend themselves. Women's physical weakness and its psychological consequences can only be overcome through developing their bodies. We demand that self defense instruction be provided by the university [of California at Berkeley], by towns, schools, businesses, welfare departments—all institutions which have control over women's lives."[34]

That demand was the opening round of a relentless campaign by *It Ain't Me Babe* to persuade women to fight back. Numerous articles offered practical tips on how women could protect themselves. Opting to defy not only the conventions of female roles but also the grammatical conventions of capitalization, one piece began: "your attitude is essential. refuse to be a passive victim. attackers assume we will attempt no self defense. many men are so cocksure that a simple kick in the shin can set you free." The article went on to advise women to arm themselves with mace ("carry this in your pocket, you may not have time to open your purse") and to kick an assailant with the side of her foot rather than the front (the side is stronger and covers more surface than the toes). The article ended by saying: "if he attempts to choke you, don't give up; both his hands are occupied and you can stab his eyes with your fingers. if he just won't quit, hit at the hollow of his throat with your finger tips. this can knock him out. if you're extremely strong and angry, it can kill him."[35]

The most extreme aspect of *It Ain't Me Babe*'s crusade against physical attacks was the paper's plan for how convicted rapists should be punished. "if men had an arm chopped off every time they raped one of us, they could not get more than 2 women." Recognizing that many readers would think that cutting off the arm of a rapist was too severe of a punishment, the paper went on to offer a defense of the radical proposal: "they are not fighting fair. if you are polite and harmless, he may get your daughter in 10 years."[36]

CRUSADING FOR ABORTION RIGHTS

The most ubiquitous issue in the women's liberation press during its early years was one that would remain a topic of rancorous debate throughout America for decades to come. In 1970, abortion laws varied widely, with about half the states allowing the procedure only when the woman's life was in danger and the other half allowing it in some circumstances, such as in cases of rape.

Although the women's liberation papers were united in their desire that abortion be legalized in all instances nationwide, they differed in the tactics they employed to show their support. On this most contentious of issues, the most strident publications spoke with a voice that was loud, shrill, and filled with a sense of outrage. One article in *Rat* read, "We pledge a campaign of terror against any man who tries to deny us the right to control our own bodies. No more passive demonstrations!" And a piece in *Ain't I a Woman?* screamed, "Sisters, remember—health care is a right and not a privilege! DEMAND THAT RIGHT!"[37]

off our backs chose a very different approach. Although the paper published many essays and editorials in support of abortion rights, most of its coverage on the topic was in the form of news stories. Hundreds upon hundreds of articles covered every aspect of the abortion-rights campaign—from speeches, debates, and conferences to mass marches, public demonstrations, and guerrilla theater productions. The paper also documented both advances and setbacks in legal cases at every level of the court system and in state legislative initiatives from coast to coast. *oob* called the campaign to legalize abortion the most important women's rights effort since the suffrage campaign, and, because of that stature, the effort deserved saturation coverage—and saturation coverage it got.[38]

Although all the stories provided the who, what, when, and where of the news event at hand, many of them clearly communicated a pro-abortion-rights point of view as well. A reporter covering a planning meeting for a national abortion-rights conference in New York City concluded her story with the comment, "I, personally, was impressed by the consistently well thought out, articulate positions presented." Likewise, an article reporting Maryland Governor

Marvin Mandel's veto of an abortion-rights bill ended with the statement, "Remember, Marvin will be up for re-election in November."[39]

In addition to summarizing the most recent developments in the abortion-rights campaign, *off our backs* also promoted upcoming events. An article about 3,000 women participating in a rally in Washington ended, "The Women's National Abortion Action Coalition, which organized the demonstration, is holding its next national coordinating committee meeting December 18th at 12 at the GWU [George Washington University] Student Center." *oob* also printed sample statements it encouraged readers to personalize and then deliver before local judges and government officials, such as, "I _____ wish to present the following personal testimony concerning abortion."[40]

off our backs readers often learned more about developments in the abortion-rights campaign than readers of mainstream newspapers did. When Dr. Ernest Lowe, chief of obstetrics at D.C. General Hospital in Washington, told women's liberation leaders that he would not allow his doctors to give abortions because the procedure was "boring and distasteful," *oob* readers heard the quote, but *Washington Post* and *Washington Evening Star* readers did not. Similarly, when Massachusetts legislator Joe Ward said he wouldn't support legalized abortions just because of "some broad who gets herself knocked up in some hotel," *oob* readers again heard the quote, but readers of the *Boston Globe* did not.[41]

It was not only *oob*'s vigilance in covering the various developments in the abortion-rights campaign that kept readers informed but also the paper's willingness to undertake investigative reporting. After abortion became legal in New York state and pregnant women from throughout the East Coast began traveling there for the procedure, an *off our backs* reporter interviewed a number of women to make sure that the various New York clinics were providing patients with proper medical care. They weren't. One clinic, the reporter wrote, gave women "a physical exam which includes complete blood and urine lab tests, a Pap test, blood pressure, temperature, listening to the heart, and a complete medical history." But a second clinic, the reporter continued, "merely asks a woman about her medical history via a questionnaire." The reporter gave the first clinic a grade of "A," the second one a "C."[42]

During the three years between *oob*'s founding in February 1970 and the U.S. Supreme Court's decision to legalize abortion in January 1973, the paper's coverage of the abortion-rights campaign was without peer—not only among women's liberation papers but among all news outlets. For no other journalistic organization in the country exhibited *oob*'s combination of a consistent focus on women's issues, its news-oriented approach to women's liberation, and its location in the nation's capital.

EXPANDING THE SECRET WAR TO THE WOMEN'S LIBERATION PRESS

It must have been excruciating for the virtually all-male FBI of the early 1970s—a legendary bastion of male chauvinism—to admit that a group of females had become such a powerful force that it was necessary for the bureau to expand its Secret War to the women's liberation press. Nevertheless, the agents rose to the occasion and made the dissident papers a target of their harassment campaign.

The FBI first set its sights on the most radical of the publications. The women who commandeered *Rat* from its male editors made arrangements with a New Jersey company to print the paper. After FBI agents visited the printer and threatened to prosecute him on obscenity charges related to *Rat*'s explicit articles about female sexuality, however, he refused to continue doing business with the paper. The women eventually located another printer, but the additional effort sapped time and energy that they otherwise could have devoted to their primary purpose of writing material aimed at liberating the American woman. FBI agents also monitored *Rat*'s mail, opening and reading correspondence before postal officials delivered it. The agents confiscated many of the letters and then harassed the women who had written them—thereby causing many readers to stop buying the paper.[43]

The FBI next focused its attention on the other vociferously radical voice of women's liberation, *Ain't I a Woman?* The agents hired a female informant to infiltrate the collective by arriving in Iowa City, claiming to be destitute, and appealing to the women to help out a sister who had been victimized by the country's patriarchal system. "We offered her a spare room in the house where our collective lived," an *Ain't I a Woman?* staff member later wrote. After the woman began asking an inordinately large number of questions, members of the collective became suspicious and distanced themselves from her, prompting the woman to leave after about two months. In the wake of her departure, however, a number of *Ain't I a Woman?* staff members had altercations with local police regarding their drug use and homosexuality. The officers were so familiar with the activities inside the collective that the information clearly had come from the infiltrator.[44]

As women's liberation gained momentum, FBI agents realized that the most effective movement publication was neither of the ideologically strident papers but the women's news journal being published in the very shadow of the bureau's headquarters in the nation's capital. So in the spring of 1971, agents from the Alexandria, Virginia, office initiated a comprehensive campaign of intimidation against *off our backs*. The opening shot came in the form of a memo to J. Edgar Hoover that criticized the most recent issue of *oob* because it featured a drawing of labor activist Mary Harris "Mother" Jones on the cover, which the agents interpreted—in quite a stretch of the imagination—as signaling that the paper's staff was planning to use racketeering tactics to force middle-of-the-road women to join the abortion-rights campaign. In reality, the cover was merely commemorating Jones's birthday by suggesting that her famous quotation highlighted on the cover—"Pray for the dead. Fight like Hell for the living"—was an apt motto for the contemporary effort to fight on behalf of women who otherwise might die while having the unsanitary abortions that women had to resort to because the procedure was illegal in many states.[45]

That memo launched an FBI effort to intimidate *oob*'s printer, the Journal Newspapers, Inc., so it would stop doing business with the women's liberation paper; that effort failed. Later memos documented the FBI's attempt to coerce members of the *off our backs* staff to provide information about the paper's internal operations; that attempt also failed. Despite the FBI's lack of success, the agents still created considerable anxiety within the collective. "We were very concerned about the possibility of government disruption of *off our backs*," two members later wrote. "Several times, women worried that other women who had contact with the newspaper might be government agents."[46]

A LEGACY BOTH NARROW AND BROAD

off our backs not only survived the FBI's covert efforts to destroy it but went on to achieve an unparalleled longevity among women's liberation publications—and, indeed, among the legion of dissident publications that erupted in the 1960s and early 1970s. Still being published today, the Washington, D.C., paper circulates to 29,000 committed readers worldwide. *Rat, Ain't I a Woman?*, and *It Ain't Me Babe* all ceased publication by 1975.[47]

From the distance of more than three decades after the women's liberation press came into being, this genre of the dissident press appears to have been effective on two distinct levels.

First, the papers provided a venue for the ideas, concerns, and life experiences of an enormous number of women who otherwise may never have raised their often-disquieting voices. In fact, the papers launched the writing careers of numerous women who went on to enjoy highly successful publishing careers.

One example is Robin Morgan. After her "Goodbye to All That" essay in *Rat* became a cogent manifesto for women's liberation, Morgan went on to publish more than a dozen books and a plethora of poems and essays. The most high-profile among Morgan's many works is *Sisterhood Is Powerful*, an anthology of essays that served as the catalyst for thousands of women to change both their personal aspirations and their daily realities. First published in 1970, *Sisterhood Is Powerful* is one of the most important feminist tracts ever written and is still being read today by new generations of feminists.[48]

Rita Mae Brown is another widely respected author whose work was first published in the women's liberation press. Brown made a major contribution to the country's perceptions of lesbians in 1973 when she wrote the best-selling *Rubyfruit Jungle*, a semi-autobiographical novel that shattered lesbian stereotypes by depicting gay women as smart, fun-loving, and beautiful. Brown has gone on to write a dozen additional books.[49]

The second legacy of the women's liberation press is in the advancements among American women that took place simultaneously with the publishing of the papers. Most significant of those victories was the 1973 Supreme Court decision that legalized abortion nationwide. That monumental event marked a watershed in the struggle for gender equality, as it established—more than any other event before or since—a woman's right to control her own body. Despite many assaults on that right, it has remained in place.

Progress has been made regarding other controversial themes raised in *Rat*, *Ain't I a Woman?*, *It Ain't Me Babe*, and *off our backs* as well. Sex is no longer seen as a pleasurable activity for men only, lesbian rights are now a staple element on the feminist agenda (including that of the National Organization for Women), equality for women of color has not been achieved but certainly has been established as a goal of most fair-minded Americans, and the abundance of self-defense classes and rape-prevention educational programs speaks to the priority that American women place on protecting themselves.

By the late 1970s, Robin Morgan had already published an inventory of other indications that the American woman had succeeded in entering a new phase in her liberation. Morgan wrote of the proliferation of women's health centers and shelters for battered women in cities and towns across the country. She also applauded the emergence of women's studies as an academic discipline on college campuses and the growing number of women's bookstores—and the thousands of feminist-oriented volumes to fill their shelves. Morgan documented an explosion of women-owned businesses, too, writing, "Restaurants, craft shops, self-defense schools, employment agencies, publishing houses, and small presses—the list goes on an on."[50]

Reinforcing her stature as one of the Women's Liberation Movement's most insightful theorists, Morgan also noted the changes that were taking place in feminism itself. She acknowledged that many critics were saying that the women's movement was dead. "Such death-knell articulations are not only (deliberately?) unaware of multiform alternate institutions that are mushrooming," Morgan wrote, "but unconscious of the more profound and threatening-to-the-status-quo political *attitudes* which underlie that surface." Feminists were not retreating, Morgan wrote, but were maturing beyond what she called the "ejaculatory tactics" of the radical early years of the movement—so vividly expressed in the most strident of the women's liberation papers—"into a long-term, committed attitude toward *winning*." The new generation of women's rights leaders, Morgan continued, "know that serious, lasting change does not come about overnight, or simply, or without enormous pain and diligent examination and tireless, undramatic, every-day-a-bit-more-one-step-at-a-time work."[51]

Refusing to take a defensive or apologetic stance regarding the less-revolutionary phase that American feminists had entered, Morgan wrote: "We've only just begun, and there's no stopping us. The American woman is maturing and stretching and daring and, yes, succeeding, in ways undreamt until now. She will survive the naysayers, male *and* female, and she will coalesce in all her wondrously various forms and diverse life-styles, ages, races, classes, and internationalities into one harmonious blessing on this agonized world. She is so very beautiful, and I love her. The face in the mirror is me. And the face in the mirror is you."[52]

The fourth generation of the dissident press bulged with five genres dedicated to effecting social change, each with a discrete mission and yet all of them some- what overlapping as well. Even though these "voices of revolution" followed the well-worn path that their predecessors had been traversing for a century and a half, they nevertheless illuminated several more overarching commonalities rel- evant to this unique form of American journalism.

THE DISSIDENT PRESS IS PARTICULARLY ACTIVE DURING PERIODS OF SOCIAL, ECONOMIC, AND POLITICAL TURBULENCE

The labor papers that launched dissident journalism in the United States in the 1820s—the *Mechanic's Free Press*, *Free Enquirer*, and *Working Man's Advocate*— reflected the concerns of an awakened working class during a time of rapid change impelled by the first stages of the country's shift from an agricultural to an industrial economy.

The most prolific period for dissident voices during the 1800s came at the end of the century as the robber barons thrust American industry into the future at breakneck speed. Recognizing that this economic surge had driven urban laborers into squalid tenements and fetid factories, socialist and anarchist pub- lications erupted in a desperate attempt to eradicate capitalism and return the nation to the working men and women who—according to the *Appeal to Rea- son*, *The Alarm*, and *Mother Earth*—had been forced into industrial slavery.

The most active period in the entire history of the dissident press was the ten years between 1965 and 1975. That single decade gave birth to four of the four- teen genres covered in this book—the counterculture, Black Panthers, gay and lesbian, and women's liberation presses—and marked the most vital period of a fifth—the anti-Vietnam War press. It is no coincidence that the period was fertile ground not only for dissident journalism but also for upheaval across the spectrum of American life. Political uncertainty surrounded the most unpopular war in U.S. history and the assassinations, in chillingly rapid succession, of John F. Kennedy, the Rev. Martin Luther King Jr., and Robert F. Kennedy. Meanwhile, social unrest spawned a defiant youth culture, rebellions on college campuses and in urban centers, and social movements led by racial and sexual minorities who demanded changes in an economic system increasingly defined by greed, consumerism, and a widening gap between the Haves and the Have Nots.

DISSIDENT PUBLICATIONS TEND TO BE SHORT LIVED

Of the thirty-three individual newspapers and magazines illuminated in this book, only thirteen survived more than ten years.

This figure shows that the life expectancy of a dissident publication is considerably shorter than that of a mainstream one. Although it is impossible to determine the average life span of the thousands of commercial newspapers published in the United States during the last three centuries, the founding dates of some of today's leading papers—1851 for the *New York Times,* 1877 for the *Washington Post,* and 1881 for the *Los Angeles Times*—attest to the staying power of the Brahmins of the American press.

One frequent cause of death for dissident publications—along with the lack of resources that results from scant advertising and circulation revenue—is the federal government. Anthony Comstock's anti-obscenity crusade in the 1870s destroyed the sexual reform press, first by entangling the editors of *Woodhull & Claflin's Weekly, The Word,* and *Lucifer, the Light-Bearer* in court cases and then by sending them to jail—ultimately shortening the lives of Ezra Heywood and Moses Harman. That same government crusade against obscene material—as defined by "St. Anthony"—killed another dissident voice in the early twentieth century when *Woman Rebel* ceased publication as Margaret Sanger fled to Europe to avoid prosecution for attempting to inform American women about birth control.

The federal government waged another far-reaching campaign against the dissident press in the 1960s and 1970s. The FBI's Secret War included a broad array of activities—many of them illegal—that contributed to the premature demise of numerous journalistic tribunes of the anti-Vietnam War, counterculture, Black Panther, gay and lesbian, and women's liberation movements.

For a dissident voice to survive beyond the ten-year threshold, the journalists supporting it often have had to pay a high price. William Lloyd Garrison endured a life of poverty and deprivation, as did his family, to keep *The Liberator* in print for the thirty-five years until slavery was finally abolished. Robert S. Abbott continued to publish the *Chicago Defender* long after the Great Migration ended, but he did so only by eliminating the militancy of his editorial content. Dorothy Day published the *Catholic Worker* for half a century, but even in her old age she suffered the emotional pain of being publicly denounced, because of her opposition to the Vietnam War, as "Moscow Mary."

IN SEEKING TO END A WRONG THAT IS DEEPLY EMBEDDED INTO AMERICAN LIFE, THE DISSIDENT PRESS OFTEN EITHER PROMOTES OR CONDONES VIOLENCE

Although most readers prefer nonviolent approaches to resolving problems and therefore may cringe at this observation, the necessity of taking up arms to battle the various evils perpetrated against the poor and the powerless throughout this nation's history was a recurring theme in the dissident press of both the nineteenth and twentieth centuries.

Abolitionist and socialist publications merely condoned violence. *The Liberator* carried articles that encouraged slave revolts, but William Lloyd Garrison, on a personal level, remained morally opposed to violence; the *Appeal to Reason* on occasion threatened armed conflict—such as in the "Arouse, Ye Slaves!" editorial—but otherwise remained firmly committed to its mantra of "ballots not bullets."

Anti-lynching and anarchist publications embraced violence unequivocally. When Ida B. Wells told *New York Age* readers that lynching had become so widespread in the South that "a Winchester rifle should have a place of honor in every black home," she was not giving decorating advice. And Albert R. Parsons of *The Alarm* was fully convinced that the violent overthrow of the government was the only way to wrest the United States from the greedy grip of capitalism, with the most memorable element in the paper being the dozens of articles and editorials praising the power of dynamite to level the nation's social, economic, and political playing field.

Numerous 1960s dissident voices celebrated violence; they saw armed revolution as the only feasible means of eliminating the pervasive racism, homophobia, and sexism that had become ingrained in modern-day America. The *Black Panther* and the majority of both gay and women's liberation papers gave their visual endorsement by peppering their pages with images of rifles, pistols, hand grenades, bombs, and clenched fists. Editorial content reinforced the point—the *Black Panther* called for all racist police officers to be killed, *Come*

Out! denounced the City College of New York as a citadel of "establishment thinking" that should be burned to the ground, and *Ain't I a Woman?* urged its readers to castrate men "because they are murderers and destructive and fucked up."

WHEN A VARIETY OF DISSIDENT PUBLICATIONS SPEAK ON BEHALF OF A MOVEMENT, THE RADICAL VOICES TEND TO EXPIRE WHILE THE MODERATE ONES LIVE ON

An early example of this phenomenon began to unfold in 1868 when *The Revolution*, with its first issue, insisted that suffrage was only the first step in the march toward women's rights, so the uncompromising newspaper campaigned hard for such concepts—ones the mainstream press would not even mention, much less support—as enacting laws to ban sexual harassment and domestic violence. The more temperate *Woman's Journal*, by contrast, limited its agenda to suffrage and such middle-class reform efforts as establishing women's clubs and encouraging women to obtain higher educations. *The Revolution*'s strident voice went silent after two and a half years; *Woman's Journal* continued without interruption for sixty-three.

The genres of the dissident press that emerged in the middle to late twentieth century provided several examples of this same tendency. *The Kudzu* and *The Paper*, two extremist counterculture papers, were both dead by 1972; the tamer *Berkeley Barb* survived until 1980. *Gay Times, Come Out!, Gay Sunshine*, the *San Francisco Gay Free Press*, and *Killer Dyke* all called for radical changes in American society, but then withered and died while the moderate *GAY* continued to publish. *Rat, Ain't I a Woman?*, and *It Ain't Me Babe*—all militant in their demands for fundamental changes in the role of American women—added three more tombstones to the dissident press graveyard by 1975; more than a quarter of a century later, the less strident *off our backs* is still alive and well and appearing with total regularity from an office in the nation's capital—both in printed form and on line.

15 DISSIDENCE IN A NEW MILLENNIUM

The phenomenon of creating a dissident press to effect social change that William Heighton pioneered when he created the first labor newspaper in 1828 did not cease after feminists published their women's liberation newspapers in the 1970s. Throughout the final years of the twentieth century and the early ones of the twenty-first, social and political insurgents have continued to define their own brand of journalism. From a historian's perspective, though, sufficient time has not yet elapsed to gauge, with any degree of certainty, the long-term impact of the dissident publications that have appeared during the last thirty years.

And yet, this book would somehow feel incomplete if it did not acknowledge and speak at least briefly, if not conclusively, about two important forces that have emerged during recent decades and that clearly have the potential to challenge the institutions and power relationships that define this nation today: the zine and the Internet.

The author of one book about zines defines them as "non-commercial, non-professional, small-circulation magazines which their creators produce, publish, and distribute by themselves." The roots of these unique publications can be traced back to science fiction fan magazines of the 1930s, but their numbers exploded during the 1980s. As Ronald Reagan set a conservative tone throughout the country, throngs of young people expressed their growing alienation with establishment society by creating an underground communication network of scruffy, inexpensive-to-produce, highly personalized zines. By the 1990s, their ranks had grown to at least 10,000—with some observers placing the figure closer to 50,000.[1]

Many zines consist of an individual writer's thoughts on a variety of topics, but others seek to transform society with regard to one specific issue and, therefore, fit securely under the rubric of "voices of revolution." And with circulations that sometimes have surpassed 25,000, the impact of these grassroots voices of dissent should not be dismissed.[2]

Brief descriptions of even a handful of the plethora of zines being published today give a flavor of both their diversity and their potential for social change.

Beer Frame is one of the hundreds of publications that focus on the theme that has emerged as perhaps the single most consistent message among zines: Consumerism is out of control. This Brooklyn-based voice of dissent exposes the strategies that some public relations firms devote to developing the hype that has become a seemingly essential element in selling a product. "How many board meetings," editor Paul Lukas asked, "did they hold to determine what a new item would look like and what it would be called?" Lukas went on to tell his readers that a particular shish kebab marinade called Spiedies tastes no different from dozens of other sauces. But this particular one became an overnight sensation in Binghamton, New York, after a phalanx of well-paid PR flacks came up with the idea of creating a "Spiediefest" to promote the product that climaxed, Lukas wrote, with the crowning of "the acknowledged king of the Spiedie"—the very restaurant that had hired the PR team to begin with.[3]

Kill Your Television is one of the most ambitious of the multitude of zines, as the tiny publication takes aim at the most powerful medium of communication in the history of humankind. "I had been watching for a long time," the anonymous editor wrote in one personal confession. "I went to sleep with the TV on, ate in front of it." But finally came the day, the dissident journalist wrote, when "something way back in my spirit said 'NO, I won't take this anymore. This is killing me, and it's either me or IT' and so I killed my TV." The Oberlin, Ohio, editor then went on to describe taking out a toolbox and disassembling the television that previously had dominated her life. By no means does *Kill Your Television* consist entirely of personal commentary, however, as the editor also praises and reprints the findings of such media watchdog and advocacy groups as Fairness and Accuracy in Reporting and the Center for a New Television.[4]

Riot Grrrl may be the most popular title in the world of zines, as hundreds of young women across America have attached that name to their written descriptions of their personal encounters with sexual abuse. Such publishing testimonies not only provide catharsis for the authors but simultaneously encourage other women to take precautions to avoid becoming rape victims. "I told him I really didn't want to," Diana wrote in her essay, "but I did kiss him." She went on to describe how the man "kept grabbing and yanking" and asking "Do you give up yet?" until she finally did. After the man forced himself onto her and then ejaculated inside of her, Diana wrote poignantly in her issue of *Riot Grrrl*, "he handed me my clothes."[5]

The second force to burst onto the dissident press landscape in recent years ultimately will have even more impact than the zine. For the Internet is a technological development that is rapidly reshaping all forms of communication to a degree comparable, at least in this author's mind, to Johannes Gutenberg's fifteenth-century invention of printing from movable type.

What's more, several of the Internet's traits have particularly stunning implications for the dissident press.

- It dramatically reduces the cost of creating and disseminating information, enabling even people with modest financial resources to become publishers—and, thereby, agents of change.
- It bypasses the information monopoly, in the form of the mainstream media, that has increasingly become the nemesis of the socially, economically, and politically disenfranchised, offering an alternative to the media conglomerates, such as Time Warner and Disney, that have mushroomed in power and influence in recent years.
- It allows, through hyperlinks from publications to permanent Websites, for readers to be informed not merely of the most recent event—as in daily newspapers and TV news programs—but to be continually reminded of the movement's overall mission statement, goals, and past accomplishments—a service that traditional news outlets refuse to provide.
- It allows individuals in far-flung locations to come together, to share, and to build the strong ties and sense of community—united in ideology even if separated by geographic distance—that foster a true grassroots movement.

So the Internet has become an enormous boon to the dissident press. Some of the anti-establishment voices that began in the 1960s and 1970s, such as Bobby Seale of the *Black Panther* newspaper and feminists who produced *off our backs*, have moved into cyberspace; some 500 additional publications are listed on just one Website, Alternative Viewpoints on the Internet. As with zines, brief descriptions of just a few of the thousands of on-line dissident publications give a taste of the range and the possibility that they represent.[6]

Real Change offers Seattle's homeless population a monthly voice. "Once you're homeless, it's so hard to get a real job," writes Rainee Maurer, "you don't have a permanent address or phone number. I don't really have anything I can put down on a resume since 1989." Maurer and others do not merely speak, as they also agitate. "We believe people have a right to be angry," the paper asserts. "We also think we have an obligation to be political." Since 1994, *Real Change* has been campaigning for the Washington state welfare system to place more emphasis on job training and for Seattle officials to create more homeless shelters and eliminate the city ordinance that prohibits homeless people from sitting for prolonged periods of time in the downtown area. "We publish quality, socially committed journalism," the mission statement promises, "and always place the voice of the people first."[7]

Earth First! is a radical environmental journal that rejects what it calls "namby-pamby" tactics, such as lobbying and letter writing, in favor of direct action. One activity *Earth First!* applauds is tree sitting, during which forest conservationists try to stop loggers not by hugging trees—but by living in them. Veteran sitters have such whimsical names as "Moonshadow," who sits eighty feet up a Colorado spruce, and "Toad," whose residence of choice is an Oregon redwood. But saving the environment isn't all fun and games or funny names. In September 1998, David Chain and eight other activists walked into an active timber harvest zone in California. When a falling tree struck the twenty-four-year-old Chain, he was crushed to death.[8]

The Week Online promotes liberalized drug laws, with particular emphasis on campaigning for marijuana to be legalized for medical purposes. "Patients suffering from AIDS, cancer, glaucoma, multiple sclerosis, and other serious conditions often find that marijuana is the most, sometimes only, effective treatment," the Washington, D.C., weekly has repeated in every issue since it began publishing. *The Week Online* also sends its 10,000 subscribers periodic "Action Alerts!"—in red letters that continuously flash on and off the computer screen—to urge them to participate in pro-marijuana rallies around the country.[9]

While the various on-line voices of dissent have not yet been in existence long enough to permit a definitive assessment of their impact, there is no question that some of the publications have helped advance their causes. When *The Week Online* began appearing in 1993, medicinal use of marijuana was a concept far beyond the pale of mainstream American life; today, voters in nine states— from Hawaii to Maine, Alaska to Arizona—have legalized the procedure. That dramatic shift in thinking cannot be attributed entirely to the on-line weekly, but neither should the power of a publication that 10,000 Americans have posted to their e-mail every single day be dismissed as irrelevant.[10]

———

As a former reporter for a daily newspaper and now a professor who helps prepare young men and women to enter the field of journalism, I want to end this book by making a final point not as much about dissident publications as about the mainstream media that have so often been their detractors.

American journalism is in trouble.

During the second half of the twentieth century, readers abandoned the daily newspaper in droves, many of them being attracted to the convenience and lively format of television news. In the 1990s, legions of Americans deserted not only newspapers but also the major networks, attracted to cable TV, the Internet, and forms of new media that are bursting onto the media landscape every day. Indeed, it has become increasingly murky exactly where people are turning for their news—or if they are simply turning *away* from news altogether.

In addition, the trust and respect that the American people once had for the institution of journalism has eroded. The public perceives the news media—and with good reason—as seeking out the most negative angle of every story, as invading people's privacy, and as twisting the facts to suit their own liberal agenda. Contemporary journalists are seen as rude, arrogant, self-righteous, cynical, irresponsible, unpatriotic, and amoral. News media executives seem to be more interested in entertaining their audience and sensationalizing their material than in informing and serving the public good; depending on whether they work for the print or electronic media, journalists seem to be guided by one of two principles: Sell papers or get high ratings. Subsequently, public esteem for journalism has plummeted, threatening the very foundation of one of the pillars of our democratic system of governance.

One place the men and women who determine journalistic values could look for guidance on how to regain a sense of mission is the dissident press. For although many of the publications illuminated in this book can be criticized on various counts, the dissident press has never wavered from being an exemplar of passion, conviction, sacrifice, and commitment to a cause.

Because of dissident journalism's single-mindedness of purpose combined with an impressive heritage of success, the mainstream news media should stop ignoring the dissident press and start emulating it. A close examination of just the "voices of revolution" that appeared during the middle to late twentieth century offers several lessons that the titans of American journalism need to learn.

The anti-Vietnam War press boldly questioning why the United States was involved in Southeast Asia speaks to the importance of news organizations remaining vigilant in the role as watchdogs over—not bedfellows with—the government. The counterculture press highlighting lifestyle issues that ultimately defined an entire generation of young people suggests that mainstream journalism should look beyond middle-aged politicians and elected officials if it truly wants to reflect the realities of contemporary life. The *Black Panther*'s commitment to providing a voice for the politically, socially, and economically disenfranchised shows the merits of not focusing exclusively on the dominant segments of society—even if they are the demographic ideal of advertisers. The gay and lesbian press demanding equal rights for sexual minorities demonstrates the virtue of supporting causes that are just and right, despite the fact that many Americans do not yet embrace those beliefs. Several different women's liberation papers all reprinting the same article because they wanted to reach as many readers as possible suggests that the cutthroat competition that drives the mainstream media—as during the fiasco on election night 2000—may feed their egos but fail to serve their readers and viewers.

Many wags will criticize these suggestions, saying that such a call for mainstream news organizations to travel the path forged by the dissident press ignores all sorts of economic factors. It is true that the proposals I am making are based on an idealistic premise that not everyone shares: Journalism that is substantive in content and strong in backbone ultimately will succeed, prosper, and serve the people. Yes, this may be a lofty goal. But if it is not the goal of the modern-day news media, I question—with considerable despair—if mainstream American journalism is still an institution worthy of saving.

ACKNOWLEDGMENTS

Much of the material that I am now publishing in this book has appeared in papers I have presented at academic conferences or in articles I have written for scholarly journals. So I want to thank the various reviewers of those manuscripts whose names are masked behind the blind review process, including many of my fellow members of the Association for Education in Journalism and Mass Communication. Among the remarkably dedicated journal editors I want to thank are Shirley Biagi of *American Journalism*, Barbara Cloud of *Journalism History*, and Jean Folkerts and Margaret Blanchard of *Journalism & Mass Communication Quarterly*.

In addition, I am sincerely indebted to three individuals who have read and commented on this manuscript at various stages. Specifically, Elizabeth Burt of the University of Hartford, James P. Danky of the State Historical Society of Wisconsin, and Norma Fay Green of Columbia College, Chicago, all provided me with supportive and insightful feedback.

I also want to express my fond and heartfelt gratitude to my mentor extraordinaire, Susan Henry. It was not until Susan read a draft version of the entire manuscript—and then I scurried to make the revisions she suggested—that *Voices of Revolution* fully came together as a coherent work.

My gratitude further extends to the American University Senate Research Committee, Dean of Academic Affairs Ivy Broder, and School of Communication Acting Dean Glenn Harnden for awarding me a university research grant. Their support allowed me to travel to important research repositories related to the dissident press.

With regard to moving my research into book form, I would be woefully remiss if I did not thank Howard Yoon, who has successfully shepherded my books through the complexities of the publishing world. Howard has enabled me to avoid the many sinkholes that, without him, I most assuredly would have stumbled into long ago. In particular, I applaud the consistently high level of integrity and professionalism that Howard and his firm, the Gail Ross Literary Agency, have exhibited in all of their dealings with me.

On a personal level, I want to acknowledge the unwavering support of Tom Grooms. Not only is he the first person to read every word that I write but also the one who must walk that precarious line between my two alternating responses to his feedback: "Why are you always so critical of my work?" and "Why don't you have more criticism? Didn't you even *read* what I gave you?"

And, finally, I want to speak to why I have dedicated this book to my son Matt and my daughter Kate. Although I am pleased that I have made substantial contributions to the body of knowledge in the areas of both American journalism and American history, it is this fine young man and fine young woman who have, on a much more fundamental level, enriched and provided the real meaning to my life.

Rodger Streitmatter
February 2001

NOTES

INTRODUCTION

1. Rodger Streitmatter, "AIDS: 'It's just a matter of time,'" *The Quill*, May 1984, 22–27.

2. For the *Native*'s first story, see Lawrence Mass, "Disease Rumors Largely Unfounded," *New York Native*, 18–31 May 1981, 7; for the *New York Times*'s first story, see Lawrence K. Altman, "Rare Cancer Seen in 41 Homosexuals," *New York Times*, 3 July 1981, A-20. For the *Native*'s first discussion of how the disease was spread, see Lawrence Mass, *New York Native*, "Cancer in the Gay Community," 27 July–9 August 1981, 20–21; details about how the disease was being spread were problematic for the mainstream press because of taboos against topics such as anal intercourse, which the *Native* was comfortable discussing.

3. The only previously published book that attempts to describe and document the significance of the dissident press in the United States during the last two centuries is Lauren Kessler, *The Dissident Press: Alternative Journalism in American History* (Beverly Hills, CA: Sage, 1984); among the many publications covered in this book but not in Kessler are the 1820s labor newspapers, sexual reform journals, anti-lynching publications, birth control magazines, and gay and lesbian newspapers. Numerous books have been written about the alternative press of the 1960s; they include David Armstrong, *A Trumpet to Arms: Alternative Media in America* (Los Angeles: J. P. Tarcher, 1981); Everette E. Dennis and William L. Rivers, *Other Voices: The New Journalism in America* (San Francisco: Canfield, 1974); Robert J. Glessing, *The Underground Press in America* (Bloomington: Indiana University Press, 1970); Laurence Leamer, *The Paper Revolutionaries: The Rise of the Underground Press* (New York: Simon and Schuster, 1972); Roger Lewis, *Outlaws of America: The Underground Press and its Context* (Baltimore: Penguin, 1972); Abe Peck, *Uncovering the Sixties: The Life and Times of the Underground Press* (New York: Citadel,

1985); Ken Wachsberger, ed., *Voices from the Underground: Insider Histories of the Vietnam Era Underground Press* (Tempe, AZ: Mica Press, 1993). Other books that contain material about some non-mainstream presses include James P. Danky and Wayne A. Wiegand, eds., *Print Culture in a Diverse America* (Urbana: University of Illinois Press, 1998); John Downing, *Radical Media: The Political Experience of Alternative Communication* (Boston: South End, 1984); Kathleen L. Endres and Theresa L. Lueck, eds., *Women's Periodicals in the United States: Social and Political Issues* (Westport, CT: Greenwood, 1996); Frankie Hutton and Barbara Straus Reed, *Outsiders in 19th-Century Press History: Multicultural Perspectives* (Bowling Green, OH: Bowling Green State University Popular Press, 1995).

4. Upton Sinclair, *The Brass Check: A Study of American Journalism* (Pasadena, CA, 1920), 184.

CHAPTER 1. FIGHTING FOR THE RIGHTS OF AMERICAN LABOR

1. Jon Bekken, "'No Weapon So Powerful': Working-Class Newspapers in the United States," *Journal of Communication Inquiry* 12(2) (Summer 1988):105; John R. Commons, David J. Saposs, Helen L. Sumner, E. B. Mittelman, H. E. Hoagland, John B. Andrews, and Selig Perlman, eds., *History of Labour in the United States*, 2 volumes (New York: Macmillan, 1921), vol. 1, 286; Foster Rhea Dulles, *Labor in America: A History*, 3rd ed. (Arlington Heights, IL: AHM, 1966), 35; Philip S. Foner, *William Heighton: Pioneer Labor Leader of Jacksonian Philadelphia* (New York: International, 1991), 26; Donald Myers, "Birth and Establishment of the Labor Press in the United States," 1950, unpublished master's thesis, University of Wisconsin (journalism), 49; Dan Schiller, *Objectivity and the News: The Public and the Rise of Commercial Journalism* (Philadelphia: University of Pennsylvania Press, 1981), 45; Alden Whitman, *Labor Parties, 1827–34* (New York: International, 1943), 32–33.

2. On the *Mechanic's Free Press*'s circulation, see William Heighton, "To Advertisers, &c.," *Mechanic's Free Press*, 23 April 1831, 4. The largest daily in the country at the time was the *Courier and Enquirer* in New York City, with a circulation of 4,000; see C. K. McFarland and Robert L. Thistlethwaite, "20 Years of a Successful Labor Paper: The Working Man's Advocate, 1829–49," *Journalism Quarterly* 60(1) (Spring 1983):35. The *Working Man's Advocate* changed names several times during its history; among those names were the *New York Sentinel and Working Man's Advocate* and the *Radical Reformer and Working Man's Advocate*.

3. This position was taken in a pamphlet that has not been preserved but the content of which was later published in the *Mechanic's Free Press*; see "Miscellany," *Mechanic's Free Press*, 21 June 1828, 1.

4. Myers, "Birth and Establishment of the Labor Press," 54; Philip S. Foner, *History of the American Labor Movement in the United States* (New York: International, 1947), 133).

5. Foner, *History of the American Labor Movement*, 122.

6. *Working Man's Advocate*, "Communications," 7 November 1829, 2; "From the Wayne County Patriot," 5 June 1830, 2.

7. Heighton, "To Correspondents," *Mechanic's Free Press*, 23 January 1830, 3; "Newspaper Reading," *Mechanic's Free Press*, 3 May 1828, 3; "To Correspondents," *Working Man's Advocate*, 9 January 1830, 3.

8. Heighton, *Mechanic's Free Press*, "Miscellany," 25 October 1828, 1; "To Correspondents," 19 April 1828, 3; untitled article, 31 May 1828, 3.

9. "Address," *Free Enquirer*, 7 October 1829, 1.

10. *Working Man's Advocate*, "Address," 7 November 1829, 1; "Prospectus," 31 October 1829, 3; "Meeting at the Masonic Hall," 31 October 1829, 3; "Signs of the Times," 8 May 1830, 3.

11. "Prospectus," *New York Daily Sentinel and Working Man's Advocate*, 9 June 1830, 1.

12. Commons et al, *History of Labour*, vol. 1, 174.

13. On biographical details about William Heighton, see Louis H. Arky, "The Mechanics' Union of Trade Associations and the Formation of the Philadelphia Workingmen's Movement," *Pennsylvania Magazine of History and Biography* 76 (April 1952):142–76; Foner, *William Heighton*; Bruce Laurie, *Working People of Philadelphia, 1800–1850* (Philadelphia: Temple University Press, 1980), esp. 74–79; Edward Pessen, *Most Uncommon Jacksonians: The Radical Leaders of the Early Labor Movement* (Albany: State University of New York Press, 1967), 12, 14, 28, 56.

14. Heighton, "To Correspondents," *Mechanic's Free Press*, 12 April 1828, 3.

15. Heighton, *Mechanic's Free Press*, "To Advertisers, &c.," 23 April 1831, 4; untitled article, 2 October 1830, 2.

16. Heighton, *Mechanic's Free Press*, "For the Mechanic's Free Press," 19 April 1828, 2; "Original Communications," 5 June 1830, 2.

17. Z. W. L., "Messrs. Editors," *Mechanic's Free Press*, 21 August 1830, 2.

18. Heighton, "For the Mechanic's Free Press," *Mechanic's Free Press*, 19 April 1828, 2.

19. Commons et al, *History of Labour*, vol. 1, 307; "To Correspondents," *Working Man's Advocate*, 7 November 1829, 3.

20. Heighton, "Gross Injustice in Some of Our Manufactories Exposed," *Mechanic's Free Press*, 21 August 1830, 2.

21. Heighton, "Gross Injustice in Some of Our Manufactories Exposed," *Mechanic's Free Press*, 21 August 1830, 2.

22. "Child Labor," *Free Enquirer*, 16 June 1832, 3.

23. On biographical details about George Henry Evans, see Lewis Masquerier, *Soci-*

ology, or, The Reconstruction of Society, Government, and Property (New York: Lewis Masquerier, 1877); "To Correspondents," *Radical Reformer and Working Man's Advocate*, 19 September 1835, 3.

24. Commons et al, *History of Labour*, vol. 1, 182.

25. Heighton, *Mechanic's Free Press*, "Original Communications," 2 October 1830, 2; "Original Communications," 29 August 1829, 2; "Public Education," 20 February 1830, 1; "Original Communications," 1 May 1830, 2.

26. *Working Man's Advocate*, untitled article, 31 October 1829, 1; "Working Men's Measures," 30 October 1830, 3; "Farmers' and Mechanics' Meeting," 6 February 1830, 4.

27. On biographical details about Robert Dale Owen, see Richard Leopold, *Robert Dale Owen, A Biography* (New York: Octagon, 1969).

28. Robert Dale Owen, "Public Education," *Free Enquirer*, 8 May 1830, 3.

29. "Public Education," *Mechanic's Free Press*, 8 May 1830, 1; "Public Education," *Working Man's Advocate*, 1 May 1830, 1.

30. "Plots and Plotters," *Free Enquirer*, 5 June 1830, 3.

31. Untitled article, *National Gazette*, 10 July 1830, 2.

32. "Address," *Free Enquirer*, 7 October 1829, 1.

33. Foner, *William Heighton*, 36.

34. Heighton, "Mr. Simpson's Reply," *Mechanic's Free Press*, 25 September 1830, 2; Commons et al, *History of Labour*, vol. 1, 221.

35. "Imprisonment for Debt," *Working Man's Advocate*, 13 March 1830, 2–4; quoted in Dulles, *Labor in America*, 49.

36. Foner, *William Heighton*, 30; "The Slave Trade," *Free Enquirer*, 13 August 1831, 1.

37. Heighton, "Address of the Working Men of Locust Ward," *Mechanic's Free Press*, 2 October 1830, 2.

38. Heighton, "Communication," *Mechanic's Free Press*, 31 May 1828, 3; Foner, *William Heighton*, 40.

39. *Mechanic's Free Press*, "Election Returns," 18 October 1828, 3; Heighton, "The Election," 18 October 1828, 3.

40. Heighton, "Address of the Committee appointed by the Working Men's Republican Association of Southwark," *Mechanic's Free Press*, 31 October 1829, 3; quoted in Commons et al, *History of Labour*, vol. 1, 205.

41. Commons et al, *History of Labour*, vol. 1, 207; Foner, *History of the American Labor Movement*, 122.

42. *Working Man's Advocate*, 31 October 1829, "The Working Men and the Commercial," 2; "The Approaching Election," 3.

43. "The Election," *Working Man's Advocate*, 7 November 1829, 2.

44. *Working Man's Advocate*, "From the Syracuse Gazette," 24 April 1830, 3; "More Triumphs," 15 May 1830, 3; "Working Men," 29 May 1830, 3.

45. Commons et al, *History of Labour*, vol. 1, 287–90; "New London Election," *Working Man's Advocate*, 19 June 1830, 3; "The Working Men Triumphant!," *Working Man's Advocate*, 10 April 1830, 2; "The Next President," *Working Man's Advocate*, 7 August 1830, 3.

46. On biographical details about Frances Wright, see Celia Morris Eckhardt, *Fanny Wright: Rebel in America* (Cambridge, MA: Harvard University Press, 1984).

47. Eckhardt, *Fanny Wright*, 2, 184, 204, 299.

48. "The American Sentinel and Poulson's Advertiser," *Mechanic's Free Press*, 16 October 1830, 3; "To Correspondents," *Working Man's Advocate*, 9 January 1830, 3; "Troy Farmer's Register," *Working Man's Advocate*, 4 August 1830, 1; "Communications," *Working Man's Advocate*, 7 November 1829, 2.

49. Commons et al, *History of Labour*, vol. 1, 215.

50. Foner, *William Heighton*, 53.

51. "Prospectus of the Working Men," *Working Man's Advocate*, 11 December 1830, 1; Commons et al, *History of Labour*, vol. 1, 326–27.

52. Commons et al, *History of Labour*, vol. 1, 327–29, 331.

53. Commons et al, *History of Labour*, vol. 1, 331–32; Jon Bekken, "The Working-Class Press at the Turn of the Century," in *Ruthless Criticism: New Perspectives in U.S. Communication History* (Minneapolis: University of Minnesota Press, 1993), 151–75.

CHAPTER 2. AWAKENING A NATION TO THE SINS OF SLAVERY

1. William Lloyd Garrison, "Black List," *Genius of Universal Emancipation*, 20 November 1829, 2.

2. Garrison, "To the Public," *The Liberator*, 1 January 1831, 1.

3. Garrison, "The Insurrection," *The Liberator*, 3 September 1831, 3.

4. "Threats to Assassinate," *The Liberator*, 10 September 1831, 1.

5. Garrison, "Vindication of the Liberator," in *Selections from the Writings and Speeches of William Lloyd Garrison* (Boston: R. F. Wallcut, 1852), 184–85.

6. *The Liberator*, M. Stuart, "Slavery Sanctioned by the Bible," 9 June 1837, 1; "The Abolitionists," 13 June 1835, 1; "Refuge of Oppression," 9 June 1837, 1; "Communication," 29 June 1833, 2; "Refuge of Oppression," 12 September 1835, 1.

7. Edmund Quincy to William Lloyd Garrison, 6 November 1843, in W. P. Garrison and F. J. Garrison, *William Lloyd Garrison, 1805–1879: The Story of His Life Told by His Children* (Boston: Houghton, Mifflin, 1885–89), vol. III, 86.

8. William Lloyd Garrison to Helen Garrison, 9 August 1847, William Lloyd Garrison Papers, Boston Public Library.

9. Garrison, "What Shall Be Done," *The Liberator*, 30 July 1831, 1.

10. On Garrison founding the abolition societies to support *The Liberator*, see John L. Thomas, *The Liberator: William Lloyd Garrison, a Biography* (Boston: Little, Brown, 1963), 139, 170.

11. Garrison, "Boston," *The Liberator*, 27 December 1834, 3.

12. Thomas, *The Liberator*, 136–37.

13. Thomas, *The Liberator*, 200–05.

14. Garrison, "Address to the Friends of Freedom and Emancipation in the United States," *The Liberator*, 31 May 1844, 2.

15. Garrison, "Speech of Wm. Lloyd Garrison," *The Liberator*, 16 December 1859, 2.

16. C. F. Hovey to Helen Garrison, 26 June 1855, in Garrison and Garrison, *William Lloyd Garrison*, vol. III, 428; Garrison and Garrison, *William Lloyd Garrison*, vol. III, 428–29.

17. Garrison, *The Liberator*, "Hurrah for the War!," 26 July 1861, 1; "The Government Forces Defeated!," 26 July 1861, 2.

18. "The Liberator Released," *The Nation*, 4 January 1866, 7; "The Last Number of the Liberator," *New York Tribune*, 4 January 1866, 4.

19. Roy P. Basler, ed., *The Collected Works of Abraham Lincoln*, vol. VIII (New Brunswick, NJ: Rutgers University Press), 266; Thomas, *The Liberator*, 425.

20. John W. Blassingame and John R. McKivigan, eds., *The Frederick Douglass Papers*, vol. 5 (New Haven, CT: Yale University Press, 1992), 369.

21. Gilbert H. Barnes, *The Antislavery Impulse, 1830–1844* (New York: D. Appleton-Century, 1933), 58.

22. On Garrison's exchanging technique, see Thomas, *The Liberator*, 136–37.

23. Garrison, "Editors," *The Liberator*, 29 January 1831, 2.

24. See Garrison's editorial battles with the editors of the *Milledgeville* [Georgia] *Journal* in *The Liberator*, 28 July 1832, 3; the *Vicksburg* [Mississippi] *Register*, 9 June 1837, 1; the *Xenia* [Ohio] *Free Press*, 11 November 1842, 3; the *Fort Gratiot* [Michigan] *Journal of Commerce*, 28 July 1832, 3.

25. On Lovejoy and the circumstances of his death, see, for example, Merton L. Dillon, *Elijah P. Lovejoy, Abolitionist Editor* (Urbana: University of Illinois Press, 1961); John Gill, *Tide without Turning: Elijah P. Lovejoy and Freedom of the Press* (Boston: Beacon, 1958); Paul Simon, *Lovejoy, Martyr to Freedom* (St. Louis: Concordia, 1964).

26. Garrison, "A Martyr for Liberty," *The Liberator*, 24 November 1837, 3.

27. Garrison, *The Liberator*, 1 December 1837, "Horrid Outrage!," 2; "Lovejoy Murdered!!!," 2. On Garrison expanding the abolition debate to include a broad range

of civil liberties, see, David Paul Nord, "Tocqueville, Garrison and the Perfection of Journalism," *Journalism History* 13(2) (Summer 1986):56–63.

28. On publicity about Lovejoy's death energizing the Abolition Movement, see, for example, Dillon, *Elijah P. Lovejoy*, 175–79; Simon, *Lovejoy*, 154–70.

29. The Fugitive Slave Law created special commissioners who only had to be convinced of a fugitive slave's identity in order to grant the alleged owner authority to seize the alleged runaway. "The Meeting at Framingham," *The Liberator*, 7 July 1854, 2.

30. "Great Anniversary Meeting of the American Anti-Slavery Society," *New York Herald*, 12 May 1841, 1.

31. "Great Anniversary Meeting of the American Anti-Slavery Society," *New York Herald*, 12 May 1841, 1.

32. "Incendiary Publications," *The Liberator*, 8 October 1831, 1; "Free Speech," *Philadelphia Ledger*, 14 May 1850, 4; the *Boston Courier* was quoted in "Selections," *The Liberator*, 1 February 1861, 4; Garrison, "An Address Delivered in the Broadway Tabernacle," *New York Times*, 15 February 1854, 8.

33. "The Liberator Released," *The Nation*, 4 January 1866, 7.

CHAPTER 3. SETTING A REVOLUTIONARY AGENDA FOR WOMEN'S RIGHTS

1. "The Women of Philadelphia," *Philadelphia Ledger and Daily Transcript*, reprinted in Elizabeth Cady Stanton, Susan B. Anthony, and Matilda Joslyn Gage, eds., *History of Woman Suffrage* (New York: Fowler & Wells, 1881), 804.

2. *The Revolution*, Elizabeth Cady Stanton, "One Hundred Thousand Subscribers," 9 April 1868, 1; "To Correspondents," 6 January 1870, 2.

3. "What the People Say of Us," *The Revolution*, 5 February 1868, Olympia Brown, 3; Elvira Wheelock, 3; Ann Raley, 2.

4. Stanton, Anthony, and Gage, *History of Woman Suffrage*, 70.

5. "The Woman's Rights Convention—The Last Act of the Drama," *New York Herald*, 12 September 1852, 2; "Woman's Rights," *New York Times*, 18 October 1851, 2.

6. *The Revolution*, 8 January 1868, "Salutatory," 1; "The Revolution," 8.

7. Stanton, "William Lloyd Garrison Crucifies Democrats, Train, and the Women of *The Revolution*," *The Revolution*, 29 January 1868, 1; Lois W. Banner, *Elizabeth Cady Stanton: A Radical for Woman's Rights* (Boston: Little, Brown, 1980), 101.

8. Elizabeth Cady Stanton, *Eighty Years and More: Reminiscences, 1815–1897* (Boston: Northeastern University Press, 1993, first published in 1898), 257–58.

9. Laura Curtis Bullard, "What Flag Shall We Fly?," *The Revolution*, 27 October 1870, 8.

10. On the suffrage press, see Lynne Masel-Walters, "To Hustle with the Rowdies:

The Organization and Functions of the American Woman Suffrage Press," *Journal of American Culture* 3 (1) (Spring 1980):167–83; Anne Mather, "A History of Feminist Periodicals, Part I," *Journalism History* 1 (Autumn 1974):82–85; Linda Steiner, "Finding Community in Nineteenth Century Suffrage Periodicals," *American Journalism* 1 (1983):1–15.

11. "What the Press Says of Us," *The Revolution*, 18 June 1868, 3; untitled article, *New York Times*, 12 January 1868, 4.

12. *Utica Herald*, reprinted in Ida Husted Harper, *The Life and Work of Susan B. Anthony* (Indianapolis: Hollenbeck, 1898), vol. 1, 367; *Syracuse Weekly Star*, reprinted in Harper, *Life and Work of Susan B. Anthony*, vol. 1, 267; *New York Sun*, reprinted in Harper, *Life and Work of Susan B. Anthony*, vol. 1, 90.

13. Miriam Gurko, *The Ladies of Seneca Falls: The Birth of the Woman's Rights Movement* (New York: Macmillan, 1974), 104; Lucretia Mott, "National Convention at Cincinnati, Ohio," in Stanton, Anthony, and Gage, *History of Woman Suffrage*, 164.

14. *The Revolution*, untitled article, 8 January 1868, 8; Stanton, "Harvard Divinity School," 7 October 1869, 9.

15. "Woman's Wages," *The Revolution*, 5 February 1868, 1.

16. *The Revolution*, untitled article, 7 January 1869, 13; "A New Work for Woman," 2 December 1869, 11; "Woman's Wages," 5 February 1868, 1; Susan B. Anthony, "The Working Woman," 7 April 1870, 12.

17. Anthony, "The Working Woman," *The Revolution*, 7 April 1870, 13.

18. *The Revolution*, Parker Pillsbury, "The Impeachment Trial," 30 April 1868, 8; "The Revolution," 7 January 1869, 14.

19. "Workingmen's National Congress," *The Revolution*, 17 September 1868, 9.

20. Stanton, "The Working Women's Association," *The Revolution*, 5 November 1868, 8.

21. Untitled article, *The Revolution*, 16 April 1868, 3.

22. Eleanor Kirk, "Startling Literary Facts," *The Revolution*, 30 July 1868, 12.

23. *The Revolution*, "Woman's Wages," 5 February 1868, 1; Frans Widstrand, "Woman's Dress," 24 December 1868, 7; "Girls and Gowns," 7 October 1869, 9; "Arrest of a Feminine Pedestrian," 19 November 1868, 12.

24. *The Revolution*, Parker Pillsbury, "Civil Service Reform," 2 December 1869, 9; Stanton, "The Family a Unit," 10 March 1870, 8.

25. Stanton, *The Revolution*, "Universal Suffrage," 30 July 1868, 9; "The Ballot," 26 March 1868, 8.

26. Stanton, "Sharp Points," *The Revolution*, 9 April 1868, 4.

27. *The Revolution*, "Petition for Equal Suffrage," 19 November 1868, 1; H.P.J., "About Petitions," 28 January 1869, 5.

28. H.P.J., "About Petitions," *The Revolution*, 28 January 1869, 5.

29. Elvira Wheelock Ruggles, "What the People Say," *The Revolution*, 29 July 1869, 7.

30. Eleanor Kirk, "A Word to Abused Wives," *The Revolution*, 18 June 1868, 13.

31. Eleanor Kirk, *The Revolution*, "A Word to Abused Wives," 18 June 1868, 13–14; "To My Friend in Rhode Island," 6 August 1868, 13.

32. Stanton, *The Revolution*, "Marriage and Divorce," 22 October 1868, 9; "The Man Marriage," 8 April 1869, 8.

33. Stanton, "Marriages and Mistresses," *The Revolution*, 15 October 1868, 9.

34. Stanton, "Hester Vaughan," *The Revolution*, 19 November 1868, 8.

35. Stanton, "Hester Vaughan," *The Revolution*, 19 November 1868, 8.

36. Stanton, "Editorial Correspondence," *The Revolution*, 10 December 1868, 2.

37. Stanton, "Hester Vaughan," *The Revolution*, 10 December 1868, 8.

38. Harper, *Life and Work of Susan B. Anthony*, vol. 1, 254.

39. On biographies of Stanton and Anthony, see Katharine Anthony, *Susan B. Anthony: Her Personal History and Her Era* (New York: Doubleday, 1954); Banner, *Elizabeth Cady Stanton*; Kathleen Barry, *Susan B. Anthony: A Biography of a Singular Feminist* (New York: New York University Press, 1988); Florence Horn Bryan, *Susan B. Anthony, Champion of Women's Rights* (New York: Messner, 1947); Rheta Childe Dorr, *Susan B. Anthony: The Woman Who Changed the Mind of a Nation* (New York: Frederick A. Stokes, 1928); Ellen Carol DuBois, ed., *Elizabeth Cady Stanton/Susan B. Anthony: Correspondence, Writings, Speeches* (New York: Schocken, 1981); Gurko, *Ladies of Seneca Falls*; Elisabeth Griffith, *In Her Own Right: The Life of Elizabeth Cady Stanton* (New York: Oxford, 1984); Harper, *Life and Work of Susan B. Anthony*; Alma Lutz, *Created Equal: A Biography of Elizabeth Cady Stanton, 1815–1902* (New York: John Day, 1940); Alma Lutz, *Susan B. Anthony: Rebel, Crusader, Humanitarian* (Washington, D.C.: Zenger, 1959); Mary Ann B. Oakley, *Elizabeth Cady Stanton* (Old Westbury, New York: Feminist, 1972); Lynn Sherr, *Failure Is Impossible: Susan B. Anthony in Her Own Words* (New York: Times, 1995); Stanton, *Eighty Years and More*; Theodore Stanton and Harriot Stanton Blatch, *Elizabeth Cady Stanton* (1922; New York: Arno, 1969). On studies of *The Revolution*, see Bonnie J. Dow, "The *Revolution*, 1868–1870: Expanding the Woman Suffrage Agenda," in Martha M. Solomon, ed., *A Voice of Their Own: The Woman Suffrage Press, 1840–1910* (Tuscaloosa: University of Alabama Press, 1991), 71–86; Agnes Hooper Gottlieb, "The Revolution," in Kathleen L. Endres and Theresa L. Lueck, eds., *Women's Periodicals in the United States: Social and Political Issues* (Westport, CT: Greenwood, 1996), 339–45; Lynne Masel-Walters, "Their Rights and Nothing More: A History of *The Revolution*, 1868–70," *Journalism Quarterly* 53 (Summer 1976):242–51; Masel-Walters, "To Hustle with the Rowdies"; Mather, "A History of Feminist Periodicals, Part I"; Steiner, "Finding Community." For the book consisting of articles from *The Rev-*

olution, see Lana Rakow and Cheris Kramarae, eds., *The Revolution in Words: Righting Women, 1868–1871* (New York: Routledge, 1990).

40. Anthony, *Susan B. Anthony*, 228; Anthony, Stanton, and Gage, *History of Woman Suffrage*, vol. 2, 373.

CHAPTER 4. PROMOTING "FREE LOVE" IN THE VICTORIAN AGE

1. "Victoria and Theodore: Free Love, Passional Attraction and the Celestial Affinities at Steinway Hall," *New York Herald*, 21 November 1871, 10.

2. Victoria Woodhull, "The Beecher-Tilton Scandal Case," *Woodhull & Claflin's Weekly*, 2 November 1872, 9.

3. For details about Victoria Woodhull's life, see, for example, Mary Gabriel, *Notorious Victoria: The Life of Victoria Woodhull, Uncensored* (Chapel Hill, NC: Algonquin, 1998).

4. "The Check Frauds," *New York World*, 20 March 1870, 8.

5. The *New York Times* and *New York Globe* comments were reprinted in "Opinions of the Press," *Woodhull & Claflin's Weekly*, 28 May 1870, 11.

6. "Woodhull & Claflin's Weekly," *Woodhull & Claflin's Weekly*, 14 May 1870, 8. Articles about Victoria appeared in the *New York Herald* on 16 and 25 April; 2, 9, 16, and 27 May; 4 and 19 June; 4 and 11 July 1870.

7. Thomas Nast, "Mrs. Satan," *Harper's Weekly*, 17 February 1872, 140.

8. Ezra Heywood, "Free Love League," *The Word*, May 1876, 2.

9. Angela Heywood, *The Word*, "The Ethics of Sexuality," April 1881, 3; "Body Housekeeping," March 1893, 3.

10. See, for example, *The Word*, "Bibles Against Usury," April 1875, 1; untitled article, April 1876, 1.

11. The *Boston Globe* and *Worcester Press* comments were reprinted in "The Opposition," *The Word*, April 1876, 2.

12. *Lucifer, the Light-Bearer*, "A Divided House," 15 April 1892, 2; "Published under Government Censorship," 13 May 1892, 1. See "James Law, "Diseases of the Generative Organs," in D.E. Salmon, compositor, *Special Report on Diseases of the Horse* (Washington, D.C.: 1890), 138.

13. The *Osawkee Times* comment was reprinted in *Lucifer, the Light-Bearer*, 29 October 1886, 1; the *Winchester Argus* comment was reprinted in *Lucifer, the Light-Bearer*, 24 September 1886, 2; the *Kansas City Times* comment was reprinted in *Lucifer, the Light-Bearer*, 25 February 1887, 2.

14. Woodhull, "Proceedings of the Tenth Annual Convention of the American Association of Spiritualists," *Woodhull & Claflin's Weekly*, 18 October 1873, 12.

15. Woodhull, "Moral Cowardice & Modern Hypocrisy," *Woodhull & Claflin's Weekly*, 28 December 1872, 3, 7.

16. Ezra Heywood, *Uncivil Liberty* (Princeton, MA: Co-Operative Publishing, 1870), 17, 20; *Cupid's Yokes* (Princeton, MA: Co-Operative Publishing, 1876), 6.

17. W. G. Markland, "Another 'Awful Letter,'" *Lucifer, the Light-Bearer*, 18 June 1886, 3.

18. Ezra Heywood, "Ethical Health—Language," *The Word*, August 1889, 2.

19. Dr. Richard O'Neill, "A Physician's Testimony," *Lucifer, the Light-Bearer*, 14 February 1890, 3.

20. *The Word*, April 1890, Ezra Heywood, "Self-Sovereignty—Plain English," 2; untitled article, 2–3.

21. Woodhull, "The Beecher-Tilton Scandal Case," *Woodhull & Claflin's Weekly*, 2 November 1872, 9.

22. "The Courts," *New York Herald*, 3 November 1872, 6.

23. Ezra Heywood, "The Use of Plain Words Defended," *Lucifer, the Light-Bearer*, 14 August 1891, 3.

24. Angela Heywood, "Sex Nomenclature—Plain English," *The Word*, April 1887, 2, 3.

25. Angela Heywood, "The Ethics of Touch—Sex-Unity," *The Word*, June 1889, 2.

26. On Comstock, see Heywood Broun and Margaret Leech, *Anthony Comstock: Roundsman of the Lord* (New York: A. & C. Boni, 1927).

27. Mary Ware Dennett, *Who's Obscene* (New York: Vanguard, 1930), xix.

28. Woodhull speech titled "Tried As By Fire, or The True and The False, Socially," delivered in 1874 and reprinted in Taylor Stoehr, *Free Love in America: A Documentary History* (New York: AMS Press, 1979), 372; Harman, "Marriage," *Lucifer, the Light-Bearer*, 13 June 1884, 2; Ezra Heywood, *Cupid's Yokes*, 3, 12.

29. *Lucifer, the Light-Bearer*, "Autonomistic Marriage Practicalized," 1 October 1886, 1; untitled article, 17 December 1886, 1.

30. *The Word*, Angela Heywood, "The Woman's View of It—No. 1," April 1889, 2; Ezra Heywood, "Trial of the Case, U.S.G. vs. E.H.H.," January 1883, 2.

31. Ezra Heywood, "Social Freedom," *The Word*, May 1875, 4; Moses Harman, "A Remonstrance and an Appeal," *Lucifer, the Light-Bearer*, 16 October 1891, 2.

32. "Letter from a Mother," *The Word*, March 1890, 2.

33. Anthony Comstock, *Traps for the Young* (New York: Funk and Wagnalls, 1883), 158.

34. Comstock, *Traps for the Young*, 159; Martin Henry Blatt, *Free Love and Anarchism: The Biography of Ezra Heywood* (Urbana: University of Illinois Press, 1989), 174.

35. The *Topeka Daily Capital* and *Kansas City Times* comments were reprinted in "The Harman Case," *Lucifer, the Light-Bearer*, 4 February 1887, 2; R.E. VanMeter,

"A Disgraceful Affair," *Valley Falls New Era*, 30 September 1886, 1. VanMeter was editor of the *New Era* as well as the Associated Press correspondent for the area.

36. Hal D. Sears, *The Sex Radicals: Free Love in High Victorian America* (Lawrence: Regents Press of Kansas, 1977), 273.

37. Stoehr, *Free Love in America*, 3; Sears, *Sex Radicals*, 37.

38. Sears, *Sex Radicals*, 267.

CHAPTER 5. CRUSADING AGAINST THE BARBARISM OF LYNCHING

1. On the number of lynchings, see, Donald L. Grant, *The Anti-Lynching Movement, 1883–1932* (San Francisco: R and E Research Associates, 1975), viii–ix; Rayford W. Logan, *The Negro in the United States* (Princeton, NJ: D. Van Nostrand, 1957), 54; August Meier, *Negro Thought in America, 1880–1915* (Ann Arbor: University of Michigan Press, 1963), 19–21.

2. "A Lynching in DeSoto Parish," *New Orleans Daily Picayune*, 25 October 1886, 8.

3. No copies of the article that originally appeared in the *Memphis Free Speech* have survived; the article was reprinted in numerous papers, including "How the Constitution Is Being Trampled Under Foot by the South," *Indianapolis World*, 2 July 1892, 1.

4. James Elbert Cutler, *Lynch-Law: An Investigation into the History of Lynching in the United States* (New York: Longmans, Green, 1905), 157–58.

5. The best sources of information about Ida B. Wells-Barnett's life are her autobiography edited by her daughter, Alfreda M. Duster, *Crusade for Justice: The Autobiography of Ida B. Wells* (Chicago: University of Chicago Press, 1970), and Mildred I. Thompson, *Ida B. Wells-Barnett: An Exploratory Study of an American Black Woman, 1893–1930* (Brooklyn, NY: Carlson, 1990).

6. "The Press Convention," *New York Freeman*, 20 August 1887, 4; T. Thomas Fortune, "Mr. Fortune on the West," *New York Age*, 11 August 1888, 1.

7. "The Press Convention," *New York Freeman*, 20 August 1887, 4; Fortune, "Mr. Fortune on the West," *New York Age*, 11 August 1888, 1; Roland Wolseley, "Ida B. Wells-Barnett: Princess of the Black Press," *Encore*, 5 April 1976, 2; Duster, *Crusade for Justice*, 35–37, 41–42.

8. Quoted in Thompson, *Wells-Barnett*, 22.

9. Reprinted as Ida B. Wells, "A Little Plain Talk," *Memphis Appeal-Avalanche*, 6 September 1891, 4.

10. Quoted in Duster, *Crusade for Justice*, 52.

11. Duster, *Crusade for Justice*, 58–59.

12. Reprinted as "Memphis Stirred Up" in the *Nashville Daily American*, 26 May 1892, 4.

13. "Colored Folk Protest," *Memphis Appeal-Avalanche*, 30 June 1892, 5.

14. Emma Lou Thornbrough, *T. Thomas Fortune, Militant Journalist* (Chicago: University of Chicago Press, 1972), x.

15. Ida B. Wells, "Exiled," *New York Age*, 25 June 1892, 1; T. Thomas Fortune, "Ida B. Wells," in Lawson A. Scruggs, ed., *Women of Distinction: Remarkable in Works and Invincible in Character* (Raleigh, NC: L.A. Scruggs, 1893), 38. The first African American newspaper, *Freedom's Journal*, was founded in New York City in March 1827 by the Rev. Samuel Cornish and John Russwurm; the paper was published weekly until October 1829.

16. Wells, "Exiled," 1.

17. Wells, "Exiled," 1.

18. Wells, "Exiled," 1.

19. Wells, "Exiled," 1; Duster, *Crusade for Justice*, 52.

20. Wells, "Exiled," 1.

21. Wells, "Exiled," 1.

22. Wells, "Exiled," 1.

23. Wells, "Exiled," 1.

24. Wells, "Southern Horrors: Lynch Law in All Its Phases," (New York: New York Age Print, 1892), 6.

25. Frederick Douglass letter dated 25 October 1892 and reprinted in Wells, "Southern Horrors," preface.

26. "His Opinion No Good," *Indianapolis Freeman*, 29 September 1894, 4; Thompson, *Wells-Barnett*, 117.

27. Quoted in Thompson, *Wells-Barnett*, 32.

28. Thomas C. Holt, "The Lonely Warrior: Ida B. Wells-Barnett and the Struggle for Black Leadership," in John Hope Franklin and August Meier, eds., *Black Leaders of the Twentieth Century* (Urbana: University of Illinois Press, 1982), 47.

29. Thompson, *Wells-Barnett*, 38–40.

30. Paula Giddings, *When and Where I Enter: The Impact of Black Women on Race and Sex in America* (New York: William Morrow, 1984), 92.

31. "How Miss Wells' Crusade Is Regarded," *Literary Digest*, 28 July 1894, 366–67; "Ida Wells Heard Here," *New York Sun*, 30 July 1894, 2; "Negroes Loyal to Democracy," *New York Times*, 4 September 1894, 1.

32. *Chicago Inter-Ocean*, "A Bystander's Notes," 24 September 1892, 4; "Another South Carolina Plan," 5 August 1893, 12.

33. Nora Hall, "Ida B. Wells-Barnett," *Dictionary of Literary Biography*, vol. 23, *American Newspaper Journalists, 1873–1900* (Detroit: Gale Research, 1978), 343.

34. Quoted in Holt, "Lonely Warrior," 51.

35. Grant, *Anti-Lynching Movement*, 65.

36. Cutler, *Lynch-Law*, 245–46; Grant, *Anti-Lynching Movement*, 68–70. The states were Georgia, Kentucky, North Carolina, South Carolina, and Texas.

37. Wells, "A Red Record: Tabulated Statistics and Alleged Causes of Lynchings in the United States,"(Chicago: Ida B. Wells, 1894). The content of "A Red Record" is reprinted in Jacqueline Jones Royster, ed., *Southern Horrors and Other Writings: The Anti-Lynching Campaign of Ida B. Wells, 1892–1900* (Boston: Bedford Books, 1997). For the photograph, see Royster, *Southern Horrors*, 118.

38. Royster, *Southern Horrors*, 135, 148–54.

39. Meier, *Negro Thought in America*,20; Logan, *Negro in the United States*, 54.

40. Royster, *Southern Horrors*, 151.

41. Thompson, *Wells-Barnett*, 47.

42. Harold F. Gosnell, *Negro Politicians: The Rise of Negro Politicians in Chicago* (Chicago: University of Chicago Press, 1935), 155, 206; Allan H. Spear, *Black Chicago: The Making of a Negro Ghetto, 1890–1920* (Chicago: University of Chicago Press, 1967), 60–61. No copies of the *Chicago Conservator* for the period in which Wells wrote for or edited it have been preserved.

43. G.S.B. "A Negro Postmaster Killed," *Charleston* [South Carolina] *News and Courier*, 23 February 1898, 1; Dorothy Sterling, *Black Foremothers: Three Lives* (New York, 1988), 99; "Mrs. Ida Wells Barnett Calls on President McKinley," *Cleveland Gazette*, 9 April 1898, 2.

44. Wells-Barnett, "Mob Rule in New Orleans" (Chicago: Ida B. Wells-Barnett, 1900). The pamphlet is reprinted in Royster, *Southern Horrors*. For the quotes, see Royster, *Southern Horrors*, 169, 170, 173.

45. Holt, "Lonely Warrior," 51.

46. Wells-Barnett, "Our Country's Lynching Record," *Survey*, 1 February 1913, 574.

47. Wells-Barnett, "Our Country's Lynching Record," *Survey*, 1 February 1913, 574.

48. Quincy Ewing, "The Heart of the Race Problem," *Atlantic Monthly*, January–June 1909, 389.

49. Madelon Golden Schilpp, "Ida B. Wells-Barnett Crusader," in Madelon Golden Schilpp and Sharon M. Murphy, *Great Women of the Press* (Carbondale: Southern Illinois University Press, 1983), 130–31.

50. Grant, *Anti-Lynching Movement*, 67.

51. Grant, *Anti-Lynching Movement*, 159.

52. Gosnell, *Negro Politicians*, 11, 15–16, 19.

53. *Chicago Defender*, "Hold Last Rites for Ida B. Wells-Barnett," 4 April 1931, 2.

54. W.E.B. DuBois, "Postscript," *Crisis* 40 (June 1931):207.

55. Meier, *Negro Thought in America*, 20; Logan, *Negro in the United States*, 54.

56. Fortune, "Ida B. Wells," 35; Lucy Wilmot Smith, "Woman's Number," *Journalist*, January 1889, 5; Cutler, *Lynch-Law*, 230.

57. Royster, *Southern Horrors*, 10.

CHAPTER 6. EDUCATING AMERICA ON THE MERITS OF SOCIALISM

1. On the number of socialist papers, see Joseph R. Conlin, ed., *The American Radical Press, 1880–1960*, vol. 1 (Westport, CT: Greenwood, 1974), 49; David Paul Nord, "The *Appeal to Reason* and American Socialism, 1901–1920," *Kansas History* 1 (Summer 1978):75; James Weinstein, *The Decline of Socialism in America, 1912–1925* (New York: Vintage, 1969), 84–85.

2. Paul M. Buhle, "The Appeal to Reason" in Conlin, *American Radical Press*, vol. 1, 50; David Armstrong, *A Trumpet to Arms: Alternative Media in America* (Los Angeles: J. P. Tarcher, 1981), 38; John Graham, ed., *"Yours for the Revolution": The Appeal to Reason, 1895–1922* (Lincoln: University of Nebraska Press, 1990), x. Curiously, the book about dissident journalism that has been most widely adopted for classroom use—Lauren Kessler, *The Dissident Press: Alternative Journalism in American History* (Beverly Hills, CA: Sage, 1984)—does not even mention the *Appeal to Reason*.

3. George Milburn, "The Appeal to Reason," *American Mercury*, July 1931, 359–71. The Socialist Party of America was founded in 1901 in Indianapolis.

4. On the *Appeal*'s circulation, see Armstrong, *Trumpet to Arms*, 38; Graham, *"Yours for the Revolution,"* 1; Abe Peck, *Uncovering the Sixties: The Life and Times of the Underground Press* (New York: Citadel, 1985), 5; Elliott Shore, *Talkin' Socialism: J. A. Wayland and the Role of the Press in American Radicalism, 1890–1912* (Lawrence: University of Kansas Press, 1988), 134.

5. On biographical details about J. A. Wayland, see Graham, *"Yours for the Revolution,"* esp. 1–7; Shore, *Talkin' Socialism*, esp. 7–31.

6. J. A. Wayland, *Leaves of Life* (Girard, KS: Appeal to Reason Publishing, 1912), 23; "One Year's Work," *Appeal to Reason*, 14 September 1907, 1.

7. Wayland, "A Vision of the Future," *Appeal to Reason*, 8 December 1906, 1.

8. Wayland, untitled article, *Appeal to Reason*, 16 May 1896, 2.

9. Wayland, untitled article, *Appeal to Reason*, 16 October 1897, 4.

10. Kate Richards O'Hare, "He Counteth the Sparrow's Fall," *Appeal to Reason*, 19 November 1904, 2.

11. Wayland, *Appeal to Reason*, 6 March 1909, "More Democracy," 4; "What Socialism Is," 4.

12. Eugene V. Debs, "The Co-operative Commonwealth," *Appeal to Reason*, 29 December 1900, 3. Debs was the socialist candidate for President in 1904, 1908, 1912, and 1920. Allan Benson, a staff writer for the *Appeal*, was the socialist candidate for President in 1916.

13. Debs, "Co-operative Commonwealth," 3.

14. "What Is Fair?," *Appeal to Reason*, 24 August 1901, 1.

15. Mary Jones, "Mother Jones in Alabama," *Appeal to Reason*, 24 October 1908, 2.

16. Jones, "Mother Jones in Alabama," 2.

17. Jones, "Mother Jones in Alabama," 2.

18. "Powerless Without the Ballot," *American Standard*, 30 March 1888, 6; "Call a Halt," *Loyal American*, 2 December 1893, 4; "Joe Howard on Foreignism," *United American*, 11 August 1894, 1.

19. Henry O. Morris, "Miners' Property Destroyed," *Appeal to Reason*, 18 June 1904, 1.

20. *Appeal to Reason*, "Dynamite Witness Suicides," 7 September 1912, 3; John Kenneth Turner, "Labor Union and Socialist Local Infested With Corporation Spies," 25 July 1914, 2; Striker, "The Battle of McComb," 21 October 1911, 1.

21. "White Landlords, Robbing Negro Tenants, Let Loose Arkansas Reign of Terror," *Appeal to Reason*, 14 February 1920, 3; Shore, *Talkin' Socialism*, 181–82.

22. F. X. Waldhorst, "How We Move in Alabama," *Appeal to Reason*, 5 September 1903, 4.

23. A. G. Edmunds, "The Work in Butte," *Appeal to Reason*, 19 August 1911, 3.

24. *Appeal to Reason*, Helen Keller, "Helen Keller Writes," 24 December 1910, 1; "Helen Keller Sends Her Greetings to Gene Debs," 17 May 1919, 2; Jack London, "A Good Soldier," 27 November 1915, 2; Martha Baker, "A Woman's Chance," 14 June 1913, 3; William Babcock, "Dives and Lazarus," 2 October 1897, 2; Clarence E. Broom, "The Farmer Division of the Appeal Army," 26 December 1908, 3.

25. "His Last Letter," *Appeal to Reason*, 7 June 1902, 2.

26. Graham, *"Yours for the Revolution,"* 11.

27. Shore, *Talkin' Socialism*, 190–91.

28. *Appeal to Reason*, "An Electric Belt Free,"24 January 1903, 5; "$3 a Day Sure," 17 December 1904, 2.

29. *Appeal to Reason*, "Keep Something Going On," 25 November 1899, 1; "Los Angeles Wins," 24 February 1900, 1.

30. Upton Sinclair, "The Jungle," *Appeal to Reason*, 29 April 1905, 2.

31. "Samuel Hopkins Adams Is Dead," *New York Times*, 17 November 1958, 31; Arthur and Lila Weinberg, *The Muckrakers* (New York: Simon and Schuster, 1961), 206; Louis Filler, *Crusaders for American Liberalism* (Yellow Springs, OH: Antioch, 1939), 163.

32. Untitled article, *Appeal to Reason*, 3 March 1906, 1.

33. Eugene V. Debs, "Arouse, Ye Slaves!," *Appeal to Reason*, 10 March 1906, 1.

34. Nord, "*Appeal to Reason*," 75; Theodore Roosevelt, "Socialism: Where We Cannot Work with Socialists," *Outlook*, 20 March 1909, 621.

35. Shore, *Talkin' Socialism*, 216–17.

36. Shore, *Talkin' Socialism*, 217–18.

37. "Appeal's Issue of June 30 Is Barred from the Mails," *Appeal to Reason*, 14 July 1917, 1.

38. Alexander Troupe, "Socialism in Paragraphs," *Appeal to Reason*, 17 December 1904, 2.

39. John H. M. Laslett and Seymour Martin Lipset, eds., *Failure of a Dream? Essays in the History of American Socialism* (Garden City, NY: Anchor Press/Doubleday, 1974); Weinstein, *Decline of Socialism*, viii–ix.

40. George Allan England, "The Story of the Appeal to Reason," *Appeal to Reason*, 30 August 1913, 2.

41. Shore, *Talkin' Socialism*, 223.

42. Bob Nicklas, "A Good First Step in a Long March," *In These Times*, 12–25 August 1981, 17.

CHAPTER 7. FOLLOWING ANARCHY TOWARD A NEW SOCIAL ORDER

1. Frederick D. Buchstein, "The Anarchist Press in American Journalism," *Journalism History* 1(2) (Summer 1974):43. The earliest anarchist publication was a weekly newspaper titled *The Peaceful Revolutionist*; it was published from January to April 1833 in Cincinnati by Josiah Warren, who is known as the father of American anarchism.

2. The first issue of *The Alarm* was published in October 1884, and the paper was suppressed in May 1886. The paper was revived from November 1887 until February 1889 with Dyer D. Lum as editor. Lucy Parsons later revived *The Alarm* again in 1915 and 1916.

3. Albert R. Parsons, *Anarchism: Its Philosophy and Scientific Basis as Defined by Some of Its Apostles*, Lucy E. Parsons, ed. (Chicago, 1887), 15.

4. Philip S. Foner, *The Autobiographies of the Haymarket Martyrs* (New York: Humanities, 1969), 30.

5. "By Night," *Chicago Tribune*, 10 May 1876, 7.

6. Paul Avrich, *The Haymarket Tragedy* (Princeton, NJ: Princeton University Press, 1984), 24.

7. Parsons, *The Alarm*, "Wage-Workers," 24 January 1885, 1; "Revolutionary," 19 September 1885, 1.

8. Parsons, *The Alarm*, "Revolutionary," 19 September 1885, 1; "Wage-Workers," 24 January 1885, 1.

9. Parsons, *The Alarm*, "Reform or Revolution?," 18 October 1884, 2; "Revolutionary," 19 September 1885, 1.

10. Avrich, *Haymarket Tragedy*, 109.

11. Avrich, *Haymarket Tragedy*, 109; "The Black Flag!," *The Alarm*, 29 November 1884, 1.

12. Parsons, *The Alarm*, untitled article, 18 October 1884, 3; "WORKINGMEN TO ARMS!," 24 April 1886, 1.

13. Avrich, *Haymarket Tragedy*, 208–10.

14. "Anarchy's Red Hand," *New York Times*, 5 May 1886, 1; untitled article, *Philadelphia Inquirer*, 5 May 1886, 4; untitled article, *St. Louis Globe-Democrat*, 6 May 1886, 6.

15. In 1893, Illinois Gov. John Peter Altgeld pardoned the three surviving anarchists who had been convicted in the Haymarket case, ruling that the evidence had not proven that any of the eight men had been directly involved in the bombing. The trial of the Chicago anarchists is now viewed as one of the most unjust in the history of American jurisprudence.

16. Emma Goldman, *Living My Life* (New York: Knopf, 1931), vol. 1, 10.

17. Candace Falk, *Love, Anarchy, and Emma Goldman* (New York: Holt, Rinehart and Winston, 1984), 36, 43, 47, 51, 55, 60–205.

18. Emma Goldman, *Anarchism and Other Essays* (New York: Mother Earth, 1911), 86.

19. "Angry Crowds Surge about the Jail where Czolgosz Is Confined," *New York World*, 14 September 1901, 5.

20. Alice Wexler, *Emma Goldman: An Intimate Life* (New York: Pantheon, 1984), 122.

21. Goldman, "End of the Odyssey," *Mother Earth*, July 1910, 162; "Bold Priestess of Reds Appears," *Chicago Daily Tribune*, 6 March 1908, 1.

22. Ben Reitman, "Boston Lecture," *Mother Earth*, April 1915, 74.

23. *Mother Earth*, Ben Reitman, "Why You Shouldn't Go to War," April 1917, 41–44; Goldman, "The No Conscription League," June 1917, 113.

24. "Emma Goldman's Speech," *Mother Earth*, July 1917, 159.

25. J. Edgar Hoover to Creighton, 23 August 1919, National Archives Record Group 60, Department of Justice, Central File #186233–13, section 3, Washington, D.C.

26. *The Alarm*, Parsons, "Your Paper," 4 October 1884, 2; Parsons, "Revolutionary," 19 September 1885, 1; "The Black Flag!," 29 November 1884, 1.

27. Goldman, *Mother Earth*, "Observations and Comments," April 1913, 37; "Self-Defense for Labor," January 1914, 328, 331.

28. Goldman, "Intellectual Proletarians," *Mother Earth*, February 1914, 370.

29. *The Alarm*, Parsons, "The Useless Classes," 1 November 1884, 2; "The Black Flag!," 29 November 1884, 1.

30. *The Alarm*, Parsons, "The Useless Classes," 1 November 1884, 2; "Some Reminiscences," 31 December 1887, 3.

31. Goldman, "White Slave Traffic," *Mother Earth*, January 1910, 344–45.

32. *The Alarm*, Parsons, untitled article, 4 October 1884, 1; Lucy Parsons, "Outraged," 13 December 1884, 1.

33. *Mother Earth*, Goldman, "Observations and Comments," March 1909, 5; Ralph Waldo Emerson, "The Law," June 1914, 114–15.

34. *The Alarm*, Parsons, "Mass-Meeting," 7 February 1885, 1; August Spies, "An Anarchist and the Ministers of the Congregational Church," 9 January 1886, 3.

35. *The Alarm*, Parsons, "July 4, 1776," 27 June 1885, 2; Parsons, "To the Workingmen of America," 18 October 1884, 3; Gerhard Lizius, "Dynamite," 21 February 1885, 3.

36. Goldman, *Mother Earth*, "A Rejoinder," December 1910, 326–27; "The Ups and Downs of an Anarchist Agitator," August 1913, 172.

37. *Mother Earth*, July 1914, "Rebecca Edelsohn's Speech," 145–46; Alexander Berkman, "A Gauge of Change," 167–68.

38. "The Black Flag!," *The Alarm*, 29 November 1884, 1.

39. Goldman, *Anarchism and Other Essays*, 64.

40. Goldman, *Anarchism and Other Essays*, 61–62.

41. Margaret C. Anderson, "Emma Goldman in Chicago," *Mother Earth*, December 1914, 321.

42. For a summary of these actions, see Rodger Streitmatter, *Mightier than the Sword: How the News Media Have Shaped American History* (Boulder, CO: Westview /HarperCollins, 1997), 85–102.

43. For a summary of these actions, see Streitmatter, *Mightier than the Sword*, 85–102.

CHAPTER 8. PROPELLING BLACK AMERICANS INTO THE PROMISED LAND

1. The Black Press: Soldiers Without Swords (video), Stanley Nelson, producer/ director (New York: Half Nelson Productions, 1998); E. Franklin Frazier, *The Negro Family in Chicago* (Chicago: University of Chicago Press, 1932), 48–49; James R. Grossman, "Blowing the Trumpet: The *Chicago Defender* and Black Migration During World War I," *Illinois Historical Journal* 78 (Summer 1985): 82; Roi Ottley, *The Lonely Warrior: The Life and Times of Robert S. Abbott* (Chicago: Regnery, 1955), 161; T. J. Woofter Jr., *Negro Problems in Cities* (New York: Negro Universities Press, 1928), 28–29.

2. Chicago's black population soared from 44,103 to 109,458 between 1915 and 1919; see Carole Marks, "Black Workers and the Great Migration North," *Phylon* 46(2)

(1985): 161. On black population growth in urban centers more generally, see U.S. Bureau of the Census, *Negroes in the United States, 1920–1932* (Washington, DC: Government Printing Office, 1932), 55; Emmett J. Scott, *Negro Migration During the War* (New York: Oxford, 1920), 3.

3. Sandburg made the statement in his *Chicago Daily News* column "Notebook" in 1919, quoted in Ottley, *Lonely Warrior*, 159; Grossman, "Blowing the Trumpet," 84; Charles S. Johnson (president of Fisk University), quoted in Ottley, *Lonely Warrior*, 9.

4. Ottley, *Lonely Warrior*, 160; Gunnar Myrdal, quoted in Ottley, *Lonely Warrior*, 2; Robert S. Abbott, "Blazing the Way," *Chicago Defender*, 12 October 1918, 16.

5. Grossman, "Blowing the Trumpet," 84; Ottley, *Lonely Warrior*, 139; Roland E. Wolseley, *Black Press, U.S.A.*, 2nd ed. (Ames: Iowa State University Press, 1971), 54.

6. Grossman, "Blowing the Trumpet," 88; Alan D. Desantis, "A Forgotten Leader: Robert S. Abbott and the Chicago *Defender* from 1910–1920," *Journalism History* 23(2) (Summer 1997): 66.

7. Emmett J. Scott, "Letters of Negro Migrants of 1916–1918," *Journal of Negro History*, vol. 4 (1919), 333; Scott, *Negro Migration*, 30; James R. Grossman, *Land of Hope: Chicago, Black Southerners, and the Great Migration* (Chicago: University of Chicago Press, 1989), 80; Ottley, *Lonely Warrior*, 8.

8. Metz T. P. Lochard, "Robert S. Abbott—'Race Leader,'" *Phylon*, vol. 8 (1947): 124.

9. *Chicago Defender*, "White Man Rapes Colored Girl," 29 April 1916, 1; "Aged Man Is Burned to Death by Whites," 31 March 1917, 1.

10. "Railroad Rumblings," *Chicago Defender*, 21 May 1910, 4; "Railroad Rumblings," *Chicago Defender*, 1 January 1916, 2; Grossman, "Blowing the Trumpet," 88; Grossman, *Land of Hope*, 79.

11. *Chicago Defender*, "An Eye for an Eye, a Tooth for a Tooth," 8 January 1916, 1; "Lynching Must Be Stopped by Shotgun," 7 March 1914, 1; "When the Mob Comes and You Must Die, Take at Least One with You," 23 January 1915, 1; "Call the White Fiends to the Door and Shoot them Down," 23 January 1915, 1.

12. *Chicago Defender*, "Below the Mason-Dixon Line," 6 May 1916, 1; "White Southerners Burn Church," 1 April 1916, 1; "Woman Brutally Murdered by Memphis," 11 September 1915, 1.

13. *Chicago Defender*, Fon Holly, "Desertion," 2 September 1916, 12; "The Exodus," 28 August 1915, 8.

14. *Chicago Defender*, Abbott, "How Much Longer," 12 February 1916, 8; "Invites All North," 10 February 1917, 3.

15. *Chicago Defender*, "Paducah Horror!," 21 October 1916, 1; "W. Allison Sweeney," 19 February 1916, 8; "W. Allison Sweeney Breaks a Memphis 'White Folks Nigger'

on the Wheel!," 8 December 1917, 12; "Struggle in South Impossible," 1 April 1916, 8.

16. Grossman, "Blowing the Trumpet," 85.

17. "Texas Mob Burns Human Being in Public Square," *Chicago Defender*, 7 August 1915, 1.

18. Henry Walker, "Southern White Gentlemen Burn Race Boy at Stake," *Chicago Defender*, 20 May 1916, 1.

19. "New Lynching Disgraces Tennessee," *Chicago Defender*, 8 December 1917, 1.

20. *Chicago Defender*, "Help Wanted," 2 September 1916, 10; "Laborers Wanted," 28 April 1917, 9; "Help Wanted," 10 February 1917, 5; "Laborers Wanted," 1 December 1917, 10.

21. *Chicago Defender*, "Our Industrial Opportunity," 12 August 1916, 12; "The Eternal Question," 12 August 1916, 12.

22. "Trooper of Company K," *Chicago Defender*, 7 October 1916, 4.

23. *Chicago Defender*, "Madame X," 29 January 1916, 5; "The Two Tutts," 29 January 1916, 5; "Theatrical Review," 6 November 1915, 6; "Eight Black Dots," 7 October 1916, 4.

24. "Owl Theater," *Chicago Defender*, 27 January 1917, 3.

25. *Chicago Defender*, "Clubs and Societies," 6 November 1915, 6; "World's Champion Is Jack of All Trades," 20 February 1915, 6; "American Giants Close Season with Victory," 20 October 1917, 10.

26. Quoted in Grossman, *Land of Hope*, 86.

27. Florette Henri, *Black Migration: Movement North, 1900–1920* (Garden City, NY: Anchor, 1975), 64.

28. "THE EXODUS," *Chicago Defender*, 2 September 1916, 1.

29. *Chicago Defender*, "Leaving for the North," 20 January 1917, 2; "Farewell, Dixie Land," 7 October 1916, 12; "300 Leave for North," 18 November 1916, 2; "200 Leave for the North," 10 February 1917, 5; "Alabama," 10 March 1917, 6; "Old Mississippi," 7 April 1917, 2; "Down in Georgia," 10 March 1917, 2; "Old Mississippi," 31 March 1917, 3.

30. *Chicago Defender*, "Still Planning to Come North," 12 May 1917, 8; "Thousands Leave Memphis," 2 June 1917, 3.

31. "Two Schools," *Chicago Defender*, 7 April 1917, 8.

32. *Chicago Defender*, "Millions Prepare to Leave the South Following Brutal Burning of Human," 26 May 1917, 1; "Lynching of Crawford Causes Thousands to Leave the South," 7 October 1916, 3.

33. Abbott, *Chicago Defender*, "Farewell, Dixie Land," 7 October 1916, 12; untitled editorial, 16 September 1916, 12.

34. *Chicago Defender*, "Defender Editor Addresses Ministers," 29 January 1916, 3; "Editor Abbott Addresses Large Rockford Audience," 3 March 1917, 9.

35. Sandburg made the statement in his "Notebook" column, quoted in Ottley, *Lonely Warrior*, 162.

36. Scott, "Letters of Negro Migrants, 333; Emmett J. Scott, "Additional Letters of Negro Migrants of 1916–1918, *Journal of Negro History* 4 (1919):420, 422, 426, 437, 448, 449; Carter D. Woodson Collection, Box 20, Library of Congress Manuscripts Division.

37. Ottley, *Lonely Warrior*, 326; *Soldiers Without Swords*.

38. Quoted in Ottley, *Lonely Warrior*, 165.

39. Ottley, *Lonely Warrior*, 165.

40. "Emigration Worries South; Arrests Made to Keep Labor from Going North," *Chicago Defender*, 24 March 1917, 1.

41. Soldiers Without Swords; Ottley, *Lonely Warrior*, 142, 145, 146, 167; Henri, *Black Migration*, 64; Desantis, "Forgotten Leader," 69.

42. Ottley, *Lonely Warrior*, 142; Desantis, "Forgotten Leader," 69.

43. Desantis, "Forgotten Leader," 69.

44. Ottley, *Lonely Warrior*, 145; *Soldiers Without Swords*.

45. Abbott, "I Appeal to All the Members of My Race Throughout the United States to Crush This Damnable Disgrace," *Chicago Defender*, 4 August 1917, 12; Scott, *Negro Migration*, 31.

46. *Chicago Defender*, "Alabama," 31 March 1917, 3; "Leaving for the East," 20 January 1917, 10.

47. "Determined to Go North," *Chicago Defender*, 24 March 1917, 10.

48. "Riot Sweeps Chicago," *Chicago Defender*, 2 August 1919, 1.

49. Desantis, "Forgotten Leader"; Grossman, "Blowing the Trumpet"; *Soldiers Without Swords*; Henry Lewis Suggs, ed., *The Black Press in the Middle West, 1865–1985* (Westport, CT: Greenwood, 1996), 49; Wolseley, *Black Press*, 54.

CHAPTER 9. DEMANDING WIDER ACCESS TO BIRTH CONTROL INFORMATION

1. An abortion could be legally performed by a licensed doctor only if it had been determined that the pregnancy placed a woman's life in danger. Mary Ware Dennett, *Who's Obscene* (New York: Vanguard, 1930), xix.

2. Sanger coined the term "birth control" in early 1914 "to get a name for contraception which would convey to the public the social and personal significance of the idea." See Margaret Sanger, *My Fight for Birth Control* (New York: Farrar & Rinehart, 1931), 83.

3. Sanger, *Woman Rebel*, March 1914, "Why the Woman Rebel?," 2; "The Aim," 1.

4. Sanger, *Woman Rebel*, March 1914, "Why the Woman Rebel?," 2; "The Aim," 1; "A Woman's Duty," 8.

5. Helena Huntington Smith, "Profiles," *New Yorker*, 5 July 1930, 22.

6. On Sanger's early life, see Sanger, *Margaret Sanger: An Autobiography* (New York: Norton, 1938), 11–45.

7. Smith, "Profiles," 22.

8. Sanger, *An Autobiography*, 92; *My Fight for Birth Control*, 56.

9. Mary Alden Hopkins, "Birth Control and Public Morals," *Harper's Weekly*, 22 May 1915, 489; Sanger, "What Every Girl Should Know," *New York Call*, 2 March 1913, 15.

10. Sanger, *My Fight for Birth Control*, 80.

11. Ruth Millard, "Birth Control Fight Opened by Margaret Sanger in 1914," *New York World-Telegram*, 23 March 1931, 14; quoted in Lawrence Lader, *The Margaret Sanger Story* (Garden City, NY: Doubleday, 1955), 54.

12. On Roberts as Sanger's lover, see Ellen Chesler, *Woman of Valor: Margaret Sanger and the Birth Control Movement in America* (New York: Simon & Schuster, 1992), 92–97.

13. On Portet and Ellis as Sanger's lovers, see Chesler, *Woman of Valor*, 108–10, 118–21.

14. Sanger, Frederick Blossom, and Elizabeth Stuyvesant, "To the Men and Women of the United States," *Birth Control Review*, February 1917, 3.

15. Sanger, "The Prevention of Conception," *Woman Rebel*, March 1914, 8.

16. Sanger, "The Prevention of Conception," *Woman Rebel*, March 1914, 8.

17. Sanger, "A Birth Strike To Avert World Famine," *Birth Control Review*, January 1920, 3.

18. "Some Letters," *Woman Rebel*, September/October 1914, 55.

19. "To Our Readers," *Birth Control Review*, April 1920, 19.

20. *Woman Rebel*, Sanger, "A Little Lesson for Those Who Ought to Know Better," September/October 1914, 53; Elizabeth Kleen, "Can You Afford to Have a Large Family?," April 1914, 23; Sanger, "Into the Valley of Death—for What?," April 1914, 12.

21. Sanger, "Soldiers and Prostitution," *Woman Rebel*, April 1914, 21.

22. Sanger, "Birth Control or Abortion?," *Birth Control Review*, December 1918, 3; "Abortion in the United States," *Woman Rebel*, April 1914, 24.

23. Sanger, "Suppression," *Woman Rebel*, June 1914, 1.

24. Sanger, " 'The Menace's' Advice," *Woman Rebel*, April 1914, 23; Sanger, "Suppression," *Woman Rebel*, June 1914, 1; Floyd Dell, "The Anti-Birth Control Neuroses," *Birth Control Review*, September 1928, 252–54.

25. Sanger, *Woman Rebel*, "The New Feminists," March 1914, 1; "The Birth Control League," July 1914, 39.

26. Sanger, "The Prevention of Conception," *Woman Rebel*, March 1914, 8.

27. Sanger, "Humble Pie," *Woman Rebel*, April 1914, 1.

28. Sanger, "Your Guardians," *Woman Rebel*, July 1914, 45.

29. Sanger, "Indictment," *Woman Rebel*, September/October 1914, 1.

30. On the growth of the Birth Control Movement, see Chesler, *Woman of Valor*, 213.

31. On Williams, de Selincourt, and Wells as Sanger's lovers, see Chesler, *Woman of Valor*, 173, 183–92.

32. On Sanger and Slee's marriage, see Chesler, *Woman of Valor*, 243–64.

33. On Child and MacDonald as Sanger's lovers, see Chesler, *Woman of Valor*, 184, 349–51.

34. "Margaret Sanger Is Dead; Led Campaign for Birth Control," *New York Times*, 7 September 1966, 41.

35. Ruth Hale, "The Child Who Was Mother to a Woman," *New Yorker*, 11 April 1925, 11–12; "Some Notes on How to Be Happy If Married," *New York Times Book Review*, 4 July 1926, 8.

36. Chesler, *Woman of Valor*, 224; "Once Imprisoned, Margaret Sanger Now Given Honor," *New Haven* [Connecticut] *Register*, 22 November 1931, 4; "She Deserves It," *New York Herald Tribune*, 13 November 1931, 18.

37. "Sanger Milestone," *Time*, 21 December 1936, 24; "Birth Control Today," *The Nation*, 9 January 1937, 34; "Margaret Sanger Celebrates a Birth Control Victory," *Life*, 11 January 1937, 18–21; Evelyn Seeley, " 'It's What I'd Have Written Myself,' Says Mrs. Sanger, Elated at Victory," *New York World-Telegram*, 21 March 1931, 5; Ruth Millard, "Birth Control Fight Opened by Margaret Sanger in 1914," *New York World-Telegram*, 23 March 1931, 14.

38. "Margaret Sanger Is Dead; Led Campaign for Birth Control," *New York Times*, 7 September 1966, 41.

CHAPTER 10. OPPOSING AMERICA'S "DIRTY WAR" IN VIETNAM

1. On the mainstream American news media supporting the Vietnam War until the Tet Offensive, see Peter Braestrup, *Big Story: How the American Press and Television Reported and Interpreted the Crisis of Tet 1968 in Vietnam and Washington* (Boulder, CO: Westview, 1977) vol. 1, xxi–xxiv; David Halberstam, *The Powers That Be* (New York: Knopf, 1979), 514; Daniel C. Hallin, *The "Uncensored War": The Media and Vietnam* (New York: Oxford University Press, 1986), 151–52, 168–69; Don Oberdorfer, *Tet!* (Garden City, NY: Doubleday, 1971), 158–59, 241–42.

2. *Report from Vietnam by Walter Cronkite*, CBS, 27 February 1968.

3. Jack A. Smith, "The *Guardian* Goes to War," in Ken Wachsberger, ed., *Voices from the Underground: Insider Histories of the Vietnam Era Underground Press* (Tempe, AZ: Mica Press, 1993), 99.

4. Kumar Goshal, "Our 'Dirty War,' " *National Guardian*, 18 April 1963, 3.

5. Dwight Macdonald, "Introduction," in the reprint edition of the *Catholic Worker* (Westport, CT: Greenwood, 1970), 11.

6. Dorothy Day, "Theophane Venard and Ho Chi Minh," *Catholic Worker*, May 1954, 6.

7. Day, "Theophane Venard," 6.

8. Thomas Merton, "The Root of War," *Catholic Worker*, October 1961, 1, 7–8.

9. Merton, "Root of War," 8.

10. I. F. Stone, "Why the AEC Retracted That Falsehood on Nuclear Testing," *I. F. Stone's Weekly*, 17 March 1958, 1; Robert C. Cottrell, *Izzy: A Biography of I. F. Stone* (New Brunswick, NJ: Rutgers University Press, 1992), 200–201; Leonard Downie Jr., *The New Muckrakers* (New York: New American Library, 1976), 202; Nat Hentoff, "I. F. Stone: The Measure of a Man," *Village Voice*, 23 December 1971, 20.

11. Robert Trumbull, "Taylor Surveys Peril in Vietnam," *New York Times*, 20 October 1961, 6; Hallin, *"Uncensored War,"* 148; Stone, "There Will Always Be a Berlin," *I. F. Stone's Weekly*, 31 July 1961, 2–3.

12. Stone, *I. F. Stone's Weekly*, "Always Be a Berlin," 31 July 1961, 4; "Will New Chances for Peace Be Another Lost Opportunity?," 28 October 1963, 2.

13. Stone, "How Super Power Becomes Super Impotence," *I. F. Stone's Weekly*, 13 May 1963, 1.

14. Stone, "Will New Chances," 2–3.

15. "What We Are Doing to Innocent Villagers in Vietnam and Cambodia," *I. F. Stone's Weekly*, 30 March 1964, 3.

16. Stone, *I. F. Stone's Weekly*, "Time for the Peace Movement to Call for an End of War in Viet Nam," 23 July 1962, 3; "The Case for a Cease-Fire Now," 15 June 1964, 3.

17. Kumar Goshal, "U.S. toll mounts in undeclared war in South Vietnam," *National Guardian*, 21 March 1963, 1.

18. *National Guardian*, David Wesley, "Is war in Vietnam America's 'Spain'?," 11 April 1963, 1; Goshal, " 'Dirty War,' " 18 April 1963, 3; Wilfred G. Burchett, "Vietnam rebels' terms for a U.S. settlement," 23 January 1964, 3.

19. Goshal, " 'Dirty War,' " *National Guardian*, 18 April 1963, 3.

20. Smith, *"Guardian* Goes to War," 99. Burchett remained the only correspondent reporting from North Vietnam for an American news organization until December 1966 when Harrison Salisbury of the *New York Times* joined him.

21. Wilfred Burchett, "How 21 U.S. jet bombers were destroyed at Bien Hoa," *National Guardian*, 6 February 1965, 6.

22. Burchett, *National Guardian*, "Slaughter at Loc Ninh: Guerrilla chief's story," 7 January 1964, 3; "Burchett exclusive: the battle of Binh Gia," 13 February 1965, 6; "Vietnam coup just juggling," 6 February 1964, 1; "The U.S. myth about Vietnam," 30 January 1964, 1; "U.S. debacle in South Vietnam," 2 January 1964, 1.

23. "Get out of Vietnam!," *National Guardian*, 13 February 1964, 2.

24. *National Guardian*, "A strange war against children and patients," 27 March 1965, 3; Freda Cook, "No. Vietnam's strength," 28 August 1965, 4; "On-spot report on No. Vietnam," 25 September 1965, 1; "On-spot report: North Vietnam under bombs," 9 October 1965, 7.

25. Robert Scheer and Warren Hinckle, "The Vietnam Lobby," *Ramparts*, July 1965, 15–24.

26. Donald Duncan, " 'The whole thing was a lie!,' " *Ramparts*, February 1966, 12–24.

27. Duncan, "Whole thing," 21–23.

28. Ramparts, January 1967, Dr. Benjamin Spock, "The Children of Vietnam: Preface," 44; William F. Pepper, "The Children of Vietnam," 5–68.

29. Stone, "Time for the Peace Movement," 3.

30. James Miller, *"Democracy Is in the Streets": From Port Huron to the Siege of Chicago* (New York: Simon & Schuster, 1987), 231; *I. F. Stone's Weekly*, 25 October 1965.

31. "Viet-Nam War Protest Is Staged by 16,000," *Washington Post*, 18 April 1965, 1, 18; "16,000 March for Viet Nam Peace," *Washington Evening Star*, 18 April 1965, 1; "15,000 Anti-Viet Collegians Picket White House," *New York Herald Tribune*, 18 April 1965, 2; "Picketing Kept Up at the White House," *New York Times*, 19 April 1965, 6; "They Came, Sang, Marched," *Washington Evening Star*, 18 April 1965, B-1; "15,000 White House Pickets Denounce Vietnam War," *New York Times*, 18 April 1965, 3.

32. Tom Cornell, "Life & Death on the Streets of New York," *Catholic Worker*, November 1965, 8.

33. "Declaration of Conscience," *Catholic Worker*, February 1965, 2.

34. James Aronson, "It's time for a broad U.S. peace movement," *National Guardian*, 9 January 1964, 1.

35. *National Guardian*, "Speak out now on Vietnam," 14 March 1964, 1; Owen Lattimore, "Outcry of Horror," 17 April 1965, 2.

36. Duncan, "Whole thing," 24.

37. James Aronson, "A Radical Journalist in the 1950s," *Nieman Reports*, Spring/Summer 1975, 39.

38. General Westmoreland gave the speech on 21 November 1967 at the National Press Club; Braestrup, *Big Story*, vol. 2, 3–10; Abe Peck, *Uncovering the Sixties: The Life and Times of the Underground Press* (New York: Citadel, 1985), iv; Orr Kelly, "War Just About Won—In a Military Sense," *Washington Evening Star*, 7 November 1967, 1.

39. Hallin, *"Uncensored War,"* 161.

40. John E. Mueller, *War, Presidents, and Public Opinion* (New York: Wiley, 1973), 201.

41. "The Logic of the Battlefield," *Wall Street Journal*, 23 February 1968, 14; Stone, "Will New Chances," 2; *ABC Evening News*, 1 February 1968; *CBS Evening News with Walter Cronkite*, 2 February 1968; Merton, "Root of War," 8; Burchett, "Slaughter at Loc Ninh," 3; Burchett, "Vietnam coup just juggling," 1; Burchett, "Battle of Binh Gia," 6; "By Book and Bullet," *Time*, 23 February 1968, 32; Scheer and Hinckle, "Vietnam Lobby," 15–24; *Report from Vietnam*; Stone, "Time for the Peace Movement," 3.

CHAPTER 11. SEX, DRUGS, ROCK 'N' ROLL . . . AND SOCIAL JUSTICE

1. On the number of counterculture papers, see Abe Peck, *Uncovering the Sixties: The Life and Times of the Underground Press* (New York: Citadel, 1985), xv.

2. *The Paper*, 22 October 1968; R.R., "The Roving Rat Fink," *Berkeley Barb*, 7 April 1967, 13; Cassell, "Miss (Plastic) America," *The Kudzu*, 3 October 1968, 3.

3. Allan, "The Beatles," *The Kudzu*, 17 December 1968, 8.

4. Max Scherr, "The BARB and the Citizen," *Berkeley Barb*, 13 August 1965, 4.

5. Stew Albert, "Try Them in the Streets," *Berkeley Barb*, 16 May 1969, 14.

6. "Wild Party after March," *Berkeley Gazette*, 31 May 1969, 1.

7. On Michael Kindman and the founding of *The Paper*, see Michael Kindman, "My Odyssey through the Underground Press," in Ken Wachsberger, ed., *Voices from the Underground: Insider Histories of the Vietnam Era Underground Press* (Tempe, AZ: Mica Press, 1993), 369–89.

8. Kindman, "As We Begin: A Loyalty Oath," *The Paper*, 3 December 1965, 1.

9. "Underground Alliance," *Time*, 29 July 1966, 57.

10. Kindman, "My Odyssey," 379.

11. Warren Hinckle, "The University on the Make," *Ramparts*, April 1966, 14, 20, 22.

12. *The Paper*, 21 April 1966, "Ramparts v. MSU v. The CIA: The University on the Run," 1; "What the hell is a university doing buying guns, anyway?," 4.

13. David Doggett, "The Kudzu: Birth and Death in Underground Mississippi," in Wachsberger, *Voices from the Underground*, 214.

14. Doggett, "Generational Revolt," *The Kudzu*, 18 September 1968, 2.

15. Doggett, "The Kudzu," 219.

16. "Kudzu Busted at Callaway," *The Kudzu*, 23 October 1968, 3.

17. Doggett, "The Kudzu," 227, 220.

18. Doggett, "The Kudzu," 219.

19. Doggett, "The Kudzu," 220.

20. Eugene Schoenfeld, "Dr. HIPpocrates," *Berkeley Barb*, 7 April 1967, 13.

21. "Personal," *Berkeley Barb*, 12 April 1968, 14; 26 April 1968, 14.

22. *The Paper*, 24 March 1969, Dave Freedman, untitled article, 4; "Jo Hooper's Platform," 16; Bob Cummings, untitled article, 10; Jo Hooper, untitled quotation, 10.

23. "Heavy Hog," *The Kudzu*, 17 December 1968, 7.

24. Eugene Schoenfeld, "Dr. HIPpocrates," *Berkeley Barb*, 7 July 1967, 13, 14.

25. *The Paper*, 22 November 1969, 11, "Outlaw this Dangerous Drug!"; "NARCS."

26. Everett Long, "The Politics of Pot," *The Kudzu*, 2 August 1969, 10.

27. "Dylan," *The Kudzu*, 18 September 1968, 3.

28. Allan, "The Beatles," *The Kudzu*, 17 December 1968, 8.

29. *Berkeley Barb*, 31 May 1968, 14.

30. Bob Randolph, "Peace Action," *Berkeley Barb*, 13 August 1965, 1. The signs made by the soldiers were not mentioned in "Another Vigil at a Troop Train," *San Francisco Chronicle*, 12 August 1965, 3, or Jerry Belcher, "6 Anti-Viet War Pickets Hurt in E. Bay Ambush," *San Francisco Examiner*, 13 August 1965, 1.

31. Bob Randolph, "August 12—Black Day for Berkeley," *Berkeley Barb*, 13 August 1965, 1.

32. *Berkeley Barb*, Randolph, "August 12," 13 August 1965, 1; Jeff Jassen, "Slug-Happy Cops Wreak Havoc in the Haight," 7 April 1967, 1; "BLOOD PURGE! Cops Ambush LA Protestors," 30 June 1967, 1.

33. *The Paper*, Jim Thomas, "Notes from Vietnam," 13 October 1966, 7; "Jim Thomas: 1946–1966," 9 January 1967, 1.

34. *The Paper*, Jack Higgins, "MSU and ROTC," 1 May 1969, 3; Kindman, "Merit Program Still Confused," 5 May 1966, 7; "Jo Hooper's Platform," 24 March 1969, 16; "The Mind that Styles Itself Radical," 27 January 1966, 6.

35. Jan Hillegas, "City Dumps on Garbage Men," *The Kudzu*, October 1969, 3.

36. *The Kudzu*, "Leland Black Students Boycott," 12 November 1968, 5; "White Repression-Black Response," undated issue published sometime in February 1969, 4; "Bombing at Bluefield State," 13 January 1969, 5.

37. Harvey Wasserman, "The Joy of Liberation News Service," in Wachsberger, *Voices from the Underground*, 53.

38. Memorandum from Director J. Edgar Hoover to all FBI offices, 5 November 1968, FBI Headquarters, Washington, D.C.

39. Final Report of the Select Committee to Study Governmental Operations with Respect to Intelligence Activities, United States Senate, Supplementary Detailed Staff Reports of Intelligence Activities and Rights of Americans, Book III (Washington, D.C.: U.S. Government Printing Office, 1976), 30–31; Geoffrey Rips, ed., *The Campaign Against the Underground Press* (San Francisco: City Lights, 1981); FBI memo from Hoover to Albany, NY, field office, 8 July 1968.

40. Newsletter for Intellectual Freedom (American Library Association), vol. XIX, no. 6 (November 1970), 90; *Final Report of the Select Committee*, 30–31.

41. Agis Salpukas, "Underground Papers are Thriving on Campuses and in Cities Across Nation," *New York Times*, 5 April 1970, 58; Rips, *Campaign Against the Underground Press*, 89–91.

42. Thorne Dreyer, "Underground Fuck," *San Francisco Express Times*, 11 December 1968, 5; Thomas King Forcade, "Obscenity, Who Really Cares," *Countdown*, 1971, 168; Rips, *Campaign Against the Underground Press*, 102–04.

43. Bayard Brunt and Albert V. Gaudiosi, "The New Revolutionaries: Head of Rebel Paper Is Central Figure in New Left Here," *Philadelphia Evening Bulletin*, 28 July 1970, A-1, B-3; Rips, *Campaign Against the Underground Press*, 108.

44. Final Report of the Select Committee, 824; David Armstrong, *A Trumpet to Arms: Alternative Media in America* (Los Angeles: J.P. Tarcher, 1981), 148; Rips, *Campaign Against the Underground Press*, 117.

45. Rips, *Campaign Against the Underground Press*, 81.

46. Final Report of the Select Committee, 30–31; Angus Mackenzie, "Sabotaging the Dissident Press," *Columbia Journalism Review*, March-April 1981, 60, 62.

47. Resist Newsletter, #48, 2 December 1970, 3.

48. "Messages," *Berkeley Barb*, 22 July 1977, A-2, A-4.

49. Armstrong, *Trumpet to Arms*; Everette E. Dennis and William L. Rivers, *Other Voices: The New Journalism in America* (San Francisco: Canfield, 1974); Robert J. Glessing, *The Underground Press in America* (Bloomington: Indiana University Press, 1970); Laurence Leamer, *The Paper Revolutionaries: The Rise of the Underground Press* (New York: Simon and Schuster, 1972); Roger Lewis, *Outlaws of America: The Underground Press and Its Context* (Baltimore: Penguin, 1972); Peck, *Uncovering the Sixties*; Wachsberger, *Voices from the Underground*.

50. Armstrong, *Trumpet to Arms*, 170.

CHAPTER 12. STANDING TALL AND TOUGH AGAINST RACIAL OPPRESSION

1. "The Black Panthers—Two Paths," *New York Times*, 24 August 1969, 24; FBI memo from Hoover to FBI field offices, 15 May 1969.

2. On the circulation of the *Panther,* see David Armstrong, *A Trumpet to Arms:*

Alternative Media in America (Los Angeles: J. P. Tarcher, 1981), 146; Charles E. Jones, ed., *The Black Panther Party Reconsidered* (Baltimore: Black Classics, 1998), 420; Clint C. Wilson II, *Black Journalists in Paradox: Historical Perspectives and Current Dilemmas* (New York: Greenwood, 1991), 85; Roland E. Wolseley, *Black Press, U.S.A.*, 2nd ed. (Ames: Iowa State University Press, 1971), 90. On the *Panther* having the largest circulation of any African American newspaper of the time, see Wilson, *Black Journalists in Paradox*, 85; Wolseley, *Black Press*, 90. The second largest black paper, the *Chicago Defender*, had a circulation of 33,000; see Wilson, *Black Journalists in Paradox*, 85.

3. Huey P. Newton, "What We Want; What We Believe," *Black Panther*, 20 July 1967, 3.

4. "Armed Negroes Enter California Assembly in Gun Bill Protest," *New York Times*, 3 May 1967, 24; JoNina M. Abron, " 'Raising the Consciousness of the People': The Black Panther Intercommunal News Service, 1967–1980," in Ken Wachsberger, ed., *Voices from the Underground: Insider Histories of the Vietnam Era Underground Press* (Tempe, AZ: Mica Press, 1993), 356.

5. *Black Panther*, John Coleman, "Chicago 8," 15 November 1969, 2; Newton, "To the R.N.A. [Republic of New Africa]," 6 December 1969, 10.

6. Dora Gray and George Dewitt, "Fascism at Central High School," *Black Panther*, 17 October 1970, 3; no coverage of the incident appeared in the *Greensboro News and Record*, the regional paper for the High Point area, during the month of October 1970. "Pigs Attack Child Care Center," *Black Panther*, 14 November 1970, 4; no coverage of the incident appeared in the *Los Angeles Times* during the two weeks following 4 November 1970, the date the incident occurred.

7. Bobby Seale, *Seize the Time: The Story of the Black Panther Party and Huey P. Newton* (New York: Random House, 1970), 181; Fred Hampton, "You Can Murder a Liberator, but You Can't Murder Liberation," *Black Panther*, 15 January 1969, 4.

8. *Black Panther*, cartoons, 28 September 1968, 4; 18 May 1968, 21; 15 January 1969, 11; 12 October 1968, 14.

9. Abron, " 'Raising the Consciousness,' " 351; "Guns and Butter," *Newsweek*, 5 May 1969, 40; Martin Rywell, ed., *Afro-American Encyclopedia* (North Miami, FL: Educational Book Publishers, 1974), vol. 1, 304; quoted in Philip S. Foner, ed., *The Black Panthers Speak* (New York: Lippincott, 1970), 82.

10. "Why Was Denzil Dowell Killed?," *Black Panther*, 25 April 1967, 1.

11. "Armed Black Brothers in Richmond Community," *Black Panther*, 25 April 1967, 3–4.

12. Newton, *Black Panther*, "Functional Definition of Politics," 4 January 1969, 5; "The Correct Handling of a Revolution," 18 May 1968, 8.

13. *Black Panther*, "On the Murder of Ronald Redrick," 21 November 1970, 8; Norman, "Out with the Old Fascist in with the New," 14 November 1970, 5; Semaj, "Pigs Let Injured Brother Lie in the Street for 36 Minutes," 21 November 1970, 13; Lynn Smith, "Avenge Raymond Brooks," 14 December 1970, 3; "Reese Drug Store New Haven, Conn. Site of Fascist Brutality Against the People," 19 December 1970, 3; Malik, "Pig Responsible for Death of 15 Year Old Brother," 17 October 1970, 2; Eldridge Cleaver, "Eldridge on Weathermen," 22 November 1969, 5.

14. Foner, *Black Panthers Speak*, xvi.

15. Rywell, *Afro-American Encyclopedia*, vol. 1, 302.

16. *Black Panther*, Newton, "Functional Definition of Politics," 4 January 1969, 5; Hilliard in "Interview with CBS News," 10 January 1970, 3.; Cleaver, "On Violence," 23 March 1968, 3.

17. Hilliard, "If You Want Peace, You Got to Fight for It," *Black Panther*, 22 November 1969, 11.

18. Newton, "What We Want; What We Believe," *Black Panther*, 20 July 1967, 3.

19. *Black Panther*, "The Ten-Point Platform and Program of the Black Panther Party," 18 October 1969, 2; "Black Soldiers as Revolutionaries to Overthrow the Ruling Class," 3 January 1970, 6.

20. Connie Matthews, "On the Vietnam Moratorium," *Black Panther*, 25 October 1969, 11.

21. Dr. Bert Small, "Black Genocide: Sickle Cell Anemia," *Black Panther*, 10 April 1971, 1.

22. Small, "Black Genocide," 1.

23. Small, "Black Genocide," 1.

24. Small, "Black Genocide," 1.

25. "Editorial Note," *Black Panther*, 10 April 1971, 1.

26. "Editorial Note," *Black Panther*, 10 April 1971, 1.

27. "The People's Fight Against Sickle Cell Anemia Begins," *Black Panther*, 22 May 1971, 10.

28. Huey P. Newton, *To Die for the People: The Writings of Huey P. Newton* (New York: Random House, 1972), 81.

29. Newton, "Huey P. Newton Talks to the Movement," reprinted in August Meier, Elliott Rudwick, and Francis L. Broderick, eds., *Black Protest Thought in the Twentieth Century* (New York: Macmillan, 1971), 506.

30. *Black Panther*, "Black Women and the Revolution," 3 March 1969, 9; "Black Woman, By a Black Revolutionary," 14 September 1968, 6.

31. Linda Green, "Black Panther Revolutionary Woman," *Black Panther*, 28 September 1968, 11.

32. Gloria Bartholomew, "A Black Woman's Thoughts," *Black Panther*, 28 September 1968, 11.

33. FBI memo from Hoover to field offices, 25 August 1967; Geoffrey Rips, ed., *The Campaign Against the Underground Press* (San Francisco: City Lights, 1981), 125; Chip Berlet, "COINTELPRO," *Alternative Media* 10(2) (Fall 1978): 11.

34. Armstrong, *Trumpet to Arms*, 146.

35. See documents introduced as evidence in the case of *Iberia Hampton, et. al., Plaintiffs-Appellants v. Edward V. Hanrahan, et. al.*, transcripts 21741–62, 21807–18, 18802, and 19483–94. Iberia Hampton was Fred Hampton's mother; Edward V. Hanrahan was state's attorney for Cook County.

36. S. K. Levin, "$1.85 Million Awarded in Chicago Panther Suit," *Colorado Daily*, 23 May 1983.

37. Abron, " 'Raising the Consciousness,' " 347.

38. Newton was shot to death in August 1989, and two years later Tyrone Robinson was convicted of the murder. Robinson was a member of the Black Guerrilla Family, a group organized to protect black prisoners from white racist prisoners. Many members of the Black Guerrilla Family blamed the Panthers for the death of their founder, George Jackson, but many Panthers believed that the FBI had instigated the rumor that the Panthers had killed Jackson.

39. The most comprehensive examination of criminal acts committed by the Black Panthers is Hugh Pearson, *The Shadow of the Panther: Huey Newton and the Price of Black Panther Power in America* (Reading, MA: Addison-Wesley, 1994).

40. Norman Hill, ed., *The Black Panther Menace: America's Neo-Nazis* (New York: Popular Library, 1971), 10.

41. Beginning in 1989, Rep. John Conyers Jr. (D-Mich.), dean of the Congressional Black Caucus, repeatedly sponsored legislation to establish a commission to study reparations. See also, Kevin Merida, "Did Freedom Alone Pay a Nation's Debt?," *Washington Post*, 23 November 1999, C-1, C-8.

42. The median black family income is $26,522, and the median white family income is $44,756; see U.S. Bureau of the Census, Current Population Reports, P60–197, *Money Income in the United States: 1996* (U.S. Government Printing Office: Washington, 1997), 14–15.

43. Rywell, *Afro-American Encyclopedia*, vol. 1, 308.

44. The 1970s books were Foner, *Black Panthers Speak*; G. Louis Heath, *The Black Panther Leaders Speak* (Metuchen, NJ: Scarecrow, 1976); G. Louis Heath, ed., *"Off the Pigs!": The History and Literature of the Black Panther Party* (Metuchen, NJ: Scarecrow, 1976). The 1980s books included Earl Anthony, *Picking Up the Gun: A Report on the Black Panthers* (New York: Dial, 1970); Armstrong, *Trumpet to Arms*; Paul Chevigny, *Cops and Rebels: A Study of Provocation* (New York: Pantheon, 1972);

Ward Churchill and Jim Vander Wall, *Agents of Repression: The FBI's Secret Wars Against the Black Panther Party and the American Indian Movement* (Boston: South End Press, 1988); Robert J. Glessing, *The Underground Press in America* (Bloomington: Indiana University Press, 1970); Hill, *Black Panther Menace*; Lewis, *Outlaws of America*; Robert H. Muller, Theodore Jurgen Spahn, and Janet M. Spahn, eds., *From Radical Left to Extreme Right: A Bibliography of Current Periodicals of Protest, Controversy, Advocacy, or Dissent*, 2nd ed. (Ann Arbor, MI: Campus, 1970); Gilbert Moore, *A Special Rage* (New York: Harper & Row, 1971); Huey P. Newton, *Revolutionary Suicide* (New York: Harcourt Brace Jovanovich, 1973); Newton, *To Die for the People*; Peck, *Uncovering the Sixties*; Robert Scheer, ed., *Eldridge Cleaver: Post-Prison Writings and Speeches* (New York: Random House, 1970); Bobby Seale, *A Lonely Rage: The Autobiography of Bobby Seale* (New York: Times, 1978); Seale, *Seize the Time*. The 1990s books included Lori Andrews, *Black Power, White Blood* (New York: Pantheon, 1996); Earl Anthony, *Spitting in the Wind: The True Story Behind the Violent Legacy of the Black Panther Party* (Santa Monica, CA: Roundtable, 1990); Elaine Brown, *A Taste of Power: A Black Woman's Story* (New York: Pantheon, 1992); Ward Churchill and Jim Vander Wall, *The Cointelpro Papers: Documents from the FBI's Secret Wars Against Domestic Dissent* (Boston: South End Press, 1990); Jim Haskins, *Power to the People: The Rise and Fall of the Black Panther Party* (New York: Simon & Schuster Books for Young Readers, 1997); David Hilliard and Lewis Cole, *This Side of Glory: The Autobiography of David Hilliard and the Story of the Black Panther Party* (Boston: Little, Brown, 1993); Jones, *Black Panther Party Reconsidered*; John T. McCartney, *Black Power Ideologies* (Philadelphia: Temple University Press, 1992); Meier, Rudwick, and Broderick, *Black Protest Thought*; Pearson, *Shadow of the Panther*; Huey P. Newton, *War Against the Panthers: A Study of Repression in America* (New York: Writers and Readers, 1996); Wachsberger, *Voices from the Underground*; Wolseley, *Black Press*. The reprinted works include Brown, *Taste of Power* reprinted by Anchor in 1994; Moore, *Special Rage* reprinted by Carroll & Graf in 1993; Newton, *To Die for the People* reprinted by Writers and Readers in 1995; Seale, *Seize the Time* reprinted by Black Classic in 1991.

CHAPTER 13. CREATING AN AGENDA FOR GAY AND LESBIAN RIGHTS

1. Alan V. Miller, compiler, *Our Own Voices: A Directory of Lesbian and Gay Periodicals, 1890–1990* (Toronto: Canadian Gay Archives, 1990); Rodger Streitmatter, *Unspeakable: The Rise of the Gay and Lesbian Press in America* (Boston: Faber and Faber, 1995), 117.

2. Author's interview with Martha Shelley, 17 July 1994.

3. Paul Berman, "Democracy and Homosexuality," *New Republic*, 20 December 1993, 22; Martin Duberman, *Stonewall* (New York: Dutton, 1993), 181–212.

4. "Hostile Crowd Dispersed Near Sheridan Square," *New York Times*, 3 July 1969, 19; "Homo Nest Raided; Queen Bees Are Stinging Mad," *New York Daily News*, 29 June 1969, 1; Howard Smith, "Full Moon Over the Stonewall," *Village Voice*, 3 July 1969, 1; Lucian Truscott IV, "Gay Power Comes to Sheridan Square," *Village Voice*, 3 July 1969, 1; Jonathan Black, "Gay Power Hits Back," *Village Voice*, 31 July 1969, 1.

5. Jack Nichols and Lige Clarke, "Pampered Perverts," *Screw*, 25 July 1969, 16.

6. Al Goldstein, "Screw You!," *Screw*, 2 May 1969, 2; Derek Miles, *Dirtiest Dozen* (New York: Midwood, 1970), 11–21. *Screw* is still being published.

7. Nichols and Clarke, *Screw*, "Homosexual Heritage," 20 June 1969, 16; "Stalls of Balls," 14 February 1969, 10; "Off the Far End," 2 May 1969, 15.

8. John Francis Hunter (John Paul Hudson) *The Gay Insider: USA* (New York: Stonehill, 1972), 171. The first issue of *GAY* was dated 1 December 1969.

9. "Bookshop Employees Arrested," *GAY*, 15 December 1970, 10.

10. The first extant lesbian or gay publication was a typewritten magazine titled *Vice Versa*; a Los Angeles woman who used the pseudonym "Lisa Ben," an anagram for lesbian, produced nine monthly issues in 1947 and 1948.

11. "Joel Fabricant Perverts Gay Power," *Come Out!*, 14 November 1969, 3.

12. "Come Out!," *Come Out!*, 14 November 1969, 1.

13. On the Gay Liberation Front, see John D'Emilio, *Sexual Politics, Sexual Communities: The Making of the Homosexual Minority in the United States, 1940–1970* (Chicago: University of Chicago Press, 1983), 233–35; Donn Teal, *The Gay Militants* (New York: Stein and Day, 1971), 38–60.

14. *Come Out!*, 14 November 1969, Gay Commandoes, "The October Rebellion," 5; Mike Brown, Michael Tallman, and Leo Martello, "The Summer of Gay Power and the Village Voice Exposed!," 10.

15. Nichols and Clarke, "The Gay Press Meets," *GAY*, 4 May 1970, 2.

16. Staff, "Dear Contributor," *Come Out!*, June/July 1970, 3.

17. *GAY*, Richard C. Wandel, "Kiss-In Staged by Young Men," 13 September 1971, 1; Nichols and Clarke, "Dancing Anyone?," 19 January 1970, 2; John Francis Hunter (John Paul Hudson), "The Rise of the New Conscience," 29 June 1970, 10–11; Nichols and Clarke, "The Editors Speak," 25 May 1970, 2.

18. Charles Thorp, "Power/Liberate Create Theory," *Gay Sunshine*, December 1970, 9; Charles Thorp, "A Gay Liberation Manifesto," *Gay Sunshine*, December 1970, 8; author's interview with Pat Brown, 6 July 1993. The first issue of *Gay Sunshine* appeared in August 1970.

19. *Come Out!*, September/October 1970, 1, 3, 4, 5; *Killer Dyke*, September 1971, 15.

20. *Come Out!*, Ronald Ballard and Bob Fontanella, "To the Gay Liberation Front," 14 November 1969, 4; "GLF News," June/July 1970, 22; September/October 1970, 2; "GLF," April/May 1970, 2; "Lesbian Demands," September/October 1970, 16; Gay Commandoes, "The October Rebellion," 14 November 1969, 5.

21. Author's interview with John O'Brien, 16 July 1993. The first issue of *Gay Times* appeared in October 1970.

22. "Killer Dykes," *Killer Dyke*, September 1971, 3. The first issue of *Killer Dyke* appeared in September 1971.

23. *San Francisco Gay Free Press*, undated issue the content of which indicates it was published in December 1970, "Pigs Sty-me Stud," 10; "Editorial," 2; Charles Thorp, "Editor-Vendor Attacked by Closet," 5; Ralph Hall, "Rising Up Gay," 10. The *San Francisco Gay Free Press* was founded in December 1970.

24. Gay Guevara, "Gay Revos Strike," *San Francisco Gay Free Press*, undated issue the content of which indicates it was published in December 1970, 15.

25. Author's interview with Pat Brown, 6 July 1993; Craig Schoonmaker, "Separatists Forming Alliance," *Gay Sunshine*, January 1971, 3.

26. *San Francisco Sunday Examiner and Chronicle*, "The Great Gay Conspiracy," 18 October 1970, 1; Leigh W. Rutledge, *The Gay Decades: From Stonewall to the Present* (New York: Plume, 1992), 13.

27. Don Jackson, "Alpine News Round-Up," *San Francisco Gay Free Press*, undated issue the content of which indicates it was published in December 1970, 3.

28. Author's interview with Shelley.

29. Author's interview with Nichols, 12 November 1993.

30. Craig Schoonmaker, "Separatists Forming Alliance," *Gay Sunshine*, January 1971, 3; Rutledge, *Gay Decades*, 13.

31. *GAY*, Hector Simms, "A Biopsy on Miss Thing," 1 June 1970, 15; Nichols and Clarke, "GAY and the Drag Queen," 22 June 1970, 2.

32. Pat Maxwell, "The Emperor's New Clothes," *Gay Sunshine*, January 1971, 16.

33. Author's interview with Shelley.

34. Shelley, "Gay Is Good," *Killer Dyke*, September 1971, 7.

35. "Free Angela Douglas!," *San Francisco Gay Free Press*, undated issue the content of which indicates it was published in December 1970, 1, 6.

36. Nichols and Clarke, "Are You a Jealous Lover?" *GAY*, 15 June 1970, 5.

37. *Come Out!*, Jim Foratt, "Word Thoughts," January 1970, 8; Joe Salata and Steve Gavin, "A Cocksucking Seminar," Winter 1972, 18–19.

38. Jim Rankin, "Jesus Is Gay," *Gay Sunshine*, October 1970, 15.

39. "A Man Loves a Man," *Screw*, 16 May 1969, 4–5.

40. Author's interview with Shelley; Bob Kohler, "I Can't Hear You—I Have a Carrot in My Ear," *Come Out!*, June/July 1970, 9.

41. *GAY*, 1 June 1970, "Gay couple files joint tax return," 3; Nichols and Clarke, "Congratulations to Dick and Bob," 2; "Two men apply for marriage license," 15 June 1970, 12; Nichols and Clarke, "Congratulations to Jack and Jim," 15 June 1970, 2; "Cornell U. GLF Holds Sit-In," 21 December 1970, 1; Nichols and Clarke, "Editorial," 21 December 1970, 3.

42. *GAY*, Dick Leitsch, "The Gay Vote," 15 December 1969, 9; Nichols and Clarke, "Bella Abzug for Congress," 8 June 1970, 2; "Bella Abzug's Victory," 13 July 1970, 2; "Editorial," 9 November 1970, 3.

43. Author's interview with Nichols, 12 November 1993.

44. John P. Leroy, "Beacon Lights on Bathing Beauties," *GAY*, 15 June 1970, 7.

45. *Come Out!*, "Come Out!," 14 November 1969, 1; "Joel Fabricant Perverts Gay Power," 14 November 1969, 3. "Gays Protest Police Raid on Bar after Young Man Is Impaled on Fence," April/May 1970, 4.

46. Author's interview with O'Brien, 16 July 1993.

47. Kathy Braun, "The Dance," *Come Out!*, April/May 1970, 3.

48. Author's interviews with O'Brien, 16 July 1993, and Shelley.

49. FBI memos from New York field offices to FBI Headquarters, 30 July 1969, 7 August 1969, 10 December 1969, 16 December 1969, 31 March 1970.

50. FBI memos from New York field offices to FBI Headquarters, 30 July 1969, 31 March 1970, 3 December 1970; author's interview with O'Brien, 16 July 1993; Anthony Summers, *Official and Confidential: The Secret Life of J. Edgar Hoover* (New York: G. P. Putnam's Sons, 1993).

51. The last issue of *Come Out!* was dated Winter 1972. *Gay Times* ceased publication in November 1970, *Gay Sunshine* in February 1971, *Killer Dyke* by the end of 1972, and the *San Francisco Gay Free Press* by the end of 1971.

52. *GAY* continued to be published until February 1974, not long after Nichols and Clarke had a major dispute with Al Goldstein. The publisher had refused to show the two editors the company's financial records, making the couple wonder if the gay portion of Goldstein's business was not more profitable than he admitted. So the editors quit.

53. Author's interview with Brown. The revamped *Gay Sunshine* continued publication until 1981.

CHAPTER 14. LIBERATING THE AMERICAN WOMAN

1. Robin Morgan, "Goodbye to All That," *Rat*, 9–23 February 1970, 6.

2. Morgan, "Goodbye to All That," 6.

3. Anne Mather, "A History of Feminist Periodicals, Part II," *Journalism History* 1 (Winter 1974–75):109. The first issue of *Ain't I a Woman?* was dated 26 June 1970,

the first issue of *It Ain't Me Babe* was dated 15 January 1970, and the first issue of *off our backs* was dated 27 February 1970.

4. Robin Morgan, *Going Too Far: The Personal Chronicle of a Feminist* (New York: Random House, 1970), 4.

5. Morgan, *Going Too Far*, 4.

6. Morgan, "Miss America Goes Down," *Rat*, 20 September–3 October 1968, 4.

7. Morgan, "Goodbye to All That," 6.

8. Morgan, "Goodbye to All That," 6.

9. Morgan, "Goodbye to All That," 7.

10. Morgan, *Going Too Far*, 121; Morgan, "Goodbye to All That," *Ain't I a Woman?*, 25 September 1970, 7; Morgan, *It Ain't Me Babe*, "Goodbye to All That," 7 April 1970, 12–13; Del Martin, "Female Gay Blasts Men, Leaves Movement," *The Advocate*, 28 October–10 November 1970, 21–22. San Diego's *Goodbye To All That* was founded in September 1970 and continued publication until May 1971.

11. Morgan, *Going Too Far*, 9.

12. Morgan, *Going Too Far*, 9.

13. *Rat*, Michela Griffo, "Women Are Rising Up—They Are Angry," 7–21 March 1970, 17; "Seize the Land," 22 May–4 June 1970, 21; "Kick Ass," 15 July–5 August 1970, 6; "Death to All Honkies!," 24 February–9 March 1970, 16.

14. Rita Mae Brown, "Say It Isn't So," *Rat*, 7–21 March 1970, 18; untitled article, *Ain't I a Woman?*, 29 Januuary 1971, 3.

15. Untitled article, *It Ain't Me Babe*, 15 January 1970, 1; "editorial," *off our backs*, 27 February 1970, 2.

16. Marlene Hicks, "the diaphragm," *off our backs*, 27 February 1970, 12.

17. "Sex: An Open Letter from a Sister," *It Ain't Me Babe*, 29 January 1970, 8.

18. "Vaginal Politics," *Ain't I a Woman?*, 19 November 1971, 2.

19. "Very Pleasurable Politics," *Rat*, 17 December 1970–6 January 1971, 12.

20. Friedan made her statement on March 4, 1973; see Leigh W. Rutledge, *The Gay Decades: From Stonewall to the Present* (New York: Plume, 1992), 54–55.

21. Untitled item, *Ain't I a Woman?*, 30 March 1972, 12.

22. Rita Mae Brown, "Say it isn't so," *Rat*, 7–21 March 1970, 18.

23. Brown, "Coitus Interruptus," *Rat*, 9–23 February 1970, 12.

24. Brown, "Coitus Interruptus," 20.

25. Martha Shelley, "Stepin Fetch It Woman," *Ain't I a Woman?*, 11 September 1970, 10.

26. *It Ain't Me Babe*, Mary, "Letter from Mary," 23 July–5 August 1970, 4; Judy, "Lesbians as Women," 21 May–10 June 1970, 7.

27. *Ain't I a Woman?*, 26 June 1970, 1.

28. "a black woman responds to women's liberation," *off our backs*, 15 April 1971, 18.

29. Some Red Witches, "An Open Letter to Betty Friedan," *It Ain't Me Babe*, 6 August 1970, 12.

30. "From Black Sisters to Black Brothers," *Rat*, 7–21 March 1970, 10.

31. Morgan, untitled article, *Rat*, 6–27 October 1970, 2.

32. "Sick Sick Sick," *off our backs*, November 1971, 7.

33. Untitled article, *Ain't I a Woman?*, 11 September 1970, 2; 1.

34. *It Ain't Me Babe*, 15 January 1970, 1.

35. "Disarm Rapists," *It Ain't Me Babe*, 23 July–5 August 1970, 13.

36. "Disarm Rapists," 13.

37. Untitled statement, *Rat*, 4–18 April 1970, 3; "Modern Midwifery," *Ain't I a Woman?*, 11 September 1970, 23.

38. fran pollner, "struggle: abortion: a woman's right to choose," *off our backs*, October 1971, 8.

39. *off our backs*, Fran Pollner, "the only good abortion law is no abortion law," Summer 1971, 27; Marlene Wicks, "Don't Fuck with Marvin," 30 May 1970, 3.

40. *off our backs*, "women march and dance for abortion law repeal," December 1971, 17; "paying court to women: 20th century version," October 1971, 9.

41. "abortions at d.c. general hospital," *off our backs*, 27 February 1970, 4; no articles quoting Dr. Lowe on his opinion about abortions appeared in either the *Washington Post* or the *Washington Evening Star* between 24 and 27 February 1970, although the *Star* covered the hearing at which he made the statement (Judith Randal, "D.C. Abortion Situation Clouded," *Washington Evening Star*, 24 February 1970, B-1). chris hobbs, " 'if men could get pregnant, abortion would be a sacrament,' " *off our backs*, 24 June 1971, 20; no articles quoting Ward appeared in the *Boston Globe* between 1 and 24 June 1971.

42. JGS, "money doesn't talk, it swears," *off our backs*, 14 December 1970, 4.

43. Geoffrey Rips, ed., *The Campaign Against the Underground Press* (San Francisco: City Lights, 1981), 84.

44. "Security," *Ain't I a Woman?*, 7 January 1972, 4.

45. FBI memo from Alexandria, VA, field office to Hoover, 18 May 1971; *off our backs*, 6 May 1971, 1.

46. FBI memo from Washington, DC, office to Hoover, 2 July 1973; Carol Anne Douglas and Fran Moira, "off our backs: The First Decade (1970–1980)," in Ken Wachsberger, ed., *Voices from the Underground: Insider Histories of the Vietnam Era Underground Press* (Tempe, AZ: Mica Press, 1993), 122.

47. Kathleen L. Endres, "off our backs," in Kathleen L. Endres and Theresa L. Lueck, eds., *Women's Periodicals in the United States: Social and Political Issues* (Westport, CT: Greenwood, 1996), 273. The major archives for the early 1970s women's liberation press is the microfilmed Underground Press Collection available at the

Library of Congress and limited other locations. The last issue of *Rat* preserved in the collection is dated 2 August 1971; the last issue of *Ain't I a Woman?* is dated May 1974; and the last issue of *It Ain't Me Babe* is dated 1 December 1970.

48. Morgan, ed., *Sisterhood Is Powerful: An Anthology of Writing from the Women's Liberation Movement* (New York: Vintage, 1970).

49. Brown, *Rubyfruit Jungle*, (Plainfield, VT: Daughters, 1973).

50. Morgan, *Going Too Far*, 9–10.

51. Morgan, *Going Too Far*, 9–10, 14.

52. Morgan, *Going Too Far*, 17.

CHAPTER 15. DISSIDENCE IN A NEW MILLENNIUM

1. Stephen Duncombe, *Notes from Underground: Zines and the Politics of Alternative Culture* (New York: Verso, 1997), 6, 14; J. Peder Zane, "Now the Magazines of 'Me,'" *New York Times*, 14 May 1995, E-4.

2. Duncombe, *Notes from Underground*, 199.

3. Duncombe, *Notes from Underground*, 111; Paul Lukas, *Beer Frame*, issue no. 1, 1994, 1.

4. *Kill Your Television*, issue no. 4, July 1994, 1.

5. Diana, "It Felt Like Rape," *Riot Grrrl 5*, March 1993, 1 (New York City).

6. See *www.altpress.org*.

7. *Real Change* (*www.realchangenews.org*), Rainee Maurer, "Down to Skin," June 1996; Timothy Harris, "No Apologies," 22 May 1998; "Unhappy Birthday," November 1998; Julie Eagleton, "Shelter Crunch," October 1995; Michele Marchand, "Shelter Shortage," January 1997; John Reese and John Fox, "Whose Seattle?," October 1994; "The Sidran Ordinance Explained," October 1994; "Mission," November 1999.

8. *Earth First!* (*www.enviroweb.org*), Almond, "Occupying Higher Ground," October 1999; Karen Pickett, "Headwaters Activist Killed," October-November 1998

9. "Medicinal Marijuana," *The Week Online*, 29 October 1999 (*www.drcnet.org*).

10. Medical marijuana is legal in Alaska, Arizona, California, Colorado, Hawaii, Maine, Nevada, Oregon, and Washington.

INDEX

ABC Television, ix, 199

AIDS, ix, xiii, 282

Abbott, Edna Brown Denison, 154

Abbott, Helen Morrison, 153–54

Abbott, Robert S., 142–58, 176–79, 277

Abolition Movement, 20–35, 39, 113

Abolitionist press, 20–35, 160, 276–77

Abzug, Bella, 252

Adams, Abigail, 1

Adams, John, 1

African American press, 80–96, 142–58, 176–79, 220–37, 256, 275–77, 281, 284

Agitator, The, 53

Ain't I a Woman?, 256, 260–63, 265–69, 271–73, 278

Alarm, The, 116, 118–20, 122, 128–34, 138, 275, 277

Alpine Liberation Front, 248

Alternate University, 253

Alternative Viewpoints on the Internet, 281

American Anti-Slavery Society, 25

American Birth Control League, 171, 174

American Sentinel, 18

American Woman's Association, 173

Anarchist Movement, 115–34, 138, 275

Anarchist press, 115–34, 138, 275, 277

Anglican Church, 173

Anthony, Susan Brownell, 37–56, 137–38, 257

Anti-Lynching Movement, 80–96

Anti-lynching press, 80–96, 137, 160, 277

Anti-War Movement (Vietnam), 184–99, 202, 205, 212–13, 225, 243, 256, 276–77

Anti-war press (Vietnam), 184–99, 219, 275–76, 283

Appeal to Reason, xi, 98–114, 127, 129, 135–36, 138, 275, 277

Argus, 216

Aronson, James, 188–89, 191, 195–96

Associated Press, 76

Atlanta Constitution, 89

Atlantic Monthly, 94

Babcock, William, 107

Baginsky, Max, 124

Baker, Martha, 107

Barnes, Gilbert H., 30

Barnett, Ferdinand L., 92–93

Beatles, 212

Beecher, Henry Ward, 70–71, 74–75

Beer Frame, 280

Belmont, Alva Smith Vanderbilt, 165
Bennett, Gordon, 39
Berkeley Barb, 200–203, 205–6, 208–13, 218–19, 278
Berkman, Alexander, 123–25, 127, 136–37
Birth Control Movement, 159–75, 177–79, 257
Birth control press, 159–75, 177–79, 276
Birth Control Review, x, 159, 166–74, 178
Black Panther, 220–37, 246, 254, 256, 275–77, 281, 284
Black Panther Menace, The, 235
Black Panther Party, 220–37, 243, 256, 276
Blackwell, Henry, 40
Blair, Henry, 90
Blatch, Harriet Stanton, 165
Blood, James, 63, 65, 73, 75
Bluefield State College, 214
Boston Courier, 34
Boston Globe, 66, 270
Brady, Ed, 124
British Anti-Lynching Committee, 88–89
Broom, Clarence E., 107
Brown, John, 27
Brown, Pat, 246, 248, 255
Brown, Rita Mae, 263–65, 273
Brown University, 65
Buck, Pearl S., 165
Bullard, Laura Curtis, 52
Burchett, Wilfred, 184, 190–91, 198

CBS Television, ix, 199
CIA (Central Intelligence Agency), 192, 215
Carnegie, Andrew, 97
Catholic Worker, 184–86, 195, 198–99, 277
Center for a New Television, 280
Central Anti-Lynching League, 92

Chain, David, 282
Charleston News and Courier, 93
Chesapeake & Ohio Railroad, 81
Chiang Kai-shek, 183
Chicago Conservator, 92, 138
Chicago Daily News, 152
Chicago Defender, x, 88, 142–58, 176–79, 277
Chicago Inter-Ocean, 89
Chicago Tribune, 94, 118, 125
Child, Harold, 172
Church of Christ, 173
City College of New York, 246, 278
City Paper (Washington), xi
Civil Rights Movement, 189, 206, 219, 225–26, 236, 243
Civil War, 27–29, 35, 39, 47, 116
Claflin, Tennessee, 40, 62, 64, 135
Clarke, Elijah (Lige), 241–42, 245, 249–51
Cleaver, Eldridge, 221, 224, 226–27, 233–34
Cold War, 183
Colgate, Samuel, 73
Columbia Records, 212, 217
Come Out!, 238–39, 243–46, 248–55, 277–78
Commercial Advertiser, 5, 18, 42
Comstock, Anthony, 73–76, 78, 136, 162–63, 276
Counter Intelligence Program (COINTELPRO), 215
Counterculture Movement, 181, 200–20, 235, 238, 256, 276
Counterculture press, 200–19, 221, 254, 275–76, 278, 283
Courier and Enquirer, 18
Crawford, Anthony, 152
Cronkite, Walter, 184, 188, 199
Czolgosz, Leon, 124–25

Daily Advertiser, 18
Daily Flash, 216
Dallas Notes, 215
Day, Dorothy, 184–86, 195, 198, 277
Debs, Eugene V., 98, 103, 111–12
Declaration of Independence, 1, 38
Delaware Free Press, 5
Democratic National Convention (1968), 233
deSelincourt, Hugh, 171–72
Disney, 281
Doggett, David, 206–8, 214
Donnelly, Dorothy, 149
Douglas, Angela, 250
Douglass, Frederick, 29, 87, 92
Dowell, Denzil, 222, 225
DuBois, W.E.B., 95
Duncan, Donald, 192–93, 196, 199
Dyer, Leonidas, 95
Dylan, Bob, 211–12

Earth First!, 282
Eisenhower, Dwight, 183
Ellis, Havelock, 165
Emerson, Ralph Waldo, 130
Espionage Act, 112, 127, 136
Evans, George Henry, 11, 56
Evening Journal, 13

FBI (Federal Bureau of Investigation), 197, 214–21, 232–36, 253–54, 271–72, 276
Fairness and Accuracy in Media, 280
Fifteenth Amendment, 47, 65
First Amendment, 72
Fortune, T. Thomas, 82, 85, 87, 92, 96
Fowler, Ebenezer, 85–86
Free Enquirer, 4–7, 10–15, 17–19, 56, 275
Free Press (Los Angeles), 216
Free Trade Advocate, 16

Freedom of Information Act, 215, 254
Frick, Henry Clay, 124
Friedan, Betty, 257, 263, 265–66
Fugitive Slave Law, 32

Garland, Judy, 239
Garrison, Helen Eliza Benson, 28
Garrison, William Lloyd, 21–35, 40, 55–56, 137, 160, 177–78, 276–77
Gay, Edward, 155
GAY, 238, 240–43, 245, 248–52, 254–55, 278
Gay and Lesbian Liberation Movement, 181, 238–56, 263–65, 276
Gay and lesbian press, 238–55, 261, 275–78, 284
Gay Insider: USA, The, 242
Gay Liberation Front, 243, 245–46, 248, 253, 255
Gay Sunshine, 238, 246, 249, 251, 255, 278
Gay Times, 238, 246, 252, 254–55, 278
General Federation of Women's Clubs, 173–74
Genius of Universal Emancipation, 21
George Washington University, 270
Goldman, Emma, 116, 122–25, 127–33, 136–38
Goldstein, Al, 243, 251
Great Migration, 141–42, 145, 147–58, 177–79, 277
Great Speckled Bird, 216
Gutenberg, Johannes, 281

Hampton, Fred, 221, 223, 232–33
Hampton, Iberia, 233
Hampton Institute, 143
Harman, Lillian, 74, 76–77, 176
Harman, Moses, 62, 67–72, 74, 76–79, 137, 176, 276

Harman, Susan Scheuck, 67

Harper's Weekly, 65

Harvard College, 43

Havel, Hippolyte, 124

Haymarket incident, 116, 120–22, 131, 134

Haywood, "Big Bill," 110

Heighton, Ann Beckley, 8

Heighton, William, 6–12, 14–16, 18, 54–56, 279

Helix, 216

Heywood, Angela, 62, 65–67, 69–72, 74, 76, 78, 138

Heywood, Ezra, 62, 65–67, 69–72, 74, 76, 78–79, 137, 276

Higgins, Anne, 160–61

Higgins, Michael, 160–61

Hilliard, David, 221, 227, 233

Hinckle, Warren, 192–93

Ho Chi Minh, 183

Homosexual Citizen, 242

Hoover, J. Edgar, 127–28, 214–15, 220, 232–33, 254, 272

Hutton, Bobby, 233

I.F. Stone's Weekly, 184, 186–90, 194–95, 198–99

Illinois Central Railroad, 142, 148

In These Times, 113–14

Indianapolis Freeman, 88

Industrial Revolution, 3–19, 59, 97, 275

Internal Revenue Service, 197

Internet, xiii, 279, 281–82

Isthmus, xi

It Ain't Me Babe, 257, 261–62, 264–69, 272–73, 278

Jackson, Andrew, 4

Jiggs, Maggie, 239

Johnson, Andrew, 43–44

Johnson, Jack, 150

Johnson, Lyndon, 183, 191

Johnson, Noble, 149

Jones, Clabrun, 150

Jones, Clarence, 150

Jones, Mary Harris "Mother," 103, 105, 272

Journal Newspapers, 272

Jungle, The, 98

Kaleidoscope, 216

Kansas City Times, 68, 76

Keller, Helen, 107

Kendall, Amos, 27

Kennedy, John, 183, 188, 276

Kennedy, Robert F., 276

Kent College, 143

Kershner, Jacob, 122

Kill Your Television, 280

Killer Dyke, 238–39, 247–49, 251, 255, 278

Kindman, Michael, 203, 205, 213

King, Martin Luther Jr., 226, 276

King, Rodney, 236

Kirk, Eleanor, 45–46, 48–49

Kois, John, 216–17

Korean War, 183, 187

Ku Klux Klan, 117

Kudzu, The, 201, 206–10, 212, 214, 217–19, 278

Labor Movement, 3–19, 103–5, 275

Labor press, 3–19, 134, 275, 279

Lee, Robert E., 29

Lennon, John, 212

Liberator, The, 21–35, 57, 64, 77, 277

Life magazine, 174

Lincoln, Abraham, 29

Literary Digest, 89

Livermore, Mary Ashton, 53

London, Jack, 107
Los Angeles Times, 276
Lovejoy, Elijah P., 31–32
Lowe, Ernest, 270
Lucifer, the Light-Bearer, 62, 67–69, 72, 74, 76–78, 137, 176, 276
Lundy, Benjamin, 21

MacDonald, Angus Snead, 172
Mafia, 239, 243, 252–53, 255
Manchester Guardian, 89
Mandel, Marvin, 270
Mao Zedong, 183
Markland, W.G., 69–70, 72
Martin, John Biddulph, 76
Masses, The, xi
Matthews, Connie, 229
Maurer, Rainee, 281
McCarthy, Joe, 263
McCloud, W.A., 153
McCormick, Katharine, 174
McGovern, George, 253
McKinley, William, 90, 93, 124–25, 134
Meat Inspection Act, 133
Mechanic's Free Press, 4–16, 19, 54, 56, 275
Mechanics' Union of Trade Associations, 4
Memphis Free Speech, 80, 83, 85, 138
Merritt College, 221
Miami Daily Planet, 215
Michigan State News, 203, 205
Michigan State University, 201, 203, 205, 213, 217
Middletown Gazette, 30
Million Man March, 236
Millsaps College, 206
Miss America Pageant (1968), 258
"Mob Rule in New Orleans," 93
Montgomery Advertiser, 154

Morgan, Frances Tracy, 165
Morgan, J. Pierpont, 73, 97
Morgan, Robin, 256, 258–61, 267, 272–74
Mother Earth, 116, 125–34, 136, 138, 275
Mother Earth Bulletin, 127
Mott, Lucretia, 42

NAACP (National Association for the Advancement of Colored People), 94, 95
NBC Television, ix
Napier, Sam, 232
Nation, The, 29, 34–35, 174, 187
National Gazette, 13
National Guard, 203
National Guardian, 184, 188–91, 195–99, 258
National Intelligencer, 34
National Merit Scholar program, 203, 213
National Organization for Women, 257, 263, 266, 273
National Sickle Cell Anemia Control Act, 230
New Appeal, 112
New England Anti-Slavery Society, 25
New Harmony Gazette, 18
New Orleans Daily Picayune, 80, 93
New Orleans Times-Democrat, 93
Newsweek magazine, ix, 212, 219
Newton, Huey P., 221, 224–27, 229, 231, 233–35
New York Age, 82, 85, 87, 138, 277
New York Call, 162
New York Daily News, 240
New Yorker magazine, 172
New York Globe, 64
New York Herald, 33–34, 39, 42, 55, 64
New York Herald Tribune, 194–95
New York Native, ix

New York Post, 186

New York Sun, 42, 89

New York Times, ix, 34, 39, 42, 64, 89, 110, 121, 172, 175, 178, 187–88, 194–95, 216, 240, 276

New York Tribune, 29

New York World, 64, 125

New York World-Telegram, 174

Ngo Dinh Diem, 183, 192, 205

Nichols, Jack, 241–42, 245, 248–52

Nielsen, Rick, 242–43

Nineteenth Amendment, 52

Nixon, Richard, 214, 227, 233, 253

No-Conscription League, 127

NOLA Express, 215

Northwestern University, 92

O'Brien, John, 246, 252–54

off our backs, 257, 261–63, 266–67, 269–73, 278, 281

Offett, William, 86

O'Neill, Richard, 70, 72

Open City, 215

Orpheus, 216

Osawkee Times, 68

Owen, Robert Dale, 13–14, 17, 56

Paper, The, 201, 203–6, 210, 212–13, 217–19, 278

Parsons, Albert R., 116–22, 128–29, 131–33, 137, 277

Parsons, Lucy, 118, 120, 130

Peabody, James H., 105

Pentagon Papers, 188

Pentecostal Church, 211

Persons, Eli, 152

Philadelphia City Council, 15, 56

Philadelphia Evening Bulletin, 216

Philadelphia Free Press, 216

Philadelphia Inquirer, 121

Philadelphia Ledger, 34

Philadelphia Record, 186

Pincus, Gregory, 174

Pitchford, Kenneth, 258

Pittsburgh Sun, 163

Planned Parenthood, 174

Plymouth Church, 70, 75

Pope, Walter, 232

Portet, Lorenzo, 165

Powers, Jerry, 215

Presley, Elvis, 211

Progressive Era, 113

Progressive Party, 188

Pure Food and Drug Act, 110, 133

Queen Victoria, 89

Rackley, Alex, 233

Rag, The, 215

Ramparts, 184, 191–93, 196, 198–99, 205

Randazzo, Roselie, 102

Rat, 256, 258–59, 261–63, 267, 269, 271–73, 278

Reagan, Ronald, 203, 279

Real Change, 281–82

Reconstruction, 80

"Red Record, A," 90–92

"Red Summer," 157

Reitman, Ben, 124

Reserve Officer Training Corps, 213

Revolution, The, x, 36–55, 57, 61, 64, 77, 134–35, 138, 257–58, 278

Riot Grrrl, 280

Rizzo, Frank, 216

Roberts, Walter, 163

Rockefeller, John D., 97

Roosevelt, Theodore, 110–11

Rosenberg, Ethel and Julius, 189

Rothchild, Peter, 216
Rublee, Juliet, 165
Rubyfruit Jungle, 273

Sachs, Sadie, 162, 165, 175
San Francisco Gay Free Press, 238, 247–48, 250, 255, 278
Sandburg, Carl, 142, 152
Sanger, Grant, 163, 165, 172, 177
Sanger, Margaret, x, 159–75, 177–79, 276
Sanger, Peggy, 163, 165, 177
Sanger, Stuart, 163, 165, 172, 177
Sanger, William, 161, 163
Scherr, Max, 202–3, 218
Schoenfeld, Eugene, 208
Scott, Lation, 148
Screw, 240, 242–43
Seale, Bobby, 221, 223, 226–27, 229, 233, 236, 281
Seneca Falls Convention, 37–39
Sexual reform press, xi, 61–79, 137, 176, 276
Sheftel, Joe, 149
Shelley, Martha, 239, 248–49, 251, 265
Sherman Anti-Trust Act, 133
Sinclair, John, 216
Sinclair, Upton, xii, 98, 109–10
Sisterhood Is Powerful, 273
Slee, Noah, 172
Small, Tolbert, 229
Socialist Movement, 97–114, 275
Socialist press, 97–114, 275, 277
Society for the Suppression of Vice, 73
"Southern Horrors," 87–88
Southern Student Organizing Committee, 206
Space City, 216
Spellman, Francis, 192
Spirit of the Age, 5

Spock, Benjamin, 193
St. Louis Globe-Democrat, 121
Standard Oil Company, 133
Stanley, Will, 147
Stanton, Edwin, 29
Stanton, Elizabeth Cady, 37–54, 56, 61, 65, 71, 135, 138, 165, 257
Stanton, Henry B., 37
Stein, Modest, 123
Steunenberg, Frank, 110
Stone, I.F., 184, 186–88, 190, 194, 198
Stone, Lucy, 40
Stonewall Rebellion, 238–40, 242–43, 245, 247–49, 253, 255
Stowe, Harriet Beecher, 70
Students for a Democratic Society, 200, 206, 211, 218
Suffrage Movement, 257
Sumner, Charles, 29
Sun, 216
Survey magazine, 94

Tennessee Supreme Court, 81
Tet Offensive, 184, 187, 197, 199
Thomas, Jim, 213
Thoreau, Henry David, 32
Thorp, Charles, 247
Tilton, Elizabeth, 70, 75
Tilton, Theodore, 70, 74
Time magazine, ix, 174, 199, 205, 212, 219
Time Warner, 281
Todd, Francis, 22–23
Topeka Daily Capital, 76
Tougaloo College, 214,
Train, George Francis, 40, 51
Truman, Harry, 183
Truth, Sojourner, 266
Tutt, William and Salem, 149

U.S. Congress, 65, 73, 90, 95, 112, 133, 136, 196, 235, 252
U.S. Constitution, 32–33, 47, 59, 178
U.S. Department of Agriculture, 67–68
U.S. Department of Health, Education and Welfare, 266
U.S. House of Representatives, 107, 155
U.S. Justice Department, 127, 136, 155
U.S. Post Office, 27, 110, 136, 155, 159, 162–63, 170–71, 179
U.S. Senate, 29, 134, 155, 177
U.S. Supreme Court, 133, 270, 273
Underwood, Mrs. J.S., 86
University of Alabama, 215
University of California at Berkeley, 200–203, 217
University of Texas, 215
Upshaw, M.D., 155
Utica Herald, 42

Vanderbilt, Cornelius, 64, 74–76, 135
Vanderbilt, William, 76
Vaughan, Hester, 50–52
Vietnam War, x, 181–200, 217, 219, 225
Village Voice, xi, 240, 245
Visiting Nurses Association, 162

Walker, Edwin, 68, 74, 76–77
Wall Street Journal, 199
Ward, Joe, 270
Warren, Fred D., 101, 109, 111–12
Washington, Jesse, 148
Washington City Post, 89
Washington Evening Star, 194, 197, 270
Washington Free Press, 216
Washington Post, ix, 194–95, 270, 276
Wayland, Etta Bevan, 99
Wayland, J.A., 99–103, 105, 107–14, 135–37

Wayland, Pearl Hunt, 111
Wayland, Walter, 111–12, 136
Wayne County Patriot, 5
Week Online, The, 282
Wells, H.G., 165, 171–72
Wells, Ida B. Jr., 93
Wells, Jim, 81
Wells, Lizzie, 81
Wells-Barnett, Ida B., 80–96, 116, 137–38, 146–47, 160, 177, 227, 277
Westmoreland, William C., 197
"Why the Colored American Is Not in the World's Columbian Exposition," 92
Williams, Billy, 171
Williams, John Sharp, 155
Wilson, Henry, 29
Wilson, Woodrow, 127
Winchester Argus, 68
Woman Rebel, x, 159–60, 163–64, 166–71, 177–79, 276
Woman's Journal, 40, 42, 53, 278
Women's Liberation Movement, 181, 256–74, 276
Women's liberation press, 256–79, 284
Women's Rights Movement, 36–53, 77, 113, 169–71
Woodhull, Canning, 62, 65, 69, 73
Woodhull, Victoria, 40, 61–66, 68–73, 75–76, 78, 135, 138
Woodhull & Claflin's Weekly, 62, 64, 66, 69, 71, 75, 78, 135, 138, 276
Woodhull Claflin & Co. Brokerage House, 40, 64
Word, The, 62, 66–67, 69–70, 74, 78, 137–38, 276
Working Man's Advocate, 4–5, 7, 9–17, 19, 56, 275

Working Men's Party, 16–18
Working Women's Association, 44
Workingmen's Advocate, 5
World War I, 112, 127, 134, 136, 141, 155
World War II, 183, 221
World's Columbia Exposition, 92
Wright, Frances "Fanny," 17–18, 56

X, Malcolm, 226

Young Women's Christian Association,
 174

Zines, xiii, 279–80
Zinn, Walter, 216